NEW DIRECTIONS IN
STRATEGIC THINKING

NEW DIRECTIONS IN STRATEGIC THINKING

Edited by
ROBERT O'NEILL and D.M. HORNER

London
GEORGE ALLEN & UNWIN
Boston   Sydney

First published in 1981

GEORGE ALLEN & UNWIN LTD
40 Museum Street, London WC1A 1LU

© Strategic and Defence Studies Centre, ANU 1981

British Library Cataloguing in Publication Data

New directions in strategic thinking.
  1. Military policy
  I. O'Neill, Robert II. Horner, D.M.
  355.03'35 VAII

ISBN 0-04-355013-4

Set in 10 on 11 pt Plantin
by Syarikat Seng Teik Sdn Bhd
Kuala Lumpur, Malaysia
Printed in Singapore by Koon Wah Printing Pte. Ltd.

Contents

Notes on Contributors

Mohammed Ayoob has been a Senior Research Fellow in International Relations, Australian National University, since 1977. He was formerly a Research Associate of the Institute for Defence Studies and Analyses, New Delhi, and Associate Professor in the School of International Studies, Jawaharlal Nehru University, New Delhi. His publications include: *India, Pakistan and Bangladesh: Search for a New Relationship*, (New Delhi, 1975); *The Horn of Africa: Regional Conflict and Super Power Involvement*, (Canberra, 1978); *Conflict and Intervention in the Third World* (ed.), (London, 1980); and *The Middle East in World Politics* (ed.), (forthcoming).

Hedley Bull is Montague Burton Professor of International Relations, Oxford University, and a Fellow of Balliol College. He taught at the London School of Economics, 1955–64. He was Director of the Arms Control and Disarmament Research Unit of the British Foreign Office, 1964–67, and Professor of International Relations, Australian National University, 1967–77. His publications include: *The Control of the Arms Race*, (London, 1961); *Asia and the Western Pacific: Towards a New International Order* (ed.), (Melbourne, 1975); *The Anarchical Society: A Study of Order in World Politics*, (London, 1977).

Johan Jörgen Holst is State Secretary in the Royal Norwegian Ministry of Foreign Affairs. He was Director of Research at the Norwegian Institute of International Affairs, 1967–76 and State Secretary in the Ministry of Defence, 1976–79. His publications include: *Why ABM? Policy Issues in the Missile Defence Controversy*, (ed.), (New York 1969); *Security, Order and the Bomb*, (ed.), (Oslo, 1972); *Five Roads to Nordic Security* (ed.), (Oslo, 1973); *A New Regime for the Oceans*, (ed.), (New York, 1976); *New Strategic Factors in the North Atlantic* (ed.), (Oslo, 1977); *Beyond Nuclear Deterrence: New Arms, New Aims*, (ed.), (New York, 1977).

Major David Horner is a regular army officer currently serving in the Department of Defence (Army Office), Canberra. He graduated from the Royal Military College, Duntroon, in 1969, and served in Vietnam in 1971. He was a Churchill Fellow in 1976 and from 1978 to 1980 was a PhD scholar in the Department of International Relations, Australian National University. He is the author of *Crisis of Command, Australian Generalship and the Japanese Threat, 1941–1943*, (Canberra, 1978); and *Australia and Allied Strategy, 1939–1945*, (forthcoming).

Brigadier Kenneth Hunt is Director of the British Atlantic Committee and was formerly Deputy Director of the International Institute for Strategic Studies. He was for some thirty years a regular army officer. He is a Visiting Professor at the University of Surrey and Specialist Adviser to the House of Commons Select Committee on Defence. His publications include: *NATO without France*, (London, 1966); *Defence, Technology and the Western Alliance*: Vol. 5, *The Requirements of Military Technology in the 1970s*, (London, 1967); *Defence with Fewer Men*, (London, 1973); *The Third World War*, (co-author) (London, 1978); *Asian Security* (ed.), (Tokyo, 1979).

Geoffrey Jukes has been a Senior Fellow in International Relations, Australian National University, since 1972. Before joining this Department in 1967 he was a member of the British Civil Service, in the Ministry of Defence and the Foreign Office, 1953–67. He has published widely in the fields of Soviet military history, naval policy, foreign policy and relations with the Third World, including the Indian Ocean. His books include: *The Development of Soviet Strategic Thinking since 1945*, (Canberra, 1972); *The Indian Ocean in Soviet Naval Policy*, (London, 1972); *The Soviet Union in Asia*, (Los Angeles, 1973).

Roman Kolkowicz is Professor of Political Science and Director of the Center for International and Strategic Affairs, University of California, Los Angeles. He was a research staff member of the Rand Corporation, 1961–66, and of the Institute for Defense Analyses, 1966–70. His publications include: *The Soviet Military and the Communist Party*, (Princeton, 1967); *The Soviet Union and Arms Control*, (Johns Hopkins, 1970); and contributions to *Interest Groups in Soviet Politics* (ed.), (Princeton, 1970); *Political Uses of Military Power*, (ed.), (London, 1980); *Problems of Conventional Warfare: The Soviet Case*, (ed.), (New York, 1980).

Richard Ned Lebow is Professor of Foreign Affairs at the National War College, Washington. He has previously lectured at The City University, New York (1968–74) and was Professor of Strategy at the US Naval War College. His publications include: *Divided Nations in a*

Divided World, co-authored with Gregory Henderson and John Stoessinger (New York, 1974); *White Britain and Black Ireland* (Philadelphia, 1976); *Between War and Peace: The Anatomy of International Crisis* (Baltimore, 1980); and *Principles of Strategy* (forthcoming).

T.B. Millar has been a Professorial Fellow in International Relations, Australian National University, since 1968. He joined this Department in 1962, was the first Head of the Strategic and Defence Studies Centre, 1966–70, and was also Director of the Australian Institute of International Affairs, 1969–76. His publications include: *Australia's Defence*, (Melbourne, 1965); *The Commonwealth and the United Nations*, (Sydney, 1967); *Australia's Foreign Policy*, (Sydney, 1968); *The Indian and Pacific Oceans: Some Strategic Considerations*, (London, 1969); *Foreign Policy: Some Australian Reflections*, (Melbourne, 1972); *Australian Foreign Minister: The Diaries of R.G. Casey, 1951–60* (ed.), (London, 1972); *Australia in Peace and War: External Relations 1788–1977*, (Canberra, 1978).

J.D.B. Miller has been Professor of International Relations, Australian National University, since 1962. He was formerly Professor of Politics at the University of Leicester and taught at the London School of Economics. His publications include: *Australian Government and Politics*, (London, 1954); *The Commonwealth in the World*, (London, 1958); *The Nature of Politics*, (London, 1962); *Britain and the Old Dominions*, (London, 1966); *The Politics of the Third World*, (London, 1966); *Survey of Commonwealth Affairs: Problems of Expansion and Attrition 1953–69*, (London, 1974); *The EEC and Australia*, (Melbourne, 1976); and *The World of States*, (London, 1980).

Professor Makoto Momoi is Dean of the Faculty of Defence Studies, National Defence College, Tokyo. A graduate of the Tokyo College of Foreign Affairs, Columbia and Harvard Universities, he became a Professor of International Relations at the National Defence College in 1962. He was appointed Director of International Security Studies in 1979 and Dean of the Faculty of Defence Studies in 1980. He was a Rockefeller Fellow at the London School of Economics in 1965 and a Visiting Professor at the University of North Carolina in 1970. He has published widely on Japanese defence issues.

Robert O'Neill has been Head of the Strategic and Defence Studies Centre since 1971 and a Professorial Fellow in International Relations, Australian National University, since 1977. He served in the Australian Army, 1955–68. His publications include: *The German Army and the Nazi Party*, (London, 1966); *Vietnam Task*, (Melbourne, 1968); *General Giap: Politician and Strategist*, (New York, 1969); *Australia in* *the Korean War, 1950–53*, Vol. I *Strategy and Diplomacy*, (Canberra, 1981), Vol. II, *Combat Operations*, (forthcoming); *The Strategic Nuclear Balance* (ed.), (Canberra, 1974), and *Insecurity! The Spread of Weapons in the Indian and Pacific Oceans* (ed.), (Canberra, 1978).

Jonathan D. Pollack is a member of the Social Science Department of the Rand Corporation, Santa Monica, California. Prior to joining Rand in September 1978, he was affiliated with the Harvard University Program (now Center) for International Affairs. A specialist on Chinese foreign and security affairs, he has published widely on these and related topics. His recent or forthcoming publications include articles in leading journals and essays in various edited volumes, including *The Soviet Threat – Myths and Realities, International Political Effects of the Spread of Nuclear Weapons*, and *China's Four Modernizations*. He is also co-editor and contributor to *Military Power and Policy in Asian States – China, India, Japan*, and author of a forthcoming monograph, *Security, Strategy, and the Logic of Chinese Foreign Policy*.

R.V.R. Chandrasekhara Rao is Professor of Political Science, Hyderabad University. He was formerly Professor of Politics at Andhra University, Waltair, and a Research Associate at the International Institute for Strategic Studies, London. His publications include: *From Innocence to Strength, Essays on World Politics*, (Madras, 1963); *Indian Unity*,(ed.), (New Delhi, 1969); *Civics*, (ed.), (Hyderabad, 1970); *International Relations*, (ed.), (Hyderabad, 1974); *Judicial Review and Fundamental Rights*, (Hyderabad, 1976); and 'Soviet Theory of International Relations', in *International Relations Theory*, (ed. K.P. Misra), (New Delhi, 1980).

Theodore Ropp has taught European, naval, military and technological history at Duke University in North Carolina since 1938. He has also taught at Harvard University, the US Naval and Army War Colleges, the United States Military Academy, the University of Singapore and the Royal Military College of Australia. He is currently completing a history of military conscription as a political issue in the English-speaking world. His best known work, *War in the Modern World*, (Durham, N.C., 1959), will be revised as soon as he and Donald M. Schurman finish their forthcoming expansion and commentary on E.M. Earle's *Makers of Modern Strategy*, (Princeton, 1941).

Warner Schilling is James T. Shotwell Professor of International Relations and Director of the Institute of War and Peace Studies, Columbia University, New York. He has contributed extensively to analysis of American strategic policy. His publications include:

Strategy, Politics and Defense Budgets, co-authored with Paul Y. Hammond and Glenn H. Snyder, (New York, 1962); *European Security and the Atlantic System*, co-edited with William T.R. Fox, (New York, 1973); *American Arms and a Changing Europe*, co-authored with William T.R. Fox, Catherine M. Kelleher and Donald J. Puchala, (New York, 1973).

Admiral Sir Anthony Synnot has been Chief of Defence Force Staff, Australia, since 1979. He has served in the Royal Australian Navy since 1939. He was a gunnery officer in the Second World War and has commanded *HMA* Ships *Warramunga*, 1956–57; *Vampire*, 1960–61; *Sydney*, 1966 and *Melbourne* 1967. He was Officer Commanding the Royal Malaysian Navy, 1962–65, attended the Imperial Defence College, London, 1968, was Director, Joint Staff, in the Department of Defence, 1974–76, and Chief of Naval Staff, 1976–79. He was President of the United Services Institute, Canberra, 1975–76.

J. Owen Zurhellen. Jr., is a recently retired American Ambassador who serves as a consultant on international affairs, foreign policy and related educational matters. He was a Foreign Service officer for over thirty years, serving in East Asia, Europe and the Middle East as well as in the Department of State in Washington. He was Deputy Director of the US Arms Control and Disarmament Agency, 1973–75, and Chairman of the US Delegation to the Preparatory Committee in Geneva for the 1975 Review Conference of the Nuclear Non-Proliferation Treaty. From 1975 to 1976 he was Deputy Assistant Secretary of State for East Asian Affairs.

Introduction

ROBERT O'NEILL

The purpose of this book is to examine major trends which have taken place in strategic thinking during the 1970s and to offer views on where these developments might lead in the 1980s. The 1970s have seen major developments across the whole field of strategic interaction, in areas such as the structure of international society, super-power doctrines, the working of alliances, the roles of developing nations, weapons technologies, tactical doctrines, arms control and political-military relations.

Their importance has been dramatised by the rise of international tensions which has followed the Soviet intervention in Afghanistan. While it is still too early to say with certainty that the world is entering a second Cold War, it is evident that military-strategic factors will play an increasingly important role in international relations during the 1980s. Hence it is particularly relevant at this juncture to appraise critically the major developments in this field over the past decade and to identify new trends which will continue to be effective in the troubled decade which appears to lie ahead. It is even more vital to foster thinking on how these troubles might be managed or overcome so that there might be a healthy and dynamic world order existing in a reasonable state of peace and harmony.

In the light of these aims, the book has been structured to examine the broader aspects of international strategic relations and then to analyse developments within particular nations, fields of warfare and areas of political-military interaction. Professor Theodore Ropp provides a broad context in the first chapter, in which he examines some of the major trends which have occurred in the development of strategy since the Second World War. Several authors then examine concepts governing super-power policies and the working of the international system: Professor Hedley Bull reviews the changing role of force in international society; Professor Warner Schilling and Mr Geoffrey Jukes respectively discuss the development of American and Soviet strategic doctrines; Mr Johan Holst analyses relations between the NATO and Warsaw Pact groupings; Dr Mohammed Ayoob investigates relations between the super-powers and the Third World;

and Dr T.B. Millar treats the changing nature of military alliances.

The focus of discussion then moves to the strategic thinking of the major Asian powers: Dr Jonathan Pollack examines Chinese concepts; Professor Chandrasekhara Rao analyses Indian ideas; and Professor Makoto Momoi discusses Japanese doctrines. Against this background the book then considers particular ways, short of nuclear war, in which force is used: Brigadier Kenneth Hunt discusses conventional warfare; Professor Roman Kolkowicz analyses limited warfare; and I examine insurgency warfare and sub-national violence. Three areas of particular importance in terms of political-military interaction are then considered: Professor Ned Lebow examines the nature of international conflict and the efficacy of the deterrence concept; Ambassador Owen Zurhellen analyses developments in the field of arms control; and Professor Bruce Miller discusses the political control of military force. Finally some concluding thoughts are offered, from differing standpoints, by Professor Bull, Admiral Sir Anthony Synnot and myself.

Planning and preparation of this volume has taken nearly two years. I was assisted in the initial stages of shaping its structure by my colleagues in the Department of International Relations and the Strategic Defence Studies Centre, Research School of Pacific Studies, Australian National University. Most of the authors were invited over a year ago to prepare their contributions. The Strategic and Defence Studies Centre, with financial support from the International Security and Arms Control Program of the Ford Foundation, held a conference at the Australian National University from 21 to 24 July 1980, at which initial versions of the chapters were presented before some 300 participants. In the light of discussions at the conference and afterwards, these chapters took the form in which they are now presented. It has been a guiding principle that the purpose of the conference was to assist in the shaping of the book rather than for the book to be simply a record of conference proceedings.

Others approaching this task might have chosen to place emphasis on different topics. Had it seemed desirable to produce a longer book, more topics might have been included and additional aspects of the present topics might have been explored. In the interests of utility to a wide cross-section of readers, both scholars and practitioners in the field of strategy, however, it seemed preferable to offer a concise treatment in a volume of something like the present size. It is left to others to attempt different approaches to examination of the problems of war and peace in the 1980s.

Finally I warmly acknowledge gratitude to the following for their assistance with the production of this volume and the organization of the Conference: Major David Horner, my co-editor; Mr J.O. Langtry, Executive Officer of the Strategic and Defence Studies Centre who bore the main burden of conference administration; Mrs Billie Dalrymple, Mrs Jocelyn West, Ms Catherine Thorpe, Mrs Patrya Kay, and Mrs Mary Manby who provided essential secretarial and other administrative assistance; Mrs Anna Booth who checked the references; Jann Little who compiled the index; and Mr Michael Holdsworth of George Allen and Unwin Ltd. for his co-operation in achieving a smooth and rapid publication.

Robert O'Neill
Canberra
October 1980

1 Strategic Thinking Since 1945

THEODORE ROPP

Makers of Modern Strategy Revisited

Carl von Clausewitz would have been only mildly surprised at an Antipodean bicentennial celebration of his birth on June 1, 1780. Nor would he have been surprised to find his "nuggets" *On War* being used to test those "complete systems" and "comprehensive doctrines" which he did not try to construct for himself from his carefully arranged "materials". Born in the 1770–89 decades when associates of the most intellectual of the Great Captains were working his maxims into a "puzzle-solving" system, Clausewitz saw it destroyed in the "crisis" of 1790–1809. After playing a significant part in its reconstruction in the decades of 1810–1829, he spent much of his time from 1818 to 1827 reflecting and writing on those mixtures of traditional and recently traumatic experiences and prophecies which his hieratic, disciplined, tradition-minded guild funds into its peacetime rules, balances, and sciences of war.

The years since Clausewitz's death on November 16, 1831 have seen two more military intellectual crises. They are related to the sixty-year major cycles of war and peace in Quincy Wright's *Study of War* (1964). Their crisis, paradigm-adaptation or reconstruction, and puzzle-solving phases are analogous to those in Thomas S. Kuhn's *Structure of Scientific Revolutions* (1962). The dates of the major wars and crises which began in 1792, 1854, and 1914 are not hard to convert into a two-decade model of military intellectual change within a civilization which, since Clausewitz's birth, has been expanding, industrializing, and increasing the scale and intensity of war, of peacetime preparations for it, and of what are now called strategic studies. If a crisis in Western strategic thought arrived on schedule for 1970–1989, it reflected the 1950–1969 puzzle-solvers' perceived inability to connect their post-Korean War conventional war formulas with those they had hastily constructed to solve the new puzzles of nuclear and unconventional warfare. And while popular military historians still deal with Great Captains, Battles, and Empires, even they now lard their traditional epics with analyses of the men, institutions, and ideas which they epitomize.

Peacetime puzzle-solvers deal first with their Most Recent Traumatic Experiences in the language of the Most Recent Winners. But each of the resulting systems for winning the last war better still reflects a connected set of ideas about societies, states, and military power, or, in Robert E. Osgood's and Robert W. Tucker's terms, about *Force, Order, and Justice* (1967). Though their balance sheets are often compared to those of war gaming, Clausewitz compared them to those of "commerce", or "*still* closer to politics, . . . a kind of commerce on a larger scale". But the balance sheets of military, political, and commercial calculations are never quite comparable. The pay-offs are in different coin; assets on one may even be liabilities on another. Like those internal balances which military strategists must cast between war's "remarkable trinity . . . of primordial violence . . . the play of chance and probability; . . . [and] policy, which makes it subject to reason alone", each entry reflects separate "codes of law, deep-rooted in their subject and yet variable in their relationship to one another. (Clausewitz, 1961, pp. 89, 149).

Many of the resulting intellectual problems are discussed in a forthcoming expansion of and commentary on Edward Meade Earle's *Makers of Modern Strategy* (1943).[1] So a summary of these earlier cycles of strategic thinking may help to chart those developments which made Makers, Modern, and Strategy look rather different in 1980 than in 1943. There had been no entry for strategy – from the Greek word for general – in Charles James's *New and Enlarged Military Dictionary* (1802). Those by Jomini and Clausewitz combined strategem — "the peculiar talent" of the French "to secure their victories more by science than by hardihood" – and stratarithometry — "the art of drawing up an army". They added maxims on the art of generalship drawn from histories, biographies, craft manuals, and letters of advice to princes written as early as the Fifth Century B.C. The military crises of the Persian and Peloponnesian Wars, like those of the contemporary Warring States of China, had produced itinerant teachers, advisers, and handbooks on many aspects of war. That strategems from writers as distant as Xenophon or Sun Tzu were still found in the works of Frederick the Great reflected the technical, economic, and military limitations of analogous agrarian societies, limitations traditionally compounded by cumulative seasonal labor investments in fixed fortifications.

The Enlightened Despots' strategic calculations had indeed been commercial. "Each government", Clausewitz remarked, "owned and managed a great estate that it constantly endeavored to enlarge. Their means of waging war . . . consist [ed] of the money in their coffers and of such idle vagabonds as they could lay their hands on". Since "each could estimate the other side's potential in terms both of numbers and time", a Great Captain such as Frederick with "relatively limited but highly efficient forces" could turn a "small state into a great monarchy". Clausewitz had no formula for this. But the "fact that a whole range of propositions can be demonstrated without difficulty: the defense is the stronger form of fighting with the negative purpose, attack the weaker form with the positive purpose . . . that strategic successes can be traced back to certain turning points", etc. meant that his maxims would bolster most of those staff planning systems which secured that "superiority of numbers" which was "the most common element in victory" in the great wars which began in 1792, 1854, and 1914. (Clausewitz, 1961, pp. 71, 194, 589).

The Prussian General Staff's successes in 1866 and 1870 made those training and logistics specialists almost wholly responsible for postwar strategic planning. Rudolph von Caemmerer's *Development of Strategical Science during the Nineteenth Century* (1904) fairly apportions credits to Frederick, Napoleon, Jomini, Clausewitz, and Helmuth von Moltke. But the planners' increased prestige and isolation had made it harder for "the inquiring . . . mind" with "the comprehensive rather than the specialized approach" to recognize new peacetime factors which they "would ordinarily miss or would perceive only after long study and reflection". Like Montesquieu, whom he was emulating, Clausewitz felt that every strategist's calculations "must be governed by the particular characteristics of his own position . . . the spirit of the age . . . and the nature of war itself". These would change the materials entered in the columns which he labelled as the moral, physical, mathematical, geographical, and statistical Elements of Strategy. (Clausewitz, 1961, pp. 102, 112, 183, 594).

Ferdinand Foch's *Principles of War* (1903) stressed "preparation . . . and *mass* multiplied by impulsion" to break "the moral and material forces of the enemy" in battle. Jomini's geometry of throwing "an army, successively, upon the decisive point of a theatre of war and also upon the communications of the enemy" demanded as many men deployed as quickly at the decisive point as possible. In war that was still becoming, in Foch's words, "more and more national . . . more and more powerful . . . more and more impassioned", the "ever increasing predominance of the human factor" would keep the offensive moving. So French revenge and German epics stressed the herioc offensive. Neo-Darwinist explanations for their new Empires stroked all Western egos. Army strategists hardly examined Alfred Thayer Mahan's Darwinist codification of Eighteenth Century naval strategic maxims. And neither military nor maritime strategy and tactics were officially questioned by independent scientific or foreign policy specialists. "Competent only by definition" in their new imperial bureaucracies, Europe's General Staffs had lost touch with what Guilio

Douhet was to call "the living, acting, operating nation". (Foch, 1921, pp. 95-96, 111, 221-222; Jomini, 1947, pp. 39-41; Douhet, 1943, p. 125).

A soldier needs peacetime intellectual security. He can practice his profession only by Douhet's "glance at the past", look at the present, and leap into the future. But this may upset doctrines which have become dogmas, and which readily suppress doubts and doubters. So peacetime strategists solve old puzzles while doubters may become unsung prophets. During the decades of 1770-1789, the Comte de Guibert had asked in 1772 what would happen if a people "arose in Europe, vigorous in spirit, in resources, and in government" with "a national militia, a fixed plan of aggrandizement, and ... a cheap war-making system, which subsists on its victories and is not reduced to laying down its arms by financial considerations". (Guibert, 1803, p. 16). Disowned by Guibert himself after he had met Frederick, this guess was so accurate that the doubters of 1830-1849 were chiefly concerned with the loyalty, logistics, and command of conscripted Napoleonic "national militias".

In 1890-1909 the doubts were technical, economic, and political. Soldiers' doubts about the tactical effects of their new rapid fire weapons were collected by the Polish Jewish economist and banker Ivan S. Bloch in six statistical volumes in *The Future of War in its Technical, Economic, and Political Relations* (1898). The new weapons would produce tactical and strategical deadlock, economic collapse, and political revolution. War had become politically impossible. Bloch's ideas were repressed, but they had some influence on the calling of the First Hague Conference and on later statistical studies of modern warfare. The first international one was set up in Berne by the Carnegie Endowment for International Peace in 1911. It was to study war "scientifically, and, as far as possible, without prejudice either for or against war", at a time when few of the subjects for its Commissions – on the Economic and Historical Causes and Effects of War, Armaments in Time of Peace, and Unifying Influences in International Life – were seen as part of the concerns of strategic science. (Clark, 1916, pp. vii-viii).

Sixty-six years after its 1914 debacle, historians are still classifying scientific strategy's critics and crisis suggestions about power balances, arms control, strategy, and tactics. F.W. Lanchester had a mathematical formula for determining the effectiveness of *Aircraft in Warfare* (1917). Douhet thought that they could "disintegrate nations". J.F.C. Fuller, B.H. Liddell Hart and others devised mechanized ground Blitzkriegs; others new submarine and amphibious tactics. Fuller thought that "the business of industrialized war demanded: ... (1) political authority; (2) economic self-sufficiency; (3) national discipline ... (4) machine weapons, and peacetime preparations". (1943, p. 35). Each great power adjusted its strategy accordingly during the Long Armistice. Once strategy had again become a joint political-military enterprise, both natural and social scientists contributed to the adjustments which led to the more-than-Napoleonic Western and Soviet victories of 1945. But the Great War idea that war was too serious a business to be left to the generals was not always replaced by the idea that it was too important to be left to any single group of either leaders or followers.

The Greening of the Military Intellectuals

The triumphs of the natural scientists and the modest victories of the social ones made strategic studies intellectually and militarily respectable. Their professors lunched with chancellors and generals, rather than with draymen and football coaches. Gaming and behavioural scientists helped Great Captains cope with scientific and technological innovation. The 1950–1969 decades produced a body of American social scientific theory – by Kenneth Boulding, Charles J. Hitch, Samuel P. Huntington, Morris Janowitz, Robert E. Osgood, Thomas C. Schelling, et al. – which helped to make postwar American strategy. But these makers were less personally influential than the Fullers or Liddell Harts of the previous decades. And the social sciences often taught in the military versions of strategic studies could be as dogmatic as the battle histories from which Foch had drawn his *Principles of War*.

The "Moral" columns of their strategic balance sheets were often as unsophisticated as those which had overstressed Napoleon's maxim that morale is to material as three is to one. These columns estimate "the skill of the commander, the experience and courage of the troops, and their patriotic spirit". Clausewitz knew that these were partially independent variables. "The wisest course is not to underrate any of them". There is too much "historical evidence of the unmistakable effectiveness of all three." (Clausewitz, 1961, pp. 183, 186). But some American balances treated the National Purpose and National Will like the Gross National Product, to be allocated by strategists to defend particular National Interests without any feedback into the National Will or Purpose. And their Traumatic Experiences with Western charismatic leaders in the 1930–1949 decades had made Communist, Social Democratic, and Liberal conflict managers reluctant to see how the rising expectations of the continuing democratic, national, and industrial revolutions might further change the "Moral" balances. Here A.J.P. Taylorish guilt over those combinations of containment and appeasement which had allegedly driven the industrial "have-nots" to war easily combined with imperialist guilt towards their new-free "sullen peoples, half-devil and half-child".

Material on the last Great Captains was overwhelming in volume and tendentiousness. Everyone soon knew all about Adolf, Monty, and Ike, less about Joe and Mao than about Charlemagne and Sun Tzu. With strategy so collectivized that historians were still arguing over the personal roles of Churchill and Lloyd George or the military genius of such amateurs as Smuts, Lawrence, Monash, and Trotsky, it was hardly time to study the German General Staff's performance in both wars as collective examples of Norman F. Dixon's work *On the Psychology of Military Incompetence* (1973). Nor have those American intellectuals, politicians, and soldiers who spread their strategic incompetence over several levels of the conflict spectrum during the late 1960's been collectively Clioanalyzed in this fashion.

The idea of a conflict spectrum was developed from the experience of Hiroshima, the early Cold War, and the Korean War. The concept was not new. It had been implicit in Clausewitz's and other strategists' comments on limited, people's, and *Small Wars*, for which the British strategist C.E. Callwell had produced a War Office handbook in 1896. But the 1950–1969 decade's first major change in the science of war was to replace the strategic calculations of Napoleonic warfare by as many as six sets of trial balances: for nuclear, conventional, limited, guerrilla, sub-national, and diplomatic coercion. And if some of the Berne Conference suggestions seemed strange to military strategists in 1911, subjects ranging from "Super-Power Policies and World Order" to "Sub-National Violence" would have again seemed stranger to military than to social scientists in the 1930's. China's accounting system, which ignorant Western strategists could only label "unconventional", eventually presented the multi-national alliances which soon filled the nationally-fragmented and strategically-unified international conflict arena with several more types of strategic calculation. Assets on one sheet might even be liabilities on another. Investment and cash flow problems increasingly depended on the accountant's own estimate of his "own position ... the spirit of the age ... and the nature of war itself". The rules by which military guildsmen had conducted wars had become separate palimpsests. Each practitioner had to read his directions with whatever part of the light spectrum he thought his society and guild chapter wanted him to use.

The Biggest Winner usually sets the tone of postwar strategic debate. So 1950–1969's topics and language tended to be as Anglo-American as they had once been French and German. The past decades' Most Traumatic Experiences were now embedded in such political codewords as Depression, Isolation, Appeasement, Maginot Line, Blitzkrieg, Pearl Harbor, Holocaust, Hiroshima, and Cold War. The nearly simultaneous Anglo-American decisions for demobilization and deterrence posed the first puzzles, established the first balance sheets for nuclear warfare, and largely determined their relations to the traditional balances of conventional and limited war. Anglo-American military scientific think tanks – institutionalized in the Rand Corporation and internationalized in the Institute for Strategic Studies – had already solved the puzzles posed by the Manhattan Project and the United States Strategic Bombing Survey. Whether their later intellectual crisis was due to the complexity of the new puzzles which they had to solve, to their overuse of statistical analysis, or to the specialization and dogmatism which came with too much success too soon is unanswerable. But by 1970 some gulfs seemed clearly apparent, to use Clausewitz's analogy, between the "analytical labyrinth" of some specialized military intellectuals and the strategic "facts of life". (Clausewitz, 1961, p. 183).

There was little immediate debate on the Anglo-American shift to the strategic defensive at "the culminating point of victory". Defensive firepower had led Bloch to conclude that war had become economically and politically impossible. Now technological "destruction by air" had become "too cheap and easy".[2] (Arnold, 1963, p. 32). Its long-term implications were discussed in Bernard Brodie's *Absolute Weapons* (1946). But natural scientists, except for P.M.S. Blackett, mostly turned to nuclear technology's puzzles, while social and military scientists turned to those of political and economic recovery, and of peacetime military organization and administration. The Korean "police action" solidified these short-term strategic solutions. Though China had been added to the balance, containment, deterrence, and a less total post-Korean War demobilization still fitted Anglo-American political, economic, and territorial interests. The end of the Anglo-American bomber and nuclear monopolies had been accounted for. The speed of Russian technological catch-up and of Western European and Japanese recovery re-enforced American views of machines as the keys to security and prosperity. For the decades of 1950–1960 they bought the West about as much security and prosperity as could have been reasonably expected. And, as Brodie, the most distinguished American writer on *Strategy in the Missile Age* admitted in his Clausewitzian *War and Politics* (1973), they were used with "critical restraint with respect to anything that might involve China or the Soviet Union ... despite the fact that the cost of that restraint was humiliation and military failure". (p. 432) (My term in international relations is "viable chaos".).

As Anglo-American strategists became absorbed in puzzle-solving, they wrote fewer general works. Fuller's last *Conduct of War* (1961) gave little support to Liddell Hart's ultimate hope – in *Deterrent or Defense* (1960) – for a reasonable return to the indirect approaches of British strategems. Other old warriors quaffed Old Nostalgia. The publishers' upbeat ending made Sir John Hackett's *Third World War* (1978) into a Pattonite best-seller. But Henry Eccles's *Military Principles and Philosophy* (1965) and *Military Power in a Free Society* (1979) were too wise and sensible to be sexy. In his still agrarian Europe Clausewitz had never seen technology as a deliberately manipulable strategic factor. More curiously, in an era in which technology has been accused of destroying so many traditional systems and doctrines, few strategists followed Andrew M. Scott's *Informal Penetration: The Revolution in Statecraft* (1960) in asking how electronic and air communications were making political, military, and ideological systems mutually permeable, segmented, frangible, and perhaps inoperable.

Many American works on air and/or nuclear strategy were unreadable. Full of distinctions without differences, they marched from massive retaliation through flexible response and finite deterrence and back to mutual assured destruction and the scholarly oblivion of their Nineteenth Century French and German puzzle-solving strategic companions. Herman Kahn's *On Thermonuclear Warfare* (1956) fed a socially useful science fiction industry which kept people *Thinking about the Unthinkable* (1962) and away from Henry Kissinger's *Nuclear Weapons and Foreign Policy* (1957) suggestions for less massive retaliation by proliferating smaller nuclear weapons. Kissinger and Kahn's work *On Escalation: Metaphors and Scenarios* (1962) took insufficient heed of Clausewitz's fear "that once barriers – which . . . consist only in man's ignorance of what is possible – are torn down, they are not so easily set up again. At least when major interests are at stake, mutual hostility will express itself in the same manner as in our own day". (Clausewitz, 1961, p. 593). For those mutually interested in staying alive, "attenuation factors" have already taken care of one official manual entry (AR 310–25): "Limited denied war – not to be used. No recommended substitute".

The officially recommended United States Air Force substitute for "victory" was "the attainment of our specific political objectives". By 1964 military power could "still be used directly, below the level of all-out war . . . only if civilian leaders regard it as relevant and usable in specific conflict situations", and were confident that it "will be applied with appropriate precision and restraint". (USAF, 1964, pp. 1–2). "Superiority of numbers" had been "the most common element" in Napoleonic victories. In situations where Brodie had been reduced to defining strategy as "the pursuit of viable solutions", (1973, p. 453) viability was still calculated in cost-effective, budgeting, and advertising numbers. Memories of Blitzkriegs and Pearl Harbor had been reenforced by the "missile gap" and Cuban missile crises to continue to fuel the air power, nuclear, missile, and space races.

After buying more arms than its Great Captain wanted, the Second Eisenhower Administration had still lost the "missile gap" Presidential election. Sixteen years later arms salesmen who had kept quiet during the Nixon-Ford Administration launched a similar "missile gap" Blitzkrieg against the incoming Carter Administration. Retired military intelligence officers challenged CIA figures. Supported by hardline scholarly panels their throw weight, megatonnage, missile, warhead, and tactical cum strategic bomber numbers got them enough high technology weapons to balance their worsening manpower figures. Russian actions helped to save the sacred cows of a weapons triad, sixteen carriers, fifteen divisions, and all-volunteer forces. SALT II was scuttled, draft registration begun, civil defence avoided, and allies told to shape up their percentages of their Gross National Products. So air power deterrence remained the core of American strategy, and resources were still allocated by those methods of statistical analysis which had built the bomb and justified both strategic bombing and the separate and primary Air Force which Douhetites had had since 1945. The new French math of nuclear sufficiency remained as contrary to arithmetical commonsense as relativity, or the Copernican system, or the statistical poisoning of water supplies with fluorides.

Figures sold the physical ("size of the armed forces, their composition, armament" etc.) and mathematical ("support and maintenance") elements of strategy. They were less use with its other mathematical ("lines of operation" and "movements wherever geometry enters into their calculation") and geographical elements. Deployment had been the foundation of Napoleonic strategic science, geopolitics a major development of the Great War decades. Anglo-American strategists had solved major deployment problems in the 1940's. But 1945 and 1954 left their demobilizing conventional forces next to the main forces of the powers which held the centre of the world island and had effectively used its interior lines during the Korean War. That similar conventional trip wire forces were being sent to as difficult geopolitical situations was partly due to an unwillingness to raise issues which might suggest Neo-isolationism or declining morale. More transport and conventional forces raised the draft issue and took money from long range missiles which could be redeployed by retargetting. So the United States Air Force steadily insisted that the whole "vast spectrum of conflict" was "a fluid, integrated whole". (USAF, 1964, p. 7–1).

Fluid it was. Integrated it was not, as Russia built up her conventional forces, re-enforced her interior position, and increasingly threatened the increasingly tenuous and demanding exterior communications of the Western allies. So new Anglo-American ideas on conventional and limited war were largely tactical, to take advantage of the defensive power of precision guided missiles. Something could be learned from the limited and guerrilla wars of 1954–1973, but their conflict arenas were so specialized that almost every war was fought under different rules in different geopolitical conditions. So Anglo-American sub-nuclear war strategies were as derivative and reactive as other powers' strategies were at the high end of the spectrum. Perhaps the American puzzle-solving system was as intellectually inflexible as those of the French and German Second Empires. Critics had seen their weaknesses, but it had been almost impossible for Napoleon III's and William II's advisers to reform a conservative and deliberately segmented polity. This view of the 1950–1969 decades may be only too American, deterministic, and masochistic. Their strategists' problems may have been largely psychological, but they seem to have been no less real for that. Containment and deterrence bought thirty-five years of general peace. The 1970 United States was not a helpless midget. It was, however, a pitiful cataleptic. Each jerk was soon immobilized by internal political and military forces. And few military historians have yet considered how its internal contradictions were related to so segmenting strategic science that policies were often mutually contradictory. Earlier examples were the militarily generated invasion scares which kept large British ground forces immobilized for much of the Great War. The idea that Western home and civil defence forces are provocative is analogous. And traditional Western blockade and boycott policies lie in similar ruins throughout the Western alliance.

A General Military Intellectual Crisis?

Did similar crises affect other strategic systems in the 1970's? War had simplified things by wiping out the German, Italian, and Japanese schools of strategy. The independent British and the French schools were gravely weakened. But Kuhn's model of crisis, paradigm-adaptation, and puzzle-solving does not require simultaneous crises among the surviving American and Russian schools, the newly discovered Chinese, and possible middle, small, or neutralist power strategies which had grown up while the great powers were destroying each other. But possible developments in these other schools may be easier to see from 1980 than from 1945. This may justify these brief comments on other systems, which are better handled by experts on contemporary strategic concepts.

A rather separated British school continued its tradition of writing for the general military and civilian public. No one reached the international position of Liddell Hart. Britain's problems were now more local. Liddell Hart and Fuller had been prophets justified by events, and many British strategists, such as Michael Howard, have been working back into the past. The British school has been chiefly concerned with traditional, commonsense advice to Washington, Paris, and Moscow, especially through the pamphlets and objective balance sheets of the International Institute for Strategic Studies. But so long as numbers dominated the game, it was hard for the layman, civilian or military, to distinguish between their balances and the scary assessments of worst case arms mongers or, on the other side, of the peace-mongering Stockholm International Peace Research Institute. But even the British school could not produce field manuals on peacekeeping or imperial devolution. The idea that blue hats, bewigged judges, and Sandhurst drilled officers were sufficient got some rude shocks in the 1970's.

The French grafted an independent nuclear strategy onto a traditional one for conventional warfare. Their long service forces, raised from conscripts selected for political loyalty, stressed, like the rather similar German forces, close relations with the civilian population, and high professional and technical standards. France gave Western Europe its own nuclear trigger force, a stake in the high technology arms and nuclear power industries, a special channel to Moscow, and a highly mobile strike force to aid the governments of former French colonies. France provided a market for new strategic and tactical ideas, and a lightning rod for Anglo-American frustrations with NATO or the European Common Market. Whether French public opinion was interested in, or even aware of, these French strategic developments is unclear. This is equally true of the reviving German and Japanese schools of strategy. There is little question about the Italians, who have other fish to fry.

Russian and Chinese strategies for conventional and unconventional war have apparently changed little since the 1950's. Strong conventional forces and the West's defensive strategy protected Russian nuclear, air, and naval rearmament. Both Marxist powers could feel that Western failures to win limited revolutionary wars presaged their eventual defeat. Conscription remained a major modernizing and Sovietizing force. Masses of solid machines were turned out by the heavy industries which both powers placed in the vanguard of their socialist revolutions. Masses of advanced weapons were now available to the Russians and their new noncontiguous allies. Both Russia and China accused each other of substituting gas for nuclear weapons. Both powers may believe that all wars, nuclear included, remain winnable. There is little evidence – in arms which are being built up in all areas – of the strategic weights given to Russian and Chinese nuclear, conventional, and unconventional forces.

Bureaucratic caution and tradition and some remaining splits in revolutionary policies may have immobilized Soviet and Chinese strategies as thoroughly as the Americans were immobilized by their inability to move very far very fast in any direction. So that lack of strategic imagination which seemed characteristic of American puzzle-solving in the 1970's may also have affected both the Soviet Union and

China. In 1945 few American futurists had seen that Soviet bureaucrats would pile up arms for thirty-five years rather than change them
to consumer goods in a society which had gone without the latter for
decades. But few Soviet futurists imagined that the Western Communist parties would mellow, or that China would come under the
nuclear American umbrella and the Japanese economy, and then try
to punish a Marxist ally for disloyalty. So the three strategic systems
which had been more or less successful since the 1930's may have
spent more time on the new puzzles presented by the new American
strategy than on developing new general ideas. It may be that the
initiative in developing strategy passed to such rising great powers as
India or Brazil, to recovering ones such as France, to the slowly growing "nuclear sufficiency" club, and to some middle and small powers
at some time around 1970.

In any case our Conference organizers saw the years from the Tet
offensive through the Yom Kippur War and the Arab Oil embargo as
ones which began "notable changes in great power balances, in the
role of force in situations short of war and in the conduct of war
itself". So an historical introduction to the baselines from which to
measure development in strategic thinking had to place the years from
1945 to 1970 in the context of previous Makers of Modern Strategy.
The model of intellectual change which has been useful in suggesting
such developments since the end of the eighteenth Century may continue to be useful for the 1970's and 1980's. There is considerable
evidence of a sense of crisis in American strategic thought, and of
public unhappiness with American strategic leadership. There is
much less evidence that these have yet "evoked an alternative candi-
date for paradigm".[3] (Kuhn, 1962, pp. 109, 143–144). Some just
might come from those middle and small power strategists who, since
the Napoleonic wars, have managed to defend Swedish and Swiss
neutrality. ASEAN is one of their presently most beset regional organizations. The Organization of American States may be the most presently successful in damping down organized political violence and in
corporative political thought and action.

The most relevant modern strategic maxim is Picasso's: "The
against comes before the for". Every historian's favorite sport is telling social scientists what went wrong. This is most relevant at the
bicentenary of that professional soldier who so distrusted "complete
systems" and "comprehensive doctrines" of war. As Kissinger remarked at Napoleon's bicentenary, "There goes Old Lyndon to St.
Helena. He won't like it there". Or Lloyd George's opener in Paris a
half century before that: "Well, Gentlemen, we won. But by God we
almost lost". Or Admiral Thucydides comment to Flight Lieutenant
Xenophon: "So your hot Spartan whirlies blew it in Persia". But we
need an upbeat prediction for the nineteenth Bloch slide show at the

Hague. As we gather from Canberra, Singapore, Stockholm, Mexico City, Potsdam, and Durham for the bicentenary of the Declaration of the Rights of Man and the Citizen not to kill each other, someone will have rearranged Clausewitz's nuggets. Our Odyssey of "Arms and the Man" will begin again where "Troy was beyond all hope of aid. I accepted defeat, picked up my father and made for the mountains".

Section One
Concepts Governing Super-Power Policies and World Order

2 Force in International Relations
The Experience of the 1970s and Prospects for the 1980s

HEDLEY BULL

In the late 1960s and the first few years of the 1970s, it was widely held in the Western world that the role of force in international relations had gone into decline. The gains that could be achieved by resort to force, we were told, were shrinking: in particular, the use of force to acquire or maintain control of overseas territories did not advance a nation's prosperity – an old liberal thesis then being refurbished to justify Britain's retreat from east of Suez. The costs of resort to force, on the other hand, were said to be rising: costs such as political opprobrium in world opinion, the enmity of Third World nations sensitive to foreign domination, domestic political turmoil, economic dislocation and ultimately, if there was a risk of nuclear war, the physical destruction of one's own society. The great success story of the West in the 1960s had been the economic growth of West Germany and Japan, achieved without resort to force and indeed in a resolutely anti-military frame of mind. The West's recent experience of war, by contrast, was associated with some bitter failures: for Britain Suez, for France Indochina and Algeria, for the United States Vietnam.

The thesis of the declining utility of force was not simply a thesis about the impact of nuclear weapons, that force cannot serve as an instrument of state policy if it leads to a generally ruinous nuclear war. The ideas of the late 1960s and early 1970s concerned non-nuclear force as well as nuclear, and treated the declining role of force in the nuclear era as the culmination of a trend that had begun very much earlier. They harked back to the thesis stated by Auguste Comte one hundred and fifty years ago, of a fundamental incompatibility between war and industrial civilisation, between (as he put it) 'the spirit of conquest' and 'the spirit of industry'. The great wars which the industrialised countries did in fact fight against one another in the first half of this century might have been thought to have disproved Comte's thesis, but he never said that industrial civilisation would extinguish war at once, and defenders of his position like Veblen and Schumpeter had been able to attribute the persistence of war in the industrial era to the survival in Germany and Japan of pockets of a pre-industrial, feudal or warrior ethos. In our own times the long post-war period of peace maintained by the industrialised powers in their relations with one another led to a revival of interest in Comte's ideas: Raymond Aron, for example, gave them a qualified endorsement in his 1957 Auguste Comte lecture at the London School of Economics, and Klaus Knorr, in a book *On the Uses of Military Power in the Nuclear Age*, published in 1966 and asserting the declining utility of force, also made use of Comte's arguments. Since the Second World War, indeed, no full-scale war between highly industrialised states had taken place, and although wars in the non-industrialised or partly industrialised Third World had been legion, this could be thought only to provide confirmation of what Comte said.

In the late 1960s and early 1970s also, a school of writers about international politics began to argue that the strategic factor in international power relationships was giving place to an economic factor. Stanley Hoffmann told us that competition for military power was only one of the 'many chessboards' on which the game of international politics was played (1968). Accounts of what was called 'transnational relations' stressed the importance in world politics of multinational corporations and other non-state actors, that were without military power (see Keohane and Nye, 1972). States that had large gross national products, but were weak in terms of military power, were accorded a new status – the classic example being, of course, Japan, proclaimed by its Prime Minister, Eisaku Sato, in 1970 to be on the way to becoming the first non-military great power in history.

It was at this time also that great currency came to be given to the American doctrine of the growing so-called 'interdependence' of the various societies of the world. In these early formulations of the doctrine, the growth of 'interdependence' was thought to be having benign effects upon international politics: societies that were more interconnected and more sensitive to one another, it was thought, were bound to develop a sense of unity and common purpose: in the highly 'interdependent' world of the OECD countries, force had been largely banished from the relations between one country and another, and as 'interdependence' spread its tentacles around the world to embrace the societies of the East and the South as well as those of the West, benign consequences might be expected to follow there also.

A local expression of this belief in the declining utility of force was perhaps Mr Whitlam's memorable statement, on assuming office as Prime Minister in December 1972, that Australia would in future have a foreign policy that was 'less militarily oriented'. As late as 1973 Alastair Buchan thought it appropriate to entitle his BBC Reith Lectures *Change Without War*. In September 1973, immediately before the October Middle East war which, I think, marks the great watershed in our perceptions of this matter, Professor Laurence Martin told the annual conference of the International Institute for Strategic Studies that 'there is a growing consensus that the utility of force has diminished, is diminishing and should diminish further' (p. 14).

Today, rightly or wrongly, the ideas I have been describing are in large part rejected. In the Western world there is now a widespread expectation that the role of force will not diminish but increase – an expectation that is borne out by the evidence of mounting arms and arms expenditures in the Soviet bloc, the Third World and the West itself. The costs and risks of resort to force may still be great, but the gains to be expected from it are thought increasingly to render these costs and risks acceptable. Nations that are rich in terms of technology, industrial production and gross national product, but militarily weak, are today thought to be dangerously vulnerable. However we assess the prospects that in the long term Comte's thesis of the incompatibility of war and industrial civilisation will be validated, no-one expects that the prophecy will be fulfilled in the foreseeable future, and it is interesting that Raymond Aron and Klaus Knorr have both now published retractions of their earlier endorsements of a Comtean or neo-Comtean thesis (Aron, 1978–9; Knorr, 1977). The growth of 'interdependence' is now more often taken to be malign rather than benign in its effects upon international conflict: defined as mutual vulnerability, its spread around the world is said to be the source of new conflicts and to provide new levers with which states can bring pressure to bear on one another. The academic thesis that economic concerns are driving strategic concerns off the centre of the stage of world politics, is now in full retreat, and power-political interpretations of international relations, a decade ago written off as obsolete, are now once again in full flood. No-one would seriously maintain that economic considerations are of declining importance in world politics, but it is no longer being claimed that these considerations are taking the place of strategic or military matters. The pursuit of wealth and the pursuit of military power, instead of being thought of as different and conflicting goals of state policy, are increasingly thought to be bound up with one another. There has been, in other words, a return to mercantilist perceptions: the pursuit of wealth is thought to require the use of force.

Why has this change of perception come about? I propose to explore this question by examining five assumptions that were made by those who proclaimed the declining role of force at the beginning of the last decade, but which the experience of the 1970s has caused us to modify, if not to abandon altogether. First, there was the assumption of a continuing process of détente between the United States and the Soviet Union, the consequence of which would be to contain the role that force would play at this major point of tension. The foundations of a relaxation of tension between the super powers had been laid with the conclusion of the Partial Nuclear Test Ban Treaty in 1963 and the series of further arms control agreements that came later in the 1960s. During Nixon's Presidency, from 1969 to 1974, Soviet-American détente was extended to embrace the SALT I Agreements of 1972 and a comprehensive package of agreements on other subjects, in the spirit of Dr Kissinger's theory of positive 'linkage'. A European process of détente led in the early 1970s to the conclusion of agreements between West Germany and its eastern neighbours, and was generalised through the 1971 four power agreement on Berlin, and the opening in 1973 of the Nato-Warsaw Pact negotiations on mutual force reductions and the wider Conference on Security and Co-operation in Europe, involving neutral countries also. The United States and China were also embarked upon a process of détente which, at least on the American side, was not directed against the Soviet Union but was rather seen as a step towards the construction of a wider edifice binding all the major powers together, a twentieth century equivalent of the Concert of Europe. For a brief period during President Nixon's 'era of negotiation' the world appeared to be in the grip of a kind of détente fever: a Vietnam peace agreement was signed, a host of other countries followed the United States in moving towards a normalisation of relations with China and contacts were even established between such unlikely partners as North and South Korea.

The period of détente gave rise to hopes for a diminished role of force that were by no means wholly illusory. The super powers did manage to translate their inchoate sense of a shared interest in avoiding nuclear war into some common rules and institutions. Throughout the 1970s the world came to feel less insecure in relation to the danger of war between the superpowers than it had done in the cold war period: not even the most serious super crisis of the decade – that which occurred at the time of the worldwide alert of United States strategic forces in October 1973 – was there felt the raw fear of the 1962 Cuban missile crisis. The SALT I Agreements of 1972, even the Vladivostok Accords of 1974, while they did not do much in themselves to stabilise the strategic nuclear balance, to control the so-called arms race or to reduce the level of armaments, nevertheless pointed the way towards possible subsequent agreements that would advance these objectives. The super powers did stake out some claims to be regarded as responsible trustees in the custody of their own nuclear weapons, and despite the opposition which was generated by the 1968 Non-Proliferation Treaty and the setback to it provided by the Indian nuclear explosion of 1974, they did provide some momentum to attempts to control the spread of nuclear weapons. The process of détente in Europe that culminated in the 1975 Helsinki Final Act did bring about a radical decline in the level of tension between NATO and the Warsaw Pact countries in Europe.

In the second half of the 1970s, the edifice of détente between the superpowers first tottered and then collapsed. As the United States sees it, this is because the Soviet Union violated the rules of détente by building up its strategic arms in the pursuit of superiority, by further developing its preponderance of military power in Europe and by embarking upon an adventurist course of naval expansion and military intervention in the Third World. As the Soviet Union sees it, the rules of détente never embraced cessation of the political and ideological struggle for national liberation in the Third World; what the Americans are reacting against is not Soviet achievement of superiority but the loss of the superiority they have themselves taken for granted throughout the postwar period; moreover, the United States, with its West European and Japanese allies and the Soviet Union's deadly enemy China, are embarked upon a policy of encirclement to which the Soviet military build-up is a defensive response.

Whatever the merits of these explanations, we now face a future in which there is no longer any momentum towards developing the structure of understanding between the superpowers, and in which some of the present structure – for example, the ABM Treaty of 1972 – is under threat of dismantlement. Not only are the SALT negotiations in limbo: a deep scepticism about the whole process of arms control has now set in, even in those quarters previously most sanguine about it, reflecting an intellectual vacuum as to how progress in this field could be made, even if the political conditions for it were less unfavourable than they are. The strategic nuclear balance itself, I believe, is still stable, but not only are there powerful technological developments working to undermine it; strategic doctrines are now in the ascendancy in the United States which, like those which may always have prevailed in the Soviet Union, treat the goal of stability as subordinate to the objective of the rational conduct of a strategic nuclear war: the Schlesinger doctrine of 'flexible options', unveiled in 1973, may have added little to the ideas elaborated by McNamara more than a decade earlier, but now that there exists the technology to make some of these options physically available, together with an apparently much stronger will to use them, the danger that so-called limited nuclear strikes may be attempted, has grown. In Europe the structure of East-West détente is still standing, but while the West European allies still clearly adhere to it, the United States itself is increasingly detached from it. The détente between the United States and China has survived and indeed has been taken further, but in the Carter era, by contrast with the era of Nixon and Ford, it has come to be directed against the Soviet Union. Of the projected concert of great powers nothing remains, unless it be the grand alliance of all the major industrialised states against the Soviet Union, which seems now to be in process of formation.

Secondly, the belief that the utility of force was in decline reflected the assumption that the world's resources for development were abundant and that access to them was freely available through the workings of a liberal international economic system. Broadly speaking, wars throughout history have been fought to advance three kinds of objective, all of them set out, as every student of International Relations knows, in Thucydides' *History of the Peloponnesian War*. There are wars fought for reasons of security, like the Peloponnesian war itself, or the First World War. There are wars fought to advance an ideology, like the Crusades or the Wars of Religion. And there are wars for economic gain, like the European trade and colonial wars of the age of mercantilism. In the first quarter century after the Second World War we had our share of wars fought chiefly for security, which is the chief motive making for a Third World War, which we have so far managed to avoid. We have also had a great many wars of ideology, in the form of the various so-called wars of national liberation, directed against colonial rule, neo-colonial domination and white supremacism. In this period, however, there do not appear to be any very convincing examples of wars undertaken primarily for economic gain. Whereas the Second World War had arisen in large measure from the German desire for the food resources and living space of east Europe and the Ukraine and the Japanese desire for access to the raw materials of South-east Asia, after 1945 wars do not appear to have been undertaken for reasons of this kind.

But in the course of the 1970s the economic or material rationale for the use of force was rediscovered, as we came to think of the earth's resources as finite and ceased to take for granted the continuation of the liberal international economic order. The year which stands out as marking the transition from the assumption of abundance to the assumption of scarcity, from liberal optimism to Malthusian pessimism, from a productionist to a distributionist or zero sum approach to international relations is of course 1973. It is true that the Club of Rome Report on *The Limits to Growth* was already published in 1972, that the strains upon the postwar liberal international economic order were already made clear by the protectionist measures passed by Congress in 1970 and President Nixon's monetary changes of 1971, and that the West's growing dependence on oil imports from the Middle East was already well known at this time. But the oil price rises, the production cuts and selective embargoes imposed by the Arab oil producers during the October War, dramatising the vulnerability of the industrialised nations of the West and the new bargaining power of some Third World countries, gave a concrete demonstration of the meaning of scarcity that has coloured all our thinking since that time.

The 1973 crisis had not been the consequence of physical limitations of resources of the kind stressed in the Club of Rome Report, but rather of local scarcity arising from political and economic circumstances: from this point on, however, a perception of scarcity, an inclination to emphasise the struggle to distribute the world product, as opposed to co-operative endeavour to increase it, came to pervade international politics. In 1974 the Third World advanced its demands for a New International Economic Order and what had previously been seen, at least by most official spokesmen on both sides, as a partnership between North and South in promoting the development of poor countries, as envisaged, for example, in the Pearson Report, *Partners in Development*, came more and more to be seen as a struggle between North and South over the distribution of wealth and power. The East-West struggle also came to be seen as in part a struggle in which each side sought to control the world's resources or deny them to the other: Soviet expansionism in Africa in the late 1970s, for example, and later in south west Asia, was interpreted in the West as directed towards control of resources and disruption of Western access to them. A scramble developed for the resources of the sea and the seabed, only partly moderated by the long and inconclusive series of Law of the Sea Conferences that began in 1974. The historic argument for freedom of the seas had been the one deployed by Grotius in *Mare Liberum*, that the resources of the sea were abundant, and that enclosure by particular states was therefore inappropriate. But the argument on which states were acting as, unilaterally or in concert, they extended their claims to territorial seas, exclusive economic zones and the exploitation of the deep seabed, was the argument that the resources of the sea were scarce, the argument of John Selden's reply to Grotius, *Mare Clausum*.

The new consciousness of the scarcity of resources did not at first result in any change in prevailing views about the utility of force. The power which the Arab oil producers had demonstrated in the 1973 crisis was, after all, not military power, and the impotence of the Western countries when confronted with it was taken to be one more sign of the ineffectiveness of military force in enabling them to obtain their objectives. The great upsurge of interest among Third World countries in the further exploitation of 'oil power' and in exploring the possibility that producers' associations might wield comparable kinds of power in other areas, was matched in the West by a flurry of interest in the possibility of fighting 'oil power' with 'food power'. The term 'resources diplomacy', when it was coined in Australia at about this time, was taken to indicate a new form of power or influence deriving from the possession of resources known to be scarce and providing an alternative to arms and alliances as the basis of a foreign policy. (It became the source, I recall, of some rather tiresome Australian cockiness).

It was not long, however, before it began to be pointed out that the power conferred by possession of scarce resources might exist only for so long as those who had superior military force chose not to use it. The militarily strong might after all decide to seize resources which they were denied, and if this were so, possession of scarce resources, instead of making a state uniquely powerful, might make it uniquely vulnerable. The new consciousness of scarcity has in fact had the result of providing a new rationale for the use of force — or, more strictly, of restoring the credibility of an old one. Strong countries threatened with denial of the resources they need have sought to exploit their military power to secure them, as the United States began to do in 1974 and 1975 when statements by President Ford, Dr Kissinger and Dr Schlesinger envisaged the possibility of the use of force to secure oil supplies from the Middle East. Militarily weak countries without control of the resources they need came to be preoccupied with the military security of access routes, as Japan came to be in relation to oil routes from the Gulf to the north west Pacific. Countries which did possess scarce resources came to be convinced that they must have the military forces to defend them: thus a scramble for naval armaments developed as nations staked out their legal claims to fisheries and offshore oil and gas fields. In the latter half of the 1970s military doctrines and preparations came to be preoccupied with resources issues. Sometimes the focus of attention has been the resource itself, as most notably with Middle Eastern oil, sometimes with access routes to it, as with the Heath Government's justification of arms sales to South Africa to help protect the route *via* the Cape. Sometimes the intention has been to coerce producers themselves, as in the case of the Ford Administration's threats in response to the oil embargo, sometimes it has been rather to deter intervention by an outside power, as in the case of the Carter Doctrine stated in response to a purported Soviet threat to the Persian Gulf. Sometimes the doctrines and preparations for resources warfare are basically defensive in intent, in other cases, perhaps, implicitly predatory. The number of actual armed conflicts that have occurred about which one can say that the resource issue was prominent in them, or may have been, is so far few: the Anglo-Icelandic cod wars, the struggle for the phosphate-rich Spanish Sahara, the Chinese seizure of the Paracels. But the atmosphere has become heavy with expectation.

There was a third assumption made by those who proclaimed the decline of military force, which was that military intervention, or at all events direct military intervention in the affairs of Third World countries, had ceased to be a viable instrument of policy and indeed had become counter-productive. When Western observers at the end of the 1960s spoke of the declining utility of military force it was above all this kind of use of force that they had in mind. The use of strategic nuclear weapons to deter attack by the Soviet Union was expected to continue; so was the function of NATO forces in confronting the forces of the Warsaw Pact in Europe. But the despatch of Western expeditionary forces or the maintenance of Western garrisons to maintain colonial rule, post-colonial positions of influence or client governments in Third World countries was thought to be part of an era of world history that was drawing to a close. Except in the Portuguese territories, colonial rule had virtually ceased to exist. The independent states of the Third World were notoriously sensitive to Western policies that smacked of military coercion. And the Vietnam quagmire was taken to have shown that Western attempts to influence the political direction of Third World societies could no longer be based on direct military intervention.

It is true that the Western retreat from direct military intervention led to a search for appropriate instruments of indirect intervention: the late 1960s and early 1970s were the era of 'the Vietnamisation of the war', the Nixon Doctrine, the Five Power Arrangements, the Shah's assumption of Britain's hegemonial role in the Persian Gulf – formulae which sought to make local governments the agents of Western policies through military assistance and extra-regional strategic and naval power, as a substitute for a Western military presence on the ground. This was also a period of increased reliance upon clandestine intervention: the overthrow of Allende in September 1973, the secret bombings in Cambodia and Laos, America's muted forms of co-operation with South Africa and Portugal. But in 1974 and 1975, under the shadow of the Watergate affair and revelations about the CIA, public opinion in the United States turned strongly against indirect intervention in the Third World also, and at the same time against the degree of Executive control of foreign policy that had allowed this form of intervention to take place. The high-water mark of American non-interventionism came in 1975, when Congress denied the Executive the funds necessary to provide support for the faction it was backing in Angola, while also preventing the extension of promised assistance to the Thieu Government in Vietnam, as it faced the coup de grâce from Hanoi.

Today in the 1980s, as the Americans prepare their Rapid Deployment Force and acquire new bases in the Indian Ocean, as the British turn once again towards recovering some capacity for military action east of Suez, the French strengthen their *Force d'intervention* and even the West German military begin tentatively to look beyond European horizons, as the East Germans have long been doing, it is clear that the era of Western military intervention in Africa, Asia and Latin America has not come to an end but is about to enter a new phase. Why has this change of attitude come about?

One factor has been, of course, the growth during the 1970s of Soviet military intervention in the Third World, both indirectly through their Cuban allies in Africa and directly in Afghanistan. Before the 1970s direct military intervention in Third World countries was the exclusive preserve of the Western powers. They were the countries which had inherited colonial and neo-colonial positions in Africa, Asia and Latin America and the habit of defending them by force. It was against these inherited positions of the West Europeans and North Americans, their colonies, neo-colonies and ties with settler regimes, that the main thrust of Third World revolt was directed. The Soviet Union was in the fortunate position of being without historical entanglements of this kind; it was free to provide military assistance to national liberation movements and militantly anti-Western Third World governments and so align itself with what it rightly saw to be the prevailing wind, with which it was genuinely in sympathy. Only in Asia, where China was denouncing the 'unequal treaties' that defined the Sino-Soviet border and mobilising Third World sentiment against the Soviet Union, and where the Soviet Union's own non-European population rendered it open to the charge of being the last colonial power, did it seem vulnerable.

As in the course of the 1970s the Soviet Union came increasingly to duplicate the West's capacity for military intervention in the Third World and also to display a will to engage in it, it was argued that the strengthened ability of Third World countries to withstand intervention by industrialised states would operate to frustrate the Soviet Union, just as it had been found to frustrate the West. The more the Soviet Union sought to wield a big stick in Africa or south west Asia, it was said, the more it would create its own quagmires. Soviet intervention, therefore, did not have to be checked by Western counter-intervention; it would be checked by the same forces of African, Asian and Latin American nationalism that had rendered the old policies of coercion counter-productive for the West. The Soviet Union's strategic airlift capacity and helicopter gunships, its blue water navy and network of shore facilities, Admiral Gorshkov's doctrines of sea-power culled from the pages of Sir Julian Corbet and A.T. Mahan, were on this view essentially anachronistic and would only provide further confirmation of Senator Fulbright's thesis of 'the impotence of power'.

A good deal of evidence has accumulated that provides confirmation of this thesis: the expulsion of the Soviet Union from Egypt and Somalia, the condemnation of the Soviet invasion of Afghanistan by the UN General Assembly and the Islamic Conference, the quagmire that may indeed be developing in the wake of that invasion. But the Soviet leadership do not appear to have grasped the point that the methods they have chosen are anachronistic. It may be doubted whether the methods that proved counter-productive for the Western countries will prove equally so also for a power that has the confidence in its historic mission, the control of its own information media, the ruthlessness in execution, to enable it to intervene decisively, as it has demonstrated in eastern Europe that it has. Forcible intervention in the affairs of weaker neighbours has, of course, been practised successfully by certain of the stronger Third World countries – during the 1970s, for example, by India, Iran, Indonesia and Vietnam. The thesis that military intervention was an ineffective instrument for promoting Western objectives in Third World countries in the post-war era is in any case, I am afraid, mistaken. It generalises from a few cases. There were some spectacular failures, like Suez and Vietnam, but given the West's objectives – of resisting Third World demands for change, or at least controlling the pace of change – force was frequently used successfully to achieve the intended results: think, for example, of Britain's actions in defeating the communist insurrection in Malaya, Indonesia's policies of confrontation of Malaysia, and the East African mutinies in 1964. One may doubt that the objectives in such cases should have been pursued, but not that force was able to accomplish them.

The revival of interventionism in the West therefore has as one of its causes a growing feeling that Soviet intervention does, after all, have to be checked by counter-intervention. In the late 1960s and early 1970s it was frequently, and I should say correctly, argued by critics of official Western policies that the challenges delivered by the Third World to the West's inherited position of dominance arose essentially from indigenous factors and not as a consequence of Soviet machinations; that the problem of the West's relationship to the Third World had to be confronted in its own right, and not treated as simply one aspect of the West's conflict with the East. I believe that this is still true, and that to proceed as if the West's principal business in the Persian Gulf or in southern Africa is to meet Soviet force with counterforce or to combine with whatever local elements are most anti-Soviet promises to lead to the same disasters for the West in the future that it has produced in the past. But it has to be acknowledged that a new situation has arisen: Soviet military intervention is now a reality and not a figment of the Western imagination, and the East-West dimension of the West's relations with Third World countries seems likely to grow.

The belief that Soviet expansion should be checked is not, however, the only or even the main cause of the revival of military interventionism in the West. This is rather the consequence of a growing conviction that the Western countries can and should defend the national interests that they have at stake in Third World countries. From the late 1940s to the early 1970s the impulse underlying Western intervention was in large measure ideological: it derived from the waning imperial ideologies of the West Europeans and the anti-communist mission espoused by the Americans. The ideological impulse does not show any sign of recovery, but its place has been taken by an impulse to intervene forcibly to protect interests in the Third World felt to be under threat. This impulse is fed by a number of causes: the new militancy of many Third World countries and the backlash against it generated in the West; the spread of zero-sum assumptions about the relationship between our national interests and theirs; the belief in scarcity of resources, to which I have already alluded; the rejection of Western values in many parts of the Third World, most dramatically in some Islamic countries, and the consequent feeling in the West that we and they no longer form part of a single moral community; the prolonged recession in the Western World that produces a grasping and ugly resolve to defend a declining standard of living by whatever means are available.

The interests the West is now prepared to defend by forcible intervention take one back to European and American interventionism in its heyday in the second half of the last century and the early decades of this century. There is intervention to protect the lives of Western citizens abroad – exemplified by the Israeli raid on Entebbe in 1976, the West German action at Mogadishu, the Franco-Belgian intervention in Zaire and the abortive United States rescue mission in Iran. There is intervention to protect Western property in Third World countries, as distinct from Western lives, which appears to be a principal object of recurrent French interventions in francophone Africa. There is intervention to protect security interests, as in the case of Israeli and South African incursions into neighbouring territories to attack guerrilla sanctuaries. And there is intervention to protect resources and lines of access to them, by maintaining pliable governments in power, and perhaps to seize these resources should these governments be replaced by hostile ones. Whether or not one thinks that intervention for reasons such as these is justifiable, it has to be noted all are condemned by Third World opinion, and that claims of a right to exercise them fly in the face of legal restrictions on the right of forcible interference that have been gathering force since Latin American states first proposed them as long ago as the Second Hague Conference in 1907.

This brings me to a fourth assumption, which was that the use of force was inhibited by its growing illegitimacy. The growth in this century of inhibitions to the utility of force as an instrument of policy has, of course, been accompanied by the multiplication of inhibitions to its legality, culminating in the UN Charter, which prohibits all use or threat of force by states except in self-defence or as part of an enforcement action authorised by the Security Council. No student of international politics would fail to recognise the capacity of states to ignore this or any other legal restriction on their right to resort to force, or minimise the differences of interpretation of the Charter which already existed at the end of the 1960s. But there was at least some core of common understanding of the principle that states should not resort to force except in self defence, and some international lawyers still found it possible to advance highly restrictive interpretations of this principle. In the course of the 1970s, however, widely differing views about the legality and, more broadly, the legitimacy of the use of force have been advanced, on the one hand by the Western powers, and on the other hand by the Socialist and some Third World countries, with the result that whatever core of common understanding there was has further diminished.

In the Western countries there has been a tendency, while still relying on the right of self-defence, to give the principle a wider interpretation, cutting away the restrictions that have been insisted upon by international lawyers of liberal persuasion, and seeking to derive from it the wide licence which it was taken to confer in the pre-1945 and indeed the pre-1919 era. For example, the doctrine that the right of self-defence can be invoked only in the case of an attack on one's territory has given place to the idea that the right may be invoked also to defend one's citizens abroad and thus to provide a justification of armed interventions in other states. The Israelis, the South Africans and the late government of Rhodesia, although admittedly without general support from Western countries, have taken the right of self-defence to include a right to attack guerrilla groups based in neighbouring states, and also to attack these states themselves in cases where they fail to exert control over locally based guerrilla groups. There have been attempts to revive the nineteenth century concept of a right to humanitarian intervention, a right to intervene militarily so as to uphold human rights in other countries, the right which in the last century provided the European powers with a principal justification for the dismemberment of the Ottoman Empire, and which during the 1970s India is sometimes said to have exercised in East Pakistan, Tanzania in Uganda and Vietnam in Cambodia.

There is, I think, a tendency at present in Western thinking about the legitimacy of force to broaden the right of self-defence into a right of self-help in enforcing legal rights of many kinds, and indeed a further tendency for the right of self-help to be presented as including a right of self-preservation, a right to take whatever action is necessary to ensure the survival of the state. The 1974 Kissinger statement, envisaging the use of force to prevent economic strangulation, amounts to a return to such a doctrine of a right of self-preservation. It is true that Kissinger is said to have intended this statement as a deterrent, rather than as an enunciation of what future policy would be. It is also true that his statement made clear that the use of force would not be an appropriate response to a mere rise in oil prices that did not carry with it the threat of strangulation. There is, indeed, an important moral distinction between military action to prevent the collapse of a whole society and economy, and action merely to preserve a particular, in this case extremely affluent, standard of living against actions that threaten to bring about some redistribution of wealth. But the right to which Kissinger implicitly appealed authorises action even against a state that has not transgressed any existing legal rule, and thus strikes at the whole basis of legality in international conduct.

In the Soviet bloc and the Third World during the 1970s great prominence came to be given to the doctrine that force could justly be used in the service of national liberation. This was a decade in which national liberation movements achieved great successes: the victories of the Viet Cong and the Khmer Rouge in 1975, the coming to power of liberation movements in the Portuguese African territories following the fall of the Caetano government in 1974, the triumphs of the Palestine Liberation Organisation in achieving recognition from the Arab League as the sole representatives of the Palestinian people at the Rabat summit in 1974, followed by Arafat's reception at the United Nations in that year, the success of the Patriotic Front in Zimbabwe in forcing the white supremacist government to make concessions and enter negotiations.

The doctrine of a right to conduct 'just wars of national liberation' is sometimes presented as a special case of the right of self-defence – the extension of this right from states to nations that are not yet states – and sometimes as a right distinct in itself. But in either case it constitutes a justification of the use of force that was not envisaged by the authors of the UN Charter, mainly Western as they were, and is certainly at loggerheads with Western interpretations of international law, then and now. This is the more so to the extent that the idea of national liberation, as it was conceived in the Third World, came to assume a form very different from the Western liberal principle of national self-determination: it involved not merely political independence but also the revolutionary transformation of the nation and it could not be brought about by constitutional processes but only by resort to force. Since 1965 UN majorities have endorsed the right of nations to resort to force in liberating themselves from colonial rule, racist rule and alien domination. They have also recognised the right of third parties to use force on behalf of nations waging just wars of liberation – the right which the Cubans claimed to be exercising in their dramatic interventions in Africa. Another corner was turned in 1977 when the new Geneva Conventions on the International Law of Armed Conflict treated national liberation wars as international armed conflicts rather than domestic ones, with the implications that national liberation movements were entitled to recognition in international law and that those fighting for them were entitled to combatant status and the protection of the laws of war.

The purported entry into international law of the doctrine of 'just wars of national liberation' is, I think, another sign of the decay of viable legal rules concerning international conflict. I make no judgement here as to whether wars of national liberation are, in moral terms, justifiable or not. But the legal principle which Third World states have created is already being turned against themselves. Who is to determine what is a nation? How is it to be decided which purported national liberation movement is the authentic representative of the nation? How are new nation states, after they have been liberated from Western domination, to be protected against separatist and irredentist movements directed at themselves, such as Ethiopia has experienced at the hands of Eritrean liberationists and from Somalia? Can the international order remain viable if sovereign states cannot make good their claims to a monopoly of the use of force? Can the distinction between combatants and non-combatants, the foundation of the laws of war, survive if the dignities of the former are to be bestowed upon members of armed bands lacking any of the normal characteristics of the regular armed forces of a public authority?

During the 1970s, there have been many instances of resort to force that have resulted in a change of territorial boundaries that seems likely to be permanent. Israel's forcible enlargement of its territory in 1967 and again in 1973, of course, has not been accepted by the international community, but we may mention the cases of India's use of force against Pakistan in 1971, resulting in the break-up of Pakistan and the emergence of the new state of Bangladesh; Iran's annexation of Abu Musa and the Tumbs in the same year; Turkey's invasion and partition of Cyprus in 1974; and Indonesia's absorption of East Timor in 1975/6. This is no more than the traditional resort to force as the main agent of change in international relations, just as the willingness of other states to accept the results of such acts of resort to force, so long as they are successful, has always provided a principal foundation of the modern international system. It is worth noting, however, how little effect our recent elaborate definitions of aggression have had on recent practice.

Let me finally mention a fifth assumption that was made by those who prophesied the decline of military force early in the last decade, which was that whether or not force was still useful as an instrument of policy it was ceasing to be acceptable to modern societies, which were not prepared to shoulder the economic and social burdens of arms, armed forces and military engagements. Stanley Hoffmann, for example, at the 1973 conference to which I have alluded, thought that the great problem of Western policy was that whereas force was still necessary as an instrument of policy, Western societies were not prepared to undertake the sacrifices to make the instrument available. The early 1970s were, of course, a period of widespread popular revulsion against the military, against defence expenditure and against conscription. It was, however, maintained that this increasing disinclination to accept the role of force was no mere short-term reaction, but reflected a long-term secular trend in which Western societies were opting for welfare in preference to power or, to go back to Comte's terms, for 'the spirit of industry' as against 'the spirit of conquest' (although Comte might not have recognised the contemporary welfare state, whose spirit is anything but that of industry, as an expression of his principles).

I do not think we can say that this assumption has been falsified: no Western, industrialised society appears today to be embracing a warrior or heroic way of life, although we have to note that Nazi Germany was an industrialised society, that Communist industrialised and industrialising societies, which in the 1970s have further demonstrated their preparedness to go to war with one another, do not treat prosperity or welfare as their primary goal, that a romantic attachment to the life of violence has been amply demonstrated over the last decade by radical elements of both the right and the left in Western societies, and that there is nothing about industrialised society which in itself legislates against a martial or warrior way of life. It is worth noting, I think, the rise in the United States of what might be called the expressive use of force: the demonstration of military power that is intended less to advance any objective of foreign policy than to give vent to feelings of frustration or national pride, a tendency which was first noticeable in the *Mayaguez* intervention in 1975 and was later illustrated by the concentration of naval forces in Iranian waters after the taking of the hostages, by the mock invasion of Guantanamo and the rescue mission in Iran. It is also worth noting that the popular revulsion against the military and against defence spending has clearly abated in Western countries.

It has not been my argument in the present essay that the arguments of the late 1960s and early 1970s have now been shown to be wrong; on the contrary, there are still strong reasons for doubting the utility of force in relation to some of the objectives for which Western countries are now being urged to resort to it. Nor do I purport here to come to grips with the large and complex question of the merits today of Comte's thesis of the incompatibility of war and industrial civilisation, a subject that would require another paper. I have attempted here only the modest task of drawing attention to a change that has taken place in the prevailing Western perceptions of this matter.

As we contemplate the prospects for the 1980s, it is difficult not to feel that in the coming decade international politics will become more Hobbesian, less moderated by the institutions of international society, than it has been in the past. The expectation that the role of force will increase seems fully justified: we face a world in which the 'adverse partnership' between the super powers is disappearing, in which the revival of mercantilism has provided a new rationale for resort to force, in which military interventionism has made a remarkable recovery, the consensus about legal restraints upon resort to force is further eroding and the societies of the world are more willing to shoulder the economic and social burdens of armaments. Projects for a greater role for international organisations in matters of peace and security, a more centralised world order based upon an expended role for the United Nations, seem utterly remote from our agenda. It is not difficult to imagine scenarios in the next decade in which states might begin to behave in ways that are very much more brutal than anything we have experienced in recent decades: a war involving the great powers, an acute energy crisis, the acquisition of nuclear weapons by so-called 'crazy states'. In this more highly militarised world, civilised values will be more difficult to maintain. We have a foretaste of it in the forces of political insensitivity, chauvinism and greed that are now in the ascendant in the greatest of Western democracies. The prevailing spirit will be one of fear and defence preparedness: those of us who work in universities have a special responsibility not to conform to it.

3 US Strategic Nuclear Concepts in the 1970s: The Search for Sufficiently Equivalent Countervailing Parity[1]

WARNER SCHILLING

> "What in the name of God is strategic parity, and what can you do with it?"– Anonymous Columbia professor

The United States confronted three important decisions in the late 1960s affecting the state of the Soviet-American strategic nuclear balance: whether to deploy antiballistic missile systems (ABMs), which had the potential of greatly reducing the destruction that a nuclear attack might produce, especially in a second strike (unless the opponent had offset the defensive effect of the ABMs by adding to its own offensive warheads); whether to deploy multiple independently targetable reentry vehicles (MIRVs), which had the potential of enabling whichever side struck first to deprive the other of its fixed-site intercontinental ballistic missiles (ICBMs) as secure second-strike weapons (unless the opponent had offset the offensive effects of the MIRVs by multiplying its fixed sites or defending them); and whether to deploy additional forces to keep pace with the additions the Soviet Union was making to its offensive forces, additions which (unless offset) had the potential of changing the strategic balance from one of American superiority to one of parity or even, perhaps, Soviet superiority.

By the mid-1970s, the United States had made all three decisions. It decided to avoid, if it could, the deployment of ABMs, and in 1972 the United States and the Soviet Union signed a treaty limiting ABMs to very low, nominal levels and banning the deployment of other forms of ballistic missile defence. In contrast to their approach to ABMs, neither the United States nor the Soviet Union made a determined effort to negotiate an agreement to ban MIRVs or to limit them to nominal levels. The United States began to deploy MIRVed ICBMs in 1970 and MIRVed submarine-launched ballistic missiles (SLBMs) in 1971. Soviet deployment began later: MIRVed ICBMs in 1975, and MIRVed SLBMs in 1978.

As for the Soviet buildup of offensive missiles, the United States decided not to match the Soviet deployments by adding to its own missiles but to try, instead, to negotiate through strategic arms limitations talks (SALT) an agreement which would place a limit on Soviet force levels. In 1972, the United States and the Soviet Union agreed to limit ICBM and SLBM launchers to the numbers they then had built and were building (2358 for the Soviet Union, and 1710 for the United States. In 1974 the two states negotiated a draft agreement that placed a common ceiling of 2400 on their total number of ICBM launchers, SLBM launchers, and long-range bombers; and the two states incorporated this 2400–vehicle limit in the SALT II treaty which they signed in June 1979.

The attainment by the Soviet Union of numerical equality with the United States in strategic delivery vehicles was an event of major military and political significance. Starting in 1964, when the Soviet Union had 389 strategic delivery vehicles and the United States had 1880, the Soviet Union had surpassed the United States in the number of ICBMs by 1970, in the number of SLBMs by 1974, and in the total number of ICBMs, SLBMs, and long-range bombers by 1972. In June 1979, when the two powers formally agreed to the common ceiling of 2400 vehicles, the Soviet Union actually had 2504 deployed delivery vehicles and the United States 2058.

The military significance of the Soviet buildup cannot, of course, be readily inferred from either the absolute or the relative numbers of Soviet and American strategic delivery vehicles. Aside from the question of what "counts" as a strategic delivery vehicle, these gross numbers take no account of differences in the number, yield, and accuracy of the warheads carried by the vehicles; of differences in their deployment, readiness, reliability, vulnerability, and their capability to be held in reserve; of differences between the two states in the strategy and tactics with which they might actually employ their weapons; of differences in the performance of their command, control, communication, and intelligence systems (C^3I) during the course of that employment; of differences in the character of the targets in each country and in the effectiveness of their air, naval, and civil defence systems.

The safest generalization that can be made in the face of all these variables is that the major military effect of the Soviet buildup to date has been to increase greatly the amount of death and destruction the Soviet Union could produce in the United States, by either a first or a second strike, without significantly affecting the amount of death and destruction the United States could produce in the Soviet Union. Indeed, measured in terms of warheads surviving a Soviet first strike, the second-strike capability of the United States was probably larger in 1980 than it was in 1964, when the Soviet buildup began.

It is difficult to venture beyond the generality of this statement on the basis of the public record, and given the number and character of the variables involved, it is obvious that even classified estimates of the specific effects (e.g., fatalities) that a nuclear exchange might have produced at any given time are unavoidably arbitrary. The available evidence would suggest, however, that the Soviet Union has moved from a position in which it could have inflicted some 20–30 million fatalities on the United States in a second strike to a position where it could inflict some 100–130 million, whereas the fatalities which the United States could inflict on the Soviet Union in a second strike have remained in the vicinity of 100–200 million. Put in other terms, a nuclear exchange in the early 1960s probably would have cost the Soviet Union some three to four times as many fatalities as those suffered by the United States, even if the Soviet Union had struck first, whereas by the late 1970s the Soviets were in a position, at least in a first strike, to inflict more fatalities on the United States than the United States, in its second strike, could inflict on the Soviet Union.

The political significance of this change in relative destructive power is necessarily a matter of uncertain judgment, if only because Soviet perspectives are shrouded in secrecy, and is inevitably, given the stakes involved, an issue for heated dispute in the United States. But few would contend that nothing of importance has happened, and most would agree that, in a meaningful sense of the term, the Soviets have moved from a position of strategic inferiority to one of strategic parity, and that this event has complicated, not eased, the American task of coping with Soviet purposes and power.

The purpose of this chapter is to review the reasons why the United States did not contest the Soviet buildup; to describe how the United States has defined its strategic objectives in the light of this buildup; to analyze some of the problems the United States has met in trying to implement those objectives; and to present some summary comments on the current state of Soviet-American parity and the prospects for the near future.

Why did the United States fail to contest the Soviet buildup? The answer must start with some conception of what the United States would have had to have done in order to have "matched" the increase in Soviet offensive forces. Would this have required the United States to have maintained its 1964 ratio of superiority over the Soviet Union in delivery vehicles or warheads? Certainly, the United States did not do this. Given the 1980 Soviet force of some 2500 delivery vehicles and 6000 warheads, the United States would now need about 12,000 delivery vehicles and 50,400 warheads, instead of its present force of some 2058 vehicles and 9200 warheads. Would the United States have matched the Soviet buildup if it had maintained its 1964 margin of superiority in numbers of delivery vehicles or warheads? Actually, in the case of warheads, the United States did do this; it had about 3400 more warheads than the Soviet Union in 1964 and about 3200 more warheads in 1980. Or, since delivery vehicles are potential targets for warheads, is the most appropriate measure the ratio between the warheads of the United States and the delivery vehicles of the Soviet Union? In 1964, this ratio was 8.7:1, and it was 3.7:1 in 1980. Does this mean that the Soviet Union has yet to achieve parity?

These numbers are cited to illustrate an obvious but important point: the differences in these or any other numbers used to measure the state of the Soviet-American strategic balance have to be related to differences in the actual results or outcomes of a nuclear war before they can be said to have any military meaning. Dropping nuclear weapons on a country is an act subject to diminishing returns. Accordingly, maintaining a constant ratio or margin of superiority over an opponent in some index of nuclear power (delivery vehicles, warheads, megatons) is not an act of constant military consequence. The military consequence, for example, of the United States' being able to deliver eight times as many warheads on Soviet cities as the Soviet Union could deliver on American cities will be significantly affected by whether the Soviet capability is 100, 1000, or 10,000 warheads.

Expressed in terms of war outcomes – i.e., the actual amount of death and destruction a nuclear war would cause to any given set of targets – a successful American effort to match or offset the Soviet buildup would have prevented the increase in Soviet offensive forces from (a) increasing the amount of death and destruction the Soviet Union could cause in the United States, and (b) decreasing the amount of death and destruction the United States could cause in the Soviet Union. Seen in these terms, it is clear that the United Stated did match or offset the Soviet buildup in the second respect. Since 1964, as best can be judged from the public record, there has been no real change in the amount of death and destruction the United States could cause in the Soviet Union in the event of a major nuclear war.

The failure of the United States to match or offset the Soviet buildup was, then, the failure to prevent that buildup from increasing the amount of death and destruction the Soviet Union could cause in the United States. How might the United States have prevented this increase? To have kept constant (i.e., to 1964 levels) the amount of death and destruction the Soviet Union could cause, the United States would have needed to add to its capabilities for damage limitation; to its ability to destroy through counterforce strikes (using its own offensive forces) Soviet ICBMs, SLBMs, and strategic bombers before they could be launched against the United States; to its ability to destroy through active defences (air and ballistic missile defence systems and antisubmarine warfare [ASW] systems) the Soviet forces which would survive the counterforce attack; and to its ability to protect through passive defences (shelters and other means for offsetting the effects of nuclear explosions) the American population, industry, and other targets of value from the explosions of the Soviet warheads that would penetrate American defences.

In the late 1960s, the ability of the United States to add significantly to its damage-limiting capabilities by adding only to its offensive forces was limited. There seemed no certain way to destroy Soviet SLBMs, at least once they were deployed on an increasing number of submarines. And while the deployment of MIRVs would give the United States the potential for counterforce capability against Soviet ICBMs and bomber bases, this potential could be exercised effectively only through a preemptive first strike, one which would catch the Soviet forces before the Soviets had actually launched their attack. This was not a strategy, however, for which there was much political support in the United States, and it was, in any event, a strategy which the Soviet Union might offset by launching its land-based forces on warning, i.e., in the interval between the time the Soviets detected that the Americans had launched their missiles and the time their warheads exploded on target.

The key to keeping the increase in Soviet offensive forces from increasing the amount of death and destruction the Soviets could cause in the United States lay in additional American programs for defence: civil defence, air defence, and ballistic missile defence. But these were precisely the programs the United States decided not to pursue, and it was through its failure to deploy these defensive systems, rather than by failing to maintain some ratio or margin in offensive forces, that the United States lost its opportunity to maintain nuclear superiority.

The decision not to deploy a major ABM system to protect American cities was the critical choice in what was, in effect, and American decision not to try to prevent, by adding to America's damage-limiting capabilities, the Soviet buildup from increasing the amount of death and destruction the Soviet Union could produce in the United States. Once the United States had determined not to defend itself against Soviet missiles, which would deliver about 90 percent of the Soviet warheads, there seemed little point in maintaining an effective air defence against Soviet bombers, and defence expenditures for this purpose were significantly reduced after the signing of the ABM treaty in 1972. And without major programs for missile and bomber defence, there was no political or military basis for generating American interest in an effective program for civil defence.

Why did the United States decide not to deploy a major ABM system for city defence? This decision was influenced by technical reservations about the efficacy of the system then available and by the belief, on the part of some, that since peace had to rest on the Soviet-American balance of terror, it would be best for each state to remain naked before its enemy. But the primary argument against the deployment of an ABM system for city defence was that it would only lead to a Soviet-American arms race without any resulting military gain.

Secretary of Defense McNamara was an articulate advocate of the thesis that, if the Americans deployed an ABM system for the purpose of reducing the death and destruction the Soviets could cause in the United States, the Soviets would respond by building whatever additional offensive forces would be required to offset the effects of the ABM system. Since the United States would do the same if the Soviets deployed an ABM system, McNamara concluded that it would be in the interest of both powers to ban the deployment of ABMs. Otherwise, the superpowers would be forced into a frightening and expensive arms race which would, at best, leave them in the end exactly where they had started in terms of the death and destruction each could cause the other.

This argument had a counter. As the US Joint Chiefs of Staff pointed out, since the United States had by far the larger gross national product, the United States could outspend and outbuild the Soviets in the deployment of both defensive and offensive forces. Thus, if the United States was willing to persist in the armaments competition and spend whatever it took, the United States would, in the end, regain and retain the ability to inflict much more destruction on the Soviet Union than the latter could cause in the United States.

Given this argument, it is clear why President Johnson decided in 1967 to seek an agreement with the Soviet Union to ban the deployment of ABMs. He was in no political position to spend whatever it took in a major new strategic arms competition with the Soviet Union. He had the Vietnam War to fight and the Great Society to finance, and he was trying to do both without putting the American economy on a wartime basis. Moreover, the Vietnam War, unlike the Korean War, had no budgetary coat-tails. Johnson could not make the Vietnam War, as President Truman did the Korean War, an opportunity to finance other major military programs. On the contrary, the Vietnam War led to a climate of opinion that was increasingly antimilitary and antidefence.

Essentially the same considerations led President Nixon in 1969 to continue Johnson's policy. Nixon, too, had the Vietnam War on his hands, and he came to office intent on reducing, not increasing, the federal budget. Moreover, both presidents confronted an American public not disposed to support programs for nuclear defence, whether active or passive. Partly, this attitude reflects the public's belief that there is no real way in which the destruction from a nuclear war can be avoided, but there is another, more underlying cause. The acquisition of offensive forces can be supported, however reluctantly, in the belief that they are necessary to prevent a nuclear war. The rationale for defensive programs, however, necessarily entails the belief that a nuclear war might actually occur, and this the public finds a very uncomfortable and therefore unpopular suggestion.

In summary, the ABM decision, given the Soviet buildup, ensured that the Soviet Union would achieve parity with the United States in terms of the death and destruction each could cause the other. The ABM decision was influenced by reservations about the military effectiveness of the technology involved and by the argument of some advocates of arms control that American security would be better served in a world in which neither superpower could doubt its ability to destroy the other. But these factors should not obscure the obvious: neither Johnson nor Nixon had any real budgetary or political choice, given the Vietnam War and their domestic programs and given a public opinion characterized by a strong antipathy to the idea of preparing to fight a nuclear war.

Why did the United States agree to the other form of parity the Soviet Union has achieved: equality in the number of strategic nuclear delivery vehicles (as SALT-counted)? The American decision not to offset the destructive effect of the Soviet buildup by increasing the damage-limiting forces of the United States was not accompanied by a decision to accept equality with the Soviet Union in the number of delivery vehicles. American intelligence underestimated the rate and duration of the Soviet buildup, and in the mid- and late-1960s, American officials continued to talk about the need for and the prospect of continued American numerical superiority over the Soviet Union. Thus, the SALT proposal designed by the Johnson administration for offensive forces called for a freeze in the number of ICBMs and SLBMs in the expectation that such a freeze would leave the United States with the larger number of missiles.

The United States never decided to seek equality with the Soviet Union in the total number of delivery vehicles; it was driven to that position by the course of the Soviet buildup. The Nixon Administration developed a proposal providing for equality in the number of ballistic missiles (but excluding bombers, of which the United States had the larger number) when it became clear that the total number of Soviet missiles would equal that of the United States. The Administration changed to a proposal for equality in the total number of missiles and bombers when it became clear that this Soviet total would equal that of the United States. Then, as the Soviet buildup continued, the Administration was driven to proposals designed simply to bring a halt to that buildup. This was finally done in May 1972, in an agreement which limited the superpowers to the number of ballistic missile launchers they each then had built or were building. The resulting numbers were hardly equal: 2358 for the Soviet Union, and 1710 for the United States. Even if strategic bombers had been counted (they were excluded because the superpowers could not agree on whose and what other kind of weapons should be counted in an overall total), the numbers would have still been unequal: about 2498 for the Soviet Union, and 2237 for the United States.

Clearly, the United States did not fare well in the bargaining, if only because it was not, like the Soviet Union, steadily building additional launchers (the Department of Defense chose to wait until new systems were ready for deployment). Congressional criticism of the numbers provided by the 1972 agreement resulted in the Jackson amendment that requested the president to seek a future treaty that would not limit the United States to levels of intercontinental strategic forces inferior to those of the Soviet Union. In 1974, the United States secured Soviet agreement to such a number: 2400 for the total number of strategic bombers and ballistic missile launchers. This limit was incorporated into the SALT II treaty in 1979, but by that time, as previously noted, the limit was below the actual Soviet total (2504) and considerably above the number of operational American forces (2058).

By the early 1970s, then, the Soviet Union had achieved parity (or better) with the United States in the total number of strategic nuclear delivery vehicles, as well as in the ability to inflict death and destruction, and this new numerical relationship was codified in the SALT II treaty. Of the two forms of parity, the numerical relationship has received by far the most attention, because of the publicity and debate associated with the SALT agreements. But the SALT numbers, whether the 2400 total or the others specified in the 1979 treaty (e.g., those relating to the numerical limits on launchers for MIRVed delivery vehicles, the maximum number of reentry vehicles permitted on various missiles, or the provisions relating to launchweight and throw-weight) fix so few of the variables that would affect the actual outcome of a nuclear war (whether all-out or limited, long or short), that they cannot be taken as a meaningful guide to either the absolute or the relative military capability of either superpower.

How has parity affected the strategic objectives and concepts of the United States? The decision not to offset the increase in Soviet offensive forces by major additions to the capabilities of the United States for damage limitation still left open the question of what the United States would do in response to the Soviet buildup. At the most general and important level of policy, the United States decided to do nothing. It decided not to change any of the three major purposes for which it maintained strategic forces: to deter a nuclear attack on the United States; to deter a nuclear attack on its allies; and to help to deter a conventional attack on its allies. The importance of this decision can be gauged by imagining the kinds of policies that would have been followed by friends and foes, as well by the United States, if the United States had decided that one or more of these purposes was no longer a desirable and/or feasible objective in an era of nuclear parity.

The question of just what strategic concepts would guide American policy in the effort to maintain these major objectives in an age of parity was formally addressed by the Nixon Administration in 1969 through the means of a National Security Council study memorandum and a subsequent NSC decision memorandum. In January 1970, President Nixon christened the results of this study the strategy of "sufficiency," and the specific concepts involved were later revealed by Secretary of Defense Laird in his annual posture statements.

In the decade since then, there have been major changes in American acquisition policy (the number and kind of strategic forces bought, or not bought); in deployment policy (where and how those forces are based and on what kind of alert); and in employment policy (the plans for actually using strategic forces). But there have been relatively few changes in American strategic concepts, that is, in the terms and propositions with which acquisition, deployment, and employment policy have been debated and justified (although not always influenced or decided), at least as those concepts have been revealed publicly by US declaratory policy. Indeed, one could have gone to sleep during the strategic nuclear debate in 1970, awakened in 1980, and rejoined that debate with remarkably little sense of intellectual loss or confusion. Whether this speaks to the sophistication or to the sterility of the American strategic debate is a matter of some moment.

The successive annual reports of Defense Secretaries Laird, Richardson, Schlesinger, Rumsfeld, and Brown have varied in their listing and description of the central elements of American strategic policy in a world of strategic parity, as well as in the lengths to which they were disposed to go to avoid the use of the term parity itself. But in essence, all of these secretaries have embroidered on the requirements first listed by Laird – that the United States should maintain strategic forces capable of (1) assured destruction and (2) flexible options; forces that are (3) equal to those of the Soviet Union and (4) perceived as equal; and forces that (5) contribute to crisis stability. This listing omits only Laird's requirement for a defence against light and accidental attacks (which was overtaken by the ABM treaty), and the quasi-obligatory references made by all secretaries to the desirability of arms control and the determination of the United States not to acquire a full first-strike capability.

Assured Destruction. The Soviet buildup has affected neither the determination of the United States to maintain a secure second-strike capability to inflict massive destruction on Soviet urban-industrial targets nor, as previously noted, the continued ability of the United States to produce such destruction. In 1965, McNamara identified assured destruction with the ability to destroy about 33 percent of the population and 66 percent of the industry of the Soviet Union. These figures owed more to his appreciation for the diminishing returns that would follow from the allocation of additional forces to produce higher levels of destruction than to any analysis of how Soviet leaders might actually weigh urban-industrial damage against the possible gains from hypothetical wars, and it is for this reason that the figures have remained relatively constant ever since. Thus, in his report for fiscal year (FY) 1970, Secretary of Defense Clifford referred to the ability of the United States, in a second strike, to destroy more than 40 percent of the population of the Soviet Union and 75 percent of its industry, and in his report for FY 1979, Secretary Brown referred to the American capability to destroy a "minimum" of 200 major Soviet cities (which would encompass about 33 percent of the population and 65 percent of the industry).

It would be a mistake, however, to conclude that American policy has defined its requirements for second-strike targets solely or even mainly in terms of blowing up people and plant in the Soviet Union. Although some commentators have recently charged that the United States has neglected to target the things which Soviet leaders really value – the military power of the state (conventional and nuclear); the party cadre; the secret police; the divisions facing the Chinese frontier; the Great Russian population – these comments, for the most part, reflect ignorance about either what can be feasibly targetted with nuclear weapons or what the United States does, in fact, already target.

American employment policy has always aimed at the destruction of military as well as nonmilitary targets in the Soviet Union, and since 1974, at least, the United States has not even targetted people or industry *per se* but rather Soviet "recovery resources," with a reported requirement to destroy 70 percent of such resources. How "recovery resources" are defined operationally is not a matter of public record, except that it is clear that they are military and political as well as economic in character. It is also clear, as Secretary Brown stated in his report for FY 1981, that the United States designs its strategic forces to destroy the military and political power of the Soviet state, as well as its cities and citizens.

Less clear is why the United States is not more explicit in its declaratory policy about its plans and capabilities for producing destruction in the Soviet Union. The purpose of the US strategic force is, after all, to deter the Soviets, not to surprise them with more or different destruction than they had expected. It could be argued that a policy of ambiguity and secrecy leaves the Soviets to imagine the worst, but military history provides some telling examples of statesmen and generals with a propensity to imagine the best, not the worst, about the plans and capabilities of their opponents.

Parity, in sum, has not substantially affected American plans and capabilities for assured destruction. The recent emphasis in declaratory policy on the American ability to destroy Soviet political and military targets (as compared to industrial-urban targets) probably reflects some changes in US acquisition and employment policy, but if so, they are developments which are evolutionary in character (rather than the result of major changes in priorities), and they owe more to changes in American judgments about the kinds of costs that will deter Soviet leaders than they do to changes in the level of Soviet forces.

Flexible Options. The United States has long had an interest in a strategy which provided it with more choices than doing nothing or launching immediate, all-out strikes against the full range of targets in the Soviet Union, and the Single Integrated Operations Plan (SIOP) has contained a number of such options (e.g., strikes against only Soviet strategic forces or other military targets) since the early 1960s. Thus, in his Ann Arbor speech in 1962, Secretary McNamara stated that the United States was prepared, even after a Soviet attack, to withhold strikes against Soviet cities provided the Soviet Union exercised a similar restraint.

The advent of parity has increased the interest of the United States in adding to the range of these choices, with respect to both the timing and the scale of nuclear exchanges with the Soviet Union. The United States has sought to maintain not only a secure second-strike capability for assured destruction but a capability that does not have to be used in a hurry, hence the US interest in acquiring strategic forces and associated C^3I systems that can endure if withheld from use. Given a Soviet capability to match the United States in the amount of death and destruction it can produce, the United States has nothing to gain from rushing to all-out war. If nuclear weapons are to be used at all, it makes more sense to use them selectively against nonurban targets, keeping the bulk of US forces in reserve to hold Soviet cities at risk and, thereby, hopefully, deterring the Soviets from attacking American cities.

What the United States has endeavoured to accomplish by the policy of flexible options, particularly since 1973, has been to add to the number of preplanned strikes in the SIOP which entail the use of less than all of its strategic forces and to design strikes using far smaller numbers of warheads than did the options previously planned for the SIOP. These plans and the forces acquired to execute them (e.g., improved capabilities for hard-target destruction and for attack assessment) have been designed for two purposes: to improve the ability of the United States to respond to limited attacks by the Soviet Union (e.g., against American strategic or other military forces), and to improve the ability of the United States to initiate limited attacks against the Soviet Union (e.g., as part of the US response to a Soviet attack on Western Europe).

The policy of planning to initiate the use of nuclear weapons to respond to what otherwise might be a successful Soviet conventional attack on Western Europe continues to be most controversial. Flexible options involving theatre as well as strategic nuclear weapons presumably have been designed for three different purposes: to make the Soviets think about the risks they are running (but what if they decide to keep on fighting?); to make the Soviets sorry by destroying targets of value, e.g., their political control structure (but how does this save Western Europe?); and to make the Soviets lose by destroying their military forces (but if the Soviets respond in kind, what keeps Western Europe from becoming a radioactive Ben Tre?).

Specialists have argued over the desirability and feasibility of such policies for more than twenty years, as well as over the desirability and feasibility of alternative policies (e.g., NATO conventional forces strong enough to defend Western Europe without relying on the first use of nuclear weapons, or the development of European nuclear forces strong enough to make a European first use credible). Parity has sharpened these arguments, but it has not been responsible for them, as their twenty-year history amply demonstrates.

At all events, it is clear that parity has not led the United States to back away from plans and preparations for the first use of nuclear weapons in defence of Western Europe. And the continued interest of the United States in coupling its security with that of Western Europe; the continued willingness of the Europeans to tie their security to the deterrent effect of the American nuclear threat, to the relative exclusion of worries about the consequences if deterrence should fail; and the continued unwillingness of both Americans and Europeans to spend the money required to make major changes in their present defence posture – all suggest that the future military policies of the United States and its allies are far more likely to build on those of the present than to depart from them in any significant degree.

The probability that the United States would actually carry out its nuclear threat, in the judgment of the present writer, has been little affected by the advent of parity, and the credibility of the threat ought, therefore, to be about as good as it ever was (a carefully chosen phrase). On the face of it, if the costs of an all-out nuclear war have risen from 40 million to 140 million dead Americans, the United States ought to be significantly less willing to risk such a war in defence of Western Europe. But this argument begs the question of how willing, on a scale of 1 to 10, the United States was to risk 40 million fatalities. More to the point, the argument assumes that statesmen have some calculus through which they can rationally weigh their objects against such variations in their risks and costs, which, of course, they do not. There is no common unit of account by which Americans can measure their stake in Western Europe against American lives. Accordingly, in the nuclear age as before, statesmen will be found risking war for objects without addressing the question of whether those objects are worth the costs of war should it materialize.

In the event, an American use of nuclear weapons in defence of Western Europe will occur when and if American leaders conclude that, if they do not fire a limited number of nuclear weapons now (to try to stop the Soviets from overrunning Western Europe), they will face a major nuclear exchange later (with a Soviet Union bloated from conquest and disdainful of American will), and for a choice of this order, the fact that the costs of a major exchange have increased will be at best irrelevant. As for the credibility of the American nuclear threat, there is certainly little political logic in the argument of those who find it hard to believe that the United States would be willing to initiate a limited use of nuclear weapons in order to keep from losing Western Europe, but easy to believe that once those weapons had been used, the Soviet Union would be quite willing to engage in a continuing and escalating exchange in order to gain Western Europe. Parity has not, after all, decreased the costs of all-out war for the Soviet Union.

Strategic Equality. The American decision not to hold the amount of death and destruction that the Soviets could produce in the United States to 1964 levels did not answer the question of whether there was any limit at all, relative or absolute, that the United States would try to place on the military consequences of the Soviet buildup.

One obvious answer was to maintain a balance in which the United States and the Soviet Union could produce equal amounts of death and destruction, and this was the decision reached by the Nixon Administration in the fall of 1969 in its decision memorandum on strategic forces. As explained later by Secretary Laird, the United States would maintain forces capable of preventing the Soviet Union from "gaining the ability to cause considerably greater urban/industrial destruction than the United States could inflict on the Soviets."

Just what "considerably greater" meant was never discussed on the public record, and it is also not clear whether this criterion was ever used to determine acquisition or employment policy. At all events the criterion was dropped by subsequent secretaries, presumably because the strategic forces of the United States could no longer maintain the objective, at least as far as population was concerned. Thus, the review of strategic policy conducted by the Carter Administration in 1977 reportedly concluded that a major nuclear exchange would probably result in a minimum of 140 million American fatalities, as compared to about 113 million Soviet fatalities.

The disparity in these **expected fatalities** (which represent about

65 percent of the American and 44 percent of the Soviet population) owes more to differences in the target structure of the two countries – the United States has a higher percentage of its population in cities – than it does to differences in their strategic forces, although if the yields of American warheads were as large as those of the Soviets, the disparity would be less marked. In the case of industry, destruction still would be approximately equal, for in this case the target structure is more nearly identical, in the sense that the percentage of industrial installations that can be destroyed by any given number of 100-kiloton weapons is about the same in both countries.

Whether the difference between 65 percent and 44 percent fatalities is a case of a "considerably greater" difference (e.g., one that would lead the Soviets to believe that they had the superior bargaining position in time of crisis: "my unmitigated horrible catastrophe would be better than your horrible unmitigated catastrophe") is, of course, a matter on which judgments can differ. But the issue does raise the question of what disparity the United States would consider significant: 70–35? 66–22? 80–20? On the public record, at least, it is not clear that the United States has a definition of strategic equality that answers this question, whether expressed in terms of a ratio it will not tolerate or a ceiling above which it will not permit American fatalities to rise. The United States, however, as noted in the discussion of assured destruction, has defined, in effect, a floor below which it is determined to prevent Soviet fatalities from falling.

In more recent years, the United States has discussed strategic equality in terms other than the extent of urban (i.e., population) and industrial destruction. In his report for FY 1978, Secretary Rumsfeld spoke of the need to ensure that the Soviet Union would not recover more rapidly, either economically or militarily, than the United States from the effects of nuclear war: hence the change to "recovery resources" as the formal targetting criterion for assured destruction, and the increasing importance assigned in the annual reports of Secretary Brown to forces which would prevent the Soviet Union from gaining any military advantage from a nuclear exchange.

Whether the United States has clear operational criteria for projecting postwar recovery rates or defining postwar military advantages is not evident from the public record. The former, at least, would appear a very difficult concept to operationalise, and definitions of military advantage could range from simple numerical measures (e.g., surviving warheads or equivalent megatons) to more meaningful (but complex) comparisons about the kind of destruction these postwar forces could produce on targets of value.

Given the complexities involved, it is plausible that the actual military capabilities which the United States has maintained during the past decade in the name of strategic equality owe more to the end products of the bureaucratic and executive-congressional politics of acquisition policy than they do to the formal guidelines for employment policy that have been associated with the strategic doctrines of sufficiency, equivalence, or countervailing power.

Perceived Equality. Throughout the 1970s, the United States has been concerned with the appearance of the strategic balance, as well as with its reality, and has been intent on maintaining forces that are not only equal to those of the Soviet Union but are perceived as equal. This concern with perceptions is the result of the fact that the pace of the Soviet buildup has enabled the Soviet Union, over time, to surpass the United States in such measures as the total number of missiles, the total number of delivery vehicles, and the total amount of megatonnage. Moreover, while the United States has retained a lead in the total number of warheads (as a result of its earlier deployment of MIRVs), the larger throw-weight of the Soviet missiles gives the Soviet Union the potential (unless its deployment of MIRVs is constrained by the terms of SALT II or some comparable agreement) to overtake the United States in the total number of warheads as well.

These Soviet numerical advantages have led many Americans to fear that the Soviet Union might be tempted to use the threat of nuclear war to intimidate or blackmail the United States, its allies, or other states. Equally disturbing to the United States is the possibility that its allies or other states, believing that the Soviet Union has the superior nuclear force, might be led to yield or accommodate to Soviet interests, and the Soviets could gain the political results of nuclear superiority without even having to threaten, much less fight, a nuclear war.

In theory, of course, the United States – in designing its own forces for assured destruction, flexible options, and strategic equality – has already built the forces it needs to deter attacks or threats by the Soviet Union and to deny the Soviet Union the ability to achieve any meaningful advantage, political or military, from a nuclear exchange, whether limited or all-out, short or long. But Washington is nonetheless seized with the worry that the Soviet Union or other states might be led to contrary judgments by examining the charts and graphs (all supplied by the United States) that compare the forces of the superpowers in terms of various static and dynamic measures: numbers of warheads, delivery vehicles, equivalent megatons, countermilitary potential, or the ratio of postexchange warheads, or megatons, etc. And it has been, therefore, US policy that all of these measures cannot be permitted to favour the Soviet Union and that a Soviet lead in some must be offset by an American lead in others.

This concern for how the strategic balance is perceived is informed by very little knowledge about how perceptions of the strategic balance are actually influenced (if at all) by such household words as throw-weight, one-megaton equivalents, or prompt hard-target kill capability. The Soviets keep their perceptions to themselves, and at all events, American perceptions about Soviet perceptions are necessarily built into the design of American forces in the first place. As for allies and other states, there is no evidence that the United States has engaged in any systematic research as to how relevant foreign élites reach their judgments about the state of the strategic balance or even what those judgments are.

It is at least plausible that most foreign élites are poorly informed about the various numerical measures that pre-occupy Washington (if not indifferent to those measures); that they confuse trends with balances (the Soviets are gaining; the Soviets are ahead) and weapon developments with weapon deployments (the Americans have tested cruise missiles; the Americans have cruise missiles); and that their judgments about the state of the Soviet-American nuclear balance are significantly influenced by their perceptions of the conventional weapons balance and by their judgments about other aspects of state power (e.g., the state of the American economy), as well as by their reactions to major foreign-policy and military events (such as Vietnam, Iran, or Afghanistan).

For all this, the American concern for how the strategic balance is perceived by friends, foes, and allies is not unwise. It is simply misplaced. What is questionable is the present American policy of focusing that concern on the numerical differences between Soviet and American forces as expressed in various static and dynamic indices. These numerical differences are of consequence only to the extent that they can affect the amount of destruction that would occur to targets of value in the event of a nuclear exchange. Accordingly, the numerical differences need to be translated into war outcomes before their military consequence, if any, can be judged.

A Soviet "lead" that could result in an adverse war outcome should, of course, be corrected. But numerical differences that cannot be related to adverse war outcomes should be addressed by American declaratory policy, not redressed by American acquisition policy. The appropriate American response in this case is not to add to some component of its strategic forces in order to change the direction of a curve on a chart, but to explain to its allies and friends (and to the Soviet Union, if need be) that the numerical differences in question would have no significant bearing on the outcome of a nuclear exchange, either in terms of the kind and number of targets the United States is intent on destroying or in terms of the ability of the United States to prevent the Soviet Union from achieving its own objectives.

Why the United States does not address perceptions of the strategic balance directly, by a discussion of war outcomes, rather than focusing attention on numerical comparisons between Soviet and

American strategic forces is a good question. In part, it is because the second is by far the easier analytical exercise. The number of assumptions that must be made to predict the outcome of a nuclear exchange (long or short, limited or all-out) are legion, and the conclusions are inevitably arbitrary and open to question. Secondly, as previously noted, for the United States to be more specific about its targetting plans and capabilities, not to mention its assessments of the results of nuclear exchanges, would require a major change in the style and content of American declaratory policy. Moreover, since American élites are by no means agreed among themselves about the kind of war outcomes US strategy and forces should be designed to produce, a more revealing declaratory policy would not be without domestic political cost. The existence of these differences over strategy also helps to explain the American preoccupation with numbers and perceptions of the strategic balance, for this concern is symptomatic of how uneasy many Americans feel about the idea of parity and, at a deeper level, how uncertain they are about what parity is or should be.

Crisis Stability. One of the most important American strategic objectives has been the maintenance of a strategic balance that provides for crisis stability: a balance in which neither side has any incentive to strike first in time of crisis. Ideally, this objective entails a balance in which neither side can see any difference between striking first or striking second, either in terms of the destruction it could cause the enemy or in terms of the destruction it would receive itself. In reality, of course, there will always be some gain from striking the first blow, if only for the disruption it would bring to the other side's capabilities for C^3I. Nonetheless, in an age of parity, the United States has everything to gain from a balance which permits the Soviets to believe that, however probable war may seem in time of crisis, they have nothing to lose by waiting, that time (and further negotiation, even at the risk of an American first strike) will not work against them.

Throughout the 1970s, the concern of the United States for crisis stability has been focused on the issue of the prelaunch survivability of its fixed-site ICBMs. Space does not permit a discussion of the history of this issue (including the reasons why the United States did not try to forestall the problem by trying to ban or limit MIRVs to nominal levels through a SALT agreement); an explanation of why the United States wants to retain land-based ICBMs (they are easier to command and control, have lower operating costs, and provide a more effective hard-target capability than the other elements in the triad, and maintaining ICBMs will provide insurance against future vulnerabilities in the other legs of that triad); or an analysis of the issues associated with the present M-X debate (whether the proposed basing mode will actually ensure the prelaunch survivability of the new missile, or the reasons why the United States has rejected alternative basing modes or placing the Minuteman force in a launch-on-warning posture).

The purpose of the present discussion is to illustrate the analytical manner in which the deployment of the M-X has been related to the objective of crisis stability. In summary form, the issues are as follows. The Soviets will shortly have the theoretical ability to destroy about 90 percent of the US ICBM force (1054 missiles presently containing about 24 percent of the US warheads), and the Soviets could do this by firing as few as 210 of their 1400 ICBMs. This capability, it is alleged, would give them an incentive to fire first in time of crisis. The United States has, therefore, decided to reduce the vulnerability of its ICBMs by deploying a new missile (the M-X) in a mobile form. But the M-X will have the capability (either in conjunction with part of the Minuteman force or alone, given a reprogramming capability) of destroying more than 90 percent of the Soviet ICBM force, which presently contains about 75 percent of the Soviet warheads. This capability, it is alleged, will also give the Soviets an incentive to fire first in time of crisis.

The United States has rejected one answer to this apparent dilemma: the deployment of a mobile missile with a less effective countersilo capability than the M-X, which would insure the pre-launch survivability of the US ICBM force without jeopardizing the survivability of the Soviet ICBM force. A major reason for this rejection, as stated by Secretary Brown, is that strategic equality (both real and perceived) requires that the United States have as effective a prompt countersilo capability as the Soviet Union and that both powers be required to cope with the costs of offsetting the MIRV threat to the fixed-site ICBM.

This position illustrates the relative priority of crisis stability among the strategic objectives of the United States. The position also appears to assume that the Soviets will respond to the deployment of M-X by adding to their submarine-launched missiles and/or expending the large resources necessary to provide themselves with a mobile ICBM, rather than choosing potentially more destabilizing responses, such as doing nothing or placing their ICBMs in a launch-on-warning posture.

The public discussion of this issue, however, has taken place without any factual information about how the countersilo capabilities involved might actually affect crisis stability. A demonstration that the Soviets could destroy 90 percent of the American ICBM force is a demonstration only that the Soviets could destroy 90 percent of the ICBM force. It says nothing about the kind of gains the Soviets could achieve in terms of damage limitation from such a strike. Obviously, if all the United States had were fixed-site ICBMs, the Soviets would gain a great deal. On the other hand, if the United States had 100,000 survivable warheads in its submarine and bomber forces, the Soviets would gain nothing by eliminating some 1900 ICBM warheads. Where, between these limiting cases, is the present strategic balance? Would a Soviet first strike serve only to reduce their fatalities from 45 percent to 40 percent of their population or the destruction of their industrial installations from 75 percent to 71 percent? What incentive would differences of this order give Soviet statesmen to strike first in time of crisis, given that the best way to avoid destruction is to avert war?

Clearly, without information about what the destruction of this or that percentage of the ICBM force would mean in terms of war outcomes, it is difficult to reach a judgment about the extent to which the vulnerability of the Minuteman force will or will not present the Soviets with an incentive to strike first in a crisis. There is, of course, no way in which that vulnerability can be seen as a gain for crisis stability, but even after the deployment of the M-X, the United States will still retain some 80 percent of its ICBMs, 65 percent of its ICBM megatonnage, and 41 percent of its ICBM warheads in the fixed-site mode. Why, then, would not the deployment of the M-X still leave the Soviets with an incentive to strike first in time of crisis?

The same lack of information renders less than meaningful the arguments of those who claim that the deployment of the M-X would undermine crisis stability by threatening the Soviet ICBM force. If numbers tell the story, the United States can pose a greater threat to Soviet ICBMs than the Soviets can pose to American ICBMs, even without the M-X. By 1982, given the information publicly available about the capabilities each side is expected to have by that date if they continue to adhere to the terms of SALT II, the Soviets could, by firing some 210 SS-18s (using some 2100 warheads) destroy about 91 percent of the American ICBMs and thereby destroy some 1950 warheads, about 18 percent of the expected US total by that date. But the United States, by firing 550 Minuteman IIIs (using 1650 warheads with the presently programmed improvements in their yield and accuracy) and by concentrating its fire on the MIRVed Soviet ICBMs, could destroy some 4280 Soviet warheads, about 39 percent of the expected 1982 Soviet total.

What difference would this make for the amount of destruction the Soviet Union could cause in the United States? Why would this not give the Soviet Union an incentive to strike first in time of crisis? Why would the deployment of the M-X give them any greater incentive, especially since the Soviets can be expected to have added greatly to their sea-based warheads by the time the M-X is deployed?

In short, the public discussion in the United States about Minuteman vulnerability, the deployment of the M-X, and crisis stability is marked by the same problems as the discussion of perceived equality. The strategic debate has focused on numbers of missiles and warheads as if they were living creatures whose survival was of value in their own right, to the near exclusion of any effort to relate these military means to potential differences in the war outcomes among which statesmen might actually be able to discriminate in terms of values about which they do care.

To conclude this discussion of the strategic objectives and concepts that have guided American policy in the 1970s, it needs to be noted that American strategy is much clearer on how it proposes to prevent nuclear war than it is on its objectives should deterrence fail and war actually start. The present strategy of countervailing power, most recently expressed in Carter's Presidential Directive 59 of August 1980, a strategy for denying the Soviets any prospect of victory on whatever political or military terms they might care to define it, has a fine Old Testament ring to it: an eye for an eye, a tooth for a tooth, and, if need be, a city for a city. But if war should start, how is it to be ended? Are the superpowers doomed to engage in a Kwakiutl Indian potlatch ceremony, tossing troops, missiles, and finally cities into the nuclear fire to show how much they value Western Europe or whatever else may be at stake in the conflict?

Clearly, more thought needs to be given to strategies for war termination, and the proper beginning is to consider how a nuclear war might begin. Given parity and the mutual destruction it presently permits, sane statesmen will have to be driven, cornered, and boxed into firing nuclear weapons. They will resort to nuclear war only in the belief that they cannot avoid it. It follows that if the war is to be stopped, statesmen will need to be persuaded that the perceptions that led them to war were wrong or that things have now changed and there is more room for political negotiation than they had earlier thought.

To this end, military policy can contribute by providing forces and strategies that permit at least the possibility of limiting the war, forces and strategies that can buy time, not consume it. The American interest in planning flexible options and in the acquisition of forces that can be withheld from use without cost to their later effectiveness is, therefore, an important step in the right direction. But it is only the first step, for, in the age of parity, once a nuclear war starts, the United States and the Soviet Union will limit damage, if at all, by the exercise of political not nuclear initiatives.

What are the prospects for strategic parity in the 1980s? An answer to this question must start with the recognition that, as a result of the experience of the 1970s, there are many Americans who now have serious reservations about the concept of parity and the SALT agreements associated with it. These American critics can be grouped into three schools of thought. There are those who believe that the United States does not have parity (that the strategic balance as codified in SALT II actually favours the Soviet Union). There are those who believe that the United States cannot get parity (that the Soviets are intent on strategic superiority, an objective which makes the effort to negotiate parity through SALT at best infeasible and at worst an exercise leading to a false sense of security). And there are those who believe that the United States should not want parity (that its own military objectives, particularly the credibility of its nuclear guarantees to its allies, are better served by superiority).

The issues associated with these three arguments are complex, and only a few general comments can be made here. With regard to the question of whether SALT II provides for parity, it is important to distinguish between numerical and military parity. The primary purpose of the treaty was to provide a means for codifying parity in the number of deployed strategic delivery vehicles, and this was done by counting silos, submarine launch tubes, and certain kinds of bombers. The terms of the treaty also allow, if the parties exercise all the options permitted, each side to have an equal number of warheads. Given the need to count weapon characteristics that could be unilaterally verified and the ambiguous character of the Soviet Backfire bomber, the treaty probably provides about as feasibly as one could for numerical equality in deployed strategic delivery vehicles.

Does this mean that the treaty provides for military parity, for equality in the ability to produce death and destruction? The answer is obvious: SALT II does not ensure military parity. There is too much left out. There are, for example, no limits on defensive systems (air defence, civil defence, and ASW systems), and there are no provisions governing the reliability of delivery vehicles or the yields and accuracies of the warheads they can carry, not to mention the absence of any terms affecting the strategy and tactics with which each side can employ its strategic forces.

The best that SALT agreements can do is to bound a few of the characteristics of each side's strategic forces. Within these limits, a number of war outcomes might be possible. Thus, to lay the burden of ensuring military equality on any SALT agreement dealing with offensive weapons is to mistake the potentiality of the instrument.

The only appropriate question to ask of SALT II, or of any comparable treaty, is whether its provisions prevent the United States from achieving military parity. In this connection, the most telling criticism of the SALT II treaty relates to the inability of the United States to persuade the Soviets to reduce the throw-weight of their strategic forces by eliminating some or all of their SS-18 missiles. The Soviet advantage in throw-weight gives them the greater megatonnage which, *ceteris paribus*, gives them a greater capability for destruction. But in comparing Soviet and American strategic forces, very little is *paribus*. Thus, if the Soviets were to substitute their "lighter" SS-19 missiles for their SS-18s or even if they were to dismantle their SS-18s in return for the dismantling of an equal number of American Minuteman III missiles, the Soviets would still retain a large advantage in throw-weight. Moreover, as previously noted, the disparity in fatalities that a nuclear war might bring owes more to the asymmetry in the distribution of the populations in the two countries than it does to the difference in their total megatonnage.

What of the argument that the Soviets are not interested in parity, in a balance providing for equal destruction, but are intent on superiority and victory? No student of military history needs to be reminded that states often come to quite divergent conclusions about the military or political import of the same weapons technology, and it would be surprising if the Soviets and Americans did share the same views about the strategic implications of nuclear weapons. And there are some significant differences in these views, although the differences are neither as marked nor as novel as some students of nineteenth-century Russian history would have one believe. Soviet declaratory policy has, for example, always placed a greater emphasis on strategies for pre-emption and launching-on-warning than does at least current American doctrine. These pronouncements have not been matched, however, by Soviet deployment policy. The Soviets keep relatively few of their ballistic missile-firing submarines at sea; their bombers are not on alert; and until recently neither were most of their ICBMs.

More consequential, in the judgment of most Americans, are the Soviet statements stressing the need for war-fighting, war-winning capabilities, in contrast to the American interest in stable deterrence through mutual assured destruction. In this case, Soviet declaratory policy is matched by a Soviet acquisition policy that is clearly intent on a damage-limiting capability. The Soviets have developed a countersilo capability with their ICBMs; they allocate large resources to air defence; they are striving to improve their forces for ASW (as is also the United States); and the Soviet civil defence program is better funded, better organized, and potentially far more effective than that of the United States.

To date, none of these efforts have gained the Soviets a major damage-limiting capability, but that does not detract from the seriousness of their effort or their determination to gain as decisive a military advantage as they can. In this respect, Soviet policy probably owes less to insights from Lenin or Clausewitz than it does to the interest of the professional military in winning not losing wars, although if the Soviet military have a clear operational definition of what would constitute a "victory" in a major nuclear exchange, it is well hid. As for Soviet civilian leaders, they are probably more interested in neutralizing US strategic power than in engaging it. If the fear of retaliation can ground the US Strategic Air Command (SAC) in the event of a European war, this is, for Soviet purposes, as good as destroying it.

Does Soviet strategy, then, make parity an infeasible American objective? Again, the distinction between numerical parity, as codified by SALT, and military parity is critical. The Soviets may well be genuine in their commitment to the numerical limitations reached in SALT and to the principle of equality in numbers of delivery vehicles or warheads. But they no doubt also see SALT, as they saw détente in general, as a framework for continued competition and are determined, within the constraints of SALT, to secure whatever military advantages they can.

American policy needs, therefore, to recognize that the case for SALT II (or any comparable agreement), as a means for placing equal numerical limits on certain characteristics of the offensive forces of the two sides, does not stand or fall on the extent of the Soviet commitment to equal military outcomes. The issue is whether the United States would find it easier to deny the Soviets any expectation of victory or advantage within the constraints of a SALT agreement or without them. In answering this question, American policy-makers also need to recognize that the particulars of any SALT agreement are the product of so much intra- and intergovernmental bargaining, that its provisions will necessarily strike any observer as less than wholly satisfactory. This said, since SALT II does not prevent the United States from deploying any weapons it presently considers necessary to implement its strategy of countervailing power and since the treaty does bound the Soviet threat in at least some important dimensions, the United States would probably find it cheaper to ensure military parity within the constraints of the agreement than it would without them.

But is parity a desirable goal? Parity, in both its numerical and military sense, may be compatible with SALT II and capable of being maintained within its limits, but why should the United States settle for a strategy of denial, a strategy that commits it to an unending effort to offset Soviet initiatives, with the consequent risk that its reactions may not always be timely? Why not, instead, regain American superiority?

A return to American superiority (to a balance in which the death and destruction in the Soviet Union would be far greater than that in the United States) would be the clearest and most decisive way of ensuring that the Soviets saw no prospect of victory in a nuclear war; would restore vitality to America's nuclear guarantees to its allies; and would help put an end to the worries (or hopes) of those who believe the long-run trends of global power are running in favour of the Soviet Union. Moreover, should deterrence ever fail, American superiority would provide a far more certain means for limiting damage than the exercise of frantic political initiatives to negotiate an end to the war before it terminated in an all-out exchange. Superiority would not, of course, ensure the United States against extensive destruction in a nuclear war, but if the United States could develop the capability to reduce expected fatalities to even 20 percent of the population, this would be an act of immeasurable political and military consequence.

As pointed out in the second section of this chapter, a return to American superiority would require the United States to do far more than add to the quantity and quality of its offensive forces (the M-X, Trident II, cruise missiles, and a new strategic bomber). To reduce significantly the destruction the Soviet Union could cause in the United States would require a massive deployment of effective defensive systems: for ballistic missile defence; for air defence; for ASW; and for civil defence.

Above all, the United States would require the determination to wage a long and costly armaments race with the Soviet Union. A Soviet Union presently intent on superiority can hardly be expected to acquiesce in a return to strategic inferiority. It will be necessary for the United States to offset the Soviet offsets that offset America's offsets to their offsets and to persist in this effort. But the United States has the larger and more efficient economy and the more sophisticated technology, and in the end, given the will (and given, especially, effective new technologies for ballistic missile defence), the United States could prevail until the Soviets were finally quantitatively and qualitatively outbuilt and outclassed.

Starting with Dwight Eisenhower, six presidents have looked at this prospect, blanched, and backed off. They must have seen something! And what they saw were inordinately high costs: war-level military budgets sustained over an indefinite number of years, with all that those budgets would entail for domestic programs and services, for the American standard of living, and for the control of the American economy. They also saw an American public and Congress, not to mention members of the executive and other élites, who showed no real disposition for preparing to fight (as compared to preparing to prevent) a nuclear war and who evidenced no faith in the arguments of those who contend that there can be significant differences in the degree of disaster that a nuclear war would bring.

Will the advocates of superiority be seventh-time lucky in the presidency of Ronald Reagan? Given time and advice, Reagan, too, is likely to back away from an effort to regain American superiority. Aside from his determination to reduce the federal budget and to address the problems of inflation and unemployment, if he is serious in his commitment to redress the deficiencies in American conventional forces, including the need to restore American naval superiority in the North Pacific while maintaining a major naval presence in the Indian Ocean, he will have problems enough in selling his budgets to a Congress which is already worried about the consequences of his policies for domestic welfare programs. In his program for strategic forces, then, Reagan is likely to settle for an increase in offensive weapons (including a new strategic bomber) and a new slogan (e.g., "strategic forces second to none") but to avoid a commitment to the acquisition of forces that would give the United States a real capability for damage limitation.

But time and advice may not be this president's lot. He has committed himself to the renegotiation of SALT II, and he comes to office with many advisers who question not only the existence of parity but its feasibility and desirability. He also comes to office when the 1972 ABM treaty is under increasing question, particularly from those who are attracted to the contribution that a missile defence system could make to the prelaunch survivability of the M-X.

There is a fair prospect, then, that the Reagan Administration could lead the United States into a "little arms race." In this future, the superpowers would fail to renegotiate SALT II and cease to observe the terms of both that agreement and the interim agreement of SALT I and, perhaps, in time the terms of the ABM treaty as well. The resulting competition in strategic arms would lead to a more uncertain and changing strategic balance and to a relationship from which the superpowers would find it difficult to return to another effort to constrain their competition through SALT. But the "little arms race" would still leave the United States without the capabilities required to achieve a decisive superiority over the Soviet Union in terms of the death and destruction each could inflict upon the other – a superiority clear enough to be recognized by all concerned in Moscow and Washington, in London and Bonn, and in Tokyo and Peking.

There is only one event on the horizon that could change this last prospect. The next Soviet-American confrontation is going to be most dangerous. The Soviets, as a result of their buildup in conventional as well as strategic forces, believe that the balance of power has shifted significantly in their favour since the early 1960s, and it is reasonable to believe that they will expect the results of the next confrontation to reflect that change in power. This time, in contrast to the Cuban missile crisis in 1962, they will expect the Americans to blink first. The United States, on the other hand, will be determined to stand fast and to demonstrate that, the Soviet buildup to the contrary, its commitments are as good as ever.

Should this confrontation result in anything that Americans might interpret as a defeat, as might conceivably happen in an area like the Middle East, where the United States is presently at some disadvantage, the American reaction will be strong and across the board, politically and militarily. Allies and alliances will be critically weighed and re-examined; the United States will want to see who was there when it needed them, and who was not. But whatever the outcome of that evaluation, Americans are most likely to associate their defeat with the change in the strategic balance and to pull out all stops in an effort to regain strategic superiority, and in this event, the "big arms race", rejected in the late 1950s and in the 1960s and the 1970s, will start in earnest in the 1980s.

4 Soviet Strategy 1965–1990

GEOFFREY JUKES

The overthrow of Nikita Khruschev in late 1964 ended a period of almost ten years in which the strategic nuclear forces had been developed, but kept small in numbers, modernisation of the conventional forces had proceeded at a steady but modest pace, while their numbers had been greatly reduced (from 5¾ million in 1955 to about 3½ million in 1964), and naval construction, after ceasing almost entirely for four years (1957–61) had resumed at a much reduced pace compared with that of the pre-1957 programme. In the fifteen years since, the steady growth of the Soviet armed forces has passed levels which many Western governments would regard as 'reasonable', and has set off a round of increases in Western defence expenditures which, insofar as they are not eroded by inflation, will raise defence spending to levels altogether unthinkable in the relatively recent past.

The large improvements in Soviet conventional forces since the late 1960s can be viewed in several ways. One is to deny their existence. This is untenable; though the quantities involved in the re-equipping may well have been exaggerated in the Western estimating process, there is ample evidence of qualitative improvement through introduction of new types. In the Naval, Air and Air Defence Forces this has been accompanied by a reduction in total numbers of ships, aircraft and men, but this does not appear to have been the case in the Ground Forces. In the Strategic Rocket Forces there has been an increase both in numbers and in performance of weapons.

Another way to view the large improvement in Soviet conventional forces is to equate it with systemic inertia, and view it as a consequence of bureaucratic politics and fascination with technology. There is much to be said for this approach, given that the same phenomenon is occasionally observed in other societies where it can be more convincingly documented, but it leaves unanswered questions of why technological fascination should, in the Soviet Union, be so heavily concentrated in the armaments sector. An answer to this can perhaps be found in recent historical experience, where the technological backwardness of much Soviet equipment in 1941 rendered the possession of large quantities of it no asset,[1] and success in the ensuing campaigns depended not merely on replacing lost inventory but replacing it with much improved equipment. A doctrinal basis for emphasis given to conventional forces has always existed in the formulation, frequently restated since 1945 (and especially when conventional forces were being reduced, or doubt cast on their utility), that victory in war requires the combined efforts of all armed services and arms of service. This formulation contends that all are necessary, but not that all are of equal importance, and is therefore flexible enough to accommodate alterations in force structure within its general theoretical framework. It is, therefore, possible to ensure a particular proportion of assets to national defence by political decision, and to leave division of it between forces to the Ministry of Defence, watched over since 1967 by a senior Party official, Dimitry Ustinov, with a background in defence procurement going back to the 1930s, as well as by Brezhnev himself, in his capacity as Chairman of the Supreme Defence Council.

A third way to view the improvement in Soviet conventional forces is to see it as part of a goal of 'superiority'. This has been put forward by several analysts, but, while it seems to explain some aspects of Soviet procurement, it raises many problems of its own. One is the problem of defining 'parity', which a policy of 'superiority' rejects, and when it has been attained or forsaken. For example, NATO doctrine does not predicate victory in general war on an advance to Moscow by its ground forces, whereas for the Soviets expulsion of American forces from Europe is a precondition for even a 'draw'; the NATO doctrine does not therefore require parity in tanks, but may well find parity in anti-tank weapons totally insufficient. Unless true parity can be judged, it is difficult to say what constitutes superiority in comparing forces with different objectives and hence different composition.

The questions 'By when?' and 'For what purpose?' also have to be asked. It is already clear that the Soviet increases are now prompting a Western response, so that if superiority by a particular date was postulated, the date will have to be postponed. But if superiority is not set for any particular time, the process of seeking it appears to be of infinite duration and hence of infinite expense.[2] As for the question of 'purpose', the range of possible answers lies between 'making it obvious to potential aggressors that they can never become strong enough to attack us successfully' and 'giving ourselves the wherewithal for world domination'. The requirements at the lower end of the spectrum are more easily attained than those at the more ambitious end, and would appear to be more consistent with a steady but relatively slow modernisation of forces, such as has taken place, and is entirely consistent with the reduction in numbers of some of the forces which has accompanied that modernisation.

I do not propose to discuss at any length the occasional assertions from within the Soviet military that it is possible to win a nuclear war. There does not seem to be anything especially sinister about assertions by professional military that they can win a hypothetical war; it is, after all, what they are supposed to do. In any event, assertions by the military that a particular war can be won do not commit their political leaders to engage in it. The Soviet political and military leaders have shown by speech and action that they are well aware of the costs of 'winning' a nuclear war, and have stated time and again that the primary function of their armed forces is deterrence. The objectives of NATO and of the Warsaw Pact are first to deter war and, if unsuccessful in that, to win. They are, in that sense, mirror images of each other, and Khruschev's insistence that only deterrence mattered was rightly seen as too simplistic by his military.[3]

Soviet strategy since 1965 has retained a basic doctrinal framework which, at least conceptually, regards all types of war as lying on a continuum with small local wars at one end, and general nuclear war at the other. In political terms this framework appears to lack the very distinct break which most Western thinkers make between non-nuclear and nuclear war, and therefore contains elements of irresponsibility. In practice what it means is that each type of war is seen as containing the elements of the next higher, so that troops must train for all types of war, including conventional operations within nuclear war.[4] It also means that because there is no concept of a 'firebreak', sub-nuclear wars are not to be lightly undertaken – it is consistent with this thinking that Soviet troops have been used in mass since 1945 only in three countries, all of which had Marxist governments and were not likely to succeed in invoking Western (especially American) military intervention in their defence. The intervention in Afghanistan marks no significant departure from this concept, but requires some discussion in this connection.

Feeling in the West and in parts of the Third World has run high over the Soviet intervention in Afghanistan, and a number of interpretations have been put forward which are unlikely to stand the test of time. It has been suggested that it is part of a plan to encircle the Gulf, and that the next step will be an invasion of Pakistan, especially Pakistani Baluchistan, with the aim of seizing a base for naval forces, probably at Gwadar. This would seem rather an unlikely form for Soviet influence-seeking to take. On the one hand, it would do little or nothing to threaten oil traffic that could not be done by air action from airfields in Soviet Transcaucasus or the airfield at Shindand in Western Afghanistan. On the other hand, it would undoubtedly open the doors of many Indian Ocean countries to the establishment of a strong Western counterpresence which they are at present reluctant to contemplate and, as a direct affront to China, which claims a particular friendship with Pakistan, would risk driving China and the West even closer together. It would certainly be viewed with grave misgivings by an India which is still regarded by the Soviets as a major friend, if not exactly an ally, in Asia. Nor is it consistent with Soviet efforts to reconstruct with Iran the cautiously amicable relationship which it had with that country under the Shah.

It is far more likely that the Soviet decision to intervene in Afghanistan was based in the complexities of the internal situation in that country and of relations of the anti-Marxist forces there with adjacent countries, especially Iran, Pakistan, and China. When the indignation has subsided, as it invariably has to over the misdeeds of great powers, the intervention is likely to be seen as the result of Soviet aversion to disorder in countries on their borders, not inherently differently motivated from American interventions in Caribbean and Central American countries in the not too distant past, or Soviet interventions in Hungary and almost in Poland in 1956, or in Czechoslovakia in 1968. It is a misuse of rhetoric to define Afghanistan as a 'free and independent country' solely in the context of a Soviet military intervention. Afghanistan had been totally dependent on the Soviet Union for supply and training of its armed forces since 1954, dependent to the extent of over 60% for its non-military aid and over 40% of its trade, (United Nations, 1979, Table 156; *Quarterly Economic Review*, 1980, p. 37)[5] and been subjected to a Marxist coup d'etat in April 1978, followed by severely oppressive measures. It is extremely doubtful whether any Western government regarded it as 'free and independent' prior to the Soviet intervention. It had virtually been conceded to the Soviet sphere of influence and the Soviets by 'intervening' in support of one political faction against another, did only what they and numerous other great powers have done before and will do again in their sphere of influence. It is a function of great powers to define vital interests as they think fit, and until some international means of restraining them are found, they will continue to do so.

The emphasis on military power in Soviet internal and foreign policy is strong. Military service is presented as an honourable duty, the role of the armed forces as protector of the Soviet state is frequently mentioned, and the conscription system was revised at the beginning of a period of demographic surplus in the late 1960s, by reducing the length of service, to ensure that the proportion of youth inducted annually was maintained at a high level. Government statements frequently assert that the armed forces will continue to be provided with all that is necessary and, though conscripts serve in the internal security and frontier guard forces, the sanctity of the armed forces proper is maintained by using them as little as possible for the maintenance of internal security. Other forces are maintained for that purpose.

This does not add up to a militarised society (there being none of the glorification of war which has marked such societies in the past), and both statements about military strength and policies aimed at achieving it have a rationale in the hardships inflicted on Russia and the Soviet Union through past lack of it, but the use of military terminology and the symbolism of conflict in political and economic matters, and the way in which all leaders of the state after Lenin have adorned themselves with military ranks and decorations point to the importance of the military factor in Soviet thinking. Whether this marks something new or merely the continuation of an old 'European' tradition may be a matter of debate, but the existence of the phenomenon is not. The absence of a readily-visible 'military-industrial complex' signifies a general public concurrence, challenged only by a very small group of dissidents in public (however much it may be disputed by technocrats in private), rather than a mere lack of debate about alternatives. Large and well-equipped armed forces, based on a system of universal conscription, are less likely to be the subject of contention in a country with long and vulnerable borders and a tradition of conscription, than in countries where the ability to rely on natural barriers and a high level of technology have rendered more natural a different pattern of defence, through small but capital-intensive armed forces, with resort to conscription only in times of acute danger.

However this may be, in the mid-1960s, Khrushchev's policies of denigrating military power, and of clear preference for upgrading consumer-oriented industries were reversed to a significant extent, and systematic modernisation of the armed forces was given very high priority. Apart from a rapid increase in the ICBM force from its very low level of 1964, it is not correct to describe what happened as a 'crash programme', but it does seem clear that for fifteen years defence expenditures have risen in proportion to, or maybe in some years slightly faster than, the GNP, i.e. that defence planners have been able to rely on an approximately constant share of GNP over a long period. Consequently, modernisation of inventory has proceeded steadily rather than by the 'batch procurement' characteristic of most other countries, the defence planners (and everyone else) have become accustomed to receiving a constant share of resources, and this appears to have become a fact of Soviet life rather than an actual necessity of force development. The tank replacement cycle, for example, has shortened from 15–16 years in the case of the T54/55/62 to less than 10 years between T62 and T72, and it may be questioned whether, with so much recently manufactured artillery, gun production need continue at the present rate. It is likely, therefore, that a review of the defence allocation is already under way, that changes in a downward direction will be sought by some elements of the leadership and planners, but strongly, and probably successfully, resisted by those responsible for the conduct and planning of defence.

The reason why this is likely is that over a long period it has become normal for about 10-12% of the GNP to be devoted to defence; the economy has adjusted to this situation, in which it has still been possible to maintain a modest but steady rate of growth and of improvement in the standard of living, even during a period when the non-Communist world has been passing through a recession. The signs of slowing down in the Soviet economy may lead to pressures inside Soviet planning circles for a reduction in the defence burden, but the most critical element is likely to be the armed forces' demands on manpower rather than the cost burden as such, and the solution is more likely to be seen in a continuation of the process of substituting mobility and firepower for manpower than in significant reductions in defence spending.

The policies followed over the past fifteen years have been characterised by both qualitative improvements and quantitative increases in the weapons inventory of the army and strategic rocket forces and of increased effectiveness of the air and naval forces within an overall numerical reduction. They have also seen similar changes in the other Warsaw Pact countries, though more limited in scope. Soviet combat forces stationed abroad have been modernised and increased in numbers in East Germany, and since 1968, deployed additionally in Czechoslovakia. In the Soviet Far East, forces along the Sino-Soviet border and in Mongolia have been increased, improved and united under an operational headquarters.

The overall effect has been a significant improvement in the capacity of 'Fortress Russia' to defend itself against conventional attack and to deter both conventional and nuclear attack by any conceivable coalition of enemies. The steady pursuit of these objectives dates from early 1965, suggesting that discontent with Khrushchev's relative disdain for defence was an important factor in his overthrow and, per contra, that improvement of the capacity of the armed forces has been given high priority throughout the years of the present leadership, notwithstanding occasional complaints by Kosygin and others about the expense involved.

What will happen during the 1980s depends on the outcome of the power-struggle which will follow the retirement or death of the present now rather old group of leaders. The transformation of the armed forces can be viewed as a generational re-equipping, substantially complete in the case of the army and strategic forces, partially so in the naval and air forces, and therefore permitting some reduction in the pace of re-equipment for about a decade. Or it can be viewed as bringing the forces up to a level at which the qualitative superiority of Western forces has been substantially eroded, and as fetching them to a plateau-point from which to make a further drive to achieve superiority by increased expenditures on attaining technological goals now felt to be within reach. Among the next leaders there will undoubtedly be proponents of both these views as well as of eclectic mixtures of them.

In the current Western mood of apprehension about Soviet intentions, it would be easy to forget the realities of East-West confrontation in predicting a Soviet drive for superiority. The reality is that the Warsaw Pact countries have a total population which, at around 400 million, is only about two-thirds that of the NATO countries, and a combined GNP which is considerably less than half that of NATO. Should conspicuous consumption in an armaments race become necessary, the NATO countries could raise much larger and lavishly-equipped forces than the Warsaw Pact if they so desired. Nothing is more likely to give them the political will to do so than the nebulous concept of superiority of an adversary. When it is also borne in mind that NATO is by no means the sum of the American alliance system, and that the Soviets have also to count China as a de facto adversary, it can be seen that Soviet advocates of the pursuit of superiority will have an uphill task against those who argue for a rough overall parity coupled with reliance on the erosive effects of history upon capitalism.

It is impossible to predict the outcome of a conflict which has not yet begun, but there are some Soviet planning practices which indicate the most likely outcome. Planning proceeds in a five-year cycle and though this has been found to have drawbacks, attempts to replace it (for example, Khrushchev's Seven-Year Plan of 1958–65) have not so far succeeded. Within plan periods, there is an observable tendency to maintain a steady level of allocation, and this means that unless the formula of Five Year Plans is abandoned (which seems unlikely), only two major reviews of allocations will take place in the next ten years. At the first, probably already under way, the defence planners will argue that allocations should be maintained or increased to match increases now taking place in NATO (and themselves largely a response to past Soviet increases). What will happen at the second is less clear, but by then requirements for the late 1990s will have begun to obtrude, with the need to replace weapons procured under the generational renewal which began in 1965 and is still under way now.

The possibility of political actions dependent on the actual or symbolic value of large and modern armed forces is a major imponderable. In the 1960s, the concepts denoted by the term 'counter-insurgency' became almost a shibboleth in some Western armies and air forces, but the Soviet armed forces remained little influenced by them, since Soviet practice was to supply weapons and training to friendly governments or insurgents, but abstain from involvement in the ensuing conflicts. The only post-war situations in which Soviet troops had seen large-scale action abroad – Hungary in 1956 and

Czechoslovakia in 1968 – had been in small and densely-populated countries where the prerequisites for a prolonged armed resistance were lacking, and were dealt with by a policy of saturation. Genuine counterinsurgency operations by Soviet troops had last taken place in the late 1940s in the Ukraine and, for obvious reasons, had not been publicised to the extent of building a body of doctrine from them. However, in the late 1970s Soviet involvement in counterinsurgency began, first through operations in Angola and Ethiopia, where Soviet participation on the ground was secondary to that of Cubans, but Soviet provision of logistical support of all kinds was crucial, continued through provision of similar aid to Vietnamese intervention in Cambodia, and finally in 1979 burgeoned into fully-fledged counterinsurgency operations in Afghanistan. Here an intervention, apparently intended to be limited to securing the Afghan Army's rear, and freeing its manpower for operations against the rebels, has increasingly had to be undertaken by the Soviet forces themselves, a pattern not unfamiliar from American experience in Vietnam.

It is too early to say whether the international repercussions of the Soviet intervention, and the difficulties the Soviet forces appear to be having in controlling the Afghanistan situation, will cause the next generation of Soviet leaders to abstain from repeating the exercise elsewhere in the Third World, but it must be noted that Soviet troops are acquiring experience which they previously lacked, and therefore widening the range of options open to the political leadership in future crises. However, at the same time they are incurring casualties and not obviously succeeding as yet in operations against very lightly-armed and only minimally organised opponents. A reputation for being 'ten feet tall' is most easily acquired by combining lavish re-equipment with abstention from actual combat, and the experience of counterinsurgency in Afghanistan is proving an expensive acquisition.

In the Strategic Rocket Forces the shape of the 1980s is already evident with the new generation of missiles, multiple warheading, increased accuracy, and the Delta-class submarine. The replacement of static by mobile missiles will do much to nullify the increased accuracy which both the United States and the Soviet Union are pursuing, and the balance between the two sides will not be significantly disturbed by this gradual shift to mobile missiles, nor by deployment of the US cruise missile in Europe if this eventuates. The Soviet capacity for overkill in Europe and China will be enhanced by new mobile intermediate range ballistic missile (IRBM) and medium range ballistic missile (MRBM) deployments, but without greatly affecting the central balance.

Soviet theatre ground forces in Europe will continue large, mobile, and of high firepower. The Soviets may have miscalculated somewhat in putting the T72 tank into mass production shortly before the arrival of layered (Chobham) armour, which will almost certainly feature in most future Western tanks, but the tank is irrevocably in service and will remain substantially unchanged for several more years. With generational reequipping with new tanks, armoured personnel carriers, artillery and missiles virtually completed, no major changes in the equipment of Soviet ground forces are likely before the end of the 1980s. Innovation in artillery is more likely to be found in ammunition than in the guns themselves.

Precision-guided munitions (PGMs), an area where an early Soviet lead has been overtaken by Western forces, will be deployed in increasing numbers, especially in view of their potential role in preserving the ascendancy of the tank, a weapon in which the Soviets have invested more than any other army has, and which has become increasingly vulnerable to Western PGMs.

Modernisation of the air forces has to some extent eroded the qualitative superiority formerly very apparent in NATO aircraft, but modernisation processes go in waves, and are not always in phase with each other, so the end of the decade may well see NATO further ahead, but with a new generation of Soviet aircraft about to come into service. The acceptance of a declaratory limit on production of the 'Backfire' bomber may have marked an important concession in Soviet arms control policy, but it may simply have resulted from awareness of deficiencies in the performance of the aircraft of which we would not necessarily be aware, as was the case with some earlier aircraft such as 'Bear', 'Bison' and the MiG-25.

Airlift, especially to and within the front line areas, will be increased and increases in longer-range mobility may well be needed because of the likelihood that manpower shortages arising from the sharp post-1959 reductions in the birth-rate will cause a drop in total forces manpower. The increased airlift capacity, significantly for areas closest to combat formations, may be viewed as partial replacement of the armoured personnel carrier by the helicopter, and of the tank by the close support aircraft. Maritime strike/reconnaissance is likely to be developed further for two especial purposes: one, for protection of nuclear powered strategic missile submarine (SSBN) 'sanctuaries' against intrusion by NATO attack submarines and, two, for 'high seas' anti-submarine warfare (ASW), particularly protection of surface forces by shipborne aircraft, an aspect of aviation which is still in its infancy in the Soviet Navy.

Developments in naval strategy for the next ten years are somewhat easier to foresee, because of the relatively long lead times and the small numbers of larger units which are building at any one time. After considerable controversy about the aircraft carrier, which Khrushchev believed too expensive for the Soviet Navy, the Kiev class, the first ships capable of operating fixed-wing aircraft, began to come into service in the mid-1970s. They are assessed as configured to serve as the centrepiece of anti-submarine task forces, and it appears that three or perhaps four of them will be in service by the middle of the 1980s, probably two each with the Northern and Pacific Fleets. Their configuration, and the heavy concentration on ASW weapons in the cruiser and destroyer classes built during the 1970s suggest that they have an important role in protecting the deployment areas of the Soviet SSBN submarines against penetration by NATO attack submarines, as well as a possible though more dubious role against American, British and French SSBN boats operating off the Soviet northern coast. Some diversification can be expected during the 1980s, most probably through extension of dual-launch capability in the missile launchers of the cruisers and destroyers, and improvement in the vertical take-off and landing (VTOL) aircraft and helicopters of the carriers.

The long periods spent in harbour by the two Kiev class ships now in service may indicate that significant design faults have been encountered, and that the class will be cut short for this reason. Whether or not this is so, the Kiev class is inherently a transistional design, and a bifurcation can now be expected into smaller ships with VTOL and helicopter capacity only, coupled with ships of Kiev size or larger capable of operating conventional aircraft, which the Kiev class cannot. There is positive evidence that the first part of this bifurcation is occurring, and less positive evidence of the second.

It is premature to attempt to evaluate the roles and functions of the newer classes of ship only now beginning to emerge, but it is clear that the trend towards larger units and nuclear power for surface warships, apparent for over a decade in the US Navy, is now perceptible in the Soviet Navy as well. A distinctive feature of some of the new Soviet classes is an emphasis on large guns. Amphibious warfare capacity, hitherto not as prominent a feature of the Soviet Navy as of the USN is clearly being developed, and improvements in the fleet train will, along with nuclear power, enhance the autonomy of naval task forces appreciably. However, the extent to which these developments will increase Soviet high-seas capabilities by the end of the 1980s depends more on building and training rates than on the mere appearance of new designs. As these new designs are at the start of their production runs, it cannot yet be said with any certainty how quickly they will come into service or how many of them will be built. It is clear, however, that conceptually they indicate at least a partial victory for the views, expressed by Admiral Gorshkov over a number of years, favouring a greater high seas capacity for the Navy, with special reference to its suitability as a 'protector of state interests in time of peace'. New building programmes were necessitated anyway because of the need to replace the large numbers of cruisers, destroyers, frigates and submarines built between 1948 and 1959, and the characteristics of the post-1967 and post-1977 generations of new construction in general follow the trend apparent in other leading navies, especially the American, in which fewer but larger ships replace those going out of service.

The Western estimates of Soviet force levels show very low manpower levels for the number of weapons said to be deployed, compared to the manpower/weapons ratios of other modern armed forces, and they assume teeth/tail ratios (troops in combat units to troops in support and supply) which are also much out of line with the rest of the world's leading armed forces, as well as out of line with the rest of the Soviet economy in which manpower productivity is not outstandingly high. They also show a tendency to retain in the Soviet order of battle large numbers of weapons which by Western standards are outdated, especially tanks, aircraft, medium-sized surface warships and submarines. The probability therefore is that, at any rate in estimates released for public consumption, they overrate the quantity of effective weaponry and underestimate the manpower consumed in serving it. If it is accepted as a working hypothesis that Western intelligence estimates are likely to be more accurate in respect to large weapons, vehicles, aircraft and ships than in respect to manpower, it would seem distinctly likely that the demands the Soviet armed forces make on manpower are greater, and possibly substantially greater, than they appear to be in estimates available in the public domain. If that is so, and I believe it is, the competition between armed forces and industry for the reduced manpower coming on to the labour market in the 1980s (a consequence of the steep decline in the post-1960 birthrate) will be very severe. There are a number of ways in which the Soviet regime may attempt to solve it:

1. By increased employment of women. The Soviet armed forces employ relatively few women and may move to increase their numbers. However, the proportion of Soviet women in the workforce is already among the highest in the world, and the scope for relieving a strained manpower situation in this way is therefore limited.

2. By increased firepower and 'automation of the battlefield' wherever possible. This is merely the continuation of a trend in military affairs. In western forces it was, until recently at least, associated with increases in the support and supply elements; partial reversal of the trend may now have become possible with PGMs, miniaturisation and improved handling methods, but in the final analysis it is the high attrition rates likely to result from increased adversary firepower which will determine force levels not the attainment of any arbitrarily-defined level of firepower by Soviet forces.

3. By increasing the mobility of existing forces. The main problem here is that Soviet forces already have very high ground mobility, as

do those of their NATO opponents. Since mobility relative to opposing forces is what counts, the ability to reduce numbers by increasing mobility exists only for small-war or single-front was operations – there is scope for 'fire-brigade' forces, but they are more likely to supplement main forces than to replace them.

4. By increasing the long-service component of the forces, and reducing or abolishing the intake of conscripts. There are a number of countries (mostly maritime nations) which do not use conscripts at all. However, a policy of this kind, while enabling capital-intensive forces to be trained to a high level in peacetime, makes it extremely difficult to produce quickly the vastly-expanded forces needed for a major war. It is of doubtful validity for maritime countries in the age of the missile, bomber and nuclear weapon, and has not been valid at all for countries with long land frontiers in this century. The Soviet armed forces may well have found already that the new technologies require a higher proportion of long-service personnel, but their leaders have shown no sign of willingness to dispense with universal military service. Nor, given the higher educational levels of present-day conscripts, and the low attractiveness of a non-commissioned military career to Soviet youth, is any change of attitude likely during the 1980s.

5. By increasing the term of conscript service. In the later 1960s, when a demographic 'bulge', resulting from the high immediate postwar birthrate appeared, the principle of universality was preserved by reducing the length of service, and thus increasing throughput without significantly altering the size of the forces. It might therefore seem logical to increase the term of service. However, this would have two undesirable effects – first, and most important, it would aggravate manpower shortages in industry and agriculture, and second, it would result in a reduced output to the reserves compared to the post-1967 system.

6. By reducing the term of conscript service, and maintaining throughput as close as possible to its present level by reducing the present fairly wide grounds for exemption, or reduction in term of service. This would reduce competition for manpower with the civilian sector, at the price of a possible lowering in quality.

7. By persuading Eastern European states to take a larger share of Warsaw Treaty responsibilities, especially in provision of ground forces. Eastern Europe contributes less to the Warsaw Pact than Western Europe does to NATO, reflecting its smaller population and more limited resources. There is undoubtedly some scope for an increase in its contribution, but so far it has not responded enthusiastically to Soviet pressures to this effect. In any event, some Eastern European countries face manpower shortages of their own in the 1980s.

8. By pursuit of reductions by agreement. Progress in the talks on Mutual and Balanced Force Reduction has been slow, but MBFR may become more urgent for the Soviets as manpower shortage begins to bite.

Most likely a combination of measures will be adopted, comprising continuation of existing trends towards increased mobility and firepower, a larger long-service cadre, selective reductions in the term of service (e.g. in the infantry), continuation of MBFR talks, pressure on allies for increased commitment, a stepping up of pre-intake induction and post-service part-time training with stockpiling of pre-positioned equipment in Central Europe, and Western and Far Eastern USSR. More generally, reorganisation to achieve higher productivity in industry and agriculture would seem to be necessary as, despite considerable progress, the civilian sector of the Soviet economy is still generally unimpressive in this respect. The predominance of vertical structuring in Soviet industry, with each producer attempting to achieve self-sufficiency by manufacture of its own components and sub-assemblies, is well suited to defence production, in which there is essentially only one 'customer', but is less suited to the achievement of high productivity in the civilian sector. A solution to the manpower allocation problem by industrial reorganisation is therefore unlikely to be achieved over the next few years. There will be ample scope both for the Soviets to represent their actions as motivated by arms control considerations if they so choose, and for Western analysts to interpret them as linked to plans for surprise attack.

The likelihood of general war initiated by either the United States or the Soviet Union is low, and that of catalytic war initiated by allies of either probably lower still. The main problems for Soviet strategy in the 1980s are those of achieving the 'side effects' of power on a global scale, and they have begun to encounter frustrations with which the United States is familiar; specifically, the refusal of allies to identify their own interests totally with those of their superpower patrons; the ability of some non-aligned countries to play off one superpower against another; the tendency for arms races to become a substitute for war, which each generation of weapons costing a great deal more than the last (a problem which has left the United States and the Soviet Union as the only two countries producing the full possible range of weapons, lesser powers either grouping together to produce the more sophisticated varieties of weapon, or dropping out altogether); inability of the most expensive and powerful systems to achieve direct effects, because of the consequences of using them.

Each of the last three decades has seen one intervention by Soviet armed forces outside Soviet borders – in Hungary in 1956, Czechoslovakia in 1968, and Afghanistan in 1979. This is in fact a low usage of military intervention compared with the United States, Britain or France, exemplifying a Soviet preference for equipping 'friends' but expecting them to do their own fighting. However, during the 1970s Soviet capacity for indirect involvement and use of 'advisers' has increased, along with that for distant-area operations by the naval and air forces. The Afghanistan operation, while not exactly a Soviet Vietnam, is probably proving more difficult and long-drawn-out than expected; it has had unfavourable repercussions on relations with the West, the Third World and Eastern Europe – significantly, unlike the invasion of Czechoslovakia, it was a totally Soviet undertaking, no attempt being made to present it as 'fraternal assistance' by the 'Socialist Commonwealth' as a whole. As in the American case, Soviet strategy divides into a multilateral regional strategy for Europe and a unilateral pursuit of objectives in other regions. Whether they will attempt regional alliance-building elsewhere remains to be seen. Their plan for Asian Collective Security, put forward in 1969, and received with coolness almost everywhere in Asia, because of its perceived anti-Chinese orientation, has almost certainly received its death-blow by the invasion of Afghanistan, not to mention the changes in Chinese policy since the death of Mao.

In summary, the 1980s are likely to see little development in Soviet strategic thought as regards operations of strategic nuclear forces, armies and air forces, and some development in regard to navies, especially in respect to shipborne aircraft and amphibious forces. The naval development will be limited by the relatively small number of the new, larger ships likely to be built over ten years, but the trend to convergence on the US Navy pattern may (not necessarily will) indicate a more sustained effort to use the Navy to project the Soviet power image in distant waters. This, if undertaken, will be subsidiary to the Navy's major general war roles, namely the protection of Soviet SSBN submarines, ASW against NATO SSBN and attack submarines (and possibly Chinese also towards the end of the decade), and elimination of US carriers, especially in the Mediterranean.

Although doctrinal changes will be minor, increased production and projection capacities will almost certainly lead to higher levels of activity outside the European and Chinese border theatres. The likelihood of a much-increased US presence in the Indian Ocean will almost certainly lead to a bigger Soviet Indian Ocean force, especially if the relationship with South Yemen remains stable enough to permit long-term use of Aden. The modernisation and upgrading of the Soviet Pacific Fleet will almost certainly lead Japan to increase its Maritime Self-Defence Force and the United States its two Pacific Fleets. It remains to be seen what use the Soviet Navy will make of the Pacific Fleet carrier *Minsk* and of other air capability ships which may follow it to the Pacific, because the operating pattern of such ships is likely to depend in large measure on that of a US Indian Ocean force which has not yet taken on any permanent form.

5 On Limited War
Soviet Approaches

ROMAN KOLKOWICZ

> Limited war requires limits ... but limits require agree-
> ments on at least some kind of mutual recognition and ac-
> quiescence. And agreement on limits is difficult to reach.
>
> Thomas C. Schelling

In his *Notebook on Clausewitz*, Lenin selected the following citation
from *On War* for particular approval: 'The conqueror is always peace-
loving, quite gladly would he march into our state without disturbance'. Lenin wrote on the margin of this citation: 'Ha-ha! Clever!'
(Adoratskii, 1931, p. 167). Clever, indeed, and also fitting the con-
tempory conqueror strategies of Lenin's successors. Soviet expansionistic policies are premised in strategies of limited 'disturbance', or
more properly in doctrines of limited war.

The concept of limited war is vexatious: Americans are said to
find it historically 'unnatural'; the Soviets have declared it to be a de-
vious capitalist ploy; and the Europeans do not like it much since
their countries would likely serve as the primary battlefields. Eminent
scholars and strategists who flirted with the idea of limited war in a
nuclear era found it necessary subsequently to recant their earlier in-
discretions (Brodie, 1957; Kissinger 1960 and 1961). Unlike the ba-
roque theoretical edifice of strategic deterrence, the conceptual structures of limited war are rather rickety. While deterrence theory refers
to a clear-cut boundary between no-war and all-out general nuclear
war, limited war doctrine is complicated by the imprecision and multiplicity of its definitions and types, including local war, theatre war,
theatre nuclear war, conventional war, limited nuclear war, war of
national liberation and so forth. And yet while the empirical validation
of strategic deterrence doctrine is ambiguous at best, what is referred
to as limited war theory and doctrine is as real and pervasive as the
last war in Asia or the next in the Middle East.

A superficial examination of the evolution of limited war doctrines in the post-war period in the East and West may possibly be
misleading. Several ambiguous and contradictory trends appear to be
operating within both the United States and the Soviet Union:

* The United States historically rejected the concept of limited war; the idea of 'hobbling' oneself was considered to be against some deeply rooted American traditions. Yet it was in the United States that modern limited war doctrine was not only developed but firmly embraced by the government and the strategic community – this despite the traditional misgivings and against some strong new resistance from certain social and political groups (Halperin, 1963).

* The Soviet Union, which historically embraced the practice of limited war (having eschewed significant development of strategic forces, weapons, technologies and doctrines while supporting and developing conventional, tactical, limited-range weapons, forces and operational principles), has in the post-war period strongly objected to Western notions of limited war. What the Soviets found particularly objectionable were Western premises about the 'logic' of limited war; that is, notions of interdependent, cooperative, and mutual limiting and controlling measures to be undertaken by belligerents during war (Progress Publishers, 1972, pp. 89, 90). These Western ideas about the 'inner logic' of limited war are alien to the Soviet tradition of *kto-kovo* belief systems that stress self-reliant, unilateral, and independent modes of behaviour in war, be it 'limited' or total.

* The United States, which by the mid-1960s had obtained a superior stategic nuclear capability *vis-a-vis* the Soviets, adopted a flexible response doctrine which in principle supported the idea of controlled, limited war, with or without the use of nuclear weapons.

* The Soviets entered the 1960s possessing massive conventional forces and minimal strategic capabilities. Yet in 1960 they formally adopted a defence policy that had all the characteristics of a finite deterrence/massive retaliation doctrine, while rejecting any concept of the feasibility or desirability of limited war (Wolfe, 1965, pp. 30–34).

At first glance, these trends and developments appear puzzling and contradictory. Yet, on close examination, they yield certain kinds of plausible explanations: a strategically inferior Soviet Union could not risk the danger of provoking or confronting a strategically superior United States in a local, limited or theatre war that might escalate rapidly into a nuclear strategic confrontation; thus, in order to forestall such a possibility, to avoid the United States calling the Soviet missiles' bluff and to play for time to build their own strategic forces to partity levels, the Soviets had to reject Western notions of controlled war, local or limited. In the United States, on the other hand, the rigidities and fatuities of massive retaliation doctrine clearly argued for greater flexibility and wider spectrum options, thus a flexible response doctrine.

In the 1970s and into the 1980s, the picture has revealed itself: the Soviet Union has obtained strategic nuclear parity and at the same time has begun to gradually accept the idea of controlled, limited war. The United States, on the other hand, has lost its strategic nuclear advantage over the Soviets and has essentially returned to a mutual assured destruction doctrine, while showing increasing concern over mounting evidence of a massive Soviet buildup of conventional, theatre nuclear and 'projective' capabilities, all with potential use in limited or local wars. (The recent Presidential Directive 59 represents a shift from the MAD doctrine of 'city-busting'. It nonetheless limits itself to a central war context, i.e., that in the event of a central war, rather than targetting cities, the United States would concentrate on 'hard' targets – counter-value vs counter-force. This does not bear on limited wars as seen in the Soviet context and to be discussed in this chapter. P.D. 59 deals essentially with collateral damage limitations in a central war context: a concept which is still roundly rejected in Soviet military literature.)

How is one to make sense of these developments? Do they coalesce into rational patterns, directions, motivations, or intent? Or are they random-unrelated developments without logical explanations? This chapter will attempt to analyse these questions and in doing so to provide an explanation regarding the role of limited war doctrine in Soviet military practices and policies.

Evolution of Military Doctrines in the Soviet Union

Limited war is the 'natural' and 'rational' doctrine for a quasi-revolutionary, expansionistic political system, like the Soviet Union, that continues to espouse a global and universal mission in an international system that is 'governed' by a balance of nuclear terror. It has been suggested that in the 1980s Soviet foreign policy objectives and military doctrine will become harmonious and congruent. Soviet foreign policy since the mid-1960s has pursued the triadic primary goals of stabilized relations with the West; containment and isolation of China; and, exploration and expansion in the Third World, generally in areas south of Russia: Sovet military doctrine coincides with these foreign policy objectives; the massive strategic nuclear shield provides a stable deterrence basis with the West; limited war doctrines and forces, with or without nuclear weapons, provide additional deterrent and war-fighting capabilities on the primary contiguous flanks of the Soviet Union (Europe and Asia); and their conventional, 'projective' capabilities provide a cutting edge and a persuasive presence in support of expanding and exploratory policies in the Third World. This triadic orientation of Soviet foreign and military policy demands a large share of Soviet resources, manpower, and managerial/political talents; however, the Soviets appear to be persuaded that the costs and risks entailed are tolerable, as measured against prospective gains (Gore, 1970, pp. 591–602). Contemporary Soviet military thinking is therefore based on parry-and-thrust concept: their vast nuclear forces are to serve as the deterrent shield against Western nuclear strategic forces, while their general purpose forces are to serve as a flexible sword probing and thrusting into the vulnerable and soft regions of the world south of Russia.

In the past, the Soviets found it difficult formally to accept the idea of limited warfare, particularly limited warfare with the use of nuclear weapons:

The idea of introducing rules and games and artificial restrictions by agreement seems illusory and untenable. It is difficult to visualise that a nuclear war, if unleashed, could be kept within the framework of rules and would not develop into an all-out war. In fact such proposals are a demagogic trick designed to reassure the public opinion (Arbatov, 1974, p. 46).

Soviet political leaders have gone on record as opposing the idea of limited warfare because of the escalatory pressures and generally unpredictable consequences. Khrushchev, Brezhnev and others have at various times reiterated the proposition that 'global wars are known to have started from local wars' and that because of 'rapid development of military technology, it will be even more difficult to put any limits on armed conflict if this conflict starts in any single region' (Wolfe, 1965, Ch. X; Progress Publishers, 1972. p. 98).

The unorthodox character of limited war (that the enemy must be hit hard enough to deter expansion of the conflict, but allowed to extricate himself without serious loss of prestige or substance) has troubled Soviet military and political leaders, particularly in the event of the use of nuclear weapons. Stressing certain inherent contradictions in the asserted logic and rules of limited war as depicted in Western strategic literature, the Soviet authors of the authoritative study on *Soviet Military Strategy* (Sokolovskii, 1975, p. 68) assert:

By its character, a limited war contains two problems: on the one hand such a war must be conducted decisively and with the best methods using the necessary forces and means to achieve the set political and military goals; on the other hand, in a limited war, the armed forces must be used in such a way as to reduce the risk of a limited armed conflict escalating into a general war to a minimum.

The Soviet strategists raised questions regarding some of the fundamental Western assumptions concerning the conduct of limited war, because 'little is known about the effectiveness of this [nuclear] weapon on the battlefield, or the possible political, military and psychological consequences of its use'. The Soviets also maintained that Western assertions regarding control, effect and consequences of battlefield uses of tactical nuclear weapons were 'based chiefly on assumptions' which are at best questionable: 'It is extremely difficult to foresee how an enemy will react to the very fact of the use of a tactical nuclear weapon, even on a limited scale'. And the reactive options available to the other side are many, ranging from refraining to employ a retaliatory limited strike, to responding with a nuclear retaliatory strike of limited scale; or even, through miscalculation, responding on a much greater scale by means of 'strategic and operational tactical means, thus unleashing an all-out nuclear war'.

This Soviet concern with keeping limited war limited was also widely shared in the West. The problem of escalation control and thresholds observance was widely discussed in the professional literature without quite resolving the issues or allaying concerns. Thomas Schelling reflected a wide consensus in describing the Korean War as having set 'patterns and precedents that have affected, and will affect the conduct of limited war and the planning for it' (1966, p. 130). But, he warned, it 'may be only one possibility, one pattern, one species of a variegated genus of warlike reactions', and this no more a model 'of what "limited war" really is than the first animal the Pilgrims saw reflected the wildlife of North America'.

In the light of the enormous conceptual, definitional and operational complexity inherent in limited war, particularly with the use of nuclear weapons, it is easy to agree with Morton Halperin's assertion that while everyone understands conventional warfare, 'neither side understands what nuclear warfare is, or whether or not it can be restrained' (Halperin, 1963, p. 64). And since the risk of central war is ever present in local or limited war through the danger of 'explosion' by preemptive incentives, and in the light of all these complications and caveats, how did the idea of limited war gain support and credibility?

Dissimilarity of Conceptual Definitions

From the strategic debates in the United States in the 1950s and 1960s there emerged a sense of what limited war, with or without the use of nuclear weapons, implied and also a sense of its then rudimentary conceptual and theoretical aspects. The term 'limited war' has since come to be identified with several kinds of restraints and limitations imposed upon the conduct of hostilities.

A war fought for ends far short of the complete subordination of one state's will to another's and by means involving far less than the total military resources of the belligerents, leaving the civilian life and the armed forces of the belligerents largely intact and leading to a bargained termination (Osgood, 1957, p. 47).

Limited war theory, unlike the sharp and satisfying definitions of strategic deterrence, remained rather difficult to define precisely because its limitations are contingent upon judgements, defined by degrees, and perceived from differing perspectives. There emerged, however, a general agreement that the following constitute the basic parameters of limited war:

– Wars which are limited in *geographic scale*, as opposed to 'world wars' that span the globe. (The Korean, Vietnam and Middle East Wars would fit this category.) The problem becomes more complicated when 'coalition wars' are involved which may remain limited in one sense, but geographically dispersed.

– Wars that are limited in their *objectives*, which could be territorial or political, but fairly specific and perceived by all sides to be so.

– Wars fought with *limited means*, in effect where the belligerents are deliberately 'hobbling' themselves with regard to the quantity and quality of weapons and technology employed. The Korean War may be used as an example, where both sides had access to nuclear weapons, but practised restraint, thus shackling their military force.

– Wars in which the belligerents limit themselves to *certain targets* and deliberately avoid other available targets.

This description of limited war and its parameters is, however, more in the nature of a normative model, an ideal type, what it ought to be, rather than a reflection of historical reality. While some of the conflicts of recent decades reflected some of these parameters, others did not, and still others seemed to fit under different conceptual or analytic rubrics. Unfortunately, the Soviet and other communist categorizations of war do not quite conform to those of the West.

In practice, the Soviets distinguish between three types of war and provide appropriate guidance for each: (1) *World War* between the two superpowers and their coalitions, with massive employment of nuclear weapons that would devastate their countries in massive salvos of strategic weapons in a counter-force and counter-value targetting mode; (2) *Limited War* that would not involve the respective countries of the superpowers, but would be fought with their direct or indirect involvement, with or without nuclear weapons; and (3) *Local War* or wars of national liberation in the Third World, which would remain non-nuclear, conventional and contained in terms of scope, targets, weapons and objectives.

Soviet analysts frequently attack what they perceive as the pernicious Western attempt to impose their own rule of the game of politics and strategy upon the socialist countries and on those countries in the Third World that are trying to emancipate and liberate themselves from colonial or imperialistic shackles:

The development of a new international situation more favorable to the cause of peace in no way signifies an interruption of the strenuous and sharp struggle which Soviet policy is waging. There are no pauses in international relations just as there is no rest in the struggle which accompanies their development (*Kommunist*, June 1972, editorial).

Marshal of the Soviet Union N.I. Krylov claimed that 'the imperialists are trying to lull the vigilance of the world's peoples by having recourse to propaganda devices to the effect that there will be no victors in a future nuclear war. These false affirmations contradict the objective laws of history' (1969). General Bochkarev asserted that 'Marxist-Leninists are not panicked in the face of the terrifying danger created by imperialism nor do they depict it as a prelude to the "end of the world"' (Gouré *et al.*, 1974, p. 61).

The Soviets do not comply with American deterrence theories, preferences, or even fantasies. Instead of confronting the US and NATO directly and frontally in the European NATO/Warsaw Pact theatre, the Soviets have chosen to probe, feign, and challenge the US and its allies in areas remote from Europe. Moreover, the Soviet challenge is undertaken indirectly, by proxies and allies. One might say that Soviet military and political behaviour reflects what might be called a 'commissar strategy', which is essentially non-confrontational, or more properly, a confrontation-avoidance under conditions of low Soviet advantage and control. It is largely a strategy that is manipulative, deceptive, theoretically inelegant, methodically "unsophisticated" and shrouded in ambiguities. It is strategy of confrontations *and* negotiations, one that rejects the stark American deterrence alternatives of either/or, preferring their own neither/nor deliberativeness. The Soviets appear to approach the problem of strategic doctrine as a highly politicized means-ends *process*, rather than the American ends-means *teleology* of Armaggedon-avoidance.

Ultimately, Western deterrence strategy is one that is logically and politically suitable to a conservative status quo and balance of power state with no territorial but widespread and vital international and economic interests; a power possessing strategic superiority whose traditional values favor minimal involvement in remote areas; a power that has historically relied primarily on technological and economic means for the implementation of its foreign policy. It is a policy for dealing with a troublesome, dangerous but weaker adversary, a policy of launching terrible threats of punishment in order to appeal to the bully's sense of survival.

Soviet military strategy, on the other hand, is more suitable to a quasi-revolutionary, expansionistic power that is interested in changing the international status quo. It is suitable to a power that emerged on the international scene after World War II as a strategic inferior and one whose traditions have been of reliance on the brute force of mass armies, guided primarily by defensive continental strategies, and with defensive coastal navies; a country that has had little experience with massive projection of its forces beyond the Eurasian mass. It is a strategy of a country with global and universal ideological and political interests and claims, but one that is not in a hurry, believing that history and time is on their side.

The times, however, have changed. The Soviet Union has become a military power at least equal to the United States and has moved from its previous continental, defensive military position into the direction of a global superpower. Soviet strategic doctrines have shown themselves to be, in the final analysis, more flexible and adaptable than those of the West. While the United States remained largely committed to deterrence strategy and some of its variations, despite the profound changes in international and regional politics, the Soviets have shown lively interest in experimenting with various strategic formulations in an effort to fit strategy to policy and to the ever-changing political and technological circumstances. At present, Soviet strategy consists of a strategic-nuclear shield for the primary purpose of deterring and thus neutralizing the threat from the West, and of a flexible and powerful strategy of engagement in the vulnerable and vital areas of the Third World by means of their conventional sword, their general purpose forces.

Limited and Local War Prospects in the 1980s

Recently-displayed Soviet interest in the feasibility of limited and local war, and their systematic preparations for such a contingency, may reflect their current strategic-doctrinal 'maturity'. They seem to understand clearly that in the nuclear era, major powers need the security of a credible nuclear strategic deterrent force before they can safely adopt limited war doctrines and policies. The reason for this lies in the 'logic' of deterrence and limited war: to remain limited, wars involving the major powers, directly or indirectly, need credible fallback reserves of a strategic (assured destruction) retaliatory threat that would act as decelerator of escalatory pressures and would provide boundaries. The espousal of limited war without such a credible deterrent retaliatory threat potential would leave a state open to manipulation and blackmail, analogous to a strategic context in which one side lacks a credible survivable second-strike capability. The Soviets have in recent years fulfilled these necessary criteria; they have built a powerful and credible nuclear deterrent as well as a vast modernized general purpose force (Bondarenko, 1968).

In a 1970 submission to the Committee on Foreign Relations (Gore, 1970, pp. 593, 594) this author stated the following:

We would want first to examine certain entrenched Western beliefs and misapprehensions about the Soviet Union and U.S.-Soviet relations. Among these beliefs are: (1) that we can 'bleed them to death economically by forcing them to keep up with us in an intensive arms race; (2) that we can still attain meaningful strategic superiority; (3) that we can expect an internal political and social upheaval in the Soviet Union or in the communist bloc.

I would suggest that such beliefs are unrealistic and are to some extent wishful thinking. It may be more realistic to assume that: (1) the Soviet Union is going to continue its arms programs, if necessary to ensure equality; (2) that the Soviet Union is not seriously interested in first strike or surprise attacks on the United States; (3) that the Soviet Union is interested in stabilizing the expensive arms race and would seek to avoid confrontations with the United States in areas of vital interests; *however, (4) the Soviet Union is also going to selectively probe in the soft areas of the world for opportunities and expansion, regardless of the SALT outcomes.*

Nothing that ensued in the intervening decade would motivate me to change that assessment of Soviet military and political calculus. As a matter of fact, the Soviets seem to have followed that projection to an amazingly close degree. Moreover, there is little reason to assume that they are likely to depart significantly from that policy line in the coming decade, since the above projection of the 'alignment of political forces around the world' reflects current Soviet perceptions and assessments.

In the mid-1960s, Thomas Wolfe observed that 'the relatively meager treatment customarily given in Soviet literature to the question of conducting limited warfare is in marked contrast to the attention bestowed on general nuclear war' (1965, p. 123). Wolfe believed that until the mid-1960s this reflected the major Soviet concern for the contingency they feared most (massive nuclear attack) and for the rapid or even 'automatic' escalatory possibilities inherent in local or limited war. He found, however, that there were already signs at that time that the Soviet doctrinal positions with regard to local and limited war had been undergoing some change. Although there was still a good bit of ambiguity and inconsistency in Soviet treatment of the subject, and no unifying doctrine of limited war appeared to evolve, there was less rigidity regarding the problem of escalation in local conflicts.

The Soviet position has undergone some substantial changes since the mid-1960s, in terms of doctrine, capabilities and utilities. Although still formally adhering to the earlier, ideologically correct position which rejects callous and deliberate uses of military power (except in 'just' wars) the Soviets appear to have appraised the implications of the changed 'correlation of power' in the 1970s and 1980s. By the late 1960s and in the 1970s Soviet analysts began publicly to consider the implications of the Soviet achievement of nuclear party with the US. A 'debate' ensued in open and classified Soviet literature (recalling the earlier 'strategic debates' of the 1950s and 1960s) that focused on the proper roles of nuclear and conventional forces in future war. Although the voice of the more conservative advocacy was heard, the position of the realists appears to have prevailed and set out the new Soviet position:

In our times conditions may arise when in individual instances combat operations may be carried out using conventional weapons. Under these conditions the role of the conventional means and the traditional services of the armed forces are greatly enhanced. It becomes necessary to train troops for various kinds of warfare.

The author, a well-known military analyst, then argues against those who would interpret such renewed emphasis on the conventional forces and limited warfare as a 'negation of the contemporary revolution in military affairs', that is negating or reducing the roles of tactical or even strategic nuclear weapons. He dismisses those backward views because 'one cannot agree with this opinion', and then lectures his more obtuse colleagues:

The point is that the new possibilities of waging armed struggle have arisen *not in spite of, but because of the nuclear missile weapons*. They do not diminish their combat effectiveness, and the main thing, they do not preclude the possible use of such weapons (Bondarenko cited in Scott, 1979, p. 55).

The point is well taken. Soviet doctrine and policy have in the past decade followed closely this sort of reasoning. In effect this means the loosening of strictures against theatre warfare, with or without nuclear weapons, and the endowment of the conventional forces with vital military and political roles in consonance with the 'alignment of political forces in the world'.

This new emphasis on the vital roles of the conventional forces and the possibility of limited and local war with conventional forces is also evident in the Defence Minister's recent statement: 'There has been a great improvement in the fire, shock and manoeuvre capabilities of troops', which makes it possible to assign them very decisive missions on the battlefield which they are capable of accomplishing without resorting to nuclear weapons' (Douglass, n.d., p. 113).

The Soviets have in the past decade been realigning their foreign policy and military doctrines in the triadic mode described above. To reiterate, their massive nuclear capabilities are to neutralize and stabilize their relations with the West; their theatre forces, both nuclear and conventional, are to enhance deterrence but also to serve as a warfighting capability in Europe and Asia, in the event deterrence fails; and their conventional forces are to serve as the vital military and political element in Moscow's new expansionistic policies in the Third World. This Soviet appreciation of realistic targets of opportunity in the Third World is reflected in their perception that the 'outcome of the historic battle between socialism and capitalism largely depends on how the revolutionary movement will develop in the non-socialist world and what path the nations liberated from colonial oppression will follow' (Gouré, et al., 1974).

The new opportunities for Soviet exploitation in the Third World endow their conventional forces with a multiplicity of important roles, including the possibility of fighting local wars. The central role of these forces is evidenced in the admission of the American author of a recent Pentagon study on Soviet theatre nuclear warfare (Douglass, n.d., p. 46). The author states that although 'this study began as an analysis of the Soviet nuclear threat to NATO ... during the course of this study it became apparent ... that the real heart of the Soviet threat has been and still is, the ground forces, particularly the tank armies and combined arms armies'. Thus even though in the European context Soviet doctrine envisages the use of nuclear weapons in theatre warfare, 'the heart of the Soviet concept is in reality not the initial nuclear barrage, but rather what might be called the exploitation forces'. These are essentially conventional forces, trained and equipped to operate in a nuclear environment, but with increasing concern 'to maintain their capability to fight and not become excessively dependent on nuclear weapons'.

As we shift our attention to the Third World we find that conventional forces and weapons and their modes of employment in 'local wars appear to be regarded as a principal mechanism to be exploited by the Soviet Union in expanding their influence and hegemony'. Since these areas appear to hold the greatest promise of Soviet exploitation, and since the Western strategic deterrence forces play a marginal role in such areas, the Soviets feel that their military doctrine for these areas is a correct one.

Indeed, the use of conventional forces in support of Soviet expansionistic pressures in the Third World makes eminently good sense. Soviet exploratory policies and tactics remain essentially prudent and cautious, and rather non-provocative or provocation-avoiding. The various roles of their conventional forces, as seen by the Soviets, include the roles of protector and patron of anti-Western regimes (Afghanistan, Syria, South Yemen, Ethiopia, Iraq, Angola, and Libya), as a factor in 'influencing building' in those regions, and as a supplier of expertise, training, weapons and intelligence to their clients and proxies. As General Epishev, head of the political organ of the Soviet military, indicated, 'the Soviet Union's ability to give assistance to the people waging revolutionary liberation struggles, and the volume of this assistance have become greater still in the present conditions' (1975). (Epishev also states, 'Greatest importance is being attached to Soviet military presence in various regions throughout the world, reinforced by an adequate level of strategic mobility of its armed forces ... In those cases wherein support must be furnished to those nations fighting for their freedom and imperialist interventions, the Soviet Union may require mobile and well-trained and well-equipped forces . . . Expanding the scale of Soviet military presence and military assistance furnished by other socialist states (i.e., proxies) is being viewed today as a very important factor in international relations'.) (Scott, 1979, p. 57).

In sum, Soviet doctrines of limited and local war, based on their achievement of strategic nuclear parity, reflect current and foreseeable Soviet political and military interests. This also suggests that the Soviets will continue to modernize and enhance their strategic, theatre and local warfare capabilities. The new global mission of the Soviet military was asserted by Marshal Grechko:

At the present stage, the historic mission of the Soviet Armed Forces is not restricted to their function in defending our Motherland . . . but to support the national liberation struggle and resolutely resist imperialist aggression in whatever distant region of the planet it may appear (1974).

Conclusions

In the 1980s Soviet foreign and military policies and strategies have become harmonious and congruent. The inherent Soviet drive to expand their political and military influence into the Third World has been matched by a capability to do so. The cutting edge of their current expansionary drive lies in their conventional capabilities and doctrines of local and limited war. Moreover, the political guidelines for these doctrines provide for non-confrontational, indirect proxy and ally based forces and operations in those vulnerable regions south of Russia. The Soviets have for decades been careful to make a distinction between wars by proxy and the great dangers inherent in intergovernmental wars. The latter involves the possibility of a formal confrontation between Soviet and American forces and should be avoided if at all possible; while the former may be pursued with tolerable risk through aid and assistance of guerrilla, proxy or controlled-regime forces.

In order to explore the Third World for targets of opportunity, the Soviets needed to neutralize American strategic preponderance, and to create credible deterrence and war-fighting forces on their two most exposed and dangerous flanks: NATO/Europe and China/Asia. The Soviets have achieved these objectives at great costs in manpower and weaponry, and in the process stirred up deep suspicions in the West and China. However, the main and primary Soviet expansionary trajectory lies neither in Europe nor in China, but rather in the direction south of Russia, particularly in the Gulf region, the Middle East and Africa.

The Soviets are generally convinced that the direct political payoff lies in a prudent and indirect use of their conventional forces in the Third World rather than in the politically inert strategic nuclear deterrent. This view has been expressed by one of the most influential Soviet analysts: 'It has become clear that this [nuclear] might is becoming progressively less usable as a political weapon' and that therefore the 'sphere of applicability' of such weapons 'for rational political ends is inexorably shrinking' (Arbatov, 1974, p. 56). Of course, this is not to denigrate in the slightest the crucial and decisive dissuasive and 'holding back' functions of the vast strategic nuclear capabilities, with which the conventional and theatre forces would become rather meaningless. It is simply that having obtained the strategic deterrence forces frees the Soviets to press on with the risky, but tempting game of expansion southward. The Soviets have turned out to be, after all, adept students of Western deterrence strategy, which has been asserting that the more stable the strategic deterrence the greater the willingness and freedom to risk the use of low-spectrum forces for political ends.

The Russians have 'rediscovered' the wisdom and relevance of their long-dead 'revolutionary' strategists, Marshals Tukhachevsky and Frunze, who preached a gospel of 'revolutionary warfare' that included concepts of highly mobile, offensive, deep-thrust, airborne military operations, not along a wide straight-line front (*a la* Stalin) but along selective points of the enemy lines; the use of surprise, secrecy, deception and pre-emption; the vital roles of armour, artillary, and mechanized infantry for the achievement of high mobility, surprise, troop dispersal and target-denial (these being particularly relevant in a nuclear battlefield environment). These aspects of 'revolutionary warfare' are being updated and used as current Soviet training and doctrinal modifications for the forces (Savkin, 1972, pp. 22, 23).

The dominant motive force of Soviet political and military action is dialectical: the compelling 'push to the utmost' derived from Clausewitz is moderated by the restraining Leninist *caveat* regarding avoidance of 'adventurism'. This Bolshevik *yin-yang* combination provided the parameters for their inherently aggressive and expansionistic tendencies during the long formative period of Soviet Russia, which was marked by perception of threat from the outside and by military inferiority and insecurity. However, the powerful restraints of the Leninist admonition against adventurism (and the risk of losing it all through high risk and foolish gambles) are eroding: the Soviets feel less threatened, they feel more secure and powerful and they sense that the Western capitalist countries are less than monolithically unified.

There is little doubt that the Soviets are committed to gradual, non-provocative but sustained exploration of the vulnerable regions of the Third World as targets of opportunity. They are building the requisite forces, weapons, and technologies for the purpose of projecting Soviet influence and power into these regions during this decade. Their doctrines, their operational and tactical guidelines, and their training programs are congruent with these objectives.

The Soviets have in the past practised confrontation-avoidance whenever a direct clash with the other superpower seemed unavoidable. In the 1980s, the situation will have changed drastically. The Soviets are at least as powerful as the United States and the theatres of most likely confrontations are logistically accessible. Given the American tradition described above and the newly gained Soviet might, a confrontation between the two superpowers in the areas of Asia, the Persian Gulf, the Middle East, or Africa would have very ominous implications: the Soviets are not likely this time to blink first in an eyeball to eyeball confrontation. Given the current trend of events, it is not unreasonable to say that the superpowers are on a potential collision course in the 1980s.

6 Deterrence and Stability in the NATO-Warsaw Pact Relationship

JOHAN JÖRGEN HOLST[1]

Introduction

The 1970s arrived in an atmosphere of détente. The *Ostpolitik* of the Federal Republic removed the obstacles to a *modus vivendi* based on *de facto* acceptance of the territorial outcome of World War II. The pattern of politics seemed to be transcending and modulating the confrontation of earlier decades. There was hope and confidence that confrontation would be replaced by cooperation, regulated competition and the crystallization of an accepted code of conduct.

The 1980s, however, had their inauguration with the Soviet invasion of Afghanistan, a serious crisis in superpower relations, and widespread questioning of the basic concept and assumptions of the policies of détente. Détente did not break down in Europe. However, its evolution and proliferation in Europe did not develop the kind of momentum which could impose upon the Great Powers the degree of mutual restraint which would be necessary in order to preserve the conditions for long-term détente in Europe.

It is important to observe that arms control played little or no role in the normalization of relations between East and West in Europe. The military confrontation in Europe has remained and the force levels as well as the complexity of the military calculus have increased. Some would argue that détente itself created an atmosphere in which democratic governments and open societies found it hard or inconvenient to recognize the sustained military build-up of the Soviet Union throughout the decade. Others will claim that it was the failure of arms control negotiations, most notably in Vienna, to stem and reverse that process which caused détente to whither away towards the end of the 1970s.[2] The hard facts of military build-up remain. Interpretation, however, is contentious and uncertain.

Impact of the Central Balance

Western Europe remains dependent on North America for its protection. The reasons for that dependence are political and psychological in nature rather than founded on resource constraints. The European political order is made up of nation-states and there is little if any prospect that they would be willing to merge sovereignties in order to permit defence efforts to reap the benefits from superpower scale. In fact, community building has been possible precisely because defence cooperation has remained external to that process. The state of political trust in Europe has not reached that stage where any European state would entrust its security to the nuclear guarantee of another European state. The American guarantee is acceptable because of American distance from the territorial texture of Europe. Paradoxically, however, that very distance, or separateness, is a recurrent theme in the periodic debates about the credibility of extended deterrence. The dilemmas involved are not soluble in any strict Cartesian sense. Will any US President be willing to sacrifice New York in order to protect Frankfurt or Munich? If the issues were ever to emerge in such clear-cut form, the answer would seem fairly obvious. However, real contingencies are likely to be much more ambiguous with respect to the challenge and response involved. Furthermore, the alternatives are likely to be at the same time less clear-cut and more numerous. The Gallois-type questioning which dominated the strategic debate of the 1960s has mellowed in the 1970s and seems unlikely to become a major debating point in the 1980s. The primary reason therefore is political. The logical consequences of the Gallois argument in terms of political action would prove disastrously destructive to the political order in Europe. Moreover, it has become increasingly clear that the social acceptability of the nuclear option is dramatically absent in most European polities. A generalization of the French conclusions would therefore not only prove disruptive to the texture and cohesion of inter-state relations, but impose enormous strains on the stability of the relationship between society and state in Western Europe.

The SALT process has tended to institutionalize and codify parity at the level of central war forces. Generally speaking this development has been perceived in Europe as constituting a stabilizing mechanism rather than amounting to an erosion of extended deterrence. The reasons behind this general but by no means unquestioned consensus probably comprise the following elements: The conclusion of the German *Ostverträge* and the initiation of the CSCE process removed or reduced the immediate source of military conflict inherent in the political order in Europe. Therefore attention was properly focussed on the task of enhancing the intrinsic stability of the central balance in order to avoid destabilizing feedback from the level of the central balance to the level of East-West relations in Europe. Furthermore, the convertibility of incremental advantages in nuclear weapon power to operational political currency had proved itself very limited during the history of the cold war period. Finally, there was, I suppose, a feeling of inevitability about the Soviet Union's eventually catching up with the United States in strategic nuclear power terms. A race to stay ahead would have had an exacerbating impact on the East-West competition and produced a basic contradiction between the political agenda in Europe and the shape and content of Soviet-American relations. It could open, therefore, for the dual dangers of European *Alleingang* and the relegation of Europe to the role of hostage to Soviet-American tensions. The Soviet Union was clearly intent on attaining co-equal status with the United States. In the predominant view it would be easier to deal with a Soviet Union which had arrived at the station of essential equivalance in nuclear weapon power than an insecure superpower still fighting to break the dual bondage of encirclement and inferiority (see Holst, 1973, 1976, 1979a).

In the 1980s the problems of maintaining stability against preemptive pressures in a crisis are likely to increase on the level of the central balance due to the emerging imbalance between weapon accuracy and target coverage on the one hand and secure modes of deployment on the other. However, explosive competition is in no way inevitable if arms control be pursued simultaneously as an integral part of arms decisions concerning posture, and through the SALT process with the aim of establishing broad envelopes of agreed constraints with respect to force size.

The Political Context of the Evolving Balance

The evolution of the central balance and the pursuit of the SALT process have focussed renewed attention on other force components which impact on the pattern of political relations in Europe. Concerns are increasing about the implications of the substantial changes which have taken place in the Soviet military posture in Europe with respect to both nuclear weapons and conventional forces. What are the options which may be opened and exploited in future if current trends continue?

The overall Soviet military effort has been on a steady increase throughout the 1970s with real defence expenditures growing at a rate of 4% per annum and accounting for some 11-13% of GNP. During the same period NATO expenditures were actually declining in real terms. In addition the Soviet Union has been able to allocate a proportionately higher fraction of the defence budget to investment and procurement as their costs for operations and maintenance are lower (particularly due to lower personnel costs).

The political saliency of the Soviet build-up of conventional and theatre nuclear forces has increased in the context of the arrival of parity at the level of central war forces. Secondly, the build-up has taken place so to speak in the shadow of negotiations for mutual force reductions in Central Europe, raising questions about the exploitation of negotiations for purposes of affecting the relative distribution of constraints with respect to force modernization.

In these circumstances European attention has turned increasingly to the structural position of the Soviet Union in the security order in Europe, focussing on the political consequences which may flow from the military posture and the framework of potential arms control arrangements.

The Soviet Union appears to be striving for a management position with respect to the security order in Europe in the sense of obtaining recognition of claims for a *droit de regard* without having to succumb to a system of constraints which would be instituted through arms control arrangements in Europe. Soviet negotiators have attempted to structure the geographical parameters for arms control regimes in Europe in a manner which will preserve for Soviet territory the privileged status of being exterior to the regime in question. The definition of the reduction zone in MBFR and the refusal to include anything more than a narrow zone of 250 km of the Soviet Union in the CSCE/CBM regime, indicate the way in which Moscow approaches arms control as a means for structuring the broader context of the political order. The French proposal for a Conference on Disarmament in Europe (CDE), envisaging a European arms control zone extending from the Atlantic to the Urals, constitutes a direct challenge to the Soviet conception.

Moscow has tended to define her security objectives in territorial rather than in functional terms. Soviet deployment of intermediate range missiles which are capable of covering the whole of Europe coupled with an insistence on defining the SALT categories for limitations in a manner which preserves formal equality of status for Soviet and American territories, increases the European fears of Soviet hegemonial aspirations and that those aspirations are structuring Soviet deployments in the context of codified parity on the level of intercontinental and submarine launched nuclear forces.

The Nuclear Imbroglio

The nuclearization of the military confrontation in Europe was initiated in the mid-1950s. It resulted in some important asymmetries which were to attract increased attention in the 1970s. The NATO build-up of the theatre nuclear forces had essentially peaked by 1967. The posture was characterized by a relatively strong emphasis on short-range battlefield weapons, particularly artillery, and a large number of warheads for the Nike-Hercules high-altitude air defence missiles. The Soviet Union by contrast had emphasized longer range capabilities, particularly M/IRBM forces, although the SCUD guided missile was introduced in front or army formations and FROG artillery rockets in division formations by about 1960.

During the 1970s the relative advantages in numbers underwent some significant changes. With respect to short range (< 100 km) systems FROG deployments increased by some 50% during the 1970s, and a new generation missile (SS-21) with increased accuracy, longer range and improved response time is under deployment. LANCE has replaced HONEST JOHN on the NATO side. However, there has emerged a 5:1 Warsaw Pact advantage in short range missiles. If we include artillery the advantage is reversed.

With respect to medium range missiles (< 1000 km) the number of Soviet systems have increased almost threefold. Successor systems to the SCALEBOARD and SCUD missiles (SS-22 and SS-23) have been developed. NATO has 180 PERSHING-I's with a range of 600 km. The NATO dual capable aircraft include F-104, F-4, BUC-CANEER and JAGUAR. The number of nuclear capable aircraft has doubled on the Soviet side, resulting in a combined medium range numerical advantage for the Warsaw Pact of about 3:1.

It is, however, long range theatre nuclear forces (> 1000 km) which have attracted the greatest political attention. Here the Soviet Union has been augmenting the SS-4/5 missile force with the SS-20 mobile MIRV'ed missile, and the medium bomber force with the new supersonic BACKFIRE bomber which has been entering the inventory at a rate of 25–30 per year. NATO's land based LRTNF force is limited to aircraft, the F-111 and the ageing VULCAN which is due to be phased out in 1982. The Soviet Union has introduced a substantial number of third generation nuclear capable fighter bomber aircraft in the operational inventory during the last decade.

In December 1979 NATO decided on modernizing its TNF posture by deploying 108 PERSHING-II launchers (with 108 single warhead missiles) and 116 Ground Launched Cruise Missile (GLCM) launchers with 4 single-warhead missiles each. Deployments would not commence till the end of 1983.

The decision followed a long period of detailed scrutiny and assessment in two special groups, the High Level Group (HLG) and the Special Group (SG). However, it is arguable that the Soviet SS-20 challenge in political terms came to preempt the process of comprehensive examination of NATO's nuclear posture which had been under way since the early 1970s by lifting out the long range component for special consideration.[3] The imperative of political options collided with the requirements of analytical method. The codification of parity in SALT and the Soviet failure to exercise restraint outside the SALT categories, as evidenced by the deployment of the SS-20, raised fears in Europe of a Soviet design to bring the shadows of military preponderance to bear on the pattern of politics in Europe. It was deemed necessary to communicate a substantive response which would challenge the notion of Soviet territory's constituting a sanctuary in war. In military terms, of course, that message could have been carried by submarine launched systems. However, in political terms as the latter were governed by the SALT constraints and as the Soviet challenge had been mounted from under those constraints, it was deemed necessary to deploy long range theatre systems on the ground in Europe.

What was lost via this process, however, was the framework and criteria for modernization and restructuring of the total TNF posture. From the point of view of stability it was necessary to consider the posture and individual systems with respect to survivability, security, flexibility and responsiveness. Furthermore, the nuclear posture should be examined with respect to combined operations, taking account of technological changes, particularly the emergence of precision guided munitions (PGMs) (See Holst and Nerlich, 1977) and the reorganization and restructuring of the Soviet forces in Central Europe.

The analytical exercise was designed also to circumvent and overcome the stalemated and bureaucratized work on NATO employment doctrine which had failed to produce any credible guidelines beyond some rather dubious notions of initial demonstrative use. It may be that the model of the high level *ad hoc* task force is the best way of dealing with complex strategic issues in the Alliance rather than relying on a permanent bureaucracy. The High Level group set out to analyse the logic of the total theatre nuclear posture. It should have produced a report pointing towards a reconfiguration of the posture which would have been consistent with the doctrinal refinements with respect to selective employment options and deliberate control which had been introduced with respect to central war forces. (See Rowen, 1979)

The changes which may take place in the 1980s include reduced emphasis on forward short range rockets, reduced emphasis on and eventual retirement of Atomic Demolition Munitions (ADMs) and a substantial reduction in the number of nuclear weapons allocated to air defence. The eventual retirement of Nike-Hercules and the deployment of the conventional PATRIOT system will further drive this issue. In basic policy terms it is desirable to reduce dependence on systems requiring early release and decision to use nuclear weapons. PGMs and earth penetrators are likely to provide conventional alternatives to the employment of nuclear weapons, enabling NATO to raise the nuclear threshold and enhance the scope for political control. Improvements are likely also with respect to the security and survivability of the special munition sites. About a third of the less than 150 current sites are associated with the Nike-Hercules air defence systems.

The December 1979 decision in NATO was a two-track decision comprising also an offer to negotiate limitations on LRTNF in the framework of SALT-III.[4] Initially the Soviet Union remained unresponsive, insisting on the unrealistic precondition that NATO undo its decision on deployment. However, Chancellor Schmidt, who had originally pointed to the strategic and political issues raised by the SS-20 deployment, (1978, pp. 2–10) managed to get the Soviet leadership to drop that precondition. Moscow insisted that the so-called Forward Based Systems (FBS), i.e. delivery systems capable of reaching Soviet territory with nuclear weapons, be included. In hardware terms it would mean the inclusion of F-111 aircraft and carrier based A-6 and A-7 fighter bombers. It is unclear what Soviet reciprocals are envisaged.

The Soviet SS-20 deployment already includes more warheads than would be deployed through a full implementation of the NATO decision from December 1979. SS-22's deployed to Eastern Europe with a range of 1000 km could constitute largely effective functional equivalents to SS-20's deployed in the Soviet Union. Hence, it would seem to NATO's advantage as well that the negotiations on TNF become sufficiently comprehensive in scope to encompass the major strike elements. The Soviet Union is likely, however, to insist on categories which highlight the threshold quality of the Soviet border and sanctuary status of Soviet territory. That particular outlook is incongruent with the emphasis on equality of status within the security order in Europe which predominates in West European capitals at the threshold of the 1980s. Negotiations about arms in Europe are not only or even primarily about arms, but about the parameters for political relations and the linkage between arms and influence.

The Conventional Dynamics

The conventional balance in Europe underwent significant changes in the 1970s. NATO's qualitative superiority in conventional weapon technology became off-set by a comprehensive modernization of Soviet forces and an overall quantitative increase. Traditionally, manpower has been considered a key to calculating the balance. However, that currency is hardly adequate for purposes of describing the balance. It is necessary, first of all, to distinguish between combat manpower and other manpower categories. Secondly, NATO actually had a small lead in ground force personnel in the late sixties. That lead was erased by a 150 000 man increase in Warsaw Pact forces. The current disparity in Central Europe is about 1.2:1. However, a rough numerical balance in deployed forces exists when French forces are taken into account. Steven Canby is probably correct in asserting that "the critical deficiency of NATO always has been the lack of combat units and operational reserves. The problem has been one of organization, not lack of total numbers. NATO Europe has sufficient manpower and even a sufficient number of militarily trained reservists, but it has never placed these reservists into organized units nor bought the necessary material to equip them". (1980)

The numerical advantages of the Warsaw Pact over NATO are much more pronounced in key equipment categories such as main battle tanks, tube artillery, and infantry combat vehicles than in manpower. The expansion in Soviet military capabilities in Central Europe in the 1970s did not take the form of an increased number of divisions. It took place rather within the divisions themselves or in Army and Front level supporting units. Thus the manpower of a Soviet motorized rifle division rose from 11 000 to 12 500 during the 1970s, while that of a Soviet tank division rose from 9 000 to 10 000. Similarly the number of tanks rose from 188 to 255 and from 316 to 325 respectively, while the number of APCs grew from 180 to 325 and from 90 to 140 in the same units. In aggregate terms the Warsaw Pact enjoys a superiority of 3:1 in tanks and 2:1 in artillery in Central Europe. There also took place a large increase in the number of artillery tubes available to both motorized and tank divisions during the decade of the 1970s. Similar significant improvements took place in Soviet Frontal Aviation amounting to a fourfold increase in payload and a 2½ fold increase in range. In the early sixties a forward deployment of the Soviet Frontal Aviation was necessary to provide combat support aircraft to one third of West Germany with the Soviet forces based in East Germany. Today Frontal Aviation aircraft operating from deep bases cover all of NATO's airfields. FLOGGER (MIG-23/27) and FENCER (SU-19) can deliver nuclear or conventional ordinance to all NATO bases even when flying at low altitudes. Soviet Frontal Aviation in Central Europe alone is equal to the total number of available NATO aircraft. 90% of the Soviet force is made up of modern aircraft.

The Soviet force posture in Central Europe acquired enhanced offensive capabilities during the 1970s, enhancing the ability of first echelon forces, i.e. the Group of Soviet Forces Germany (GSFG) and the Central Group of Forces (CGF), to launch surprise or short warning attacks. Second echelon forces, i.e. Northern Group of Forces (NGF), and third echelon forces (drawn from the Western Military Districts in the USSR) could in principle become engaged only after the initiation of hostilities. This enhanced offensive option is the result of modernization and restructuring with respect to the major combat functions such as suppression, manoeuvre, defence and combat support.

It is far from clear what intentions are imbedded in the expansion of Soviet offensive capabilities in Europe during the 1970s. From the

Soviet perspective it may constitute an investment in options for an uncertain future both with respect to the social stability of Eastern Europe and the political configuration of Western Europe. It has occurred simultaneously with the arrival of parity with the United States on the level of strategic forces and constitutes a potential instrumentality in support of a political strategy designed to increase a Soviet *droit de regard* in the management of the security order in Europe.

NATO has in Central Europe 28 in-place divisions with approximately 6 500 main battle tanks. These forces are to take rapid defensive action implementing the concept of forward defence until such time as European reserves raised by mobilization and reinforcements from North America are available.

It is often asserted that the Eastern numerical advantage in tanks is off-set by a Western numerical advantage in anti-tank guided missiles (ATGM). However, that numerical advantage appears to have dwindled by the end of the 1970s. Moreover, ATGMs will not fire at ATGMs. Their number has to be compared with the number of targets, and the targets include not only main battle tanks (MBT), but also light tanks, armoured personnel carriers and armoured reconnaissance vehicles. The number of armoured targets on the Eastern side outnumber NATO's ATGMs and anti-tank guns approximately by a factor of seven.

The US commitment of army ground forces to the defence of Europe remained essentially unchanged from 1950 through the mid-1960s. Under the impact of the Vietnam War it was decided to reduce the Seventh Army by some 35 000 men, while introducing the dual basing concept whereunder the units maintain prepositioned equipment in Europe and periodically return to Europe on deployment exercises. The qualitative and quantitative levels of the US Army have been negatively affected by the introduction of the all-volunteer force (AVF) (See Coffey, 1979).

The strategic effort of the 1980s is likely to be dominated by the broad scale introduction of precision guided munitions and the enhancement of strategic reinforcement capabilities. The usefulness of early reinforcements of the central front will depend in large measure upon the status of prepositioned equipment stockpiles, or POMCUS (prepositioning of material configured to unit sets). At present the forward deployed US ground force of five division equivalents and two armoured cavalry regiments could be augmented within ten days by some two and one third division equivalents for which there is prepositioned equipment in Europe. As part of the NATO Long Term Defence Programme it was decided in the late 1970s to provide POMCUS for three additional divisions by Fiscal Year 1982. The long term goal is six additional sets by the late 1980s. (Brown, 1981, pp. 210–211; Coffey, 1979, p. 127) Augmentation in airlift capabilities and war reserve stocks would have to match the POMCUS expansion.

The Long Term Defence Programme identifies ten discrete areas where improvements should take place. Some of the plans look like shopping lists, while others reflect more stringent priorities. It seems reasonable to expect the major effort to be focussed on rapid reinforcements (to counter enhanced Warsaw Pact offensive capabilities), communications, command and control(C3) and Long Range TNF modernization in the first half of the 1980s. (See Holst, 1979b, pp. 310–333)

This chapter is focussed on the NATO-Warsaw Pact balance in Central Europe. It is necessary, however, to point out certain linkages between the Northern and Central regions in Europe. There is no local military balance in Northern Europe. However, the NATO states of Northern Europe have obtained general drawing rights on the general equilibrium in Europe. It is possible for NATO plausibly to deny any would-be aggressor the option of limited attacks against Norway by the implementation of incremental adjustments with respect to the equipment of local forces and prepositioning for external reinforcements. (See Holst, 1978, 1980) The forces that would need to be committed to an attack on the Northern region would be diverted away from the Central region, affecting the balance of escalation in the core area. Extension of deterrence to the Northern region is predicated on NATO's ability to control the process of escalation in the Central region. However, the integrity of the Northern region is of vital importance to that ability. Technological changes, particularly with respect to airpower, during the 1970s have affected a stronger link and interdependence between the two regions from the point of view of strategy.

The maritime links are particularly important in this context. NATO's ability to deal with second and third echelon forces committed to an attack in the Central region, will depend critically on its ability to bring forward across the Atlantic Ocean large volumes of reinforcements, supplies and replacement equipment for North America. Control over the Norwegian coastline and air bases in Norway could be critical for the protection of sea lines of communication (SLOC) along which the bulk of the reinforcements would have to be carried. This observation does not amount to postulating preparations for another battle of the Atlantic. It merely draws attention to the importance of the SLOCs for the calculation of the escalation balance in Central Europe, and of the Northern region in that context. (See Bertram and Holst, 1977)

This chapter does not purport to draw up a balance sheet of force relations in Europe. It merely outlines some critical parameters in a complex picture. There is a multitude of uncertainties and unknowns involved in assessments of military balances. The logistic systems of neither side have been tested in large scale war. We have no real knowledge of the effect of nuclear weapons on the battlefield. Nor do we know what would happen to C3-systems in face of modern electronic warfare. There are also the unquantifiable factors of morale, motivation, generalship, professionalism and luck.

With respect to technological developments which will shape the calculus and force planning in the 1980s, they will affect the rapidity with which war may be initiated and forces concentrated. Furthermore, they will affect the intensity of battle by increasing the rate at which targets are acquired and killed and ordnance is expended. Similarly they will affect the rapidity of movement of the battlelines. There will be increased emphasis on measures of obfuscation (jamming, smoke, etc.) and a general increase in the reliance on stand-off weapons. But all this belongs to the microstructure. The critical issues involve the shape and nature of political relations and, most critically, the influence of arms of the shadow of arms on the pattern of the 1980s. The pursuit of arms control seems likely to constitute the preferred approach for dealing with that overall dimension of the security issues in Europe.

Arms Control Revisited

MBFR has focussed on manpower as the unit of account and category of limitation. That focus reflects the initial impetus which was the NATO need to contain the threat of unilateral US manpower withdrawals via the Mansfield Resolution. Since then the perceived threat from the US Congress has been replaced by a reconfigured Soviet Army. Present disparities are larger, and growing, with respect to major equipment categories than manpower levels. Verification of manpower levels is inherently uncertain. The present impasse over data seems unlikely to be resolved on the basis of the prevailing approach to manpower levels. Since support organization and overhead constitute inherently ambiguous categories and since reducing the threat of large scale offensive action is the primary security concern from the NATO perspective, attention should probably be focussed on combat manpower and associated equipment. For reasons of geography the United States is dependent on prepositioned equipment in order to compensate for Soviet contiguity. That dependency is likely to grow in the years ahead. The systemic implications thereof need examination from the point of view of reducing preemptive incentives.

Focussing solely on equipment withdrawals may seriously degrade NATO's ability to maintain the equilibrium. Force to space ratios for defence against concentrated attacking forces must be assessed also when contemplating force level reductions. An agreement based on withdrawals of combat manpower combined with a commitment to store equipment which is not withdrawn in certain agreed and verifiable equipment parks may constitute a possible model for agreement.[4] It would limit the ability to carry out surprise attacks by moving troops rapidly into combat ready positions. It would increase predictability by drawing lines and it would shift the MBFR negotiations in the direction of dealing with the problem of blunting the offensive potential of the Warsaw Pact posture in Europe.

In the NATO view an agreement on force reductions in Central Europe should be accompanied by an agreement on the institution of associated measures for stabilisation, verification and non-circumvention. They should apply to areas outside the reduction zone, including portions of the Soviet Union, for purposes of stabilising an agreement on reductions, but also in order to prevent MBFR from compartmentalising the established coherence of the security order in Europe or from promulgating a privileged sanctuary position.

It is difficult to establish relevant criteria for functional arms control in Europe. In the context of the prevailing military realities and political framework the emphasis is likely to be on crisis control and confidence building measures (CBMs). With respect to the latter some basic reconceptualization is in the offing with the aim of preventing a codification of Soviet preponderance and exclusivity. A territorial conception of a CBM regime embracing Europe from the Atlantic to the Urals is emerging under French stimulation. A reconceptualized approach would focus on the construction of comprehensive packages encompassing measures with respect to information, notification, observation and stabilization. The purpose would be to create greater transparency, predictability and stability. The objective would be to enhance agreed standards and patterns for routine military activity, through agreed guidelines for reporting, observing and eventually limiting the size and scope of military activity. The perspective would be that of inhibiting the show or use of force for political purposes as well as to provide reciprocal assurance against surprise attack. Some of the conceptions and ideas from the early 1960s may get a new try. Hence it is possible that the 1980s may provide opportunities for fulfilling some of the aborted dreams and visions of the 1960s.

The Limits of European Independence

Whilst NATO may develop a more coherent conceptual approach to arms control, the odds seem slimmer that the military strategy of the Western alliance will exhibit similar trends. The general framework of 'Flexible Response' is sufficiently permissive to contain the prevailing contradictions. Doctrine has had the primary function of facilitating internal management in NATO rather than structuring deterrence of the Russians. The 1970s did not see the great strategic debates of the previous decades. The defence planning process had become institutionalised. Detailed examination of Force Goals and Ministerial Guidance replaced the theological discussion of strategic concepts. Major decisions concerning posture, such as the Long Term Defence Programme (LTDP) and the decision on Long Range Theatre Nuclear Force (LRTNF) modernisation were prepared by *ad hoc* high level working groups. Follow-up, however, will to a considerable extent be the responsibility of the permanent machinery (some of the *ad hoc* groups may in fact evolve into permanent mechanisms).

Compartmentalism and incrementalism prevail with respect to the approach to strategy. The basic conceptual framework for relating naval strategy to the defence of the central front or extra-European contingencies to European security is notably absent. The revival of notions like burden sharing cannot substitute for conceptual clarity.

The major innovation of the 1970s as far as strategy is concerned was the refinement of the doctrine of limited nuclear options and the crystalisation of selective employment plans (SEP). However, with respect to theatre-nuclear force doctrine the intellectual and operational stalemate persists. Nevertheless, the classical dichotomy of conventional versus nuclear defence has largely disappeared. The concept of combined operations focussing on the synergistic effects of conventional and nuclear options has produced the primary analytical framework. The role of nuclear weapons in the defence of Western Europe remains, however, politically contentious. The degree of social acceptability is inversely related to the degree of nuclear emphasis.

Strategic theory of the academic variety had little impact on defence decisions or discussion throughout the seventies. However, the emergence of new conventional technologies with respect to target acquisition, target destruction, area coverage and earth penetration raise issues which require some basic architectural efforts on the conceptual level of analysis as we enter the decade of the 1980s. (For an early attempt see Holst and Nerlich, 1977)

During the 1970s the Soviet Union acquired the means to sustain the option of a major offensive combined with versatility in respect of the choice of warfare method. The Soviet posture in Central Europe is based on armoured mobility and fire power. The 1970s saw the introduction of fourth generation tanks (T-64/72) and infantry fighting vehicles (BMP), as well as fourth generation ATGMs (AT-4 SPIGOT, AT-5 SPANDREL). The first self-propelled guns (SAU-152) were introduced in the mid 1970s and three low-level field air-defence missile systems were fielded during the decade (SA-6 GAINFUL, SA-8 GECKO and SA-9 GASKIN). Soviet doctrine remained ambiguous on the interrelationship between the nuclear and conventional phases of a major war, but with increased attention paid to the conventional option. In general the Soviet posture of the 1970s was rendered more consistent with the doctrine developed in the late 1960s.

The point about the evolution of the military balance in Europe is not that the Soviet Union is likely to attack Western Europe in the expectation of being able to win or to exploit a temporary window of opportunity. The uncertainties will remain enormous, and the consequences of miscalculation disastrous. Soviet military power may, however, stimulate intransigent behaviour and heavy-handedness during crises as well as in the diplomatic process. The shadow from trends in the direction of substantial Soviet numerical advantages may generate a sense of insecurity in Western Europe leading to uncoordinated policies and decisions which could prove destructive to the established order, particularly with respect to nuclear insurance and the pursuit of policies towards the East.

There is a natural desire within Europe to protect the pattern and temperature of interstate relations in the old world from becoming hostage to political volatility and strife outside Europe. Part of the strains flowing from alliance dependence in the 1980s may be caused by its tendency of generalising conflict. The rhetoric about the indivisibility of détente obscures the real issue which has to do with the option of defining parameters and linkages in concrete circumstances. European and American perspectives and perceptions may not always coincide. It is possible, of course, that European insularity would encourage Soviet interventionist behaviour outside Europe and that the military build-up in Europe is meant in part to stimulate European insulation. Maintenance of an essential balance in Europe would in this perspective serve also as a constraint on interventionist behaviour outside Europe.

It is important also in this connection that towards the end of the 1970s some of the old controversies seemed to be fading or acquiring new accents. Britain and France reaffirmed their commitments to maintaining their separate brands of national deterrents as they entered the 1980s. When Her Majesty's Government decided to modernise the Polaris fleet by acquiring Trident C-4, it was hailed in Washington, which claimed to attach 'significant importance to the nuclear deterrent capability of the United Kingdom'. (Carter, 1980) London has decided to acquire four Trident-submarines with an option on a fifth one, at a total cost of £5,000 million over the next fifteen years.

The French modernisation programme is more extensive. The eighteen medium range ballistic missiles in the Plateau d' Albion will be moved out of the silos and mounted on mobile launchers. A sixth nuclear submarine, characteristically named the *Inflexible*, will be added to the deterrent fleet. By 1985 the new submarine will be equipped with sixteen missiles each carrying seven independently targetable reentry vehicles (MIRV). Four of the five older submarines will be similarly armed later. It has been suggested that $US20 billion at current values will have to be spent on modernising the French nuclear force during the decade of the 1980s. (*Time*, 21 July 1980, p. 8)

It has become part of the conventional wisdom that the British and French forces add to strategic deterrence by residual uncertainty. However, in view of the conventional force challenge in central Europe, serious gaps may develop in the 1980s between the British and French nuclear modernisation programmes on the one hand and the priorities and productivities from the point of view of NATO's requirements on the other. With Bonn wishing not to exceed a commitment of 50% of the total NATO military manpower in Central Europe, internal tensions may arise over the allocation of resources, and the failure to establish a credible conventional defence in Europe. In addition political tensions may arise on the level of SALT and, more particularly with respect to LRTNF negotiations if Moscow were to decide to demand formal compensation for non-US nuclear forces and, most particularly, if a demand for constraints on such forces be raised.

The national deterrents are, of course, also parts of the British and French investments in intra-Western influence. However, the combination of rhetorical inflation and nostalgia harbour the danger of disruption, particularly in a period of a double crisis with respect to superpower relations and American leadership. The French call for a 'renaissance of European influence' and the 'reappearance of an independent and self-assured Europe in world affairs' during the President's state visit to Bonn in July 1980 contains the seed of such disruption. As *The Economist* so aptly noted '. . . to be independent . . . means having the capacity to act separately and differently from America not just in side issues, and matters of tactics, but in the heart of the matter; which is the business of keeping Western Europe out of the Soviet sphere of control' (19 July, p. 13). That is clearly not within the power of the states of Western Europe in the forseeable future. Thus, we are back where it all started in the 1940s. The basic facts are still valid, and likely to remain so throughout the decade if not longer.

7 Autonomy and Intervention
Super Powers and the Third World

MOHAMMED AYOOB

The 1970s saw the culmination of some important processes at work within the post-1945 international system which have had major effects on super power relations with the Third World[1]. These developments have, however, not been able to modify to any significant extent the basically hierarchical nature of the international system. By and large, although with some relatively significant exceptions, the countries of the Third World have remained at the bottom of the international pecking order. What these developments, which gained such prominence in the 1970s, have done, however, is to challenge, at least to some extent, the political and intellectual validity of the assumptions on which this hierarchically organised system is based. This challenge, and the occasional demonstration of the political and economic clout, however limited and unidimensional, of certain Third World countries (for example, the Organisation of Petroleum Exporting Countries, OPEC, and particularly the Organisation of Arab Petroleum Exporting Countries, OAPEC) have forced strategists and policy-makers within the dominant powers themselves to rethink their assumptions regarding great or super power relations with the Third World in general, and some of its regions in particular.

The foremost among the processes at work within the post-World War II international system referred to above has been the closing of the strategic gap between the US and the USSR. This has had important political repercussions as well. It has, among other things, led the super powers to compete for the allegiance of the Third World on terms of greater equality with each other. Throughout the 1950s and most of the 1960s, despite the gradual increase in Soviet capabilities, the West in general and the US in particular enjoyed political and military preponderance (in addition to the economic preponderance which they still continue to enjoy) in the Third World. It was only towards the second half of the 1960s that the Soviet Union was able to change its status from that of a regionally dominant power with certain global aspirations to one of a *real* super power with effective global reach. The change was simultaneously translated in the political and military confidence that now marked Moscow's relations both with

Washington and with the Third World.

The second development which reached its culmination in the 1970s was the process of decolonisation in the Third World. The emergence of a host of newly independent countries in the 1960s, particularly in Africa which had hitherto been an almost exclusive Western preserve, contributed significantly to the transformation of the super power balance as it pertained to the Third World. While it was in the 1960s that most of this decolonisation took place, it was not until late in that decade that the Soviet Union was able to capitalise upon this process. As the residual business of decolonisation – namely the end to white settler rule in southern Africa and the expulsion of the Portuguese from their African territories – reached the top of the international agenda in the 1970s, an increasingly confident Soviet Union was in a much better position to take advantage of Western, and more particularly US, weaknesses than it had been a decade earlier. These Western, and especially American, weaknesses were not primarily military in character, as they were made out to be by certain Western analysts in the wake of the Angolan episode. They were largely the result of America's close political and military association with fellow NATO member Portugal and its (and Western Europe's) economic and strategic links with white-ruled South Africa.

The combination of these two factors – the Soviet Union's increasing global reach and the increasingly indefensible alignments of the Western powers in Africa – in the context of an increasingly assertive Third World majority in the UN helped significantly to alter the balance between the super powers, especially as it pertained to super power influence and prestige in the Third World. This was nowhere better demonstrated than in Soviet actions during the Angolan crisis. The Soviet success in Angola is thrown into sharper relief particularly if one compares it to the failure of Moscow's strategy at the time of the Congo crisis of the early 1960s. While the Congo episode demonstrated both Soviet impotence and (in the support extended to US-sponsored UN actions by the Third World) the lack of Soviet credibility in the Third World, the Angolan episode was a demonstration both of the political and military prowess Moscow had built up over a decade, and of the greater credibility and legitimacy that Soviet actions had acquired in the eyes of the Third World. This was especially the case when Moscow was pitted (as it was in Angola) against Salazar's erstwhile friends and Pretoria's and Salisbury's *de facto* allies.

Another important trend was manifested in the Third World in the 1970s. This was the logical corollary of the emergence of the Third World into political independence during the 1950s and 1960s, but it also had a major impact on super power relations with the Third World. This trend was best portrayed by the dramatic developments around the OAPEC embargo (and the simultaneous oil price rises announced by OPEC) in 1973–74 and the developments surrounding the Iranian revolution of 1978–79. While the first event demonstrated both the increasing (if limited and selective) economic clout of at least certain Third World countries and their willingness (however haltingly) to use such clout for political ends, the second demonstrated the capacity of dissident elements in Third World countries successfully to use indigenous ideologies for purposes of social and political change. The fact that such change could be brought about despite the open opposition of one super power (which backed the Shah) and the hardly-concealed dismay of the other (on whose borders the transformation was taking place) was testimony to the importance of the Iranian experiment.

Both these developments – and their corollaries in relation to the pricing, output and flow of oil as well as the political resurgence of Islam — were signals aimed at the super powers that the drive for autonomy in cultural and economic matters in the Third World was becoming increasingly stronger and that these cultural and economic trends were bound to manifest themselves in the political realm in anti-hegemonial, anti-Western (which in the cultural sense includes the USSR) and, therefore, anti-super power terms. These developments, although territorially limited to the Middle East-Persian Gulf region, therefore, reinforced the lessons which intelligent analysts had drawn from the US encounter with Vietnamese nationalism in the 1960s and the early 1970s.

These trends relating to Third World aspirations for cultural and economic, and, therefore, political, autonomy have been further strengthened by the debate in international forums over the New International Economic Order (NIEO) proposals and the parallel process of the North-South dialogue. The transformation of the Non-Aligned Movement in the 1970s from its 'outside the contest' posture of the 1950s and the 1960s to one which has made it the political arm of the Group of 77 – which is itself close to becoming the trade union of the Third World – has been yet another major demonstration of the change that has occurred in the last decade in the equation between the super powers (and the international establishment which they represent) on the one hand and the Third World on the other.

What does all this portend for the 1980s? There are more than one aspect of this question, and although they are interrelated, they need to be answered separately for purposes of analytical clarity. The first relates to super power responses to developments in the Third World that one of them might interpret as being so disadvantageous to its global and/or regional objectives that they need some sort of military response. This, of course, is a situation not unique to the 1980s. Both super powers have on occasion intervened militarily outside their borders more than once since 1945. The landing of US marines, for example, in the Dominican Republic or in the Lebanon, in order to prevent political changes which Washington considered would be deleterious from its point of view, had become almost normal routine during the 1950s and the 1960s. The US military involvement in Vietnam was, of course, the high point of this exercise. It was the negative outcome of the Vietnam adventure that led the US to exercise greater military restraint in its dealings with the Third World during the 1970s.

On the other hand, Moscow's new-found capacity to intervene (outside of Eastern Europe, its traditional preserve), coinciding as it did with the US withdrawal from Vietnam and the post-Vietnam self-examination that America underwent, led to the impression both in the Soviet Union and outside that it could intervene with relative impunity in various parts of the Third World. The Soviet involvement in Ethiopia (although by Cuban proxy) was, at least partially, the result of this newly felt sense of self-confidence.

The Soviet intervention in Afghanistan took this strategy one step further but, as Marshall Goldman has pointed out, it was not Moscow's preoccupation with the question of energy supplies, whether in relation to natural gas or oil, that prompted the Soviet Union to take the fateful decision to intervene militarily in Afghanistan. To quote Goldman, while 'it is difficult to reconstruct Soviet thinking, ... apparently the Soviets decided to act because they saw their influence in Afghanistan diminishing. They feared the situation would soon be out-of-hand and concluded that they could occupy the country, eliminate the trouble and do it so quickly and cleanly that there would be only minor protest from the rest of the world. As they have now come to realise, this was a serious miscalculation'. (Goldman, 1980, p. 6) The Soviet action, therefore, was the result of Moscow's calculation that unless it intervened militarily its influence in Kabul would be drastically reduced either by Amin attempting to play the role of an Afghan Tito or by the total collapse of the Marxist government and its replacement by an anti-Soviet coalition. Moscow, for obvious reasons, was unwilling to accept either of those outcomes.

The Soviet Union, therefore, was not doing anything very different from what the US had done in Vietnam in the middle 1960s, and this explains partially the violent US reaction against the Soviet move into Afghanistan. Moscow could not be allowed to succeed where Washington had failed.

The US response to Soviet moves in Afghanistan, of course, has another and equally important dimension which one should not overlook. This is related to US concern for oil supplies from the Gulf for its European and Japanese allies, but above all for itself. (See Conant and Gold, 1978; Stobaugh and Yergin, 1980, pp. 563–595). This concern has been heightened since the Arab oil embargo of 1973–74 and particularly since the fall of the Shah and the drastic reduction in Iran's oil supplies which accompanied the virulent outburst of anti-Americanism in that country.

The Arab embargo of 1973–74 had brought forth a spate of comments from official and non-official sources in the US regarding US intentions about and/or capabilities for taking over oil fields of the Gulf if supplies of oil to the US were threatened again.[2] It was rather ironic that in most of the officially sponsored studies prepared in the US on this issue, the oil fields of Saudi Arabia (the staunchest Arab friend of the US and one of the two pillars of the 'twin pillars' US policy in the Gulf during the 1970s) were projected as the most likely targets for a US bid to take over oil fields in the Gulf in order to ensure supplies of oil to the industrialised countries.[3]

The Soviet military intervention in Afghanistan came in the wake of the Iranian revolution which had already curtailed oil supplies to the West, and, more importantly, by aligning Iran with the mainstream Arab position on Palestinian self-determination, had threatened to cut off almost all Gulf oil supplies to Israel's allies if tensions escalated in the Middle East as a result of the failure of the US-sponsored Camp David process to resolve the issue of Palestinian rights. The Soviet move into Afghanistan, therefore, provided the US Administration with the excuse and the opportunity to implement plans for the escalation of military presence in the western Indian Ocean region, particularly in the vicinity of the oil-rich Gulf, which were already being contemplated following the fall of the Shah.

The holding of American hostages by Iranian militants has further legitimised this American move, which encompasses the up-grading and expansion of the Diego Garcia facilities, the construction or use of base facilities in Oman, Kenya and Somalia and the deployment of an impressive US naval force, including two aircraft carriers, just off the Persian Gulf. Moreover, as indicated by a statement from General Paul Kelley (USMC), Commander of the Rapid Deployment Force, (RDF), plans in the US for the deployment of a 'rapid deployment force' seem to be going ahead, (Allan, 1980, p. 8) particularly with the latest disclosure that seven 'prepositioning' ships are to use the expanded facilities at Diego Garcia as an anchorage beginning in mid 1980. According to one reliable report,

These 'prepositioning' ships . . . will carry the heavy equipment and supplies (including fuel, ammunition and even water) for . . . [a] marine brigade training in California and its two squadrons of aircraft [some 12,000 men with a squadron of Phantom fighters and another of A-6 Intruder attack aircraft]. The ships will stay at Diego Garcia . . . until it looks as if the brigade might be needed. The men and aircraft will then be flown into an airfield somewhere near the trouble spot, and the ships will move to a port where they can hand over the equipment. The join-up point could be one of the three 'forward operating locations' – Mombassa in Kenya, Berbera in Somalia and a port in Oman – which are now the subject of negotiations between those countries and the United States. The equipment could also be unloaded in any other convenient seaport which had an airfield nearby. (*The Economist*, 7 June 1980, p. 40)

These preparations, although ostensibly meant to counter the Soviet move into Afghanistan, are perceived in large parts of the Third World as part of a US strategy of military intervention in the oil-rich Gulf when its interests in the region are threatened not so much as a result of a Soviet drive towards the oil reservoirs of the Gulf as of another outbreak of hostilities in the Middle East or an escalation of tension in the region following the collapse of the Camp David process.[4] Either of these possibilities could lead to another total or selective OAPEC embargo on oil supplies which would in all probability be joined by Iran. Such a threat to US interests would, therefore, emanate from indigenous forces in the Gulf (particularly if a nervous Saudi elite, increasingly concerned about its lack of legitimacy at home and in the region, joins mainstream Arab opinion on the issue) rather than from Soviet moves whether through Afghanistan or otherwise. (See Ayoob, 1981). Contrary to the objectives of the regional forces as far as they pertain to oil supplies, the Soviet Union despite, or rather because of, the fact that it is likely to become a net importer of oil before the decade is over, would be as interested in maintaining the free flow of Gulf oil as are the Western powers. This would be particularly the case since the USSR would also have to take into account the possibility of US attempts militarily to seize Gulf oil fields, the consequent sabotage and disruption of supplies and even attempts (which even if partially successful can considerably impede the flow of oil from the Gulf) to close the Straits of Hormuz by indigenous actors working independently of either of the super powers.

The situation in which the countries of Southwest Asia – the Gulf and Afghanistan – find themselves today epitomises the problems that the Third World in general faces vis-a-vis the super powers, especially in terms of actual or potential acts of military intervention. It must be clearly recognised that these acts have been undertaken, are being undertaken, and are likely to be undertaken when either of the super powers feels threatened not so much by the other super power as by certain indigenous forces operating within Third World countries which act autonomously of both the super powers. This has been the pattern from the Suez intervention (although the direct intervenors there were not super powers but European great powers), through the Lebanon, Cuba, the Dominican Republic, Vietnam, the Horn of Africa and now Afghanistan (and who knows tomorrow Saudi Arabia?). It is interesting to note that in almost all these instances the intervening super power has used the pretext of its rival's likely involvement in a particular situation to justify its own act of pre-emptive intervention. Even in the latest cases, the Soviet Union has accused the US (and China) of acting through proxies (presumably Pakistan) to destabilise the Afghan situation in order to justify its military intervention. The US seems to be adopting the same strategy by using the Soviet intervention in Afghanistan as the pretext for building up interventionist capabilities targeted on the Gulf, particularly on Iran and Saudi Arabia.

The challenges to super power domination which preceded such intervention came from local forces, whether represented by Nasser, Castro, Ho Chi Minh, Hafizullah Amin or Ayatollah Khomeini. The reason why the intervening super powers are unwilling publicly to accept the fact that these challenges are indigenous in inspiration is based on their realisation that such interventions would be considered less illegitimate and less unjustified by the majority of nations if they are presented as responses to challenges posed by the rival super power. This is especially relevant in the context of the changing international consensus as represented by the Third World majority in the UN that is firmly opposed to super power intervention in Third World countries irrespective of the particular circumstances surrounding each intervention.

Such interventions however, are likely to become more numerous and occur with increasing frequency in the 1980s, and for two reasons: first, with the Soviet attainment of near-parity with the US in terms of its global reach and spreading network of interests and influence in the Third World, we now have two rather than one global actor with a finger in almost every Third World pie. Moreover, the US now in its post-post-Vietnam stage is once again beginning to flex its military muscles, and may well revert to its pre-Guam doctrine strategy, particularly since that doctrine has been discredited with the fall of the Shah.

Secondly, the Third World has, so to say, come of age. This would mean further and more dramatic demonstrations of Third World autonomy from the managers of the international system, in political, economic and cultural terms.[5] Such gestures of autonomy are bound to run into increasing resistance on the part of the dominant powers who would find their interests, individually and collectively, threatened as a result of this development, particularly if they feel that this 'infection' is liable to spread.[6] In the long run, the Soviet cause for alarm on this count would in fact be greater than that for the US. Since the epicentre of autonomous, revolutionary activity seems to be moving closer to Soviet borders, the fall-out effect of such activity on the 'Third World' regions of the Soviet Union could be conceivably much greater than, and qualitatively different from, what the US would have to face.

The 1980s are, therefore, expected to bring forth a greater spurt in interventionist activity on the part of the super powers aimed at containing this 'infection' of autonomous activity in the Third World. The US Administration, having failed to do anything about the Iranian revolution, would be under increasing pressure to intervene if a similar development took place in neighbouring Saudi Arabia. The Soviet Union, in search of its own Vietnam to demonstrate its super power status, might decide to airlift its own troops to Ethiopia if the Cubans are unable to perform their assigned role in Eritrea and the Ogaden. And, Afghanistan, on present indications, is likely to tie down an increasing proportion of Soviet political and military capabilities for the next few years. (See *The Economist*, 14 June 1980)

While on the face of it, it may appear that the existence of two major external actors, capable of bringing force to bear at long distances within the Third World, would help to neutralise each other and particularly neutralise each others' interventionist proclivities, this does not seem to be the case. Given the state of nuclear deterrence and the stability of the central balance, as well as the stake which both the super powers have in maintaining the stability of the international system as a whole (which is perceived largely as the sum-total of 'regional stabilities'), an unwritten and implicit agreement seems to have been reached between Moscow and Washington that frees them to intervene in Third World regions as long as they do not overstep certain boundaries and do not directly threaten the other super power's vital interests. (See Ayoob, 1979a, pp. 197–205). It is as a result of this unstated compact that the super powers, by following Hedley Bull's prescription about 'managing the balance of power between them, and by exploiting their joint predominance in relation to the rest of the world', (1971, p. 146) are able to effectively dominate the international system.

Whether it is in relation to Ethiopia or Afghanistan, or earlier in relation to Vietnam or the Lebanon, *de facto* spheres of influence are recognised and while signals are sent off warning the intervening power not to step beyond certain limits – territorial, military and political – the principle of the 'sphere of influence' is by and large scrupulously honoured. Even in the latest case of Afghanistan, about which such hue and cry was made in the US, the signalling was aimed primarily at warning the Soviets not to step beyond the borders of Afghanistan rather than at forcing them to vacate their aggression in that country. Afghanistan, despite recent disclaimers, had, in fact, been accepted by the US as *de facto* within the sphere of Soviet influence almost a couple of decades ago.

When and where this concept of 'spheres of influence' has been challenged it has been challenged by indigenous Third World forces – with Iran as the most outstanding recent example. In other cases too, as for example in Egypt, the Sudan, Ethiopia and Somalia it is the native ruling elites that have decided to move away from and/or expel their super power patron and sometimes accept the patronage of the rival super power. As far as the two super powers have been concerned, throughout the 1970s they have been more than willing to accept the mutual benefits that accrue to them from their reciprocal recognition of *de facto* spheres of influence and activity. This does not mean that they have not indulged in low level diplomatic and intelligence activity within the other's sphere, but these have been usually kept at mutually acceptable levels. It is only when the old order in individual Third World countries or regions seems to be breaking down as a result of internal challenges, that such activity has been escalated to take advantage of an already disintegrating structure. This pattern is likely to continue through the 1980s.

The question of indigenous Third World forces challenging 'structures of stability' supported or underwritten by one or the other super power, brings us to the next crucial question regarding the 1980s. What are the major areas where such challenges are likely to emerge? In my view the two most prominent candidates for this honour would be the Middle East (including the oil-rich Gulf) and southern Africa. In both these cases, it is the West in general, and the US in particular, which is preceived as committed to the *status quo* that is and would be the target of attack by local forces working for change. Therefore, if and when these regional structures undergo transformation it will be the US rather than the Soviet Union which would emerge as the major loser in these regions. Given the strategic location of these two regions as well as the concentration of strategic resources – oil and minerals – in the Middle East and southern Africa, the losses would be much more far reaching than even the 'loss' of Vietnam.

It would be worthwhile pointing out here that in both these cases – on the question of the end to apartheid in South Africa and the end to Israeli occupation of Arab territories occupied in 1967 – the Third World consensus is firmly on the side of those who wish to change the *status quo*. Moreover, in both cases the US is perceived as being committed to the current 'stable' structures as a result of its identification with Israel on the one hand and the white regime in Pretoria on the other. While in the latter case, Washington has recently attempted (particularly since the collapse of the Portuguese empire in south-central Africa in the mid-1970s) to distance itself from the white regime, its earlier stance (based on Kissinger's National Security Study Memorandum 39 of 1969 – See El-Khawas and Cohen, 1976) as well as its, and its West European and Japanese allies', economic (and in some cases military) links with Pretoria make its anti-apartheid rhetoric appear less than sincere. This image is further augmented by America's, and Western Europe's, continuing refusal effectively to support economic and military sanctions against the white regime in South Africa. Only a radical change in the style as well as the substance of US policy towards South Africa will be able to change the American image of *de facto* commitment to Pretoria and thus preserve at least some of its credibility on this issue with Azanian nationalists within South Africa, with the African countries at large, and with the Third World which is united on the issue of majority rule in South Africa. Since, on present indications, it appears that the South African situation will probably reach critical stage sometime in the 1980s – especially since the domestic, regional and global environments in which apartheid has operated have undergone radical transformation in the 1970s (See Ayoob, 1980, pp. 156–160) – it would be essential for such a change in US policy to be introduced soon if Washington is not to be faced with irreversible losses in the region. This becomes particularly important since, once the revolutionary process gets underway, the Soviet Union can (with limited amounts of military aid) reap considerable economic and strategic benefits and at minimum cost and risk to itself.

In many ways the situation in the Middle East, particularly on the issue of Palestinian self-determination (and the Israeli vacation of Palestinian territory which must accompany if not precede it), is similar to that in South Africa. On the one hand, there is a broad Third World consensus about the need to change the *status quo* in Palestine. On the other hand, once again the US is perceived as committed to an unjust *status quo*. Moreover, despite President Carter's feeble attempts to prod the Israelis into accepting some change, the US commitment to Israel is generally perceived in the Third World as not only a committment to Israeli *security* but to Israeli *expansionism* as well. Israeli intransigence, especially on the issue of West Bank settlements, and the half-hearted US response (particularly as demonstrated by the flip-flop on the Security Council vote on the settlements in May 1980) to this Israeli defiance of international opinion further augments the image of US support to Israel's expansionist designs.

Given the links that this central issue in the Middle Eastern region has with the politics of the Gulf – and, therefore, of oil – the opprobrium which attaches to US policy as a result of Israeli intransigence is bound to have an effect on the questions of oil production, oil pricing and the supply of that strategic commodity to the West in general, and the US in particular. (See Ayoob, 1981; Ball, 1979–80, pp. 231–256). In the absence of a satisfactory solution to the Palestinian issue, the Saudi search for legitimacy both at home and in the region might prompt Riyadh increasingly to distance itself from the US. This would, of course, have a direct effect on the volume of oil produced for export as well as on the price of oil. As the Saudi example demonstrates, even the most conservative Arab rulers of the Gulf have become increasingly nervous at the lack of genuine movement on the issue of Palestine, particularly since they feel that in the absence of such movement their own identification with the US undermines their legitimacy at home and opens the way for their violent overthrow. Of course, if that happens US interests in the region would be even further adversely affected. If the US is then prompted into taking military action in the Gulf, presumably sometime during the 1980s, it would open a veritable Pandora's box leading to a drastic reduction in oil production, sabotage of pipelines and installations, attempted blockage of the Straits of Hormuz and further radicalisation of the Arab world. Once again, the main external beneficiary of these developments would be the Soviet Union which would be able to pose as the defender of Arab rights and sovereignty, and would be able to do so possibly at relatively little cost to itself.

The pervasiveness of the Palestine issue in the Middle East is the major reason why the US has not been able to take advantage of the Muslim world's revulsion against the Soviet intervention in Afghanistan. A senior Kuwaiti Minister summed up Arab/Muslim feelings on the issue very well when he remarked:

'The crisis of Afghanistan should not divert our attention from the real problem. Jerusalem is more sacred to us than Kabul'. (*Newsweek*, 18 February 1980, p. 11)

To sum up therefore, given the current US postures and policies towards the two most likely flash-points in the Third World in the 1980s, it appears that, unless Washington is able to make radical departures from its current policies, the Soviet Union, notwithstanding its involvement in Afghanistan, is likely to make further short-term gains in the Third World as a whole and in Africa and the Middle East in particular in the next decade. This would be due not so much to the intrinsic merit of Soviet policies regarding the Third World in general, or in the major crisis-areas in particular, as to the lack of sensitivity on the part of the US to the susceptibilities and demands of Third World actors, especially those most directly involved in the unfolding dramas in the Middle East and in southern Africa.

However, the current state of Soviet-Third World relations is far from satisfactory. The Soviet intervention in Afghanistan is only the last of a series of acts that has upset a sizable section of the Third World. And, as one analyst has argued, given the fact that 'the future ... will surely bring deeper Soviet involvement in the Third World, both politically and economically ... the Soviets will run the risk (as the example of Afghanistan dramatically demonstrates) of producing among the nonaligned [read 'Third World'] a new set of grievances which are anti-Soviet rather than anti-Western in character'.

(Leo-Grande, 1980, p. 52)

It is interesting to note in this context that attempts made by Cuba and a few others to sell the Soviet Union as the Third World's 'natural ally' were firmly turned down at the last summit of non-aligned countries in Havana. Third World leaders, even those closely identified with Moscow, realise that any alliance with the Soviet Union is a temporary affair and purely an act of convenience. As long as that convenience lasts so will the alliance. It would not be wrong to state, however, that it is US policies which seem to be prolonging that alliance beyond its natural termination point.

In fact, US policies, because of their relative lack of responsiveness to Third World aspirations are unable to capitalise upon the more fundamental and in-built contradiction between the Soviet Union and important segments of the Third World, a contradiction for which the Afghanistan crisis merely performs the proverbial role of the tip of the iceberg. For, if the US has important Third World constituencies within its political system – the Black-and Spanish-Americans – the Soviet Union embraces a sizable chunk of the Third World itself within its polity, a chunk that in demographic terms seems to be growing in geometric progressions. (Rywkin, 1979, pp. 1–13). If this segment of the Soviet population is denied adequate participation in the Soviet decision-making process (as seems to be the case until now), and with the Muslim world around it in political ferment, one should not be surprised if the ideology of 'Muslim National Communism', so popular in the Muslim Republics in the years immediately following the Russian Revolution, once again raises its head in the Muslim regions of the USSR. One should not forget either that it was Mir-Said Sultan Galiev, a leading ideologue of Muslim National Communism in the 1920s, who first propounded the theory of 'proletarian nations' (by which he meant the Muslim regions of the erstwhile Tsarist Empire as well as what is now generally known as the Third World), much before the Chinese had realised its political significance, and decades before the leadership of the Third World had even become aware of the term. (See Bennigsen and Wimbush, 1979; Critchlow, 1972, pp. 18–28; Bennigsen, 1980, pp. 38–51). For, all said and done, once South Africa is liberated and the problem of Palestine settled, Central Asia would remain as the only unfinished business of the colonial era. However, to capitalise upon this inherent contradiction between the Soviet Union and the Third World, which would probably take a generation to reach its culmination point, US and Western policies must respond quickly and adequately to Third World demands in the 1980s. The next decade will be the crucial one in this respect, for the major outlines of the next generation's conflicts would emerge in the 1980s, just as the processes at work during the 1940s and the 1950s have produced the major confrontations of the 1970s and the

1980s. Also, it will be in the next decade that the Third World will begin to make up its collective mind as to who its allies and its adversaries will be in the first decade of the 21st century.

8 Alliances in the 1970s and 1980s Problems of Cohesion and Effectiveness

T.B. MILLAR

In his first volume of memoirs, (1979a, p. 78) Henry Kissinger refers to his book on NATO, *The Troubled Partnership*, and mentions that it sold modestly almost everywhere except in one town where the main bookstore had placed it on the shelf concerned with marriage manuals. Perhaps the bookseller was not wholly in error. An alliance is a form of marriage, or at least a liaison for certain purposes, with all the problems of compatibility, pride and varying expectations.

The present strategic balance – if "balance" is the right word – exists between two very different alliances, or alliance systems, both of which *de facto* have existed for more than thirty years, and both of which are likely to continue throughout the next decade. Yet both have gone through processes of change since their inception, and we must assume that such processes will continue.

These two alliances, NATO and the Warsaw Pact, are of course not the only alliances in existence, even if they are the most strategically important and the most clearcut. The mutual security treaty between the United States and Japan is undoubtedly an alliance. The treaty relationship between the United States and the Republic of (Nationalist) China was an alliance – a relationship between allies. One could probably say the same about the American treaties with the Philippines, and with Australia and New Zealand (ANZUS). Was the Baghdad Pact an alliance? Or the US treaty with Pakistan? There is a wide margin to the definition, and whether a relationship is inside or outside the definition or fuzzily in the margin will vary with circumstances. In that phrase beloved of American treatymakers during the Dulles era – the commitment to "act to meet the common danger in accordance with constitutional processes" – there exists a margin of indefinable width. To "act" may be to express token regret, or it may be to put 5 million men into battle, or unleash a nuclear war.

Again, in the wording of most Soviet treaties ("of friendship and co-operation") negotiated during the past twenty years, there is an at least equivalent uncertainty. For example, the wording of the November 1978 treaty between the USSR and the Socialist Republic of Vietnam, in the relevant clause, is almost identical to that of the August

1971 treaty between India and the Soviet Union, yet India (a non-communist country) would strenuously deny that it is an ally of the Soviet Union, whereas communist Vietnam would presumably acknowledge that something close to an alliance exists.

"The essence of a genuine alliance system," writes G.F. Hudson (1969, p. 178), "is that both the commitments and the aid to be expected are precisely defined." This may be the ideal, but it is never the reality. In practice a treaty of alliance will affect each ally differently, offer greater or less security, demand greater or less contributions, risks, sacrifices. It is a mutual insurance policy among unequal contributors and beneficiaries. But whereas an insurance policy for an individual has fixed premiums and known returns, the premiums in an alliance are the continuing subject of bargaining, and the returns can only be guessed at until the policy "matures". The premiums may even all turn out to have been paid in vain; or, like the labourers hired for the vineyard harvest, a small contributor may be just as well served as a large one. [1]

If Napoleon in fact said, as reported, "Give me allies to fight against," he was at least premature in his expectations. The allies defeated him in the end, just as another group of allies defeated Hitler. Alliances have their problems, but they exist because they have more than compensating advantages.

Alliances as such cannot usually be said to have a purpose: it is the states composing the alliance, or the governments of those states, that have a purpose in concluding the alliance, a purpose *for* the alliance. Although the existence of an alliance requires a broad consensus about its objectives, the various national purposes will not be identical, because no two states are in identical situations. Most alliances are concluded by governments who perceive a common threat, such as Western Europe against the Soviet Union – which keeps the balance in the region[2]; or the USSR and China (1949) against the United States – an agreement that probably deterred the US from bombing targets in China during the Korean War. But the perceptions and expectations will differ in detail and perhaps (as with France in NATO) in substance.

Alliances exist because they are believed to add external power to the power of each member (Spanier, 1972, Ch. 7). They may be defensive or offensive or both, but are customarily negotiated in a spirit of common defence: to prevent attack, or at least to make the potential attacker think more carefully before launching his assault. They may also be used to define a strategic frontier, to signal (as with both NATO and the Warsaw Pact) the principal powers' front line of defence. Such a signal may discourage adventurous behaviour; or it may act as a challenge to the opposition, may create hostages for the principal power, or may incite the frontier state to more provocative actions than a less assured security would allow. As John Foster Dulles knew only too well, there can be advantages in leaving uncertain the nature of a response.

Once an alliance has been negotiated, it has an inertia or momentum that keeps it going. The members develop habits of thought as well as habits and machinery of co-operation. There are all kinds of political implications short of physical conflict. The world changes around the members, and they and their circumstances change, so that the purpose of, expectations from, influence in or contributions to an alliance will change also.

As suggested earlier, those purposes, expectations and contributions are never just of a military/strategic nature. Physical security is a pre-requisite both for political stability and maximum economic progress. All contributions to an alliance have political implications, and all that are not simply intellectual are fundamentally economic: they cost money, they involve industrial production, research and development, taxes, foregone opportunities in other areas. They are measured, publicly, against GNP, and that proportion is compared with the proportions expended by allied or opposing powers[3]. For a quarter of a century, the dominant fact of the Western Alliance was the economic power of the United States.

It might seem reasonable to assume that the value of an alliance is in some proportion to the degree of voluntary participation of the members; that an imposed alliance will *ipso facto* be more fragile than one that is freely negotiated. This is too simple a proposition. Many factors contribute to the readiness of a people to engage in war or to prosecute it once engaged, and there are few, if any, direct correlations.

How then does one measure the cohesion or the effectiveness of an alliance in advance of its being proved by action? Cohesion and effectiveness are functions of each other, but it is not simply a 1:1 relationship. There are also questions of comparative military strength and political will. Military strength can be measured by rough indicators; if made comparative with other nations, there is a much greater likelihood of error. Political will is very difficult to assess ahead of a crisis[4]. There are indicators of alliance cohesion: readiness to contribute to the alliance budget, to make armed forces available, to engage in planning and in training exercises, to co-ordinate defence production, accept installations on one's soil, etc. These also are only approximate guides. Even more important to political leaders are the general attitudes of other governments, their loyalty to the alliance "party line", their readiness to go along with the urgent preoccupation of the dominant member, and the support their populations give to the alliance. It is on the superpowers' enthusiasm for the alliance that the distinction narrows most between the "coercive" Warsaw Pact and the "voluntarist" NATO, i.e. on the enthusiasm of the protector to protect. Finally, effectiveness as a combination of the other factors is at best an impression, a calculated guess. Cynics in Europe say that if the Russians attacked West Germany on a Friday afternoon they could be through to the Channel by Monday morning, but no Soviet government would be wise to base its planning on such a judgment.

There is no space here to consider all the alliance arrangements in existence, and it is proposed therefore to look at several based on the United States and two based on the Soviet Union.

Apart from the United Nations Charter, the first post-war agreement involving the United States was the Inter-American Treaty of Reciprocal Assistance negotiated at Petropolis near Rio de Janeiro in August 1947 and known as the Treaty of Rio. Eighteen Latin American republics plus the United States agreed to submit any disputes between themselves to peaceful settlement. They agreed also that an armed attack on any of them would be considered an armed attack on all of them, and each undertook "to assist in meeting the attack". There was to be an "organ of consultation" to examine and agree upon collective measures to be adopted. The whole arrangement was incorporated into the Organization of American States (OAS). Through the Treaty of Rio and associated documents, the OAS thus became an alliance for common defence and a collective security system for solving regional disputes.

In its second role, the OAS has had about a score of useful successes. As an alliance, its record is much more equivocal, and since 1970, as a positive alliance system, the OAS has been ineffective. It is broadly if selectively supportive of American foreign policy, not wholly resistant to Soviet penetration, still porous to American capital and enterprise, and has provided in Cuba the renegade who "joined the enemy" and made possible the Soviet military penetration of the African continent. It seems that Cuba's military value to the Soviet Union as a thorn in the side of the United States is once again on the increase. Yet both the Cuban and Soviet leaders know how dangerous a fire this is to play with, and the 40,000 Cuban troops and advisers cannot stay in Africa forever, at some cost to the Soviet exchequer. In various ways Cuba is moving back into the Inter-American system, which is its natural environment. Geography has a tendency to overcome history. If the next few years can be weathered, it should be possible to return Cuba fully into the system – a system which is decreasingly the vehicle of American strategic policy and increasingly part of a pluralistic world, of a world in which Switzerland and West Germany can ignore vigorous American protests and sell nuclear power facilities to Brazil.

The security treaty between Australia, New Zealand and the United States (ANZUS) signed on 1 September 1951 constituted an alliance of a very different order. Two small, stable states are partners to a superpower, supplicants for possible future protection for which they are prepared to pay in repeated instalments that the superpower finds useful for its diplomacy and global strategic capacity. There are few problems of cohesion in the alliance. The three states share broad national objectives, basic principles on the values and organisation of society, and even a language that is on the whole mutually understandable. The question of effectiveness is a different one for each partner, and varies according to its changing needs. In the 1950s and 1960s, the United States wanted its two partners' flags alongside the Stars and Stripes in Asia, and *they* wanted the Stars and Stripes there as a protection against militant Asian communism. In the 1960s and 1970s, the United States wanted also and received facilities in the antipodes for its global strategic communications and missile launch detection program. Australia and New Zealand wanted favoured access to American intelligence and military equipment. The favours were small but acceptable, and the cost – vulnerability to Soviet missiles - was considered a fair burden for the protection that made those missiles less likely to be fired.

This is the continuing situation for the 1980s, given emphasis by the chronic world oil situation and the increasing Soviet military and naval presence in South-west and South-east Asia and the Indian Ocean. Fear of that presence has increased the conservative Australian government's desire to be of service to its great ally (e.g. offers to the US Navy to "home-port" ships in Western Australia, and to the Air Force to use airfields in northern Australia). In effect, ANZUS, designed and specifically declared to relate to the Pacific, has been extended to the eastern Indian Ocean. Yet if the United States takes up the invitation to base US ships or aircraft on the Australian mainland, *the nature of the alliance will change.* There have been no American combat bases in Australia since World War II. Australia's diplomacy since then has made use of that fact. The possibility of nuclear missile storage near a major city is alarming to many people. And the American government and military industrial complex run hard-nosed, unsentimental operations. The full costs of the new sense of dependency may take years to work themselves out.

The United States has three alliance treaties with East Asian states which are vital to the strategic balance of the region: with Japan, the Republic of (South) Korea, and with the Philippines.

The most important, the alliance with Japan, was a direct result

of the Korean War – a war made possible by Soviet arms and at least
acquiesced in by the Soviet government. The United States went to
the help of South Korea, and soon found itself in a sizable and difficult
conflict. Its armed forces needed access to military and naval facilities
in Japan, but the United States could not afford to continue to occupy
Japan and subsidise its economy. Under the 1946 constitution, presented to Japan by the US, Japan had renounced forever the use of
armed force as a means of settling international disputes. This was
perhaps an understandable imposition by victors who had suffered
greatly, but it made no political or strategic sense. The peace treaty or
8 September 1951 thus recognised Japan's "inherent right of self-
defence" under the UN Charter. A bilateral security treaty signed on
the same day granted the United States exclusive rights "to dispose
US land, air and sea forces in and about Japan" for the defence of
Japan and for "the maintenance of international peace and security in
the Far East."

This 1951 treaty gave Japan full protection while it rebuilt its
economy and its dignity and established what were euphemistically
called "self-defence" forces. A new treaty which better reflected the
formal political equality of the two states was signed in January 1960.
American forces retained access to their bases in Japan. Article 5
stated: "Each party recognises that an armed attack against either party *in the territories under the administration of Japan* would be dangerous
to its own peace and safety, and declares that it could act to meet the
common danger in accordance with its constitutional provisions and
processes" (emphasis added). What the treaty in effect said was that
the United States would continue to protect Japan, but if Japan were
invaded its armed forces – new, small, and with little domestic support – would help.

This is broadly the situation today, but the treaty has had to bear
and the two partners to reconcile its deliberate ambiguities,
the different objectives of the two governments, and the different
cultural backgrounds of protector and protected (an aspect Kissinger
documents in *The White House Years*).

If Japan disastrously lost the war, by taking a very energetic, firm
but "low" posture it has unquestionably won the peace. Ruled continuously by conservative (Liberal Democratic Party) governments,
under American protection it has developed into the world's third
largest economy, has consistently spent less than one per cent of GNP
on defence, and has been rigorously uninvolved in the conflict and
tensions that have boiled up around it. The problems of the alliance
have been turned to good account. Do the countries and peoples of
the region have vivid memories of Japanese aggression? Then while
the United States fights in Korea, in Vietnam, and stands ready to
defend Taiwan, Japan will stay neutral and provide bases, arms,

equipment and supplies at handsome profits. The United States wants a military partnership? Then it must also provide an economic partnership. It wants Japan adequately armed? Then it must provide Japan at reasonable price with the technology to produce those arms. It wants Japan not to be a nuclear weapons state and to shelter under the US nuclear umbrella? Then it must acknowledge the sensitivities of the only people who have ever been subjected to atomic bombing, and not bring nuclear weapons into Japan. The United States wants Japan as a democratic state? Then it must take account of the pressure of Japanese public opinion on all these matters, including opinion against rearmament (See Langdon, 1973). The fact that public opinion was by no means wholly supportive of the alliance gave the Japanese government anxious moments at home but increased leverage in Washington.

While the treaty has done all these things, Japanese economic competition with the US has subjected the alliance to psychological strains. It has not rewarded Japan's new economic strength with appropriate political influence. Japan has felt compelled, like a proper wife, to follow American foreign policy a step or two behind, especially with respect to China, and to accept with equanimity the "shocks" of the new opening to Peking and harsh economic measures introduced without consultation.

The 1970s revealed Japan's almost total vulnerability to pressure from the Middle East oil producing states. They saw the end of American involvement in Vietnam and a turning away from military commitments to Asia, a decline in the value of the dollar compared with the yen, and more assertive Soviet policies in Asia partly due to the rapprochement of the United States and Japan with China. Gauche Soviet diplomacy strengthened Japan's commitment to the American alliance, but a weakened American defence capacity has troubled her ally[5].

Important though the alliance is to Japan, it is not the dominant preoccupation of Japanese foreign policy. As Saburo Okita wrote for *Foreign Affairs* just before becoming Foreign Minister:

Japan has a highly organised and tightly compacted economy. (Japan's per acre GNP, for example, is about ten times that of the United States.) Thus a few hydrogen bombs could completely devastate the entire country. Under these circumstances the best strategy for Japan is to avoid any possible military attack by following a prudent diplomatic course. (1979, p. 1109)[6]

One manifestation of that prudent diplomatic course in 1978 was to sell the Soviet Union on credit an 80,000-ton dry dock for Vladivostok, capable of taking the latest Soviet aircraft carrier, and (as reported) to refuse a US proposal for an additional carrier base on Japan's west coast.

A sense of vulnerability, prudence, economic advantage: these will continue to characterise Japanese policies towards the American alliance, and will keep them out of any proposed wider alliance to include China, Thailand or Australia (*The Times*, 10 July 1980).

North Korea's invasion of South Korea brought American troops to the defence of the latter, and the possibility of a repeat performance has kept them there. The Carter administration wanted to disengage from Korea as it disengaged from Taiwan, and began to withdraw US forces and to assist South Korea to modernise its military machine. The South Korean economy was capable of bearing the defence of the country, but the withdrawal stopped when the US realised that it was alarming both South Korea and Japan and could seriously destabilise the balance of power in the region. The effectiveness of the alliance is directly related to the presence of US ground forces, and their "tripwire" effect, and to the political stability of the Republic. This is now increasingly uncertain. The cohesion of the alliance is reduced by American reluctance to work too closely with a military dictatorship, and is strengthened by its fear that South Korea might otherwise develop nuclear missiles. The only escape from this Catch-22 situation would be a political solution to the North-South confrontation.

The third Asian treaty, with the Philippines, makes available the major American air base at Clark Field and naval base at Subic Bay which are essential to American military power in the central western Pacific and the Indian Ocean. Successive Filipino governments have made the Americans pay increasingly dearly for the bases, which are thus a splendid source of revenue but also a potential target for nationalist dissent. They could only be replaced elsewhere at enormous expense.

Western interests in the Pacific depend on the United States and the several alliance "spokes" of its strategic policy. In Europe and the North Atlantic, it is one treaty, NATO, that holds the ring against what are seen as the potential depredations of Soviet power. Since the Korean War, the United States has been the only link between the two alliance systems, the backbone of both[7]. Thirty years after NATO was signed, it is relevant to recall the events that prompted the alliance: the Soviet Union had made clear that it had no intention of withdrawing its forces from Eastern Europe. It had abandoned any pretence to democratic principles and had installed subordinate communist regimes in every state under its control. It used continuously obstructive and offensive tactics in the organs of occupation. It supported communist insurgency in Greece, made territorial demands on Turkey, threatened Yugoslavia, and refused for a time to evacuate the occupied parts of Iran. For nine months it blockaded Berlin against access by land, in direct breach of the occupation agreement. It is not surprising that the United States and West European powers saw these activities as a threat to their security.

The Truman Doctrine for Greece and Turkey, the Marshall Plan, the Brussels Pact and the North Atlantic Treaty together made possible the economic and psychological recovery of Western Europe, and the reconciliation of France and Germany.

Article 5 of the North Atlantic Treaty stated:

The Parties agree that an armed attack against one or more of them in Europe or North America shall be considered an attack against them all, and consequently they agree that, if such an armed attack occurs, each of them, in exercise of the right of individual or collective self-defence recognised by Article 51 of the Charter of the United Nations, will assist the Party or Parties attacked by taking forthwith, individually and in concert with other Parties, such action as it deems necessary, including the use of armed force, to restore and maintain the security of the North Atlantic area . . .

The strength of NATO has lain in the power of the United States, and in the fact that the fifteen[8] member states have combined their military efforts within a single organisation and command structure. In these strengths lay also weaknesses: the problem of taking urgent or even non-urgent decisions by so large a group; the fact that the direct threat has been in Europe, but the United States with its global interests lies 3,000 miles away on the other side of the Atlantic, and all reinforcements have to cross that distance, mostly by sea; the fact that the protector and the protected have different perspectives of the same problem, and that American psychological and physical commitment to the containment of Soviet power has enabled the West European governments to pay less than their share of defence costs; and the fact that the European members are proud sovereign states with a variety of languages, cultures, mental processes, electorates, per capita incomes, ambitions, and accumulated resentments.

All the problems of any voluntary alliance are found in NATO. Hans-Peter Schwarz noted that in the mid-1970s there were 23 different kinds of combat aircraft in NATO, 7 different groups of combat vehicles, 8 different groups of transport tanks and troop transport vehicles, 22 different anti-tank systems, 36 different models of radar guidance and targeting systems, and more than 20 different calibres in weapons up to 30 mm (1979, p. 233). There is also of course some rationalisation in major defence systems, defence co-operation on development and production, production under licence, and local off-set arrangements. NATO powers (such as Belgium) have found that they can negotiate successfully on these issues, and do not have to accept on instructions American equipment at American prices.

The fact that the Europeans have had different perspectives among themselves and with the United States has not prevented NATO from being a formidable military alliance. Partners in any alliance will never be sure when or how other partners will act. The remarkable thing about NATO is not the degree of mistrust but the degree of final trust among its members, even though this may be a trust founded on necessity. Even de Gaulle predicated his maverick policies on the ultimate protection of the United States. NATO's great political achievement, despite Gaullism, has been the continued strategic and economic partnership of France and Germany; its great strategic achievement has been the security of Europe under American patronage.

The 1970s saw considerable changes in the central power balance, changes which almost wholly favoured the Soviet bloc: the steady increase in Soviet conventional and nuclear power so that it became preponderant in Europe, and eventually selectively superior in the strategic nuclear confrontation. American involvement in Vietnam had weakened the West in Europe, which was the Europeans' main complaint about the war, and when it ended in 1972 (with Kissinger's hollow promises to South Vietnam) Europe did not receive the benefit because the American mood was one of retrenchment at home and detente abroad. Willy Brandt's opening to the East was timely, but it aroused in Washington and in parts of both Western and Eastern Europe two related concerns that have been repeated over Schmidt's mid-1980 visit to Moscow; (1) that it represented political weakness and could lead to the "Finlandisation" of Western Europe; and/or (2) that it was a prelude to a deal between Moscow, Berlin and Bonn for the reunification of Germany, with all the potentially ugly consequences for the peace of the continent. While both Brandt and Schmidt went out of their way to reassure their allies on these points, the prospect of reunification – a West German article of faith written into its constitution – has been the persistent shadow of the Federal Republic's commitment to the North Atlantic Treaty, the death's head at the feast of détente. Were Bonn to trade reunification for a neutral foreign policy, NATO would collapse and the future of Europe be plunged into uncertainty.

The 1970s also saw the legitimation of the Soviet Union's wartime and post-war territorial acquisitions in Europe[9] through the Final Act of the Conference on Security and Co-operation in Europe, signed at Helsinki in late 1975. Recognition of the new boundaries was afforded by the Western powers in return for a "basket" of largely spurious Soviet concessions on human rights.

The Soviet Union can chalk up other strategic benefits for the 1970s: the 1974 Turkish invasion of Cyprus, the even wider Greece-Turkey dispute and the expulsion of Americans from bases in Turkey for several years; the successful (on balance) diplomatic offensive in Africa, backed by Cuban troops and Soviet arms and logistics, and the ousting by Iranian revolutionaries of the Shah plus his numerous

American military suppliers and advisers. The effect of the first was to weaken NATO; the last two, together with the Soviet invasion of Afghanistan, have reinvigorated American resolve and strengthened the alliance by re-emphasising the thrust of Soviet power. They have also raised European fears of a global war not of Europe's making, provoked by perhaps hasty American reactions in times of heightened tension to adversities in places like the Persian Gulf. Such fears have not been assuaged by the Carter Administration's incompetent diplomacy, as over the sudden shift in SALT II, the on-again-off-again neutron bomb, the immovable Soviet brigade in Cuba, the attempt to dictate Europe's civil nuclear policies, and the sad but perhaps saving failure of the mission to rescue US hostages in Tehran.

In the background to these events have been two disturbing facts that have altered NATO. The first is the relative decline of the American economy, and the rise of Europe (especially West Germany) to a position of close to equal partnership with the United States. This has altered the tenor and confidence of the alliance. The second is the increasing nuclear weapons capacity of the Soviet Union, challenging the whole basis on which the alliance was predicated: American invulnerability through nuclear superiority. This invulnerability began to disappear in the late 1950s, as de Gaulle kept telling everyone while he took France out of NATO's military organisation, and the growing doctrine of mutual assured destruction by nuclear weapons was a doctrine not for the prevention of all war but only for the prevention of nuclear war, unless a reasonably certain escalation from local conventional to global nuclear war acted to restrain the opening shots.

In a lecture in late 1979, ex-Secretary of State Henry Kissinger, who in office had preached the doctrine of mutual assured destruction, declared that "it is absurd to base the strategy of the West on the credibility of the threat of mutual suicide" (1979b, p. 7). This shook the chancelleries of Western Europe, except in Paris which had always believed it. In fact the strategy of the West had been based for fifteen years on the deterrent capacity of such a threat *as the last stage* of confrontation. For a long time, the NATO powers who possessed them had been prepared to use battlefield nuclear weapons in the event of a conventional Soviet breakthrough, because of the superior Soviet conventional forces. But in the late 1970s the Soviet Union had begun to deploy in its territory, outside the reach of tactical nuclear weapons based on Western Europe, mobile nuclear weapons (the SS-20s) targeted on Western Europe. The Kissinger message was in fact designed to encourage West European governments to accept on their soil a new generation of tactical nuclear weapons that could retaliate against Soviet territory and not depend on American strategic weapons, located outside Europe, to do so. This "modernisation" of the theatre nuclear force (TNF) has since been substantially agreed to, despite (or perhaps because of) a Soviet campaign to prevent it, thus closing a gap in the escalation process and hopefully opening the way for SALT III negotiations from a basis of a broad theatre equality.

Apart from the modest but not discountable independent British[10] and French nuclear forces, all tactical and strategic nuclear weapons in the European theatre are under American (or joint) control, as the Russians well know. What the US government therefore assumes is that, out of fear of mutual assured destruction, the Soviet Union will not escalate a conflict beyond the European theatre. This does not calm European apprehensions that the United States might not resort to theatre nuclear weapons at all for fear of Soviet escalation, but such apprehensions discount the tripwire effect of several hundred thousand American servicemen and their families located in the Federal Republic of Germany.

Whether or not the alleged "window of opportunity"[11] for the Soviet Union will exist in the early 1980s, there are so many aspects to it, to the strategic nuclear balance, and to the Soviet Union's need of Western food and technology, that no Soviet government could with any rationality risk a pre-emptive strike "through" the window. Yet the more that responsible Americans lament the supposed existence of the window, the less confidence will Europeans have not only in American capacity but also in American will. That confidence could only be restored by a US nuclear force structure which Americans can trust to protect themselves against a Soviet first strike. It is a matter of debate whether the addition of the MX missile later in the decade, the Trident submarine missile, and air-launched cruise missiles will provide such a structure, and what will be the effect of American failure to ratify SALT II. For the present both sides have good reasons to act as though SALT II, with its ceilings on nuclear weapons, were in effect. If the European powers implement their decision, taken with some US twisting of arms, to increase defence spending by 3 per cent per year, this should enable the conventional force structure in Europe to appear a more credible deterrent. At present it would be quite inadequate on its own to stop the Soviet and East European armies. The northern flank is but lightly defended and the southern is in disarray.

One aspect of NATO in the 1970s that seems unlikely to apply to the 1980s is the possibility that one or more of the European states (Italy, France) could include Communists in the government. "Eurocommunism", to use the inadequate but common term, rose and fell in the 1970s, yet in Italy especially it is by no means a spent force, still holding 30 per cent of the votes. There are few grounds for confidence that a NATO government with communist participation would remain loyal to the alliance.

NATO periodically goes through crises of confidence: of American confidence in Europe's cohesion, military capacity, and readiness to contribute; of European confidence in American leadership, will and sophistication; of both in the NATO machinery and NATO cohesiveness. It is not surprising that there should now be a crisis of European confidence in American leadership, but there are signs that this one is different in kind and degree from earlier crises. The European powers have rebelled at US dominance of alliance foreign policy, and especially its handling of the Middle East (Arab/Israel) situation. Most of them rejected American pressure to ban attendance at the summer Olympics in Moscow. They have not found requests for sanctions against the Soviet Union and Iran to be convincing. This may reflect a narrower perspective; it may be a passing phase of discontent; or it may be a realignment of power within the alliance, even a degree of "decoupling" by Western Europe from the global preoccupations and problems of the United States. Were that to take place, it could cause a more permanent American disenchantment with Europe, a situation which for the foreseeable future Europe cannot afford, any more than it can afford to give the Federal Republic the degree of leadership to which its power may entitle it but which would only dismay its allies and alarm its enemies.

The Warsaw Pact as a treaty organisation was a direct response to NATO, to the accession of West Germany (via the West European Union), and the East German uprising two years earlier (1953), but it largely formalised an already existing situation begun by Stalin in 1948 and linking the states of Eastern Europe (except, initially, East Germany) to the Soviet Union and to one another by a series of bilateral security agreements[12]. Comecon or CMEA, similarly began in 1949 as the Soviet Union's pale but authoritarian version of the Marshall Plan, with the economic benefits tending to move in the reverse direction, i.e. towards the USSR. By late in that year all six states (Poland, Hungary, Romania, Bulgaria, Czechoslovakia and East Germany) as well as Albania, had governments subservient to Moscow, constitutions modelled on that of the USSR, a communist party modelled on the Communist Party of the Soviet Union (CPSU) and closely connected to it, with personnel and policies subject to CPSU control or review.

What keeps NATO together is fear of the Soviet Union. What keep the Warsaw Pact together is also fear of the Soviet Union. There are some 20 Soviet divisions in East Germany, 5 in Czechoslovakia, 4 in Hungary, 2 in Poland. They may serve a dual purpose, but it *is* *dual* – occupation and defence. The Pact is also held together by a

web of agreements and institutions, by Polish and Russian fears of a
rearmed Germany, and by common public dogma. Among the ruling
elites, there must also be concern at the presence of NATO forces,
and still more concern at the liberal ideas which permeate the Western
powers and which, if allowed to spread in Eastern Europe or the
USSR, would mean the end of the existing governments, the people
running them and the systems they administer.

The Warsaw Pact does not have NATO's problems of cohesion,
or does not have them to anywhere near the same degree. No member
except the Soviet Union is a sovereign state even in the way Luxem-
bourg is. There is some bargaining, some dissent, even some determined refusal on occasions to implement particular Soviet requirements, but the organisation is fundamentally monolithic and an instrument of Soviet foreign and defence policies. The controlling Permanent Commission is in Moscow. The Joint Secretariat is headed by a
Soviet official and is located in Moscow. The Commander-in-Chief is a
Soviet Military Officer, and he is chairman of the Military Council.
The post of Chief of Staff and most of the key positions in the Joint
High Command are held by Soviet officers or officials. The air defence system has its headquarters in Moscow. The forces of each
member state are operationally subordinate to the Soviet High Command. Almost all the weapons systems are Soviet, as with a few exceptions are the military doctrine, organisation, training and communications.

Article 1 of the Warsaw Treaty states:

The Contracting Parties undertake, in accordance with the Charter of the
United Nations Organisation, to refrain in their international relations from
the threat or use of force, and to settle their disputes peacefully and in such
manner as will not jeopardize international peace and security.

Article 4 sets out the commitment to assist one another in the
event of an armed attack on one or more of the Parties. In article 8,
each Party undertook to adhere to "the principle of respect for the
independence and sovereignty of the others and non-interference in
their internal affairs."

The post-war history of Eastern Europe has demonstrated both
the strength and the limitations of Soviet power, the cohesion and the
strains of the bloc. The Soviet Union was unable to force Yugoslavia
to accept Soviet domination, yet the post-Stalin uprising in East Berlin was brutally put down by Soviet occupying forces. Articles 1 and 8
of the Warsaw Treaty went by the board in Hungary in 1956, when
Soviet tanks crushed the attempted liberal reforms. The Pact was only
invoked ex post facto. In August 1968 it was the Pact – the forces of
five nations – that massively invaded undefended Czechoslovakia to
achieve a similar purpose. It brought another result – the final withdrawal of Albania, which had long been restive against Soviet hege-

mony, but which had no common border with the Soviet Union and had developed links with the People's Republic of China.

Romania since the early 1960s (following the withdrawal of Soviet occupying forces in 1958) has shown, within limits, a determined freedom of attitude in foreign affairs, bought partly by a rigid doctrinal conformism in domestic policies and the fortunate possession of extensive oil deposits. It does not take a full part in Warsaw Pact manoeuvres. It recently refused Soviet instructions to boost defence spending. It condemned the Soviet invasion of Afghanistan. It would almost certainly refuse to take part in any military assault on Yugoslavia, and would probably do all it could to discourage the passage of Soviet forces across its territory for that purpose. The Romanians, a Latin people, periodically demonstrate a cordial dislike of the Soviet Union.

Bulgaria has no common border with the USSR, and also has no Soviet occupation forces. It does not need them. It is considered the most docile of the satellites, a Soviet province in all but name. If the Soviet Union wished to launch an attack on Yugoslavia, Bulgaria would probably be the most enthusiastic of partners, seizing the opportunity to dismember its neighbour and "recover" the province of Macedonia. Yet, again, the Bulgarian people, though acquiescing in the system that rules them, appear to have little respect for the Soviet Union.

Despite a persistent and lively spirit of resistance, there is little likelihood that Czechoslovakia, crushed, cowed and occupied, will be other than a "loyal ally" of the Soviet Union and politically subservient. As 1968 showed, it is totally vulnerable to Soviet and other Pact forces. Hungary and Poland are in a different category. Poland lies across the historic invasion route to Russia, and in reverse it provides the essential communications channels from the Soviet Union to the western limits of the Soviet "empire". No Soviet government will be likely to allow any threat to Poland's full participation in the Pact, and despite the people's strong Christianity, inner strengths, and rejection of rigid communist doctrine, no Polish government is likely to forget the fact. It may take initiatives to lessen East-West tensions, but it will not deviate from the strict line of Moscow policy. Hungarians, a flexible and calculating people, learned their lesson in 1956. The forms are preserved, but within them there is considerable deviation in domestic policy.

The (East) German Democratic Republic is the forward battle zone of the Warsaw Pact, and thus has least flexibility of all. Successive governments have tried to use the Pact in order to protect the Republic from the possibility of being bypassed in West German reconciliation with the Soviet Union and the rest of Eastern Europe. More recently it has been coming to its own prickly but economically profitable accommodations.

What a strange, restive, frightened, formidable alliance this is, a pack dominated by a whip! It is certainly a more "efficient", more disciplined and regimented alliance than NATO. Its military exercises are public demonstrations of considerable power. It gives the Soviet Union control over the great glacis of central Europe. It is poised to exploit any weaknesses in its Western opponents. Yet all the participating governments know that none of them is there by the freely-expressed will of the people; that the Soviet Union is popular nowhere in Eastern Europe. While armies tend to do what they are told, all the peoples of Eastern Europe are strongly nationalistic, and it seems inconceivable that they will permanently accept one more foreign hegemony in their long history.

Too little is yet known about the Soviet "alliance" with Vietnam. It has made possible Vietnam's dominance of the whole of Indo-China. In return, Vietnam is tied firmly into Soviet anti-China strategy; it provides the Russians with a communications station and access to naval and air bases from which surveillance can take place over the whole South-east Asian region from India to Australia. The Vietnamese economy is dependent on Soviet aid. But the Vietnamese have a history of militant independence, and the alliance will last only so long as they feel they require it.

Alliances are created by nations that believe they need them. Despite appearances, they mean no more at any time than the need for them, except to the extent that a degree of assumed obligation puts a gloss on the degree of need.

Where will alliances go in the 1980s? Some suggestions have already been made. In East Asia, there are moves towards a de facto alliance between China, Japan and the United States, but a formal treaty would be too strong a "China card" for Washington to play without upsetting (perhaps disastrously) its relations with the Soviet Union; and Japan is too nervous a neighbour of both China and the Soviet Union to take sides in their confrontation. An intelligent Soviet diplomacy would woo Japan into a more central, more neutral position between the three major powers. This would involve a less blustering general assault on Japanese sensitivities, and some concessions over the northern islands, a proposition probably beyond the range of consideration of the Soviet machine. As a Soviet Foreign Office official concerned with Japan said to me in Moscow in 1979: "Every rock we have, we hold".

This is probably a statement representative of Soviet attitudes to the outside world and to its European alliance. Every position of military, political, or economic strength that the Soviet Union has, it will attempt to retain. But in the alliance it is not dealing with rocks, with territory, but with people, with non-Russian people. Gandhi once said that if the Indians had got together, they could have thrown the British out years before independence. For a subject people to get together is always difficult and dangerous, but the harder the lid is held on, the more likely is the pot, eventually, to boil over.

NATO and the Warsaw Pact have much in common. They are not mirror images of each other but each exists because the other exists, each acts because the other acts. How can these two alliances be decoupled, released from their posture of gladiators? The answer lies not only in Moscow. I see the most hopeful route through the growing contacts, the economic interdependence between Eastern and Western Europe. Romania has now followed Yugoslavia into a special relationship with the European Community. Yet the overall relaxation of tension and confrontation will be a long, slow and dangerous process, with one alliance attenuated by democracy and the other attenuated by dissent.

It is hard to foresee any other situation where the commonality of interest and the strength of continuing fear will be such as to create anything more than a passing, *ad hoc*, coalition. Perhaps the nearest approach to an alliance is slowly taking shape between members of the Association of South East Asian Nations (ASEAN). There are already bilateral defence links, but whether these develop further into a formal alliance will depend on the degree to which the members see Vietnam as a common threat to their peace and security.

One would like to think that the fear which produced the age of great, confronting alliances is on the decline; or that the demands of a world where increasing population presses ever more relentlessly on resources may force governments to shift expenditure from military to economic alliances, from producing arms to providing food, clothing, shelter, education and employment for the vast mass of desperately underprivileged. It will take a major shift in the attitudes of the industrialised states, all of which are members of one or other alliance system, before this begins to happen.

Section Two
The Strategic Thinking of the Asian Great Powers

9 The Evolution of Chinese Strategic Thought

JONATHAN D. POLLACK

China as an Object of Study

Among the emergent powers in the last decade, none has assumed more global and regional significance than the People's Republic of China (PRC). To be sure, China was hardly an inconsequential actor in previous decades; by virtue of its size, population, and past greatness as a civilization and empire, she has long exerted a considerable hold on thinking in the West. Equally significant, during their three decades in power Chinese leaders have continuously devoted a very substantial portion of their national resources to the defence sector. In absolute terms, China maintains the world's largest ground forces, third largest navy and air force, a modest but growing array of strategic nuclear forces, an armed militia numbering in excess of seven million, and an indigenous defence industrial system whose production capacities rank among the largest in the world. While there have been periods since 1949 when the relative emphasis given military needs has diminished somewhat, the general commitment to mobilising a vast number of men under arms has never been seriously questioned. Indeed, as the Chinese Communist Party (CCP) enters its fourth decade as a ruling institution, most of its senior leaders (no matter what their present positions in the hierarchy) remain military men[1]. In view of their early experiences as revolutionaries, it is doubtful whether very many of them have thought about, much less planned for, a world without weapons. The Chinese see no means of being taken seriously in the contemporary international system without first possessing weapons in significant numbers, and without demonstrating a willingness to use them, even in the face of severe risk. This is not to suggest that those who govern China are thinly disguised militarists, or that they are unjustifiably or unnaturally wedded to the use of force. Rather, they are persuaded that China must never again remain exposed, vulnerable, and unprepared in the face of adversaries generally far stronger, wealthier, and technologically more advanced than the PRC.

Much of the knowledge about modern military institutions and strategic thought that is simply taken for granted in the West remains unknown or little known with respect to contemporary China. While the Chinese in recent years have initiated a major reassessment of their defence planning and military policies, its results remain inconclusive. As a consequence of such activity, however, observers and officials from the West have gained a degree of exposure to the Chinese decision process which would have been unthinkable only a few years ago. It is critically important to understand the technical, organisational, and manpower base from which China derives its military strength. Despite China's absolute power, in relative terms it remains a poor and woefully under-educated society. These facts must be reflected in the quality of men and machines which China deploys for its own defence, and in the military doctrines China's leaders espouse.

Yet to focus exclusively on China's technical and material deficiencies in relation to the West loses sight of some essential considerations which those responsible for China's security have always understood. First, numbers count. The fact that China's combat aircraft lag several decades behind the USA and the USSR with respect to avionics or airframe construction is important to know and bear in mind, but it also helps explain why the Chinese armed forces fly in excess of 5,000 jet aircraft. China's military commanders know that their aircraft are outmoded and vulnerable; they expect to lose far more planes than they might destroy in air exchanges with most potential adversaries; they therefore compensate for such weakness by assembling the world's third largest air force. A comparable logic applies to explaining the size of Beijing's ground and naval forces, though not to the PRC's strategic forces, a point to which we will return.

Second, absolute power and sheer size often matter as much or more than relative power. China's *per capita* gross national product of approximately $440 suggests only China's relative poverty. In aggregate terms, however, the PRC already ranks among the world's largest economies. It is worth noting, for example, that the production level of China's present heavy industrial base equals that of Japan during the mid-1960s – hardly an inconsequential amount[2]. Countries and economies of this size are thus able to generate significant quantities of resources critical to the exercise of power in relation to the external world. Thus, while China may not be wealthy or developed by Western standards, it is not without very significant assets to enhance its national power.

Third, putting aside numbers and size, mere possession of certain instruments of national power *ipso facto* confers widespread recognition of great power status. When Mao Zedong asserted in 1956 that "if we are not to be bullied in the present-day world, we cannot do without the [atomic] bomb," he revealed an acute understanding of one of the principal functions of a nuclear weapons capability, no matter how modest (Mao, 1977, p. 288). The fact that China in 1980 became the third state to fire a full-range ICBM does not provide the PRC with genuine "equivalence" in relation to either the USA or the Soviet Union. But it is a strategic breakthrough of singular significance, provided the PRC neither overstates nor understates its worth for greatly reinforcing the *perception* of China as a great power. Thus, China does not need to deploy vast numbers of missiles in order for the PRC to receive acknowledgement and recognition as a major power, a fact understood by Chinese decisionmakers since they first acquired the means to deliver strategic weapons almost a decade and a half ago.

Fourth, the Chinese clearly reject – and with good reason – an exclusively technical approach to warfare. They maintain an enduring concern with the "human factor" in armed conflict, in particular the morale, organisation, and social cohesion of their armed forces. To some extent this makes a virtue out of necessity, but it is readily substantiated by their own experiences, both during and since the conclusion of the Chinese revolution. China's military commanders have long been sensitive to how seeming weakness can be turned to advantage, and how and why technological enhancement *per se* cannot be an exclusive or preeminent organisational goal.

Fifth, and perhaps most important, Chinese strategic thinkers (whether in past dynasties or the contemporary period) do not subscribe to a purely military conception for achieving security. The advantages accruing to those adept at employing psychological and political means in pursuit of strategic goals are readily apparent in the Chinese case. The limits of Chinese resources alone offer sufficient cause for China's willingness to live with far greater ambiguity and seeming vulnerability than is deemed tolerable in the West. Moreover, as a major Chinese assessment of political-military strategy has noted: "Compared with wars in the past, a large-scale modern war is even less a purely military question. Its preparations cannot but be closely interwoven with such factors as domestic, financial, and economic affairs and external relations." (Editorial Department, 1977, p. 34).

Put briefly most Chinese thinkers remain largely or wholly convinced of the virtues of what Liddell Hart termed the "indirect approach" to strategy (Liddell Hart, 1964). Their decided preference for a "conservative" rather than "acquisitive" approach to grand strategy has served the PRC extremely well since 1949. To be sure, there are very considerable dilemmas and complications in such a strategy. In particular, the somewhat rarified logic of grand strategy pays insufficient heed to the exigencies and threats for which a military planner must prepare. Yet Chinese sensitivity to time as a variable and their avoidance of the fixation on situational logic so prevalent in American military thought have recurrently demonstrated their worth. Reliance on an indirect approach proved pivotal and ultimately successful in Chinese dealings with the USA as a major military adversary in the 1950s and 1960s (Pollack, 1980b), and a strikingly similar logic is increasingly discernible in China's long-term competition with the Soviet Union (Pollack, 1981b). Nevertheless, the Chinese often fail to demonstrate with much clarity the specific interrelationships between various levels of strategic thinking discernible in their writings and military practices.

Varieties of Chinese Strategic Thought

Chinese officials and analysts repeatedly stress the need to approach the analysis of the world situation from "the higher plane of global strategy". They further suggest that most observers and politicians in the West are unable or unwilling to view the world on these terms. Yet the Chinese themselves are often frustratingly vague about this issue. There is no convenient distillation of PRC views or a primer on Chinese strategic thought; either would tend to "freeze" the analysis of events at a given moment in time, thereby belying the dynamic and at times unexpected logic of strategic analysis (Pollack, 1981a). Thus any study of Chinese strategic thinking must be largely inferential and somewhat equivocal in its judgments, for at least four reasons. First, as noted above, the dominant assumptions underlying such analysis are rarely if ever specified; even less frequently does one encounter detailed discussion within a single document. Second, unlike the Soviet case, there is no highly institutionalised tradition (at least in a public sense) of the analysis of military doctrine, or a fully developed field of military science, though key Chinese officials now openly advocate its creation (Ye, 1978). To the extent that these questions are addressed, it is often through the rather problematic filter of CCP military history or allegorical writings based on Chinese dynastic history. Such accounts are usually an instrument of policy debate within the leadership and are politically tainted in ways which diminish their worth for the study of strategy *per se*.

Third, as the above points suggest, the entire realm of defence strategy remains an extremely sensitive one in China. A number of key issues long overdue for an airing within the military elite – the relationship of technology to strategy and doctrine, alternative approaches to the deployment of Chinese forces, and various measures to more fully professionalise the Chinese officer corps – have long remained almost wholly beyond the realm of public debate, except by euphemism or indirection. In the less restrictive political atmosphere evident in China since Mao's death in the fall of 1976, a small circle of China's senior military leaders have begun to voice such concerns, but only guardedly.

Fourth, all students of Chinese military affairs require periodic reminders of the role of deception in Chinese strategy. The present leaders are the legatees of a rich historical tradition in China, best embodied in the writings of Sun Tzu (Sun, 1963). While a more detailed discussion of this perenially fascinating issue is beyond the scope of the essay (see Boorman, 1972), it raises yet again the difficulties of inferring "real" attitudes. We are left, therefore, with considerable uncertainty, if not confusion about how best to confront the diverse levels of contemporary strategic thought in China. At a minimum, these varied levels encompass: (1) discussions of the grand strategy of enemy intentions and actions; (2) assessments intended to sketch or suggest the appropriate strategy for deflecting and ultimately defeating China's enemies; (3) analyses of nuclear strategy, principally of the superpowers but intermittently that of the lesser nuclear powers, including China; and (4) the articulated principles and specific military doctrines advocated for the armed forces of the People's Republic. Each of these levels of strategic thought reveals a particular sensitivity to the relationship between general strategic principles and the manner in which they are served by the acquisition and application of military power.

The Use of Force in Chinese Military Strategy

Very little has been said or written publicly by the Chinese about the actual military operations conducted by the People's Liberation Army (PLA) since 1949[3]. While some excellent case studies have been undertaken on various Chinese decisions to use force, this research has only intermittently addressed the specific doctrines or strategies governing the application of military power and their relationship to broader foreign policy objectives. Chinese officials have recurrently insisted that their military strategy is the necessary concomitant of a foreign policy which is purportedly non-coercive and non-threatening to all other states. Thus, Chinese pledges to "never seek hegemony" in international relations and "not to seek an inch" of anyone else's territory presuppose that war will be imposed upon China by others, rather than vice versa, and that China need only prepare to resist aggression and defend PRC territory. The Minister of National Defence, Xu Xiangqian, has asserted that: "Engaging the enemy outside the gates has never been a good method of fighting. Ours is a socialist country and our social system determines that our strategic principle must be one of active defense. In coping with invaders, we must strike at the enemy after letting him in, and strategically we strike only after the enemy has struck." (Xu, 1978, p. 10).

Since the PRC's experiences in the diplomatic and security arenas over the past thirty years have so often been reactive rather initiatory, few attempts have been made to consider the premises and purposes underlying China's application of military power. Yet authoritative statements on Chinese defence policy, even when asserting that PRC military planning is wholly defensive, acknowledge that such operations encompass a significant range of potential actions: the protection Chinese territorial integrity, natural resources, and air space; the deterring of armed attack against the PRC; and (when necessary) actions intended to defeat, expel, or punish those committing such aggression. Such tasks have obviously required that Chinese forces do far more than (as the mythology would have it) rely almost totally on a "people's war" strategy of "luring the enemy in deep". As Xu Xiangqian has further noted:

Our country has vast territories with a large population and varied national conditions. This invariably imposes different demands on national defense. Our country shares far-flung borders with the big and small hegemonic countries [i.e., the Soviet Union and Vietnam]. It has vast expanses of territorial air space and waters. It has different types of geographical and climatic conditions. The armed forces in different areas have different combat tasks and different targets of attack. (Xu, 1979, pp. 45–46).

Indeed, over the past three decades the PLA has resorted to the use of force beyond the territory physically controlled by the PRC on eleven different occasions (Whiting, 1972, 1975; Pollack, 1980a). While none of these episodes reveal marked departures from coincident activity in Chinese foreign policy, the readiness to resort to force – including the initiation of military hostilities – is clearly deserving of more careful consideration.

It seems readily apparent that the PLA's combat needs require a diverse array of military plans and policies. Such variation has been explicitly noted by Su Yu, perhaps China's leading military strategist:

Our method of fighting should vary in different wars or in different stages of a war, in different times and places, with different enemies or with different weaponry or equipment. It is necessary to flexibly deploy troops and employ tactics, change tactics, and study and master the latest tactics developed along with new technology and equipment (Su, 1977, p. E21).

Such statements indicate that Chinese military behaviour has proven highly adaptive and varied. Indeed, very little evidence suggests that China's military leadership remains rigidly wedded to a "guerrilla mentality". Even a cursory review of Mao's own writings on military affairs reveal his scarcely disguised contempt for mechanistic conceptions of warfare that pay inadequate heed to the conditions and circumstances affecting a specific campaign or battle (Mao, 1963).

In an earlier study (Pollack, 1980a), I suggested that there are seven overall forms of warfare for which PLA commanders have either actively prepared or actually employed force. While some have been used in conjunction with others, each form has required a distinctive organisational effort in terms of training, tactics, and the level and type of military technology. These comprise five actual forms of fighting and two geared largely to deterrence: (1) main ground force operations; (2) small unit border operations; (3) coastal defence operations; (4) coordinated air and sea operations; (5) linear defence (the protection of airspace and territory); (6) nuclear deterrence; and (7) people's war. Such a diverse array of military actions and preparations permit much more specific judgments about Chinese views on the utility of military force.

The role of ground forces has been critical to Chinese security in past decades, and their importance does not seem likely to diminish appreciably in the 1980s. The Chinese clearly believe that large ground forces are an essential component for military planning in a number of key areas, both beyond China's borders (Korea, India, and Vietnam) and within China should an armed attack on whatever scale occur. They convey seriousness of intent and commit a nation's power in a far more graphic, meaningful fashion than any other type of capabilities. At present, the overwhelming preponderance of China's ground forces consist of infantrymen. Many of these forces provide essential assistance in a purely domestic context; this includes extensive involvement in the running of the civilian economy (for example, factories and railroads) and the internal security apparatus. In this manner, more effective use can be made of organised, well-trained manpower, especially since the likelihood of combat involvement for most of these forces is very low.

There seems little doubt, however, that a major effort has begun to reequip and refurbish those ground forces more central to Chinese military planning. Greater mobility, increased firepower, and improved armour and anti-tank capabilities are central to this effort, since these will all enhance their capabilities as an actual fighting force. Even with increased mechanisation, however, certain combat terrains remain generally unsuited to more complex combined forces operations, especially where elements of surprise and deception are extensively employed.

In the 1970s, however, the Chinese have had to confront Soviet ground forces which (in conjuction with their tactical air power) are enormously superior in quality if not quantity. It remains difficult to foresee the circumstances under which the Soviet Union might choose to attack in strength across the Sino-Soviet border. Should a major attack occur, however, Chinese commanders would seemingly confront impossibly difficult defence tasks. PLA deficiencies in firepower, mobility, reconnaissance, anti-tank weaponry, and close air support – to name only the most obvious shortcomings – seemingly leave the North China plain extremely vulnerable to a Soviet combined forces assault. Within the limits of Chinese equipment and personnel, however, PLA commanders have sought to reduce these vulnerabilities. Approximately two-thirds of China's front line infantry divisions are located in the Beijing and Shenyang military regions. The bulk of China's tanks and armoured personnel carriers are also in these locales. Similarly, as tensions along China's southeastern coast diminished, many tactical aircraft were redeployed to the North. Chinese forces are therefore not prepared to yield the incalculably valuable political and economic assets of northeast China without a significant frontal battle.

Moreover, Chinese commanders still insist (at least publicly) that invading Soviet armies would ultimately have to fight the type of war that China would want to see fought (Middleton, 1978). Such expressions of confidence are premised on a belief that the ultimate form of a Soviet attack must be an all-out effort to subjugate and occupy the PRC, no matter how implausible this might seem. Yet the Chinese at the same time have obviously sought to create a viable defence line. Can this disparity be reconciled? Chinese confidence in the high morale and inexhaustible reserves of infantrymen represent the irreducible core logic of a vital dimension of Chinese military strategy: no rational enemy will ever again commit an army to invade China. The fact that war has not occurred during more than a decade of Sino-Soviet tensions and enormous disparities in fighting power further confirms this belief. It also suggests that various levels of Chinese military preparation are intended both to repulse enemies and (by virtue of the depth and diversity of military preparations) persuade a would-be aggressor that the potential gains are not possibly worth the costs. Much like their counterparts in the Soviet Union, Chinese strategists believe that an enemy can be dissuaded from attacking only if one demonstrates the steadfastness and seriousness with which one is prepared to fight. At selected levels of PRC thinking, therefore, the calculus of warfighting and deterrence is inextricably intertwined.

Small unit border operations and coastal defence operations have frequently demonstrated considerable value, as well. They testify to the commitment of Chinese forces, frequently to remote, highly inaccessible locations. They provide a ready military instrument for limited, low-level military engagements which can be linked to diplomatic efforts to publicise growing tensions in various theatres. Inasmuch as their technological needs are modest, they cost little to maintain. Given that they reduce the prospects for undetected intrusion and interference by various adversaries, their worth seems clearly justified.

Co-ordinated air and sea operations are both qualitatively and quantitatively different. In the 1950s, major operations which were conducted quickly and decisively garnered considerable success; those that did not ended in ignominious failure. With such capabilities in place, the possibility for sudden, resolute action – in effect, a *fait accompli* strategy – has been repeatedly demonstrated. Moreover, in the 1970s, as China voiced growing concern about control over offshore resources and sought to establish unquestioned control over various contested island chains in the South China Sea, the importance and degree of effort attached to this mission expanded very significantly. Notwithstanding the defensive justification offered for these forces, the style of operation and the military requirements deemed necessary to effect them are without question offensive. They fit very well a principal maxim in Chinese military planning: retain a clear capacity for surprise, take the initiative, and force others to respond only after Chinese forces have acted.

The tasks of air and territorial defence are among the most costly, complicated, yet essential operations for which China's armed forces must prepare. From the time of the PLA's initial exposure to the uses of airpower in Korea, there has been considerable awareness of the potential vulnerability of Chinese airspace to enemy penetration. The measures taken to counter such vulnerability run wholly contrary to the assumptions underlying a "people's war" strategy of "luring the enemy in deep" and "trading space for time". However, the overall record since the early 1950s is a very mixed one, and with good reason. In this realm, Chinese forces must react rather than act, nor do they have forces of the quality to prevent a determined and technologically superior adversary from initiating moves against China. The PLA's retaliatory capabilities are also severly limited.

In few areas, therefore, are China's military weaknesses and seeming vulnerabilities more starkly revealed; it is thus no surprise that air defence modernisation constitutes one of the preeminent tasks for China's military modernisation program in the 1980s. Recent efforts to improve existing air defence capabilities encompass both anti-aircraft and reconnaissance measures as well as ongoing development programs for more modern generations of interceptor aircraft. Acquisition of Western production technology for more advanced engines and an array of sophisticated electronics constitute two of the principal areas where these efforts have been undertaken. In this realm, there is no alternative but to seek more advanced technology from abroad which will be integrated with ongoing indigenous design and production efforts. The budgetary investment and manpower resources devoted to this question all suggest that air defence will continue to be taken very seriously in the 1980s.

Deterrence in Chinese Military Strategy

China has invested very heavily in the development of nuclear weaponry – more heavily, in fact, than in any other military program.

Along with the doctrine of people's war, it constitutes one of the two pillars of Chinese deterrence theory at the "unthinkable" end of the spectrum. As I have elsewhere considered the origins, accomplishments, and consequences of this program in some detail (Pollack, 1977, 1979), I will instead focus attention on the same issue discussed in the previous section: how do particular military capabilities "fit" in an overall conception of the utility of force?

To the extent that Chinese decision makers have discussed use of such capabilities publicly, they have attached virtually no military utility to their acquisition. Nuclear weapons have generally been deemed suitable only for purposes of intimidation, and for countering any attempts at blackmail. Whenever their possible military use has been discussed, Chinese spokesmen focus in particular on their limited relevance to any hypothetical conflict involving China, given the country's continued effort at dispersal of population and industry. As Su Yu has asserted: "Everybody knows that when both sides have nuclear weapons, the threat is much greater to imperialist and social-imperialist countries where industries and population are highly concentrated." (Su, 1977, p. E22). Any effort to assert the decisiveness of nuclear weapons has been comparably challenged. Yet no one has suggested that nuclear weapons would not be employed against China, or that China would foreswear employing its own nuclear weaponry against anyone launching such an attack.

Trends in PRC nuclear deployment since the late 1960s, however, have generally suggested a program restrained in size and intended almost exclusively to deal with only the most extreme of contingencies – i.e., as a limited means of retaliation against the prospect of any irrational or preemptive nuclear attack on China. Indeed, notwithstanding endless Chinese assertions about the supposed inevitability of war between the USA and the USSR, Foreign Minister Huang Hua has asserted that "when the superpowers ... come into conflict, they may fight a nuclear war, but it is more likely that they will fight a conventional war." (Huang, 1978, p. 10).

A potentially significant exception to this overall judgment concerns Chinese evaluation of tactical nuclear weaponry. For example, a Warsaw Pact proposal in late 1976 that all signatories of the Helsinki agreements sign a no first use declaration was greeted contemptuously (if somewhat tardily) in the Chinese press. Notwithstanding the PRC's long-held insistence that all the nuclear weapons states agree to such a declaration, this particular proposal was judged a ruse which would "be favorable only to the Soviet bloc which enjoys superiority in conventional forces in Europe, while enfettering NATO's defense." The NATO Secretary-General, Joseph Luns, was further quoted approvingly for asserting that the proposal was an attempt "to reduce the deterrent effect of NATO's nuclear arms by prohibiting their defensive first use". (Xinhua, 1976, pp. A2-3). Descriptions of the "neutron bomb" have discussed its possible utility in comparable terms. If such arguments are deemed appropriate in a European context, they possess equal or greater relevance with respect to Chinese vulnerabilities. In view of the fact that large areas of China (especially in the Northwest) remain largely undefended and perhaps even indefensible, the Chinese in the 1980s might well decide to undertake a far more extensive effort in the area of tactical nuclear capabilities.

Thus, Chinese nuclear strategy seems premised on an expectation of not fighting yet being prepared to fight, even with some of the PRC's own nuclear weapons being used on Chinese soil. The probability of nuclear weapons actually being employed, however, is deemed exceedingly slight, even though recent articles have begun to discuss Soviet nuclear strategy much more extensively, including analyses of Soviet limited nuclear options (Special Commentator, 1980, pp. C3-4). By unambiguously conveying a readiness to fight, even under the most adverse if circumstances, if not specifying precisely when, where, or how, the Chinese undoubtedly feel deterrence is heightened.

Similar judgements apply to the "people's war" strategy. The Chinese do not believe that anyone would be foolish enough to undertake a full scale war on Chinese soil. But they reinforce this belief by preparing for this least likely of contingencies, thereby enhancing the credibility of Chinese resolve. It also helps explain why the Chinese with good reason remain unpersuaded of the supposed irrelevance of people's war in the contemporary era. As Xu Xiangqian has noted:

If any enemy should dare invade China . . . everyone will be a soldier, every village a fortress and every place a battlefield; no enemy can stand such attack and attrition no matter how numerous his troops are. Didn't certain people in the West with military foresight say that attacking China is militarily speaking a taboo and that whoever gets involved will have no hope of getting out again? This is indeed perspicacious. People's war is extremely powerful and can achieve much. (Xu, 1978, pp. 9-10).

Here and elsewhere, therefore, Chinese military thinkers tend to adopt an essentially if not exclusively conservative strategic logic. It is assumed that, barring accident or irrationality, total war on Chinese soil will never again be fought. By conveying *behaviourally* that China is prepared to fight a conflict that should never occur, the Chinese have sought to persuade their principal adversaries in both the past and present that the effort is not possibly worth the costs or risks.

As Xu Xiangqian further noted, however, such a strategy can "achieve much", but not all. In the late 1970s, Xu and others conceded that history has not stood still. Any future war, therefore, would be a "people's war fought under modern conditions", thereby paying heed to the vast changes in warfare in recent decades, but especially those technological changes evident in the 1970s. The Chinese are noticeably vague about the precise areas where change must occur. At a minimum, however, a deterrence doctrine does not address the full spectrum of political objectives which the Chinese find well served by the use of force.

The Purposes of Military Power

What are the underlying objectives which China seeks to advance by acquiring and employing military power? Six purposes in the employment of military power can be discerned in Chinese strategic thinking and military actions. Since this essay is concerned only with the exercise of military power by one state in relation to other states, one of these six (revolution) will not be discussed. Moreover, the Chinese have generally foresworn an activist role in the promotion of revolution or wars of national liberation; the degree of Chinese participation in this activity in the past was no doubt considerably overstated, as well.

The first major category, therefore, is *deterrence*, especially nuclear deterrence. As noted previously, Chinese thinking on this issue seems in critical respects much closer to Soviet beliefs than to the long dominant if not universally accepted American logic of mutual assured destruction. It clearly differs with Soviet planning, however, in the number and characteristics of deployed weaponry, though this is obviously much affected by China's more limited technological and economic base. The Chinese appear to believe, however, that they can avoid such a war only by demonstrating a very serious commitment to fight by all available means. Various active defence measures within China such as the digging of shelters are also significant in this regard; their possible effectiveness in war is less important than that they contribute to the impression of steadfast resolve, both for China's adversaries and for the Chinese populace. Although Chinese military thinkers do not believe that such a war will break out, nor that if nuclear weapons are employed they will suffice to realise underlying strategic objectives (Su, 1977, pp. E21–22), they regard the objective of deterrence as a paramount goal in its own right, and that it cannot be separated from the tasks of war fighting; the two realms are inextricably linked.

The second principal goal is *defence*. In view of China's vulnerability over the past century and a half to penetration and subjugation from abroad, there is a particular historical importance to this objective. A "never again" mentality is readily discernible in Chinese discussions of this topic. Indeed, in the prevalent Chinese view, it matters less that one is wholly successful in such efforts, and more that the "good fight" is fought. Even in failure, therefore, China will have let its enemies know that (as Mao noted in 1949) "China has stood up". Equally important, the resolve and determination of China's populace and military forces will be comparably strengthened, if not by losses in war then by the very act of preparing and defending China in a major way, even in the absence of armed conflict. The fact that the encroachment of enemies on Chinese territory has been so sporadic, especially in the past decade, can only further strengthen one's confidence in the absolute necessity of national defence. Moreover, by virtue of their defensive or protective deployment, the actual disposition of Chinese forces can contribute substantially to conveying military restraint (for example, during the mid-1960s along the Vietnam border and during the 1970s along the Sino-Soviet frontier).

The third principal objective is *assertion*. This goal involves the readiness and willingness to use force quickly and decisively, and with little or no warning. It is the realm of what was described earlier as a *fait accompli* strategy. However much Chinese officials might wish to stress their defensive orientation, this area is clearly offensive in design and execution. What is at stake is the taking of territory whose ownership is disputed by China and other parties. The goal of assertion came increasingly to the fore in the 1970s, and there seems little doubt that China's military capacities to realise this objective will grow appreciably in the 1980s. By rapidly mobilising massive power with which to overwhelm an opponent, the Chinese can resolve claims to disputed territories by force of arms. The obvious successes in this realm demonstrate that it will remain a valuable tool in Chinese military planning, and could well increase in importance as the control of the sea's resources becomes an even more vital issue.

The fourth principal goal is *demonstration*. Mao Zedong once flippantly asserted that "on occasion, China likes to make a loud noise". Efforts taken in this area are very much for political effect. They involve a conscious Chinese decision to escalate military hostilities where there is no immediate danger of war, although local tensions may exist. China's 1979 attack into northern Vietnam is an excellent example of such activity. By intervening on a very considerable scale, one establishes a clear precedent for the willingness to use force on subsequent occasions. The specific calculations seem clear: attack in strength; achieve specific tactical objectives (these can obviously vary widely); and cease military activity as soon as is practicable, but not in such a way as to suggest that one's forces might never return. In the attack against Vietnam, for example, the Chinese suffered very considerable casualties, but they also exacted an extremely heavy toll against Vietnam. By launching a limited invasion in defiance of Soviet treaty obligations to Vietnam, the Chinese demonstrated that even in the face of severe risk the PRC would be heard from and respected within the Southeast Asian region. The parallels to tributary relations between China and vassal states in past Chinese dynasties cannot be altogether pleasing to various states in the area.

The consequences for more long term Chinese objectives may be even more important. Following their withdrawal from Vietnam, Chinese forces have remained in considerable numbers in nearby locations, thereby compelling Vietnam to redeploy many of its best forces to its northernmost provinces. China, with vastly more men under arms, can readily spare the troops on a prolonged basis, with periodic threats to teach Vietnam a "second lesson" more than sufficient to keep many of Hanoi's best forces tied down and hence unavailable for operations elsewhere. Pursuing such an objective is possible only in the context of China maintaining very large military forces with a demonstrated capacity to fight.

The fifth principal objective is *expansion*. In Chinese views, it represents the forbidden fruit of which the superpowers have been tempted to partake, but which China continues to foreswear. Both in declared policy and in their present military capabilities, the Chinese have yet to venture into this realm. It is in this area that the potent Chinese critique of great power military conduct assumes such a conspicuous and forceful quality. The hallmarks of such an "acquisitive" approach to grand strategy – forces deployed abroad, extensive alliance commitments with lesser powers, oceangoing navies, and a capacity to use force at considerable distance from one's territory – are not evident in present Chinese military beliefs and practices. The test in the 1980s is whether the temptation to use power in this manner will increase as China's technological and economic capacities progress and as the PRC's political stake in global politics also grows. While present judgements on this issue must remain inconclusive, it obviously represents an issue of enormous potential consequence for the international system as a whole, and therefore merits continuous close scrutiny.

It should be clear, therefore, that the Chinese have thought very carefully about the purposes, limits, and consequences of military power. They view the accumulation and exercise of such power as essential to their capacity to retain initiative and independence in an unsettled and frequently threatening external environment. Whatever burdens China has incurred over the past thirty years in acquiring such power, it is doubtful whether very many Chinese leaders would question their worth.

The Future of Chinese Strategic Thought

Military power in its numerous dimensions has had a recurring and even pivotal influence on the development of modern China; it was central to China's subjugation in the nineteenth century, and was equally critical to China's revolution and resurgence in the twentieth century. There are no serious suggestions or indications in the contemporary period that this influence will soon or substantially diminish.

However, those Chinese responsible for the exercise of such power have understood better than most both its potentialities and limitations. Military power is undeniably an indispensible agent in the present and foreseeable efforts of the PRC to gain greater security or (perhaps more appropriately) reduce Chinese insecurities. But there is nothing foreordained in how the Chinese will use such power. This is not to suggest that Chinese military doctrine is so culturally or organisationally distinctive as to elude the grasp of analysts not privy to the inner workings of the Chinese decision process. What the PRC has clearly sought to understand, however, is how and where the development and use of military power fits in relation to political and psychological tools in Chinese security strategy. Chinese strategists realise that security calculations do not embody a series of discrete simultaneous equations, but rather a more complicated, less orderly, and at times vastly less predictable phenomenon. They have therefore devoted very considerable energies (to use Stanley Hoffmann's felicitous phrase) to employing *both* "muscle and brains".

This process has always involved a readiness and willingness to fight. However, beyond that minimal consensus, considerable divergence exists within China. As I have argued elsewhere, leaders in the People's Republic will continue to debate five key questions pertaining to modern arms: "what to acquire, how much, how quickly, by what means and for what purposes". (Pollack, 1980a, p. 86). For much of the past three decades, China's overall security policy has been largely reactive to external pressures and imperatives. In various situations, however, they have been prepared to resort to force when conditions permitted or compelled its use; there seems little reason to believe that they will be significantly less reluctant to do so in the future. As China increasingly acquires or develops more sophisticated military capabilities in the coming decade, the opportunities for a more expansive conception of national security may also grow.

The test in the 1980s, therefore, will be for China to define an appropriate purpose or role for modern arms. It is far from clear that present Chinese strategic concepts have outlived their usefulness. The fact that there is now a large Western foot in the Chinese door provides no real assurance that the Chinese will view political and military strategy as officials and scholars in the West might prefer. The Chinese have gone to great lengths to achieve relative autonomy in security affairs, if not in the weapons they may deploy, than at least in the concept and practices they espouse and pursue. The degree to which they are prepared to mortgage such independence is far from clear. At a minimum, Chinese military thinkers and political strategists have many of their own ideas, even if some of them may be regarded as questionable in the West. They are no doubt fully capable of continuing to do so in the future. To this extent, the dominant conceptual directions in Chinese strategy will be determined by the Chinese and are unlikely to derive from either technological or doctrinal imperatives suggested by others. How successful China might be in continuing to chart its own course in the 1980s will remain a fascinating question to follow throughout the coming decade.

10 Strategic Thinking in India in the 1970s: Prospects for the 1980s

R.V.R. CHANDRASEKHARA RAO

India is a unique example of a country which for sometime put strategic thought at a discount but which at the onset of changes in its security environment chose to re-examine past premises and reformulate its framework of security. Three periods can be identified in Indian strategic thought.

The period, associated with Jawaharlal Nehru, from Indian Independence to the Sino-Indian war is the first, in which strategic concepts, particularly middle-range concepts like buffer states, balance of power and spheres of influence, were shunned or rejected as imperialist legacies. (Kapur, 1970, pp. 434–446). Many critics have traced the sorry state of India's defence preparedness in 1962 to Nehru's summary rejection of these considerations. (Sen, 1960, p. 122; Chakravarthi, 1962, p. 56). It could, of course, be argued in Nehru's favour that while dismissing the orthodox strategic ideas he was not blind to security needs. His prescription of non-alignment could in itself be regarded as a macro-level strategic concept, in the sense that its pursuit diminished the chances of involvement in conflicts on the one hand and created a climate of understanding between nations on the other. The Chinese invasion, however, compelled an agonising reappraisal of the policy by Nehru himself. It was a reappraisal not merely of foreign policy; a gradual reformulation of defence policy also took place in the 1960s which could be regarded as the transition period.

The second major stage started in the second half of the 1960s when India shed its sentimental posture about the renunciation of nuclear weapons, and a greater readiness to anticipate and react to changes in the surrounding environment could be seen in Indian policy.

If the 1960s saw India's adopting new perspectives on security, the 1970s marked the inauguration of the third period in which consolidation and even refinement of these perspectives was in evidence. The readiness to assert a regional role as exhibited in its intervention in the Bangladesh war in 1971 and the nuclear explosion of 1974 is a good example of this trend.

With this background, an analysis of India's strategic thinking in the 1970s and the prospects for the 1980s could be attempted under the following headings.

1) Symptoms and causes of changes in strategic thinking;
2) Changes in strategic thinking and security postures; and
3) Prospects for the 1980s.

Symptoms of Changes in Strategic Thinking

The first symptom was the appreciable growth in defence expenditure that occurred after 1962. While in 1961 India spent only $911 m on defence, from 1963 annual military expenditure never fell short of $1800 m. In fact it frequently exceeded $2000 m. In terms of GNP, whereas before 1962 military expenditure hardly constituted 2 percent, from 1963 it invariably stood above 3 percent. (SIPRI, 1979, pp. 42, 43).

Hitherto neglected areas of the services, the Navy in particular, began to receive attention. Proposals for a blue water naval capability were canvassed in some quarters. Though these were not seriously taken up, they reflected changes in the climate of security thinking. The establishment of the Institute for Defence Studies and Analyses in 1968 further underscores the point that strategic analysis is no longer at a discount but is regarded as an essential input for policy making. Indeed, much of the canvassing for tougher postures both on nuclear policy and on the issue of attaining autarkic strategic capability came from this Institute.[1]

The Indo-Soviet treaty of 1971, the Bangladesh war and the nuclear explosion of 1974 are other obvious symptoms of India's concern with strategic thinking.

Causes of Changes in Strategic Thinking

The first major cause, India's defeat at China's hands in 1962, resulted in it's adopting immediate remedial steps like augmenting mountain divisions and acquiring capability for high altitude warfare. Macro-level strategic responses also ensued, the best example of which is the change in the Indian stand on the unconditional renunciation of nuclear weapons. The adoption of more flexible norms in the practice of non-alignment can also be cited. The early Nehruvian position that even seeking arms from a super power would be a violation of non-alignment, to the later position of India seeking a special connection with the Soviet Union, is a long haul indeed.

If the Chinese threat constituted one major cause for awakening India's strategic concern, the Chinese nuclear explosion of 1964 served as another spur to that awakening. It forced India to rethink its nuclear policy. The debate over nuclear proliferation occured in the late

1960s and this further pushed India into shedding its idealism and into taking a stand in favour of keeping its options free on the nuclear capability issue.

The British withdrawal from the Indian Ocean was another cause. Though ostensibly welcomed as yet another stage in the withdrawal of imperialism, the prospect could not but have caused some anxiety in India, as the British presence served as a security shield for India too. The withdrawal was regarded as a challenge and an opportunity. The period witnessed neighbours like Indonesia augmenting their naval strength very appreciably and assuming strident postures in the region. Indonesia, it may be recalled, claimed exclusive jurisdiction over the Malacca straits and even demanded that the Indian Ocean be renamed the Indonesian Ocean. (Kohli, 1975, pp. 133, 134). These developments among others made Indian naval circles canvass for an expanded role. Though initially dismissed as preposterous (Thomas, 1978, p. 205), plans for naval expansion soon materialised. For the implementation of these India turned to the Soviet Union as the Western powers were reluctant to help. (Jukes, 1973, pp. 262–268; Larns, 1978). The acquisition of submarines from the Soviet Union was the first high-water mark of this trend which became more conspicuous in the 1970s. The salience of Indian Ocean politics had increased by then and the rise of regional powers like Iran presented India with new challenges.

Changes in Strategic Thinking and Security Postures

Along with shedding prejudices over strategic ideas, there has been assertion of the need for indigenous strategic theory. To an extent this is a reaction against attempts of Western analysis to lay down the parameters of strategic thinking premised on either superpowers' or Western interests. In particular the plenitude of facile theorising about nuclear non-proliferation provoked some Indian thinkers, who saw in this an attempt at intellectual browbeating to buttress superpowers' condominium over the third world. Mr. K. Subramanyam, Director of the Institute of Defence Studies and Analyses, warned the Third World against the hold of the military – industrial – academic and media complex. (1980).

One significant example of indigenous strategic thinking was the introduction of the concepts of *horizontal* and *vertical* proliferation which India counterposed against the undifferentiated application of the concept of non-proliferation sought to be thrust on the non-nuclear powers alone. (Kaushik & Mehrotra, 1980, p. 1). The distinction has proved to be an immense moral and diplomatic weapon to expose the onsidedness of the goal of non-proliferation as sought by the world powers today.

Yet, the case of the indigenous strategic thinking can be over-stated. One cannot merely dismiss the entire range of strategic concepts in use as irrelevant to the Third World.

The Sino-Indian war has vindicated many critics of India's action in recognising Tibet as a fullfledged part of China and thus trifling with the well-tested strategic asset of a buffer state. A more positive attitude towards conventional security policies resulted, as reflected not only in the reviewing of Indian defence policies and increasing defence investment but in other aspects also.

From Disarmament to Deterrence

Stress on disarmament characterised India's defence posture as well as its diplomacy till the early 1960s. On the nuclear bomb issue, in particular, Indian diplomacy was untiring in its advocacy of disarmament. Nehru proclaimed India's unilateral renunciation of nuclear weapons thus:

"No man can prophesy the future. But I should like to say on behalf of my Government – and I think I can say with some assurance on behalf of any future Government of India – that whatever might happen, whatever the circumstances, we shall never use this atomic energy for evil purposes. There is no condition attached to this assurance, because once a condition is attached, the value of such an assurance does not go very far." (Department of Atomic Energy, 1970, p. 107).

But the war of 1962 and China's acquisition of the nuclear bomb led to a critical modification in Indian policy. Lal Bahadur Shastri, then Prime Minister, expressed it in the following manner: "*I do not know what may happen later*, but our *present policy* is not to build an atom bomb, and it is the right policy". (Yueh & Liu, 1972, p. 69) (emphasis added). It is important to note that though apparently reiterating the policy of renunciation, the first two phrases in the statement have since come to signify the reservation of an 'option' to go nuclear. In view of the Chinese threat as perceived by India, the notion of a deterrent against China, howsoever small it may be, has emerged since 1964. (Kapur, 1970, pp. 145, 186). Though at the level of declared policy India had disavowed any intention of acquiring nuclear weapons, both at the official and non-official levels one could discern intimations of the doctrine of deterrence. (Kapur, 1970, p. 173). Some publicists and analysts not only justified the 'Shastri option' but also urged the early redeeming of the option, and various cost estimates of the bomb appeared.[2]

The debate on the bomb in India picked up further momentum as the nonproliferation debate proceeded in the international forums. In these forums India became the principal opponent of the nonproliferation strategy which it felt would leave some countries vulnerable to aggressive nuclear neighbours and would even impede scientific research.

There are two other indicators to show that India envisaged its potential weapons capability as a deterrent. First, it refused to take notice of the no-first-use declaration repeatedly made by China. (Noorani, 1967, pp. 490, 502). India in other words, did not feel confident of Chinese assurances and thus very seriously thought in terms of containing China through a nuclear guarantee secured from without or through an indigenous nuclear capability. As the prospect of an outside guarantee disappeared, India had to think in terms of its own potential nuclear capability. The Indian objection to the Pakistani proposal for a nuclear weapons free zone in the subcontinent, on the ground that as long as China was not included in the scheme the whole exercise was meaningless, constituted the second major indicator of the Indian anxieties vis a vis China's nuclear capability. (Singh, 1977, pp. 242–257).

Obfuscation in Indian Policy

It should be admitted that there was considerable obfuscation in Indian policy in this matter. To start with, the Shastri statement did imply that India reserved an option on acquisition of nuclear weapons. But, during the global debate over non-proliferation, the Indian objection was mainly based on the double inequity of (1) attempting to prevent horizontal proliferation only while allowing vertical proliferation to continue unabated and (2) putting a tighter lid on nuclear research and technology. Thus, Indian objection to the NPT was not primarily based on its desire for a bomb, though, this was certainly a latent factor. (Kapur, 1976, pp. 138, 139). The hiatus between the explicit and the implicit reasons led to considerable confusion during the Janata regime (1977–79). Prime Minister Morarjee Desai, while firmly refusing President Carter's plea to India to agree to full-scope safeguards over its nuclear installations, at one stage stated in his characteristic moral tone that if only the two superpowers declared their intention to scale down their nuclear arsenal, he would commit India to the NPT regime. (Rao, 1979, pp. 136–138). This was getting perilously near the position that if only vertical proliferation was contained India would abide by the ban on horizontal proliferation. Again, it was during the Janata regime that India gave up its active opposition to the idea of a nuclear weapons free zone in the region. Desai also gave his personal assurance that whatever happened, India would not develop nuclear weapons. With the return of Mrs. Gandhi to power the above ambivalences no longer exist and the implied option of relying on the idea of a deterrent will persist.

There is a problem unique to India which complicates the deterrent argument. The Indian claim for a deterrent is much more warranted than the British and French claims for independent deterrents against the Soviet Union. For India did not have a superpower guarantee against its potential enemy as the British and French always have had. Yet the fact that India perceives two distinct security threats, China and Pakistan, leads to the operation of a chain-reaction in the logic of deterrence, for if India needs deterrence against China would not Pakistan need one against India? In fact the Indian situation is unique when compared to that of other threshold nuclear powers like Israel and the Arab states who are aspiring for deterrence against each other. Their acquisition of nuclear capability would not provoke a third party to acquire a counter deterrent, as an Indian nuclear deterrent would provoke Pakistan. Most Indian writings are silent about the inherent potential for this chain reaction. Probably, underestimation of Pakistan's ability to catch up accounts for this omission. With Pakistan poised to reach nuclear capability one is now witnessing the unfolding of the full logic of the situation. In view of this logic, it is quite improbable that the Indian decision-makers ignored the prospect of Pakistan catching up when they gave the green signal for the Indian explosion in 1974.

Indian Perceptions of the Superpower Détente and the Indo-Soviet Treaty, 1971

Indian perceptions of the superpower détente have not been very sanguine. (Jain, 1977, pp. 242–257). Mrs Gandhi often asserted that détente did not prevent and rather encouraged superpower rivalry in the Asian and African regions. As the superpower détente flourished elsewhere, India's own security postures assumed shapes less soft than before as the assertion of its regional role since the early 1970s demonstrated. The Indo-Soviet treaty of 1971 is directly related to the Indian reading of superpower intentions in the regions. The treaty illustrates well the impact of objective strategic developments and the way they are perceived by countries like India. It would therefore be useful to discuss the interplay of events that formed the background to the treaty.

To Indian thinking the United States was trying to manipulate the détente to serve its purposes in South and South East Asia, particularly to checkmate the role of less pliable powers like India. This perception was confirmed by the US policy of propping up local powers like Iran as proxies to serve American interests. During the Bangladesh crisis of 1971, in particular, American diplomacy under Kissinger touched the nadir of anti-Indianism. It appeared that Kissinger would rather condemn the brutal suppression of human rights in East Bengal than reconcile to a situation that would even remotely favour India. He has since accused Mrs. Gandhi of not being primarily interested in the rights of the people of Bangladesh but only in the dismantling of Pakistan. (Kissinger, 1979, pp. 881, 914). But his memoirs testify that he was himself not even secondarily solicitous of the rights of the Bangladesh people. He admits to ordering his office to show a 'tilt' against India. (p. 897). The Sino-American détente in July 1971, accomplished through Pakistani mediation, and the hint to India then that if in a future Indo-Pak confrontation China were to come to Pakistan's aid India could not count on American help, seemed calculated to scare India so that it would not do anything to aid the people of Bangladesh and thereby reap the strategic profits also. (Rao, 1973, pp. 2059–2065). To India, it appeared that Kissinger had erected a Sino-Pak front with American blessings to subdue India into a quiet acceptance of the situation. It was under these circumstances that India decided to move closer to the Soviet Union in search of firm diplomatic backing and potential strategic support. Thus resulted the Indo-Soviet treaty, 1971.

Whatever may be the truth about Kissinger designing a Sino-Pak coalition against India during the nearly year-long crisis in Bangladesh, it is on record that during the period of hostilities in November–December 1971 he actively advised Pakistan "to work out a common position with the Chinese". (Kissinger, 1979, pp. 907; Singh, 1980, pp. 112–116). Kissinger would argue that he had to use the Chinese to prevent Moscow from supporting India militarily then. But Kissinger did bank upon the Chinese coming in on Pakistan's side. He confirmed this when he said that part of the reason for sending the American Task Force into the Bay of Bengal was because "we had to be ready to back up the Chinese if at the last moment they came into it after all". (p. 912). As is well known the Chinese never 'came in after all'. Is it then a case of the Chinese restraining the Soviet Union or the Soviet Union restraining the Chinese and thus frustrating Kissinger's strategy? Kissinger's own analysis in no way disproves the probability that but for a Soviet warning to the Chinese not to join the fray, a Sino-Pak coalition would have posed a great threat to India's interests then. The Indo-Soviet Treaty thus had a strong deterring effect.

It cannot be denied that as the Bangladesh crisis evolved Indian perspectives were also changing. The thought of exploiting the situation must have figured prominently in the minds of Indian policy-makers. But the point is that it was not a simple case of Pakistan's adversity being exploited by India. Pakistan's cynical disregard of the aspirations of the people of Bangladesh and India's patience during the months when millions of refugees poured into India had created a formidable cushion of moral legitimacy for India to rely upon. Ironically enough, Kissinger himself reflects this fact when he bemoans that the American Congress and the American media were overwhelmingly sympathetic to India during the crisis. (pp. 916, 917). Mrs. Gandhi, thus, had not only the will to power but also the proper diplomatic environment to translate that will to power. It is a moot point whether Nehru with more diverse inhibitions would have proceeded the way his daughter did in the crisis. It should, however, be realised that the environment counted for as much as the personality of Mrs. Gandhi in the situation.

India as a Regional Power – Aspirations and Capabilities

The dexterous exploitation of the events of 1971 to India's advantage was followed up by India in augmenting its security potential commensurate with its perceived role. True, the strategic advantage flowing out of the Bangladesh war has to an extent been neutralised by the souring of Indo-Bangladesh relations since 1975. Yet, the events of 1971 can be regarded as inaugurating the projection of India as a full-fledged regional power. This is a good example of the strategic trend so aptly characterised by the International Institute for Strategic Studies as one of Diffusion of Power and Proliferation of Force.[3] The indicators in terms of conventional capability are significant. Since 1971, Indian defence budgets have exceeded the $2,000 m. figure and since 1976 the figure has been above $2,600 m. (SIPRI, 1979, pp. 42, 43). As for individual wings of the armed forces, the Air Force is being strengthened with deep-penetration strike aircraft. India is also manufacturing these under licence. The Navy, in particular, has progressed from the modest expansion programme of the 1960s to a more concentrated growth in the 1970s, exemplified by indigenous manufacture of medium-sized vessels under licence. A second fleet has been established and there is a very distinct possibility of a third fleet coming into existence. Yet, the Indian naval profile has been a restrained one with rhetoric of naval doctrine (as the one so frequently articulated by the late Shah of Iran), being conspicuously absent. However, a robust demand for greater naval role has been heard in recent years. (Kohli, 1975, pp. 103–105). A blue water role may no longer be only a remote possibility.

Putting up with Regional Rivalries and Suspicions

The last decade witnessed not only India's emergence as an eminent power, it also made India experience the problem of rivalry with other emerging regional powers. Indo-Iranian relations are a good example. Iran under the former Shah aspired for a significant regional role. Superpower linkages compounded the rivalry. The Shah saw in the Indo-Soviet and the Soviet-Iraqi treaties a design to encircle Iran. The US-Iranian link, with Pakistan and China on the wings, was read by

India as part of a strategy to contain India. However, both India and Iran were able to contain their perceived conflicts of interest by wisely exploiting the potential for co-operation on the economic front. The rhetoric of confrontation was substituted by the diplomacy of economic co-operation. Indo-Iranian trade during 1973–1978 registered phenomenal growth. The Indo-Iranian interaction in the short period had become a good example of a potential conflict situation being converted into one of mutual appreciation of each other's interests. It even appeared that this regional détente might have a wider effect in easing the tensions between India and Pakistan, Pakistan and Afghanistan, and Afghanistan and Iran. One fondly hopes that recent events in Iran and Afghanistan have only interrupted this trend.

The rise of the Persian Gulf and Western Indian Ocean Area into prominence has increased India's own naval consciousness and has led to India's paying closer attention to the western direction than to the eastern. Apart from cultivating cordial relations with most of the littoral states in this region, special linkages with Iraq and Mauritius have been established.

Yet, both in capability and will, serious limitations to the future Indian naval role can be seen. With only two fleets, Western and Eastern, and a very long coast to guard, even a flag-showing role is only a limited possibility. In the east, in spite of the opportunities for economic political and security interaction with South-East Asia and Australia, Indian contacts are far below the optimum. In fact the countries in this region do not regard the Indian presence as weighty enough to be counted. When in 1974, the then Australian Prime Minister, Gough Whitlam, floated the Asian-Pacific Community idea, India did not figure as a participant in the scheme.

The projection of a regional role presents India with the burden of learning to live with the suspicions of smaller neighbours. India has to realise that these neighbours are no less concerned about the potential strength of regional powers than they are of the big powers. This is prominently illustrated by the proposals to declare the Indian Ocean as a zone of peace and to the creation in South Asia of a nuclear weapons free zone.

Both proposals reflect the smaller powers' attempts to restrain the salience of force in the region. Though India became an active champion of the proposal to declare the Indian Ocean a zone of peace, in the beginning it was hesitant about the idea. With respect to the proposal for a nuclear weapons free zone, which was directly reflective of the smaller powers' fears of the nuclearisation of regional powers, India, as mentioned earlier, expressed its disapproval on the ground that to be effective, the scheme should cover a wider area than South Asia (Singh, 1977, pp. 240–257). Misgivings about the potential effects of Indian military power will become manifest in one form or another. It

will be India's endeavour to remain prominent without appearing to
be preponderant, recognised to be weighty without throwing its
weight around, and to be respected as a good neighbour without being
feared as a big brother.

The Defence-Development Equation

Yet another pointer to a strong orientation towards defence lies in the
change that has taken place in the thinking about the equation between defence and development. Nehru's thinking corresponded to
the classical model of 'guns and butter'. He ardently favoured low
defence expenditures because India could ill-afford diversion of its
scarce resources to military ends. It could be said that he preferred
non-alignment as a kind of substitute for conventional instruments of
security. After the war with China it was inevitable that India would
spend more on defence, but as an unavoidable evil. An altered perception emerged towards the defence-development equation, and increased defence spending was sought to be a parameter of development on the basis that defence spending does indirectly promote development. Still, basically the inherent incompatability was not
ignored. However, by the late 1960s very strong pleas came to be
advanced when the equation was altered and defence was almost equa-
ted with development. One prominent strategic analyst argued in 1973
that defence and development ought to be treated as positively corre-
lated and bemoaned that "unfortunately till this day, in our policies
there is no clarity of concept and this equation between defence and
development is not reflected. We still persist in all dichotomies such
as plan vs. non-plan, defence vs. development and growth vs. social
justice". (Subramanyam, p. 4)

These views did not get translated into official policy, as Indian
defence expenditure mostly stayed at a level of 3 per cent of the GNP
even in the post 1962 period. Yet the thinking as reflected in the
above quotation is an indicator of the mood conditioning defence policy making.

PROSPECTS FOR THE 1980s

Impact of the Afghan crisis on Indo-Soviet Relations

India's strategic posture in the decade just begun will no doubt be
influenced by the critical events in the region such as the Russian
intervention in Afghanistan. On the Afghanistan situation, India on
the whole will continue to favour the Russian stand. There have been
rather ambivalent stances exhibited by the Indian leaders during the
last year. Prime Minister Mrs. Gandhi has repeatedly stated that the
Russian intervention is the result of American provocative behaviour

in and around the Persian Gulf.[4] The Indian Foreign Minister, Mr. P.V. Narasimha Rao, has suggested a possible way out of the situation by proposing that the Soviet Union should start withdrawing from Afghanistan (*The Hindu*, 6 July, 1980). In recent months in particular India has been more forthright in emphasising the need for Soviet withdrawal. But it is almost certain that the level of Indo-Soviet contacts will in no way depend upon the future Soviet response to the Indian feelings in the matter.

If the dynamics of the situation result in a closer co-ordination of Pakistani and Chinese efforts to destabilise the Afghan regime, then the scenario of two polarised groupings, an Indo-Soviet one on the one hand and a Pakistani-Chinese (with the US in the wings) on the other, is a very likely reality. Whether in this eventuality India would move closer to the Soviet Union by seeking a more intimate security linkage will remain an open question. As it is, in 1980 the Soviet Union agreed to supply $1.6 billion worth of military equipment, ranging from new generation tanks to multi-role aircraft (Doder, 1980; *The Statesman* 14 July, 1980). Would this trend be likely to lead to a more intense defence collaboration, such as India extending its naval bases for Russian use? On present indications this seems very unlikely.

What of the contingency of the Soviet Union cutting off the already disaffected Baluchi areas from Pakistan as a retaliation for the latter's support of the Afghan rebels? Would India aid such a Soviet operation. Professor J. Erickson of Edinburgh, in his analysis of the Russian intentions presented to the Foreign Affairs Committee of the British House of Commons, expressed the view that the Soviet action is potentially linked to Indian interests, in that the Soviet Union could close in on Pakistan "by instigating a reconstituted Afghanistan to apply pressure on [Pakistan held] Kashmir". He also said that the Soviet strategy might further develop into "offering Baluchistan up for partition to please both Afghan and Iranian appetites, leaving a weakened Pakistan to Indian claims and competition". (*The Guardian Weekly*, 17 August, 1980). It is very improbable that India has any aspiration to gain by the Soviet action. Whatever may be the rights and wrongs of the Indian view that the Soviet action is purely defensive in nature, there is no evidence that the Indian support for the Soviet Union is motivated by the temptation to benefit from the potential opportunities in the situation. On the contrary, India has tried to demonstrate its concern for the Pakistani anxieties by more than once trying to facilitate a Pak-Afghan dialogue over the crisis. (*The Times of India*, 19 April, 9, 15 May 1980). It can be said that India has a vested interest in the stability of Pakistan as it would feel vulnerable to have on its Western borders an unstable medley of breakaway states.

India's aim is on the one hand to see the Soviet Union withdraw, and on the other to ensure that outside intervention does not provide further cause (or pretext) for continued Soviet presence. Thus India would prefer Pakistan to develop a dialogue with the Soviet Union and Afghanistan. Islamabad may not be too willing to allow India to take the credit for any major initiative, but if Indian diplomacy could persuade the Soviet Union to make Kabul give worthwhile guarantees to Pakistan, that could pave the way for an eventual reconciliation. One significant step could be Afghanistan's recognition of the Durand Line, the existing international boundary between Pakistan and Afghanistan which the latter so far has refused to recognise.

Irrespective of the implications of the Afghan crisis, the Indo-Soviet connection will certainly endure at the present level of intensity. It has for all practical purposes become an item of all-party commitment in India, as the Janata Party's attitude during its short spell demonstrated. Starting with a programme to reduce the salience of the Soviet connection the Janata government had, in fact, continued the special connection with Moscow (Rao, 1978).

India-China Relations

The China factor is also an important one. China has recently hinted that the territorial quarrel could be settled if India gives up some of its claims in return for a reciprocal adjustment of Chinese claims. The real implication is that India should be reconciled to the Chinese occupation of the Western sector (which has already become an integral part of China's strategic road system) in return for India keeping the disputed territory in the North East frontier. (Rao, 1980). Ultimately, a settlement of this sort may become inevitable. But in the near future India may not be anxious to arrive at such an agreement. In the meanwhile, considering the turmoil in the North Eastern region, India cannot but keep a vigilant watch over China. India's recognition of the Heng Samrin regime in Kampuchea only underscores the point that India is not overconcerned about Chinese sentiment.

India-Pakistan Relations

The Indo-Pakistan relationship will remain an uncertain item. Strangely enough, the Afghan crisis did not result in any deterioration in the existing level of relationship in spite of their mutually conflicting perspectives. On the contrary both the countries showed mature understanding of each other's view-points. While there is no unanimity in the views, a line of communication has been firmly established between the two countries. As already mentioned, New Delhi could encourage the Soviet Union and Afghanistan towards extending an assurance to Pakistan about the inviolability of the Durand Line. This would eliminate the original *casus-belli* between Pakistan and Afghanistan.

India could take an important confidence-building step in the area of regional disarmament. Another round of an arms race is now visible in the sub-continent, with so-called security needs being advanced as justification. Given Pakistan's feelings of insecurity arising out of the Afghan development, the recent Indian decision to acquire more arms from the Soviet Union cannot but frighten Pakistan. It is here that an Indian initiative for disarmament could be beneficial to a regional détente.

However, if Pakistan's senior allies, the USA and China, succeed in superimposing their own interests on those of Pakistan, then a conflict of interests between India and Pakistan will manifest itself more openly. Advising America to understand the Russian motivations in proper perspective is of paramount importance to regional détente too. The Western European perspective on the situation, with which the Indian view largely coincides, may prove effective in softening the American reaction.

There is not likely to be any appreciable change in the Indo-Pakistan equation even in the event of change in the internal power structure in Pakistan. On the crucial Afghan issue, important sections of the present Pakistani opposition are more restrained in their reactions and hence seem amenable to a settlement with Afghanistan and not unduly suspicious of India's role in the matter.

A Nuclear Race?

It cannot be denied that beneath the surface of diplomatic dialogue there is the latent prospect of a nuclear race. Pakistan's quest for a nuclear explosive capability is nearer fruition, though estimates differ in this regard. (Palit and Namboodiri, 1979; Sinha and Subramanian, 1980, pp. 130–145). Prima facie, a Pakistani nuclear explosion will constitute a major independent variable in the strategic situation in the sub-continent. To be sure, a Pakistani nuclear explosion should not come as a surprise to India, for it is safe to assume that in 1974 the Indian policy makers took it for granted that Pakistan would seek nuclear parity with India. Still if Pakistan actually tests a device India, as stated by Mrs. Gandhi, may relax its self-imposed moratorium and resume its own tests. The International Institute for Strategic Studies suggests three possible alternatives in this regard; (1) Pakistan developing its centrifuge facility but stopping short of a test explosion; (2) a Pakistani test followed by the shelving of Pakistan's programme and continued Indian restraint; (3) limited Indian and Pakistani testing and stock-piling of nuclear weapons but without creation of a dedicated nuclear force. Of these three, the spiral is not likely to go beyond the second stage. (IISS, 1980, pp. 19, 20).

Relations with Bangladesh

India's relations with Bangladesh will continue to be characterised by external cordiality and latent suspicion. The Janata government was very eager to accommodate Dacca's demands as the Farakka agreement illustrated. Mrs. Gandhi's new government on the other hand is more circumspect. It perhaps feels that the post-Mujibur regime in Dacca is prone to picture India as a big brother.

There is also feeling that Bangladesh is seeking deliberately to widen purely bilateral issues like riparian disputes. Such conflicts in perception will continue to plague Indo-Bangladesh relations. India would do well to accept the demand for a multi-lateral approach to the river water dispute by inviting Nepal into the talks, thereby showing that it has no intention to gain by insisting on bilateral solutions alone. With the widespread eruption of violence in its North-East, India is likely to be chary of Bangladesh's role also, particularly because of latent but persistent fears of possible China-Bangladesh collusion to destabilise India's North-Eastern borders.

Trends in India's Defence Capability

In view of the likelihood of Pakistan acquiring a nuclear capability is it probable that the sub-continent may in the future witness a nuclear war? Maybe. But analysis can safely proceed on the assumption that for the coming decade conventional war remains the pattern. In terms of the Army, now that its strength has reached the one million mark no further quantitative growth will be seen in the coming years. Acquisition of more sophisticated armour, particularly tanks, will receive priority. The Airforce is already scheduled for a more than modest expansion programme. Under the Jaguar deal, by the mid 1980s Britain will have supplied 40 Jaguars with about 110 more to be manufactured in India under licence. Thus 150 of these will have been added by the end of the decade. (IISS, 1977–1980, pp. 55, 56,; Niesewand, 1980). A new arms race already underway may be manifested more conspicuously in the acquisition of newer and better aircraft both by India and Pakistan.

But it is in the naval field that the expansion of India's defence capability will be manifested prominently. Trends indicate that the regional environment will be crisis prone and India will try to hasten towards attaining a naval strength commensurate with its perceived role. Though a precise definition of such a role cannot be given, it would be a combination of roles ranging from coastal surveillance, and patrolling of the Indian Ocean, to a capability to engage in hostile action, including antisubmarine warfare. (Kohli, 1975, pp. 105–112). To be sure, even with an appreciable expansion only a very modest capability in these functions would be possible. Yet in terms of a symbolic projection of power as well as an ability to measure up to the capabilities of other regional powers, India will feel it worthwhile to undertake further expansion. As a former Chief of Naval Staff has said, "up to 1971, Indian maritime strategic thinking was largely focused on the north Arabian Sea and north Bay of Bengal. Today, it is obvious that it must look south of the latitude of Mangalore-Madras". (Kohli, 1975, p. 145). (Mangalore-Madras lie about 12.5 degrees north of the Equator). In fact, this trend continued throughout the decade. So India will have to diversify its concern particularly in the south-easterly direction. The defence of India's off-shore positions, particularly the Andaman and the Nicobar island groups, is receiving greater attention. Strategically these islands, if properly exploited, are as much an asset as they are a liability if neglected. These islands are now being garrisoned by the Army. The need to make the islands into a major naval centre is now recognised, and a tri-service base is a distinct likelihood.

Greater naval activity will also be accompanied by increased economic and political contacts. But, while naval contacts between India and the South East Asian countries may increase, any degree of naval co-operation is improbable. India's connection with Vietnam will remain close and this to a degree may inhibit any major ventures in Indo-ASEAN cooperation.

It is important to mention that the reluctant consensus that emerged in the last decade about containing the superpower rivalry in the Indian Ocean can no longer be sustained. This seems to be a certain casualty of the Russian intervention in Afghanistan.

Insurrectionary Activity

One of the important dimensions of security, especially in developing countries, is the challenge posed by insurrection. India has so far experienced insurrection on a fairly intensive scale, though its vastness and a successful nation-building process have contained the problem at a manageable level. Two types of insurrection could be identified. The first arose in the North Eastern border areas in which ethnic and historic diversities played a role. It is more secessionist in character. Since these areas are adjacent to China the role of the external factor in the spread of insurrection was considerable. India has handled this danger by eliminating disaffection in critical areas and by consolidating links with the masses of the population.

The second type of insurrectionary activity is connected with extreme leftist revolutionary ideologies tracing their pedigree from Mao to Ho Chi Minh to Che Guevara. Ideologically these movements also have external linkages. The Indian government treated this type of movement as a straight law and order problem entrusting the problem to the police and not to the Army. Viewed in terms of Thompson's three stages of revolutionary warfare, namely subversion leading to insurgency, guerrilla warfare and takeover, (Laqueur, 1977, p. 378), the Indian insurrections never came even within the sight of the third stage.

As for the future, some theories of insurrection link the phenomenon with unrealised aspirations for social change. A recent predictive study of world security endorses the view that in future peasant revolutions it will be the middle rank peasant proprietor rather than the landless labourer who will spearhead an uprising. (Brown, 1977, p. 142). But in India, whatever ideological insurgency is there seems to spring from the grass roots level of landless labourers though often inspired by urban intellectuals. These uprisings will not pose a serious threat to India.

The prospect for a secessionist type of insurrection is more complex. The North Eastern marchlands have once again become extremely sensitive. Unprecedented agitations in Assam and other areas occured in 1980 and the role of India's neighbours in these agitations is not above suspicion. While genuine local inequities will have to be sorted out by negotiations, any drift towards secession will have to be tackled as a strategic challenge.

One last but light-hearted point. In their book *The Third World War* Sir John Hackett and others predict an India divided into a plurality of sovereign states; some inclined towards the American bloc and some Soviet oriented. (Hackett, 1979, pp. 33, 67). Even for a futuristic analysis, this is plain imagination. While the inherent potential for India breaking up cannot be overruled, the trend has been in the direction of blunting its edges and building a process of legitimacy for united India. The prospect for the survival of India as a political entity is extremely encouraging.

11 Strategic Thinking in Japan in the 1970s and 1980s

MAKOTO MOMOI

The End of the Old Illusions

Japan has been, still is, and for some time will remain a barren land for sophisticated strategic thinking, much less for doctrines or theories. After the signing of the Japanese surrender on the battleship *Missouri* in September 1945, anything related to military affairs, ex-military officers, facilities, bases, and even people who thought about those things, was considered to be evil. Until very recently military affairs were socially unacceptable. Indeed until a few years ago, the term strategy (senryaku) had been a word for businessmen and sports commentators; in the climate of self delusion, seldom had the word strategy been used as military terminology.

However Japan's climate has changed and a limited number of her academic, bureaucratic and journalistic brains have shifted their attentions to strategic and military issues. Nevertheless there is still a fear of provoking the immediate neighbours, the Soviet Union, North Korea and China, as well as the United States. Whenever in the past Japan has suggested building up armaments to a high level there has been some disquieting noise from Washington saying that Japan should rely on the US. But when Japan has said that it will rely on the US then the Warsaw Pact has asked why Japan does not act more independently. The fear of provoking other countries has remained unconsciously in the minds of Japanese political leaders. This lack of sophisticated thinking about strategic issues in Japan is a result of the rare luxury of living in a dreamland of self-created illusions.

The first illusion was that Japan's geopolitical situation assured her safety for all time. An archipelago surrounded by seas, Japan would be safe from hostile armies unless they acquired effective amphibious or air-lift capabilities to launch an attack. The Japanese believe that as a country in the Far East, superficially armed, bound by an "exclusively defensive defence policy" under constitutional restriction, they will not become a target of major military destruction. Even the Soviet Union's confrontations with the United States did not seem to threaten Japan, for they appeared more interested in expansion to the South or West or directing their missiles northwest towards the US across the Pole. It was only in the past decade that the Soviets seemed to direct their national attention to expansion eastwards – that is into the Pacific Ocean, manifest by gigantic projects like the building of the second Siberian railway and the construction of another pipeline for oil and gas. These have been quite legitimate undertakings and the Soviet desire to increase their Pacific fleet to protect the projects has been understandable. This change to Japan's geo-political environment has come about so quickly that initially few Japanese noticed. But when the people realised that there was an impressive Soviet presence in their immediate neighbourhood the illusion of Japanese safety began to disappear.

Expert Sovietologists have conflicting views as to what the Russians are doing in the Pacific. One view, to which I do not subscribe, is that the Russians have a certain grand strategic design. Another view is that they are simply following the inertia of bureaucracy. They started to build a navy, and when they had the ships they merely distributed them to the northern seas, the Baltic and Black Seas and to the Pacific. But that does not explain why the Russians have about 30 percent of their navy in the Pacific where their supply lines are long and they have no appropriate air cover or air bases to protect their ships.

Whatever the reason for the Russian presence, the expansion of their Pacific Fleet, and in particular the arrival of the *Minsk* has had an important impact on Japanese mass-media. Four to five years ago the Japanese Self-Defence Force provided the newspapers with pictures of Russian ships but could not persuade the newspapers to publish them. Now the Self-Defence Force has merely to tell the press where they can find a particular ship, and they hire their own aeroplanes to fly in very close to take their pictures – often they are better pictures than the defence force reconnaissance planes can take.

The second illusion concerns the perception of contemporary war held by most Japanese. They believe that despite the fact that there have been a minimum of 64 wars in the past 35 years, armed conflict will not affect Japan seriously or directly. This naive notion is in part due to Japan's historical experience or lack of it. Japan has witnessed no land war or foreign invasion of her archipelago in her history. A single exception was in 1274 when Mongolians occupied a portion of Hakata city in Kyushu for about a week. It is true that Japan was bombed very heavily and effectively by the American airforce in the Second World War and suffered tremendous casualties, but there was no land warfare in the homeland. So whenever people talk about war they speak of war not in terms of war in the homeland, but something that has been and will be a foreign, distant war in which Japan will not be involved or affected seriously.

This notion of a distant war has been strengthened by the fact that most of the wars in Asia, with the peculiar exception of two wars, have been either short in period, local in theatre, or limited in violence, and often possessing all of those qualities. Even the Korean War did not have an adverse effect on Japanese life. In fact the Japanese profited economically by helping the US in terms of logistic supply. Most Japanese believed that the Vietnam War would not effect their security – not even in terms of threatening the sea lines of communication.

But in recent years the Japanese perception of war has been changing. After the Middle East War of October 1973, and the subsequent oil shortage, the Japanese public felt the impact of a foreign distant war on their own economic life. Since then, whenever there has been a major armed conflict somewhere in the world the Japanese have become alarmed. For example, after the seizure of the US Embassy in Iran people began to discuss whether Japan was going to face another oil shortage. But despite this change in perception many Japanese do not anticipate that some foreign war might spread to their part of the Pacific and alter their strategic environment. Nevertheless the net result of the events since 1973 has been that military affairs can now be discussed in public. National security has become a respectable word. Indeed in 1979 the late Prime Minister, Ohira, appointed a committee to study what he called "a comprehensive security policy". The report was submitted after his death. Thus, while it is true that a level of sophistication is still lacking in Japanese strategic thinking, at least it can be said that some people are directing attention to strategic issues.

The third illusion concerns the US-Soviet military balance and the belief that the US has been and always will be stronger than the Soviet Union. Thus, since Japan is a security partner of the United States, the Soviet Union will be deterred from waging a major military action against Japan. Usually each Japanese foreign or prime minister when he assumes office travels to Washington, and every time a joint communique is issued which includes the statement that the security treaty with Japan will be "firmly maintained". The illusion that the United States will assist Japan, whatever happens, becomes even more fixed.

The belief that Japan can rely on the United States for her security is based on three assumptions. First, Japan perceived that in relative terms the United States would always be superior to the Soviet Union. Second, the Japanese believed that the United States commitment and action would stop the numerous armed conflicts in the world from escalating to major wars, and third, US military presence and relative "dominance" over other powers in the Pacific-Asian region would be maintained.

Today all these assumptions are challenged. The super-power balance might remain "essentially equivalent" in a purely static analysis, but may turn fluid in a dynamic strategic assessment. The Soviet Union may now believe it is profitable to contemplate a first strike against the US with increased precision and other qualitatively improved strategic offensive systems while their homeland (plus most of the leaders) can expect to survive US retaliatory attacks thanks to the enhanced strategic defence systems. This, of course, remains an untested, unproven war plan, but one cannot rule out a possibility that Kremlin leaders, looking at a numerical balance sheet, might gain politico-psychological overconfidence that in turn could be translated into overbearing attitudes in their diplomatic negotiations with not only the US, but also other nations. To that extent the security of these nations might become unstable in dealing with Moscow.

Since the announcement of the Nixon Doctrine, the US has opted for what her allies perceive to be a worrying selectivity in her security commitment, while the Soviet Union has acquired capabilities to project its politico-military influence to areas distant from Moscow, i.e. Africa, the Middle East and Indochina. Hence local conflicts may increase in their frequency and even escalate in their intensity while Moscow may have better chances than ever of exploiting local situations.

In the Pacific-Asian region, US allies perceive, wrongly or inevitably a general trend of declining US military presence, if not an erosion of US will. One can, of course, argue, as did Secretary Brown in his posture statement in 1978, that China can be a "strategic counterweight against the Soviet Union", but this thesis may be valid only in terms of primarily a land confrontation along the Sino-Soviet border. In a general Japanese perception, the "China card" is not a favourite subject in Japan. In reality, she has no tradition of playing cards or a game of power politics. Nevertheless, the pronouncement by some Chinese leaders supporting the US-Japan Security Treaty has focussed Japanese public attention on the potential Soviet threat and has helped the Japanese public to change their mind about the old illusions.

Previous Japanese Strategic Concepts

During the 1950s Japan had no defence conception at all. Indeed I have elsewhere described this as the period of "total reliance" both physically and conceptually on US initiatives. (1977). In these years a Japanese premier could not even refer precisely to national security or defence, but to "what one might call defence". Toward the end of this period, which coincided with the first revision of the Mutual Security Treaty in 1960, the defence (ground force) build-up was used as a political instrument in bargaining for the early withdrawal of US troops from Japan.

In the first half of the 1960s, the period of "partial reliance", total reliance on the US became impractical, and Japan began to pay for or produce arms itself. During this period, Japan slowly developed a concept of combining its own "strategic defence" with America's "strategic offence" under a conceptual barter arrangement that continued to provide for US base facilities in Japan. Nevertheless, the exchange was far from equal; Japan still depended on US protection or automatic US military involvement. At the time, the US-Japan joint communique of 1965 which stressed that the US was committed to defending Japan "against any armed attack", was highly valued in Tokyo.

In the last half of the 1960s, the period of "selective reliance", the concept of relying selectively on the US was evident in the Third Build-up Plan, which stressed Japan's own capabilities for dealing with air and sea aggression "most effectively". The idea of "autonomous defence" also began to appear in official statements, although there was still little concrete idea of how to achieve it. At the same time, reference to US military help in a Japanese land war virtually disappeared, and the expectation of immediate US assistance in air and sea combat operations was, perhaps inadvertently, played down.

The 1970s, however, turned out to be the period of "conceptual de-Americanization", which gradually emerged after the announcement of the Guam (Nixon) Doctrine. First came the draft Defence White Paper of Arita Kiichi which gave top priority to "autonomy" in Japan's defence posture and spoke of a possible "delay" in the arrival of US help. Nakasone Yasuhiro, who succeeded Arita as Minister for Defence in January 1970, published the White Paper in October of that year, but unlike Arita's draft it did not emphasise a "rejection of non aligned neutrality", but stressed the need to reverse the manner in which the Japanese viewed their security relations with the US. Nakasone urged increased expenditure on arms but could not push his plans through Parliament.

A year later the Minister for Defence, Nishimura Naomi explained his "philosophy on self-defense – on a strategy of limited response" to foreign correspondents in Tokyo (October 11, 1971). The basic strategy, which he admitted was still in the conceptual stage, was based on the belief that there is a "natural limit for any country, whatever its economic, technological, or spiritual potential, to counter military threat with military power". Moreover, "every country has its own list of priorities at a given time for the allocation of its resources". Therefore, the Japanese should (1) "objectively assess our own strategic and geopolitical vulnerability"; (2) "plan our comprehensive national security policy to maximize the effectiveness of our limited capabilities"; and (3) "make realistic options in terms of the most likely contingencies and our own limited capabilities for dealing with possible threats, both manmade and natural". Based on this line of thinking, Nishimura outlined his "three-point comprehensive national security policy":

(a) To maintain the minimum level of defence capability necessary to deter and resist an aggression against Japan whatever the changes in both threats and international environments;

(b) To secure air and sea safety in Japan's peripheral areas in a manner that will not threaten Japan's neighbours;

(c) To endeavour to stabilize Japan's diplomatic relations with others and to extend nonmilitary assistance to the rest, in particular to Asian nations.

Nishimura's thesis, although primarily philosophical, did define Japan's defence posture as one of limited response, which presumably ruled out the possibility of acquiring most "counterthreat" capabilities. Unfortunately, Nishimura left office before he had time to elaborate his concept further.

The Arita paper, Nakasone's "autonomous defence first" thesis, and Nishimura's "strategy of limited response" all represent the first serious Japanese efforts to develop their own defence concept. Most important, all avoided the previous Japanese tendency towards wishful thinking and proceeded to assess Japan's strategic environment more realistically. None of these plans survived in its original substance. Arita's was perhaps too provocative in the political climate then prevailing in Japan; Nakasone's was too ambitious budgetarily if not conceptually; and Nishimura's was too philosophical to gain public acceptance. Nevertheless, the changes in the international strategic environment that have developed since the October (1973) War in the Middle East have undeniably revealed the extent of Japan's strategic vulnerability. Japan's strategic options are indeed limited, but such limitations might impose a conceptual framework for the future development of Japan's strategic thinking.

Towards the late 1970s, the Soviet Union increased its presence in the Pacific and expanded its naval activities; their improved capabilities had been demonstrated in their global exercises in 1970 and 1975. The naval presence per se, however did not alarm the Japanese public. What did shock the Japanese was the Soviet invasion of Afghanistan in the closing month of the 1970s. It was a bonanza for Japan's defence circles in terms of public relations; the public was awake and strategic "talks" now acquired a new citizenship in the Japanese community which had remained closed to military affairs, more or less.

Until then Japan in general remained confused in her strategic discussion, mainly due to her inexperience in, and her traditional (postwar) attitudes towards, strategic issues. Post-war Japan turned passive in her approaches to strategic affairs: the long continued, almost exclusive reliance on US strategic policies, a unique concept of "exclusively defensive defence" was the basic guideline of defence preparedness and produced a long standing policy of not possessing strategic weapons, i.e. long range bombers or any others that might reach targets in territories of other countries.

Current Problems in Japanese Defence Planning

An enduring problem in Japanese defence planning is her geo-political position. With a land mass of 372,488 square kilometres Japan is less than one twentieth the size of Australia, and only one-fifth of its land is relatively flat. Furthermore, the country is divided into four islands, so there is little scope for mobile defensive operations. There is no strategic depth. Japan is also close to the Asian continent – China and the Soviet Union are only some 400–500 kilometres away across the Yellow and Japan Seas. The entire archipelago is within range of Soviet TU-16s, not to mention medium range ballistic missiles, and the northern part can even be reached with MiG 21s or IL-28s.

Japan's demographic distribution makes defence even more difficult. Of a population of some 120,000,000, about 24.5 percent live in the vicinity of Tokyo and a further 14.2 percent live in the Osaka-Kobe area. Thus some 40 percent of the population can be hostage to a single submarine with 16 missiles which could be lurking somewhere near the Philippines. The submarine could distribute eight missiles to each population area.

By contrast the Soviet Union has about 25 percent of its population living in one hundred large cities. A similar percentage of the American population lives in ten large cities. In China, about 14 percent of the population lives in over one thousand large cities. Therefore it is not possible for Japan to have a meaningful nuclear weapons system. If Japan is to have a second strike capacity, the people have to be persuaded to accept the possibility of losing between 24 and 40 percent of their population.

In addition to these geopolitical facts, Japan has decided that she will not produce nuclear weapons, will not acquire nuclear weapons and will not allow deployment of nuclear weapons in the homeland. It is not known whether the Soviet Union believes that Japan will maintain these principles, but whatever the Soviets believe, Japan must rely upon the "regional nuclear umbrella" of the United States.

In terms of conventional defence Japan faces considerable problems. The army now spends about 80 percent of its budget on manpower; the navy and airforce spend 45–46 percent of their budgets on manpower. Yet conscription does not seem feasible. Furthermore, modern technology requires long periods of training and in return the services need personel who will serve for many years.

At the moment the government is attempting to raise the expenditure on defence from 0.9 percent to 1.0 percent of the GNP over the next two or three years. But consensus has to be built slowly. Perhaps a target of 1.2 percent will be possible by 1990. The argument always comes back to the problem of the social acceptability of defence.

Japan's Strategic Concepts

At the moment Japan has a tactical territorial defence programme which is heavily dependent on closer ties with the US in terms of naval-air operations, but what is Japan's underlying strategic concept? In determining a strategic concept Japan's first problem is in understanding the world military balance in general and the Pacific military balance in particular. It is recognised that numbers do not automatically foretell the outcome of battles; yet they represent the easier indices for the public to perceive the existing state of static factors in the military balance – quality, command, control and communications, logistics and morale are more difficult for the public to appraise.

Static figures are easy to understand; hence the public is impressed when given the figures of 785 ships of 1,520,000 tons in the Soviet Pacific Fleet in 1980 compared with some 50 US ships of about 706,000 tons. Furthermore the Russians have 120 submarines, 16 of them nuclear powered, in the area, most of them operating out of Petropavlovsk on the Kamchatka Peninsula. They are therefore free from any blockade of the three straits of Japan, and are well placed to operate against the shortest lines of communications between Japan and the United States.

Japan has become worried by the Russian behaviour. In the last OKEAN exercise in 1975 the Russians used the Japanese archipelago as a dummy target for their amphibious and bombing exercises. It is true that the Russians find it extremely difficult to resupply the Petropavlosk base, for it has no overland supply lines and all supplies must be brought in by ship. The sea lanes for this resupply are through the Kurile Islands, four of which the Japanese claim is their territory. But nevertheless, the Soviet Pacific fleet is a formidable force.

If there is some assymetry in the conventional military balance, for example, in naval forces, what should Japan do? Should she increase her capabilities to fill the gap? But an even more important question is how to recognise this assymetry. The Chairman of the US Joint Chiefs of Staff claims that the Soviets are a threat, but the Congressional Research Bureau says that in overall capabilities the Soviet Union is far behind, and this latter view seems to be designed to discourage Japan from increasing her defence capabilities. If the majority of the Japanese public are persuaded that the Soviet Union is an increasingly menacing power to be reckoned with in the Pacific, then there may be wider support for an increased Japanese naval build-up, but this will most likely stop short of a substantial quantitative increase. It may take years, longer than a decade, before the public will develops faith in a balancing game.

The military balance is not therefore a good starting point for developing Japanese strategic concepts. A more viable approach is the scenario-contingency approach. This emphasises the dynamic aspects of crises; by definition it assumes (at least theoretically,) that the US deterrence has collapsed, either totally, leading to nuclear exchanges and with conflicts spreading globally, or partially.

The Japanese tend to focus their attention on the latter, since for most of them the former is difficult to envisage in concrete terms. In thinking about the thinkable (the latter), moreover, the Japanese are psychologically prepared for the worst case scenarios:

a) Circumstances, either external or internal, might keep the US from commiting herself to the direct defence of Japan *in time*, or

b) What the US can commit might be the crisis deployment of her naval/air forces for either tactical deterrent or localization purposes, or

c) If involved in the direct defence of Japan, the US might stop short of a wholesale counterbase retaliatory offence of fear of escalation.

The contingency-scenario approach does not seem appropriate for developing Japanese strategic concepts since it might result in increased defence spending which is unpopular. The most appropriate approach is therefore to avoid conflict or to manage crises.

In the Japanese view there are three factors in avoiding conflict or managing crises, and each factor can be divided into three elements. The first factor is that it is considered that relative international peace primarily depends on continued US-Soviet detente or a reduction of the risk of global nuclear exchange, internal politico-economic stability of resource-supplying states, and the relative safety of surface and air lines of communication. The second factor is that it is considered that regional security in Asia can be best maintained by a balance of politico-military influence among intra- and extra-regional states, economic-social stability of regional nations, and minimum gaps in economic-industrial growth among the nations. The third factor is that it is considered that Japan's own domestic stability will continue so long as she maintains relative politico-social stability or recoverability of a balance if and when it is undermined, her favourable economic growth, and her territorial integrity by both her own efforts and the stable and close security ties with the US.

All these three factors (nine sub-elements) are not mutually exclusive but interdependent. A striking element of such security perception is a relative downgrading of military power. It certainly remains a vital ingredient of Japan's security, but is far from a dominant element. On the other hand, under this perception, a strong emphasis is placed on three measures in terms of policy: first, identifying the causes of conflict, both military and non-military; second, managing crises under preplanned scenarios and in collaboration with other states concerned; and third, terminating the conflict before it develops to an unmanagable degree.

This chapter does not attempt to give a value judgement on the Japanese approaches to her strategic thinking. In all fairness the third (conflict cause/issue) approach is more comprehensive than the others; in fact it incorporates – in different degrees – both the military balance and the scenario-contingency approaches. Nevertheless, Japan most likely will continue to perceive her security environments by mixing the three approaches.

Each has its particular merit. For intelligence (and public relations) purposes, the military-balance is valuable and easily perceivable; for defence planning the scenario-contingency approach is indispensable. The demerit of the two lies in their primarily regional/territorial nature. The strength of the third approach is its global character; its defect is the absence of concrete policy proposals. How then can Japan contribute to the relative international peace and to the regional security?

One idea is to allocate a certain percentage of GNP (say, 3 to 7%) to the three basic security factors and to give the flexibility of changing the percentage of suballocation to the nine subelements in accordance with the degree of need or crisis aspects. Such a money-oriented ("buy friendship") policy inevitably has its own built-in limits.

Sooner or later, perhaps by the late 1980s when new generations of leaders will be in power throughout the world, Japan will have faced a hard decision; how to go beyond the money-oriented policy in contributing to international peace and regional security. Japan may soon start talking about the regional aspects of her security environment; but it will take some time for her to formulate policies and undertake actions.

In the meantime, the Pacific-Asian region will remain potentially unstable. Most of the regional states enjoy (or suffer from) economic growth of different magnitudes; political systems are different country by country. In this region there are three nuclear powers involved directly; it is also in this region where three major issues are potentially in dispute – territories, offshore oil deposits, and choke points.

These issues could at any time flare up; major regional disputes could escalate quickly if extraregional powers are involved. If the Pacific is to remain the ocean of peace, its security and stability ought to be reviewed in a global context, in particular in a closer connection with those of the Atlantic.

Conclusion

The first task for Japan is to analyse and attempt to understand US policies. This is the most difficult task. Second, Japan has to make every possible effort to make it easier for the United States to fulfil its commitments. Third, there has to be a division of labour with the United States in strategic matters. If these tasks can be undertaken then Japan can make a contribution, if only indirectly, to the overall security status of the Western alliance.

But it is only in recent years that Japan has taken an interest in the Western alliance. The first stimulus came with the oil price rises of 1973–74, has been continued by economic pressure from Washington over the sales of cars, television sets and electronic goods, and has culminated with the events in Iran and Afghanistan. There has, however, been a reluctance to actually joining an alliance with the West. Historically Japan has enjoyed relative peace when allied with one country; the Anglo-Japanese alliance in the first part of the century and the US-Japanese alliance today. It was a big mistake to abrogate the Anglo-Japanese alliance. Instead Japan took a multiple alliance with Germany and Italy that brought catastrophe. So historically Japan feels better allied with a single powerful country, that is the United States. And even if Japan formally joined the Western alliance there is a limit to what she can contribute in material terms.

Japan might be able to undertake the following programmes. First, surveillance capabilities could be increased. These would include land-based aircraft and submarine surveillance in Japanese waters and to a certain extent in neighbouring regional areas. Second, sea control capabilities could be increased, particularly around the straits. Third, there should be capacity to provide logistic support for US forces. Fourth, there should be economic and technical cooperation with countries possessing resources used by Japan and countries on the edge of Japan's sea-line of communication. Fifth, Japan should develop a better crisis management system, including national command posts. All this, of course, means an increased expenditure on defence, and that depends, as stressed previously, on public support. Thus until public opinion changes, Japanese strategic thinking will continue to remain unsophisticated.

Section Three
The Development of Concepts Governing Non-Nuclear Warfare

12 The Development of Concepts for Conventional Warfare in the 1970s and 1980s

KENNETH HUNT

Introduction

It is said that generals always plan to fight the last war. There is obviously at least some truth in this: they lean on their experiences, on received doctrine, on weapons that are no more than improvements of older ones. And new technology tends to be brought in incrementally, so that change comes slowly. Established methods are often adapted rather than supplanted by others designed to take full advantage of the opportunities that new weapons give.

There are now not all that many generals who fought in World War Two, but some of those who did will have been influenced by the battles in which tanks and air power played such a part, and those that have followed them have read their history. So it is possible to see the practices of 1945 still there in the concepts in Europe now, on both sides. But the lessons of other wars have been drawn on too, notably those of the Middle East, which have provided a convenient laboratory in which tactics and the comparative performance of weapon systems were on test, with the Israelis energetic and intelligent demonstrators. It is worth noting in passing though, that the young Israeli generals were not proof against the old adage either: their initial setbacks in October 1973 were the result of their leaning too simply on the experience of June 1967.

It is fair then to make the point that the conventional concepts of the 1970s still owed much to the campaigns of a quarter of a century before. It must immediately be added, though, that the introduction of nuclear weapons in the intervening years had its own radical effect. Deterrence rather than just defence became the basis of the security policies of those nations that had to take nuclear weapons into account, and budgets and thus armies were tailored accordingly. Indeed there was a period in the 1950s when the role of conventional forces in NATO strategy was a very subordinate one, a mere trip-wire for nuclear retaliation. Their task was to deal with infiltration and minor aggression, leaving response to major attack to the nuclear strike forces. French strategy much later than this assigned to the conventional arm no more than the job of recognising that major aggression had occurred (*agression caracterisée*), after which the nuclear *force de frappe* would threaten Soviet cities if it did not stop. There was a phase in the 1960s in NATO too, when the idea of battlefield nuclear war-fighting had its adherents, and the *Davy Crockett* was introduced so that even infantry companies could have their own nuclear weapons. It seems extraordinary that the thinking behind such a proliferation should have taken hold, but more of this later.

The concept of the very early use of nuclear weapons gave way within NATO in 1967 to the strategy of Flexible Response. This was designed to meet an attack with whatever level of force was needed to defeat it, including the use of nuclear weapons if necessary, but was clearly intended to put off this nuclear use for as long as possible, making the conventional forces the first line of defence (unless an attack was a nuclear one). Outside Europe, concepts remained conventional, either because there were no nuclear weapons (though Israel may have had a bomb), or because, as in Korea and Southeast Asia, it was not thought politically acceptable to use them.

Since Europe is the theatre where the major armed confrontation has persisted and to which most military resources have been devoted, it seems appropriate to look first at how concepts have been developed there.

The European Theatre

NATO Strategy

The concept of Flexible Response was only agreed upon within NATO after a bitter debate lasting several years. When it was finally adopted, France refused to go along and left the integrated military organisation, preferring her own strategy of immediate nuclear retaliation against Soviet territory to anything more graduated in nature. But the other European allies had their own problems with it too, and with its inherent requirement for a stronger conventional element in the defence. They accepted the need for strong conventional forces, because these could defend territory as nuclear weapons could not and could cope with lesser contingencies while doing so. They also saw their utility as the first stage of deterrence, offering the chance of putting off a nuclear decision which began to look increasingly uncomfortable as Soviet nuclear strength grew. They did not, however, want conventional forces that were *too* strong, did not want a purely conventional defence because this would not pose the same level of risk for the Soviet Union as would a strategy patently prepared to use nuclear weapons. And they recoiled from the idea of a long-drawn out conventional war in Europe. Hence the Europeans were not prepared

CONVENTIONAL WARFARE IN THE 1970s AND 1980s

to build up conventional forces to the point at which the nuclear element in the strategy was evidently downgraded. This policy was convenient because it saved money. Deterrence thus remained essentially nuclear, based, as has been sharply observed, on conventional insufficiency.

The Flanks In practice the argument was mainly about the defence of the central sector, since the strategy for the flanks while nominally the same looked as if it could be applied differently.

On the *Northern Flank*, Norway had an aversion to nuclear weapons and would allow none on her soil. The rugged nature of the terrain coupled with the climate provided the framework for a purely conventional defence concept built around nationwide mobilisation. Light infantry and coastal batteries offered the chance of fighting holding or delaying battles in a region deeply pitted with fjords and with few roads. To help redress the numerical imbalance – Norwegian forces could be heavily outnumbered by Soviet divisions from the Kola region – reinforcement by allies was counted on, and reliance was placed on NATO navies to keep Soviet forces from the Norwegian Sea. A nuclear threat could in fact be posed if needed, since there were nuclear weapons on NATO aircraft and ships, but the Norwegian intention was fairly clear, to organise the defence otherwise. Nothing has altered this approach since 1967, though the growth of the Soviet Navy now makes allied operations in the Norwegian Sea hazardous, making sea reinforcement of the northern part of the country more difficult.

Denmark's attitude to nuclear weapons was rather similar, but with some ambiguity: she allowed none on her soil, but acquired dual-capable launchers for nuclear warheads which remained in American custody elsewhere. Her defence faced different problems, tied up closely as it was with the adjacent central sector, with a flat terrain utterly different from that of north Norway and also exposed to attack from the Baltic. Again, a national call-up was planned and allied reinforcement and naval assistance expected, but Danish defence almost certainly had the conventional phase of Flexible Response largely in mind.

On the *Southeast Flank* there was, on the face of it, no such ambiguity: both Greece and Turkey acquired nuclear weapons launchers, ground and air, and permitted the American-held warheads to be stored locally. But in Turkey at least, there was a possibility of a lengthy conventional defence, given the terrain and the large numbers of strong and tough Turkish forces, so that any need for nuclear weapons might well not come until after that stage had been reached in the central sector, by which time the whole course of the war was unknowable. The implementation of the strategy could therefore be different. However, Turkish defence does not look at all the same now. The armed forces were considerably weakened in the 1970s by the US Congressional arms embargo imposed after the invasion of Cyprus, and their ability to operate with ill-equipped, largely infantry divisions against the mechanised forces opposing them, and with a very rundown air force, must be in question. It will take many years to put right the damage and the country's economic and social problems now aggravate the situation alarmingly. Furthermore, the allied ability to help militarily has become circumscribed. The US Sixth Fleet in the Eastern Mediterranean, designed as a projection force to be able to take part with aircraft and amphibious forces in the land battle, is now opposed by a strong Soviet naval squadron supported by *Backfire* land-based anti-ship aircraft. The Sixth Fleet can give little support to Greece and Turkey until it has first won the sea battle, an important time constraint. Given the importance that the Soviet Union must place on the seizure of the Turkish Straits, allied defences now have obvious problems. The Soviet Union has, by deploying naval force, succeeded in impeding the NATO concept of projecting force on land.

The Central Sector   The logic of the adoption of Flexible Response was, and has been since, that the conventional forces should be strengthened, since they were being required to fight for longer. The air forces in particular had to plan on engaging with conventional weapons targets that had previously been nuclear, a much more demanding task. In fact there has been little strengthening and since Soviet forces have been built up considerably, the NATO relative position is worse than it was in 1967. And measures taken in the 1970s to make Soviet forward divisions less reliant on prior reinforcement has had the effect of reducing the warning time that NATO can expect, thus making its own timely reinforcement harder.

NATO conventional ground forces have a purely defensive layout and little ability to move forward other than for local counter-attack or with air strikes. The deployment is based on the concept of forward defence, so as to be able to hold territory and implement deterrence right on the inner-German border. From the time that West Germany joined the Alliance it was clearly essential to defend the country from the front, so to speak, and the build-up of German formations in the late 1950s and 1960s made possible the move forward from the earlier rearward defences on the Rhine and Weser.

Forward defence is necessary for both political and deterrence reasons, but it has often been observed that the border may well not be the best place to stand and fight, there may be obstacles or other terrain features further back which could make defence easier. Thus militarily it might be advisable once fighting started to give ground in places. And it might be unwise to put too many forces far forward, since they could be cut off by a successful enemy penetration, leaving the defences weak. Obviously commanders do have some tactical flexibility, but they must nonetheless defend well forward. There is no alternative, politically or militarily.

The Layout Since it is essential to be able to start fighting on the frontier, light armoured screening and delaying forces are deployed across the front, as a peacetime presence and to give warning in war. They can fight for information and are strong enough to force the enemy to deploy and thus to impose delay, to give time for the main NATO forces to reach their operational areas from their peacetime locations often well to the rear, and for reinforcements to arrive. These reinforcing units and formations are mobilised from reserves in the continental European countries or come into the theatre along with air squadrons from the United Kingdom, the United States and Canada, marrying up with prepositioned equipment so as to allow for speedy air movement with only personal weapons.

Behind the screening forces are the ground holding formations, mechanised for the most part, with some organic armour and increasingly more anti-tank capability. The defence – which is divided into national sectors, a structure which has its political importance but military weaknesses – thus has a linear look about it dependent on the number of troops available in each sector and on the nature of the terrain. Immediately behind the ground holding divisions are the armoured counter-attack formations, though in one or two of the weaker sectors armoured or mechanised divisions are committed to ground holding since they are the only ones available; their reinforcements, often lighter in armour, would have to be used for counter-attack, a reversal of roles dictated by a shortage of resources. Further back, behind the counter-attack formations and under the operational control of army commanders or the Supreme Allied Commander, Europe, (SACEUR), as theatre reserves, are such divisions or brigades as can be kept back from the initial battle or accumulated from incoming reinforcements.

Tactical doctrines Tactical doctrines can vary between sectors, being governed by equipment availability, terrain or national styles. The US Army, deployed where much of the ground lends itself to defence and heavy in armour, plans on fighting a battle of attrition, wearing the enemy down. Much reliance is placed, as is the American habit, on fire-power including that from army fixed-wing aircraft and helicopters. The German Army counts on a much more mobile battle, using manoeuvre to cut off and destroy enemy attacking forces, and to do this has developed armoured vehicles from which infantry can fight (as distinct from using them only to get to the scene of the fighting). The British forces plan an enfilading battle, harrying penetration from the flanks and counter-attacking with armour, tactics influenced both by the ground and the lack of numbers to provide sufficient operational reserves.

Ideas on the control of tactical air forces also vary. The US plans to operate in force at medium height, using aircraft together for defence suppression and interdiction, with airborne early warning and control aircraft (AWACS) directing air defence fighters on to incoming aircraft. Other air forces favour very low-level, under-the-radar penetration of enemy defences by small numbers of aircraft. Control would ideally still be at the highest level possible, but it is envisaged that the confusion of the battle might mean aircraft being directed by wings. These national differences stem to some extent from different resources, but the various air headquarters are probably flexible enough to adapt operations to suit the conditions. Steadily improving Warsaw Pact air defences are in any case likely to compel most aircraft to fly very low, perhaps later to be replaced by cruise missiles for some tasks when these become available for the conventional role.

Warsaw Pact Concepts

Put simply, the Warsaw Pact, with formations heavy in tanks and supporting armoured vehicles, is thought to have developed a concept of simultaneous assault right across the front so as to tie down all NATO defences and initially conceal the point of decisive attack, but with the main weight directed at only two or three points. There would probably be a separate thrust into Schleswig-Holstein and Denmark, so as to cut off that sector and seize the Baltic exits. Armoured spearhead formations would try to penetrate NATO defences deeply on relatively narrow fronts, continuing the battle by day and night, with the leading divisions being changed as necessary, like a bit on a drill. Success would be reinforced and formations that succeeded in breaking through the defences would fan out so as to cut off NATO from its reinforcements. Artillery and rocket launchers would be used to suppress anti-tank defences. Close air support would be provided for leading units and interdiction attacks mounted against reinforcing columns and against HQ. Airborne troops might disrupt rear areas and seize key points. Electronic Counter Measures (ECM) could be widely used against ground and air links and against radars. Chemical weapons could also be used as part of the main attack or selectively against important targets.

The Development of the Concepts

The Warsaw Pact

There is a familiar look to the Pact concept described above: it is not at all unlike that attempted by the German Army in World War Two, but with notions of Soviet mass and fire-power superimposed. It relies heavily on tanks and on the armoured mobility which the German forces did not often have, since their armoured divisions were few. Soviet divisions are very strong in firepower but relatively lean logistically, relying on support from behind.

The concept is thus partly new to the Soviet Union but not to the theatre. Whether the Soviet soldier can adapt and extemporise at speed, free of central direction, as could the German soldier at all levels, and whether the Soviet society's predilection for central direction will allow him to do so, is uncertain. Perhaps things would be rather more deliberate, more cautious than the pattern described.

The concept has been refined as more armour and more self-propelled artillery and the like has become available. In earlier years there was much emphasis in Soviet writing on the notion that all wars would be nuclear, that the nuclear weapon was another form of fire-power that would be used to accompany any major attack. This use of nuclear weapons from the outset certainly cannot be ruled out; they are more accurate now, with smaller yields. But Soviet ground forces have also achieved conventional superiority in Europe and thus have some incentive to try conventional attack first, thus avoiding the nuclear retaliation on Pact allies or Soviet territory that a nuclear attack would surely bring.

In the 1970s there has been much more emphasis in the literature, training and equipment, on the conventional battle. And there has been heavy investment in chemical weapons, perhaps as a substitute for early nuclear fire. Yet the development of more accurate medium-range missiles such as the SS-20 has taken place at the same time and prompted fears in the West that they are designed to be used selectively in conjunction with conventional attack, with the aim of destroying NATO command, control and communication (C3) networks and nuclear launchers, crippling both the conventional defence and the ability to retaliate with theatre nuclear weapons. There is no means of knowing whether there is any such Soviet plan, but if there were it would have to weigh the risk of immediate nuclear retaliation from surviving systems or from outside the theatre. On balance, the choice of the conventional option first seems more likely.

NATO

The NATO concept has, almost from the beginning been shaped by the imperative of holding territory, in face of the Soviet expansionism that established a hold over Eastern Europe and led to the formation of the Alliance. It has always been a defensive one as far as the conventional ground forces are concerned. There has never been any serious notion of moving into Eastern Europe nor the ability to do it, beyond air strikes.

The concept has largely pitted tank against tank, only slowly taking advantage in the late 1970s of the new anti-tank guided weapons (ATGW) to give infantry and lighter formations some ability to defend against armour and so free the tanks for their proper role of mobile fire power. Reliance on close air support, more likely to be available in earlier years, has now lessened as it has become clear that the tactical air forces, outnumbered, could not achieve air superiority and, faced with the necessity to penetrate dense air defences, would have few aircraft to spare for ground support. While the introduction of armed helicopters has done something to ease this situation, they are not plentiful and would have to be husbanded.

The other side of the coin, the fact that Soviet tactical air forces have been changing their role from one of primarily air defence, now taken over largely by surface to air missiles (SAMs), to offensive action with aircraft newly designed for the purpose, has meant that NATO defending forces have had to give belated attention to their own air defences. Without some improvement – and this is an area where NATO is arguably at its weakest – the mobility needed to be able to make best use of stretched resources and to counter attack could be sharply limited by enemy air action. The problem of providing air cover for troops on the move or at least for a limited time or space, is one that has to be solved. Combat divisions must somehow keep the enemy air off their backs. There is a renewed emphasis on mobile multi-barrel guns and SAMs and on all-arms air defence weapons. There has been rapid improvement in fire-direction radars, aided by the miniaturisation of electronics and the development of airborne warning and control radars, to detect low flying intruding aircraft and direct interceptors on to them.

The alternative way of dealing with enemy aircraft, to put airfields out of action, if only temporarily, received a stimulus from the wars in the Middle East. Air delivered munitions have been developed specifically for this purpose, notably earth-penetrating weapons and fuel-air explosives (which are also effective against air defences). Since NATO airfields are few and crowded, a good deal of effort is put into rapid runway repair and indeed to rapid aircraft repair, so as to patch them up temporarily and get them back into action again quickly.

Area weapons are now important to the ground forces, with the Warsaw Pact being quicker to introduce rocket launchers on a large scale. NATO has however introduced air and rocket delivered minelets, that can be strewn in the path of oncoming armour, thus canalising movement or slowing down or breaking up an attack. Fuel-air explosives could also have a devastating effect on troop concentrations.

Artillery has been much improved, with faster rates of fire, much increased accuracy and mobility. But as with missiles, the capacity to destroy a target has run ahead of the ability to find it. Target acquisition by a variety of means, for example drones with cameras or TV transmitting information in real time, is being developed to overcome the age-old problem of seeing what is on the other side of the hill. Troops can, however, now see much more easily what is coming towards them. Portable infantry radars and sensors give warning and night vision devices extend the daylight.

The mechanisms of command, control and communication, including the dissemination of information, have progressed enormously, though the problem of handling the mass of material that is now available and making intelligent evaluations from it quickly, is a difficult one. Radio links, particularly for front-line units, are now much more reliable, compact and easy to handle. But ECM hovers as a shadow in the wings, since it can be used to black out whole networks or disrupt air and ground weapon systems by interference with their radars. Frequency changing has to be given attention both by users and designers of equipment.

The Influence of Nuclear Weapons

If ECM is there waiting, so are nuclear weapons, and they exercise a inevitable influence over the battlefield.

Conventional battles are best fought by concentrating troops so as to achieve local superiority, at any level from platoon to army. But troops concentrated are potentially valuable nuclear targets, so when there is danger of nuclear weapons being used they must stay dispersed when they can, using long-range fire-power to cover the gaps between units or detachments. If they do concentrate they must be ready to disperse at once, yet stay in good tactical order. This is far easier said than done, but if they simply stay dispersed all the time they may lose the battle conventionally.

But lose the war? Here nuclear weapons appear again, since NATO strategy envisages threatening or using them if the conventional defence cannot hold. Nuclear weapons have therefore been made organic to forward formations. And some aircraft are dual-capable, which may mean they will be husbanded in the conventional phase, in reserve for a nuclear phase which might follow, with its own doctrines and concepts. The advantage of substituting cruise missiles for aircraft in the theatre nuclear role is that tactical aircraft can then be released for the conventional role for which they would be badly needed.

France should perhaps be given special mention again. As has been remarked, French forces remained wedded in the 1960s and early 1970s to a token conventional defence only, leaving major attack to be met with the threat of a nuclear riposte against Soviet territory. But a short-range battlefield missile, *Pluton*, was then deployed in 1974, with a range of no more than 75 miles. It was to be used in conjunction with conventional forces, in Germany no doubt, but in what sort of engagement was not clear. *Pluton* thus put the original nuclear reprisal doctrine in some confusion. Now a slightly longer range missile is being developed, but still only able to reach targets in Germany (or in Eastern Europe if deployed well forward), which may have an Enhanced Radiation ("neutron") warhead to reduce the collateral damage it might do when fired on allied territory. It would be used, perhaps, when the conventional battle was moving towards France and not before, but whatever is contemplated, some element of the flexibility to which France took such objection in 1967 seems to be creeping in. The observation might be made at this point, not altogether kindly, that French nuclear strategy has on its own showing been designed solely for the defence of France and has had almost nothing to do with the defence of anyone else. Yet it has always seemed probable that French forces would in fact take part in any battle in Germany, if only because it is a glacis, and that such fighting would be conventional so long as NATO armies were fighting that way. So there has been some ambiguity about French concepts and still is, but the conventional forces may in future be less subservient to nuclear weapons than they have been.

The Intensity of Operations

The concepts on both sides have, then, been influenced by World War Two, perhaps not surprisingly since Europe was at the centre of it and the weapons used then were not so different from those of to-day. To be sure, the forces are more mobile though more cumbersome. An infantry battalion in central Europe now has a large number of armoured troop carriers and heavy weapons and so a correspondingly heavy maintenance and logistic problem. Artillery regiments have armoured self-propelled (SP) guns and sophisticated electronics. Digging equipment, cranes and other mechanical devices abound. The whole operation of ground forces is much more complex and demanding.

With this has come greatly increased fire-power and accuracy which, as was seen in the October War, discussed later, promises far greater intensity of fighting, casualties and much faster use of munitions. This has reinforced a feeling in the West that, given a possible recourse to nuclear weapons as well, no major war could be of long duration. So warlike stocks on the ground and in reserve are now measured in terms of the consumption rates anticipated for a matter of weeks rather than months, with few nations having any plans at all for the full-scale industrial and manpower mobilisation of the World Wars. The conventional eggs are in effect limited in number and placed in a nuclear basket.

The Future

Will these concepts last through the 1980s? If, for the purpose of this chapter, the assumption is made that the European alliance systems endure, it is tempting to say that they will. But a further assumption has to be made, that nuclear developments let them – it is not possible to treat conventional concepts in Europe in a discrete fashion. For there have long been those who claim that large manpower-intensive armies, which have large economic and social costs, are no longer necessary: nuclear weapons can not only provide deterrence, they can fight the battle too. Warheads with fractional yields (well below one kiloton) could threaten immediate retribution on any attacker setting foot across the border, without the need for messy conventional fighting and retreat. They could thus seal off frontiers better than tanks.

But, of course, there are snags. All wars would be nuclear wars, something which many in the Atlantic Alliance would find unattractive. And what happens if the enemy fires back? Nuclear war-fighting arguments can be made seductively and will be put forward with the assistance of technology. But they look better from Arkansas than from Aachen and seem unlikely to prevail. There seems no satisfactory substitute for men when it is needed to hold national territory. While the strategy in Europe is likely to have a nuclear kernel, conventional forces look like keeping their present role and importance.

But other ways of saving manpower and strengthening the defences have been suggested. There are proposals to reorganise forward formations so as to make ground-holding divisions less mechanised or heavy in armour, using the money and tanks saved to provide thicker and deeper anti-tank missile defences and more counter-attack formations. Greater use of fire power rather than men to hold ground could be complementary to this, giving small detachments weapons with long-range that would enable them to cover large areas of ground and, incidentally, remain relatively dispersed. More promising, perhaps, is a more thorough-going use of reserve manpower, particularly in conjunction with ATGW and lightweight air defence guns and missiles. All conscript systems produce each year large numbers of trained men, relatively few of whom are likely to be used in a short war. Anti-tank, air defence, light infantry and pioneer units could be formed from them in large numbers, to give defence in depth and relieve active army units for front-line tasks. To some extent this is happening now, both Germany and Britain embodying reserve units in their order of battle for immediate action, but more could be done. While money would be needed for their equipment, such units are much cheaper than active ones, since they are paid less and their equipment is used less. Reserve soldiers can and do form pools for reinforcing active units, but not enough use is made of them. The Soviet Union bases its whole military system on such reservists.

All in all, the 1980s do not seem likely to see dramatic changes in concepts in Europe. Technology will make important differences in some operations, of course, but with the long lead times needed to develop new weapon systems, most of those that will be in service in the decade are known about now. Tanks will remain a powerful influence on the battlefield, with frontal armour proof against smaller ATGW becoming widespread. But other armoured vehicles will remain vulnerable since to make them otherwise would drive up costs and weight too far. So the constraints on armoured operations that ATGW have already imposed should continue, with the equation being tipped a little further against the light armoured vehicle by improved mines and weapons.

The Neutrals and the Non-Aligned

There are, of course, nations in Europe outside the alliances who have developed their own conventional concepts. Worth particular notice are three neutral or non-aligned nations, Sweden, Switzerland and Yugoslavia, who have all used national mobilisation as the basis for their defence.

Sweden has modern nationally-built weapon systems and a comprehensive defence that envisages resistance with everything from home guards to armoured brigades on land; with a missile-equipped navy and an air defence with advanced interceptor aircraft. The concept thus ranges across the board, from purely local defence using the terrain and climate, to open fighting with formations where appropriate. It has changed little in the 1970s, beyond taking advantage of more modern weapons and warning systems.

The defence is built around the national policy of non-alignment with a view to neutrality in war, but undoubtedly gains from the existence of NATO. Its problem, however, is the increasing cost that national self-sufficiency is imposing. To develop another advanced fighter aircraft nationally is probably beyond Sweden's means and the burden of the heavily-armed defence is imposing economic strain. The general concept seems likely to endure in the 1980s, rooted as it is in Swedish political attitudes, but financial stringency may force it to be implemented with less ambitious weapon systems. It will therefore be less strong, but will still fulfil the Swedish aim, of making clear that the price of any attack on the country would be very high.

Much the same remarks might be made about *Switzerland*. Here again the natural geographical strength forms the basis of an independent defence built on everything from infantry, mountain and armoured units to modern air defences. The economic burden falls less heavily than in Sweden, partly because far less has been devoted to the national development of weapon systems, and because of the existence of an armaments industry that engages in the overseas sales that Sweden has largely shunned. The concept is tailored very much to the mountains and is somewhat more free of the warning problem that Sweden has, since Switzerland is buffered by other countries. Thus it is likely to be retained in its present form, taking advantage of the modern technology that Switzerland is able to afford and, like Sweden, well able to assimilate.

Yugoslavia presents a rather different case. Politically it occupies a very sensitive position between the Warsaw Pact and the Atlantic Alliance, and the importance of its territorial integrity to the West has been made very clear. NATO would have obvious problems if Yugoslavia were to adhere to the Warsaw Pact or be forcibly occupied: the Soviet navy would have access to Adriatic ports and Italy would have a hostile frontier.

Yugoslavia has however long been intent on maintaining her independence and since she seized this herself has been prepared to defend it through her own efforts. Resistance was originally planned throughout the country based on the partisan campaigns of World War Two, which used the mountains and the tough people to make military occupation by an invader too expensive.

The Soviet invasion of Czechoslovakia in 1968 suddenly heightened a sense of threat and an awareness of Yugoslavia's vulnerability to invasion by heavily armed Pact troops. The result was an overhauling of the whole defence concept and the creation of a Territorial Defence Force (TDF) one million strong, organised down to regions and backed by an active army, navy and air force of some 260,000. TDF tactics were to be based on the World War Two experience; active force tactics were to be used for normal infantry, mountain and armoured engagements when appropriate or demanded; and for air and coastal defence.

The problem though is that all the equipment is old and not very plentiful. There are few modern anti-tank and air defence weapons and aircraft are no match for those in the Soviet air forces. The concept is sound, given the wish for non-alignment, but still has some limitations: it would be difficult even with modern weapons to resist a thrust across the northern part of the country to the sea by a heavily-armoured attacking force, or defend against modern aircraft for long with a small air force. But resistance could no doubt be continued in the mountains and thus offer the possibility of a drawn-out war which an invader might baulk at. The price of invasion would therefore be high; no one doubts the Yugoslav passion for independence.

The concept itself may therefore not change – provided that Yugoslavia remains intact as a country in face of its own divisive nationalities – though the balance between resistance by the active forces and retreat to the mountains may alter if new weapons can be obtained. Economic difficulties stand in the way of this and the West has been reluctant to give much help (the political conditions under which this might be otherwise are outside the scope of this chapter). The whole form of the Yugoslavian defence is, however, a very interesting one, for rather special circumstances.

The Middle East

In the 1960s and 1970s the most important field for the development of conventional concepts was the Middle East. The Arab-Israeli Wars of 1967 and 1973 were closely watched for their tactical lessons and for the comparative performance of weapon systems of Soviet or Western origin.

The 1967 war was dominated by the Israeli air force, which virtually neutralised that of Egypt at a blow and then, in the open skies and terrain of the Sinai, disrupted the movement of Egyptian ground forces, destroying or dispersing them piecemeal. Fast-moving Israeli armoured columns, commanded from well forward, took advantage of air superiority to attack rapidly, dispensing with slower moving support and relying on the fire-power of the tanks. The enemy forces were routed and territory seized, the return of which was the cause of the next war (and plagues us to-day).

These Israeli ground concepts were not much different from those that had been practiced in the Western Desert in World War Two, and the forces were very ably led, from generals to NCOs. The air force was very professional, central control making the best use of resources, backed by rapid turn-round of aircraft.

Israel's whole strategy was to keep the war well away from her territory, with its acute lack of depth and vulnerable populations. Attack accordingly became the means of defence, to keep the enemy at a distance; there was nothing static or passive about Israeli concepts, aggression and movement were the keynote.

The October War of 1973 showed that the Egyptian forces had learned some lessons from 1967, above all the vital necessity to defend against the Israeli air force (IAF). Egypt invested heavily in SAMs and gun defences, with the result that the IAF was severely inhibited in operations around the Canal. Egyptian infantry made good use of ATGW in the early stages, so that an Israeli armoured column repeating the dashing tactics of 1967 found itself in severe difficulties and with no accompanying infantry or artillery to suppress the ATGW. This particular lesson has since been drawn: the Israeli Army now has the mobile infantry and artillery so effective in desert warfare in World War Two and has re-emphasised the necessity for combined all-arms action.

The October War dramatised three things at least: first, the value of surprise and the fact that it could be achieved even in such an intense and continued confrontation as that in the Middle East; second, the part that ATGW could now play; and third, how an air defence umbrella could effectively cover a defensive position.

The role of the ATGW was in fact over-dramatised, with many commentators seeing in it the demise of the tank, an altogether premature burial. Certainly, armour no longer had the free ride of 1967, but properly handled it still had a prominent place. Soldiers need firepower; they need to be able to move it about over bad terrain; and they need to protect it and protect themselves; – not a bad prescription for a tank.

The Egyptian forces found their air defence invaluable in the semi-static operations of the Canal crossing and in the consolidation on the other side, but were not able to move it forward to cover later offensive operations (which included a tank v. tank slogging match at close-quarters, in which ATGW and mobility played little part). Clearly air cover can be moved and there are now plenty of mobile systems which, while they are vulnerable to ECM, anti-radar and area weapons, can raise the cost of tactical air operations to the point where surface-to-surface missiles may prove more cost-effective than aircraft – at least until a gap has been made in the air defences through which aircraft can go. But a dense barrier of air defences makes the operation of friendly aircraft also difficult, perhaps possible only on a time and space basis.

Both 1967 and 1973 showed the vital importance of leadership and morale, though Israeli dominance in 1967 led to over-confidence in 1973 and to a re-creation not only of Egyptian spirit but of the army as a whole, one determined to learn the lessons of their previous humiliation.

In any future wars of this kind, technology will play an increasing part, If this were not clear from the way Israeli forces are being equipped, it would be the course that would naturally be taken to make up for Israel's smaller numbers and geographic vulnerability. But technology makes it harder to continue to keep war at as distance, since long-range missiles can hold populations hostage, though mutual vulnerability may neutralise this threat. Air defence will be at a premium, as will its opposite, defence suppression. ECM will be much more widely used in future and its effect against ground communications and radar systems could be considerable, indeed could achieve a form of surprise that could put defences in temporary disarray. But **all** in all, the special nature of the region and its people; the terrain **and** short distances; good weather and preoccupation with territory; **all** suggest a continuity of the concepts already seen, but with Israeli ingenuity at work to keep them abreast of weapons developments.

The Persian Gulf

The West is much preoccupied since the revolution in Iran and the invasion of Afghanistan, with a possible military threat to the oil in the Gulf. With the collapse of the Shah the whole of the Western strategic position in the region crumbled. Soviet forces then dramatised this by flowing into Afghanistan, potentially opening a new front in an area where the West no longer had any strength. The fact that the oil fields are relatively near the Soviet Union and a very long way from the United States made clear the military problem that the West faced.

Thus the Soviet capacity to get ground forces into the Gulf quickly is far greater than that of the United States, particularly since it has eight airborne divisions well-placed for intervention. The imbalance could only be rectified if US forces were to be stationed in the Gulf in some numbers, but since this is politically unlikely, much attention is now being given to how forces could be got there in a hurry and how they might then be used.

By the nature of things, forces moved quickly over some 7,000 miles from the United States could bring only light equipment. Marines in the Indian Ocean might draw on floating stockpiles for heavier weapons, but both types of force would face the problem of getting from their equipment marrying-up point to the eventual area of operations, which could be slow if by sea and impose equipment limits if by air. Air cover would have to be provided along the whole supply route, over arrival airfields, equipment stockpiles, onward movement and the area of operations. Air offensive action would have to be mounted against enemy intervention forces, which might use airborne forces to secure bridgeheads. All of this argues for the acquiescence, indeed support, of host countries, but this, in the context of a Soviet military incursion, can perhaps be expected.

To get there first is part of any effective deterrent posture. Being there second is quite another matter: the longer Soviet forces had to establish themselves the harder they would be to dislodge. Air action to break up Soviet intervention would have a very high priority, from regional airfields or from carriers in the Arabian Sea or in the Gulf itself – said to be possible if there are enough carriers on station. Clearly, an enemy airborne operation could be severely disrupted if American fighters got in among the transports.

Ground operations in the Gulf could vary from actions in open desert or pipeline patrolling to mountain warfare, in Iran for example. For the former the concepts would be governed sharply by the forces and equipment available in time, and perhaps on any local forces that could help. Soviet airborne divisions have light armoured vehicles not matched by their Western counterparts, which would have to rely more on anti-tank weapons and mines in the early stages. None of the problems on the ground are new, including the important one of acclimatisation, though US forces may not have too much experience of them. Here local experience could be of great help.

Mountain warfare would be something quite different, for which any Western forces introduced would be ill-equipped. Light infantry with good tactical mobility and light weapons would be needed, backed by tactical air action against enemy columns. Little more than delaying action could be undertaken, though the problems that Soviet forces would face should not be under-rated.

There is an air of improbability about some of this, but the subject needed introducing to show that concepts of operating with light forces at great distances are having to be re-examined. Strategic mobility has been well demonstrated by the United States in the past, though largely as a means of reinforcement as in the case of Israel or Europe, or of a slow build-up as in Vietnam, or by the US Marines with their great amphibious capacity. The 1980s finds us looking at this again, but with the much more demanding task of getting combat troops on the ground urgently, ready to fight at once.

It would be unfair not to mention that France has indeed organised forces for this, the *force d'intervention*, and used them in the 1970s in Africa, with some success. They have shown how decisive a small force of well-trained men can be when deployed rapidly. Britain, which practiced such techniques widely, is now herself returning to them with the recent organisation of a small paratroop force for the purpose.

China

The country with the largest army in the world has done little for new concepts in the 1970s and seems likely only to adapt those of others in the 1980s, when re-equipment allows.

China has in effect two sets of conventional concepts, People's War and, subordinate to it, the infantry-type operations of the Korean War model.

People's War would take advantage of a massively mobilised nation, rugged terrain and great depth, to draw in an enemy and then exhaust him and 'drown him in a sea of people'. Guerrilla tactics would be combined with more conventional actions when opportunity offered. If the enemy is willing to oblige by mounting a major invasion, offering war on Chinese terms, so to speak, the concept has obvious merit and can make the best use of the aged equipment that is all the Chinese People's Liberation Army (PLA) has. But if the enemy – the Soviet Union in this case – chose instead to launch more limited operations, to seize Sinkiang, say, or Manchuria, using armour and air power that China could not match, then People's War would have little application. Neither terrain nor population would allow it in such areas, and a strategy which involves giving up an area as economically important to China as is Manchuria has obvious limitations.

China is clearly casting around for modern methods and weapons to enable her to meet such a threat, or deter it, and to be able to match Soviet forces on the frontier. There are economic and political problems outside the scope of this chapter, which make military modernisation a very lengthy process, even for part of the PLA. In the recent campaign against Vietnam, the limitations of Chinese military skills and equipment were demonstrated. The tactics used, in close and difficult country, emphasised little but infantry actions taking advantage of Chinese numbers, supported by conventional artillery bombardment. The air force was used hardly at all, perhaps because of a concern that aircraft could not match those facing them.

In the 1980s China will presumably try to bring up to date her conventional methods, as equipment and training permit, possibly drawing on European and Soviet concepts where appropriate notably for the handling of mechanised formations and air power. People's War will form a backstop, not least for political and resource reasons. So perhaps nothing really new will appear, simply something appropriate to local circumstances and conditions, taking advantage of the asset which China has, her huge numbers.

Conclusion

This chapter has not attempted any discussion of naval warfare except in its projection role, as an adjunct to the land battle. It has covered only some tactical aspects of air operations. It has not looked at internal security operations nor counter-insurgency nor fighting in jungles.

Nothing has been said here about the war in Vietnam, since it is to be dealt with in Chapter Thirteen, but some aspects do have general application: the demonstration of strategic mobility; the use of carriers in the land-battle; tactical mobility including the use of the armed helicopter; confirmation of the national style of the United States, to use fire-power and equipment to solve problems rather than men wherever possible. Minor tactics, like the use of non-lethal gas in conjunction with high explosives, have relevance elsewhere. The development of Precision Guided Missiles – the smart bomb – was accelerated by Vietnam and has now stamped the concepts in use everywhere.

The picture which emerges as a whole is that in the West there has been a gradual evolution of concepts for ground forces rather than a revolution such as was prompted by the introduction of the tank or the aircraft, and which stimulated such thinking between the wars. In the Soviet Union the approach has been a single-minded search more for security and equality with the West, than for the superiority which their doctrines call for. The result has been a formidable military machine with a coherent concept, tailored to the particular aims of the Soviet Union, both defensive and offensive.

There is a good deal of inertia and resistance built into most military organisations, and the cost of new equipment makes for slow and uneven introduction of new weapons, particularly in an alliance. Heretical thought or thorough change finds more acceptance when armies are being built from scratch, as in Germany in the inter-war years, or Israel after her foundation, or when there is wholesale modernisation, as with the Soviet Union after World War Two. Evolutionary change may not necessarily be wrong, of course, but the reasons for it can often be found in bureaucratic politics and inter-service competition, in which old fiefs are preserved and new ones very difficult to carve out or pay for.

It is impossible to set conventional concepts other than in the context of nuclear weapons in such theatres as Europe and perhaps in the future in others too. For the advanced states in Europe, complete reliance on conventional forces is hardly possible with any prudence, so defence policies and strategies are adjusted accordingly. The role of conventional forces is then anything from a trip-wire to a strong barrier, to raise the level of deterrence and the nuclear threshold at the same time. These are two very different tasks at the extreme but may tend to get blurred together in practice. Perhaps to the private soldier there is no real difference anyway: whichever concept is in force requires him to get up and take the first perilous step forward.

13 Insurgency and Sub-National Violence

ROBERT O'NEILL

> Any nation that uses [people's war] intelligently will, as a rule, gain some superiority over those who disdain its use. If this is so, the question only remains whether mankind at large will gain by this further expansion of the element of war; a question to which the answer should be the same as the question of war itself.
>
> Clausewitz, *On War*,
> Book 6, Chapter 26.

In offering this somewhat Delphic judgment on the utility of people's war, Clausewitz has no doubt as to its military value. What troubled him was the more fundamental question as to whether or not 'mankind at large' would gain from the development of this new (to him) form of warfare. He recognised that people's war is simply one manifestation of what he defined as 'merely the continuation of policy by other means' and as such carries implications no better or worse than the genus of which it is one form of species. One senses from his definition of war that he regarded the answer to his question as of no value as a guide for the shaping of policy. War is a tool of the statesman, like a hammer to the carpenter, capable of being used for good or evil but not something which can be called good or evil in any sense apart from the policy which it is employed to serve. At the very outset of his work, in Book 1, Chapter 1, Section 2, Clausewitz defines his subject: 'War is thus an act of force to compel an enemy to do our will'. It is important to note that from the beginning Clausewitz assumes the existence of an enemy. He does not consider it fruitful to inquire whether there need be an enemy, whether we can shape our world so that hostile relationships cease to exist. He accepts as a fact of life that enemies do exist and that force will be exerted by one group on another as a normal means of furthering its aims.

In discussing the subject of insurgency and counter-insurgency we might do worse than to follow Clausewitz's philosophy in this regard. It does not seem possible to judge insurgency and counter-insurgency operations to be either good or evil without considering the policies which they serve. Our judgments on that question will be determined subjectively by the way in which particular conflicts affect our interests. While many chose to criticise American intervention in Vietnam as immoral, it was not an issue around which consensus developed. The issue which was substantially agreed upon was that American policies were not winning the war. Similarly, although many condemn the morality of insurgent or terrorist groups which employ violence around the world today, few of us would wish to foreclose our options to use precisely this kind of violence in defence of our own liberties if they are ever threatened by an invader.

Clausewitz was writing about people's war as a new type of occurrence: 'In the civilised parts of Europe, war by means of popular uprisings is a phenomenon of the nineteenth century'. Given that he was writing in but the third decade of that century, he was saying that people's war was an important new development with considerable potential for the future. Not bound rigidly by his own experience, he was chancing his arm a little in drawing his readers' attention to something which he believed would become more important for both students and practitioners of war. Clausewitz, as Bernard Brodie notes in his commentary on the Howard-Paret translation of *On War* (Clausewitz, 1976, p. 691), does not mention the Peninsular War, on which he bases much of his analysis of the conditions which determine success or failure in people's war. Prudently, he did not analyse this topic at length, nor did he discuss it outside of the framework of 'The Defence', the subject of Book Six. But amongst his writings he made four penetrating observations on people's war which experience of the past two decades shows to be worth application to any current analysis of insurgency warfare. They are:

1. A general uprising ... should be nebulous and elusive; its resistance should never materialize as a concrete body, otherwise the enemy can direct sufficient force at its core, crush it, and take many prisoners. ... On the other hand, there must be some concentration at certain points: the fog must thicken and form a dark menacing cloud out of which a bolt of lightning may strike at any time.

2. Without ... regular troops to provide encouragement, the local inhabitants will usually lack the confidence and initiative to take to arms. ... But there are limiting factors ... experience tends to show that too many regulars in an area are likely to decimate the vigour and effectiveness of a popular uprising ...

3. ... one of the basic principles of insurrection ... is the principle of seldom, or never, allowing this important strategic means of defence to turn into tactical defence ... a national uprising cannot maintain itself where the atmosphere is too full of danger. Therefore, if its fuel is to be fanned into a major conflagration, it must be at some distance, where there is enough air, and the uprising cannot

be smothered by a single stoke.

4. A government must never assume that its country's fate, its whole existence, hangs on the outcome of a single battle, no matter how decisive. Even after a defeat, there is always the possibility that a turn of fortune can be brought about by developing new sources of internal strength or through the natural decimation all offensives suffer in the long run or by means of help from abroad. There will always be time enough to die; like a drowning man who will clutch instinctively at a straw, it is the natural law of the moral world that a nation that finds itself on the brink of an abyss will try to save itself by any means (Clausewitz, 1976, pp. 480–3).

Although these conclusions were drawn over 150 years ago, few, if any, theorists or practitioners of insurgency warfare have left us, in the space of several pages, a more succinct contribution towards its understanding. The French soldiers, Marshals Bugeaud, Gallieni and Lyautey, writing in the nineteenth and early twentieth centuries, developed a sophisticated approach to the problems of counter-insurgency warfare, based on their experiences in Algeria, Indo-China and Madagascar. Bugeaud not only developed effective military means for defeating the restive Arab tribes of Emir Abd-el-Kader but also combined them with a political strategy to weaken his enemy by creating internal discord. Gallieni, assisted by Lyautey, laid the basis of the modern technique of pacification. With a few thousand men and modest resources they achieved amazing results in Tonkin, the most rugged of the provinces of Indo-China. They eschewed the hard-hitting mobile offensive column penetrating deep into enemy-held territory, the equivalent of the air cavalry of the 1960s, in favour of slow steady expansion of the frontier of control, employing both political and military means to bring the principal populated areas under control. Later, in Morocco, Lyautey developed this approach further and characterised it as the *tache-d'huile*, the slowly spreading oil patch, a concept which was employed with notable success by the British in the Malayan Emergency (see Gottman, 1943, pp.243–59).

During the First World War, T.E. Lawrence practised and later wrote about insurgency with an orginality and lucidity that still repay study. In the following three decades other writers and practitioners, particularly Mao Tse-tung, adapting brilliantly ideas as old as those of Sun Tzu, made further contributions which laid the basis for the conduct and understanding of that post-Second World War phenomenon, wars of national liberation.

The Concepts of Vo Nguyen Giap

The most well known of the insurgent texts of the recent period is Vo Nguyen Giap's *People's War, People's Army*, published in 1961. This book was not conceived as a whole and, like most of his others, is a collection of articles and speeches which, although generally concerned with the question of people's war, do not cohere particularly well. This difficulty is accentuated by a heavy overlay of propaganda which the reader has to sweep aside in order to grasp the significant doctrinal points which Giap was making to his followers.

Giap's techniques of insurgency warfare embody four notable elements: a clear primacy accorded to political aspects of the struggle; a phased approach to the structure of a campaign; combination of irregular and regular forces; and imaginative tactics for both types of force to use. Let us explore them in a little more detail.

The most important elements in implementing Giap's strategy, from the 1940s to the early 1970s, were the political cadres, the trained, dedicated grass-roots leaders, teachers and organisers who lived in or near village communities and linked them with the central leadership of the Communist Party. The political cadres were the spearhead and *sine qua non* of the insurgent campaign but their importance was largely ignored by their opponents until much too late, and even then its magnitude was underestimated.

Giap structured his campaigns imaginatively and boldly into different strategic phases. He did not make the mistake of pressing forward for victory by military means in the early stages but concentrated on the political offensive. In the mid-phase of his campaign against the French he allowed his judgement to be carried away by early military successes and severe tactical reverses followed. His offensives against the de Lattre Line in early 1951 resulted in heavy losses, but, as a flexible strategist he reverted to a slower but more effective form of indirect strategy. Before launching into his final strategic offensives in 1954 and 1975, he employed wide-ranging tactical mobility to induce overstretch in his opponents, thereby offsetting their superiority in some dimensions of the military balance. He prepared his victories by political means and carried them off by dramatic use of military force.

He was no naive idealist who eschewed use of regular forces. Rather he built them up carefully and fielded them in a relatively dispersed manner to support guerrilla forces in the mid-phases of his campaign, before concentrating them to win smashing military victories over well-equipped enemy forces. He proved adept at orchestrating artillery in 1954 and armour in 1975 to shatter his opponents. He resisted the temptation to launch these strategic offensives prematurely, despite the many pressures which must have been acting on him to do so.

Finally, in his tactical methods and his more purely military strategy he showed ingenuity and originality. Once his forces had entered the transition from strategic defensive to strategic offensive, they were at their most vulnerable. Large numbers of men were concentrated together, offering suitable targets for enemy air, airborne and land offensives. However, the outstanding mobility of his main-force elements enabled him to retain the initiative and keep his powerful opponents off-balance. The wide-ranging series of pressures he exerted against the French in 1953 and the South Vietnamese in 1973–74 tied them to tactical defence operations and deprived them of any substantial manoeuvre force with which to regain the initiative. Vast areas of the countryside were thus left free for his forces to move through.

It is interesting to assess Giap's performance against the four above-mentioned criteria enunciated by Clausewitz. 'Nebulous and elusive' is an apt characterisation of the Viet Minh and Viet Cong forces in the 1940s and 1960s. Giap was masterful at concentrating the fog of his scattered guerrilla bands into 'a dark and menacing cloud' and loosing 'a bolt of lightning' at his opponents. His use of regulars to support both local forces and political cadres in the mid-stages of his campaigns, without robbing the people of vigour and effectiveness in the crucial early stages, appears to have been fully as Clausewitz had envisaged. Rarely, if ever, did he allow his forces to be drawn into tactically defensive operations in which casualities would have been heavy. On one or two notable occasions, such as at the Hue Citadel in 1968, he deviated from this principle and paid heavily for his independence. He never took a defeat as final but, as Clausewitz predicted of a wise leader, followed any tactical defeat by a process of fostering the internal unity and morale of his forces. Thus, according to Clausewitz's prescription, Giap was an excellent insurgent leader. This conclusion perhaps strengthens one's admiration for Clausewitz's perception in defining the essence of people's war so incisively without direct experience of it.

American and Allied Concepts of Counter-Insurgency

While insurgencies conducted in other parts of the world in the 1970s have drawn from and adapted the ideas of the Vietnamese, it is less clear that the precepts of their opponents, principally the Americans, have been followed by other counter-insurgents. Certainly counter-insurgency has not been attempted with the same application of men, fire-power and material resources in other parts of the world since the early 1970s. It appears safe to conclude from the public debate of the late 1970s that much of the American style of counter-insurgency operations has been repudiated by others.

Before considering the extent to which others have or have not followed American practices, the question should be asked as to why American doctrines were not more successful. The question is extremely complex and deserves a book-length study rather than a few pages. Two sub-questions must be asked in answering the main one: was there an identifiable American doctrine; and how far was lack of success due not to American shortcomings but to those of the South Vietnamese?

In answer to the first of these sub-questions, there were several American doctrines in use during the Vietnam war. The Marines, the Special Forces, the infantry divisions, the air cavalry and the armoured cavalry all had highly individual approaches to the conflict. These differences were due in part to the fact that United States forces are trained to meet a wide range of contingencies and, with the exception of the Special Forces and the Marines, counter-insurgency warfare did not rate high on their scale of priorities in the 1960s. These variations were also caused by the organisation and equipment of many of the forces which the Americans sent to Vietnam. I remember my first meeting in Vietnam with an officer of the recently-arrived Eleventh Armoured Cavalry Regiment, with its hundreds of armoured personnel carriers and tanks, and dozens of helicopters. When I asked him what use this expensive, ponderous organisation would be against lightly armed, silent guerrillas, he assured me that the regiment was in Vietnam to exercise its normal doctrines of mobile fire-power. If any Viet Cong emerged in the midst of one of the regiment's sweeps through the countryside, they would be destroyed. If not, at least the regiment would have had some good training. This officer and his colleagues seemed to lack any understanding of the counter-productive nature of their approach. In particular, without economy of effort, the United States would be unable to maintain its commitment for the length of time necessary to achieve a victory. Admittedly these armoured formations were very effective in clearing main force Viet Cong and North Vietnamese out of their concentration and base areas. They inflicted heavy casualties on rash Communist commanders who launched attacks in their vicinity. However by the time of the final phase of the war, the North Vietnamese strategic offensive, when such forces would have been optimally effective, they had already been withdrawn back to Germany and the United States.

The Special Forces and the Marines at least emphasised in their doctrines the importance of the political and economic dimensions of the war. The Marine Corps text *The Guerrilla – and How to Fight Him*, advised:

To beat the guerrilla on his own ground, the first essential is knowledge — knowledge about the enemy himself, his methods, strengths, weaknesses, tactics and techniques. More than that, to beat the guerrilla means to fight not in the sharp black and white of formal combat, but in a gray, fuzzy obscurity where politics affect tactics and economics influence strategy. The soldier must fuse with the statesman, the private turn politician (Greene, 1967, p.v).

While the feasibility of the last sentence may be open to question, it must be admitted that the Marines and the Special Forces made a major effort to understand the nature of the war. Unfortunately the Marines were stationed in the far north of South Vietnam, in I Corps area, where they were heavily committed to conventional defensive operations to hold the southern edge of the De-militarised Zone against determined North Vietnamese attacks. They played a vital role in this area, in hard-fought actions such as at the Rockpile, Con Thien and Khe Sanh, but their knowledge of counter-insurgency techniques was not fully applied. The Special Forces, although used more in accord with widely accepted counter-insurgency doctrines, were too small and specialised in their function to have other than a minor, catalytic effect on American approaches to the war.

The most substantial elements of the other American forces in Vietnam, the infantry divisions, were introduced to effective counter-insurgency methods in training but the lessons taught were rarely fully absorbed, particularly at senior command levels. As a result, many American unit and formation commanders conducted the war with emphasis on body-counts and search-and-destroy missions, while the main populated areas behind them were not effectively isolated from the Viet Cong provincial-mobile and main-force elements. As a consequence these American formations fought an expensive and ineffective war, in terms of both men and money, largely on ground of their enemy's choosing.

It may be argued that the security of the populated areas and the fostering of political support for the Saigon government was essentially the task of the South Vietnamese authorities. To a large extent it was, or it should have been but, to answer the second sub-question, the South Vietnamese administration, police and local government apparatus, proved incapable of meeting these responsibilities and thereby contributed substantially to the final allied defeat. Thus one of the major foundations of British success in the Malayan Emergency was missing and was never properly developed. The South Vietnamese administration was not uniformly bad. Parts of it were outstandingly good and some officials achieved a high degree of local popular support for the Saigon government, but they were exceptional. The system as a whole did not compare in effectiveness with the political and administrative infrastructure of the Communists. Perhaps it never could have, but at least greater efforts should have been applied in this area if there was to be any hope of a successful outcome to the conflict for the Republic of Vietnam. In the late 1960s and early 1970s much greater efforts were applied by the Americans to these aspects of the war but they came too late. The high casualty and economic costs of the first four years of the war, coupled with the demonstration provided by the 1968 Tet Offensive that this expenditure had apparently achieved relatively little, undermined the essential base of political support for the war effort in the United States and other western countries.

It is little wonder, then, that the American style of counter-insurgency operations has disappeared during the 1970s. At least the Americans did not force their allies in Vietnam to adopt their approach to the war. Australian forces which operated in Vietnam based their doctrines on extensive experience of the Malayan Emergency. Australian Army advisers had served in Malaya from 1950 and a battalion had operated there from 1955. In the initial years of the Australian Army's commitment to Vietnam, most battalion and company commanders were selected from men who had had personal experience of operations in Malaya. They knew that if the war in Vietnam was ever to be won, it would require a commitment of allied assistance over many years. No 'quick fix' of a few years' duration could be effective. Hence the level of commitment provided by allies had to be acceptable to their own public opinion over this period. They appreciated that losses and costs would have to be justified by results. While some results, such as destruction of Viet Cong main-force elements, would take a long time and cost heavily, restoration of government control and initiation of rural development programs could be achieved relatively quickly, once the Communist cadres and forces were cleared out and kept out of the populated areas.

These thoughts were the guiding principles of much of the Australian Army's activities in Vietnam. They worked tolerably well in Phuoc Tuy province, although frequent absences of Australian units caused by American requests for support in neighbouring provinces allowed ample opportunities for Communist re-infiltration of the populated areas and sabotage of development projects. How long it would have required for these Australian methods to have become so effective that local forces could have faced the Communists unaided is impossible to tell. Perhaps they never would have achieved such effectiveness. Perhaps the South Vietnamese administration was incapable of playing its essential role. But at least this doctrine did achieve more results at less cost, both militarily and politically, than some American counterparts.

Insurgency and Counter-Insurgency in Rhodesia

Some, but not many, of these ideas were used in the second most celebrated guerrilla war of the 1970s – the Rhodesian campaign. Despite the enormous political handicap of the Smith regime in terms of winning support from the black population, it attempted at the outset of the war in 1972 to fight back with political means. Economic, military and manpower problems prevented the Rhodesian government from making rapid progress in this direction, but it did embark on the construction of Protected Villages in order to break contact between rural villagers and insurgent main-force units. This program was not executed well and many of the Protected Villages were squalid camps, situated several miles away from the inhabitants' fields. No compensation was paid to the blacks who were uprooted from their villages and relocated in this way.

The size of the problems facing the Rhodesian Security Forces was such that they were soon forced by cleverly deployed, although badly trained, guerrillas to concentrate their efforts on more purely military problems. With a deployable force of some 25,000 whites and blacks at any one time, the government had to control an area of over 150,000 square miles and a border of nearly 2,000 miles. It was not long before its forces were overly stretched, reacting chiefly to guerrilla incursions and incidents as they occurred, or embarking on the more dangerous strategy of cross-border, pre-emptive raids. Four mobile 'Fire Forces' were stationed around the country, consisting each of a company of regular infantry, four or five helicopters and one C-47 Dakota aircraft. When guerrillas were reported, the nearest Fire Force sped to the scene by helicopter (Downie, 1979, p. 343). Generally the kill-ratio was six to one in the favour of the Rhodesian Security Forces, a figure which might have suggested that the government was winning. However, given that the government had only a small, specialised pool of persons on which to draw, even this disparity in loss rates weakened the counter-insurgent forces faster than those of the guerrillas (Arbuckle, 1979, p. 27).

While the guerrillas were poorly trained and equipped for military combat, they were more adept in performing the political functions which were vital to their role. Operating from wide sanctuary areas across the borders of Rhodesia, they infiltrated the Tribal Trust lands, where two-thirds of the black population live. Their political cadres then built a firm base and supporting infrastructure amongst the black population, exploiting social injustices, such as wage discrimination, lack of access to higher education, poor medical care and housing, social attitudes of the whites and indiscriminate killing of non-guerrilla blacks by the Security Forces. They then carried out what was in military terms a relatively inefficient campaign of attacks against white farms, road and rail links, schools, council offices, beer halls and black-owned businesses in order to undermine the political basis of government authority. The high loss rate which the guerrillas suffered did not matter greatly because they were not short of numbers. They quickly induced over-stretch in the Security Forces and prevented their employment in a more political role (Arbuckle, 1979, pp. 27–31).

Perhaps the main lesson of long-term significance to come out of the Rhodesian conflict is that a small, proficient counter-insurgency force can stave off a large, militarily inefficient guerrilla force for a long time. The war ran for over seven years and although there was, by 1979, no doubt that the insurgents would win, a total military defeat of the Security Forces appeared still to be a long way off. A corollary to this lesson is that any insurgent group which wishes to avoid an extremely protracted campaign would be wise to lift its level of military proficiency before confronting the opposing security forces.

Sub-National Violence

Sub-national violence and terrorism are frequently omitted from discussion amongst strategic analysts, perhaps on the ground that in many cases they tend not to transcend national boundaries and so should not be regarded as part of the agenda for our consideration. This reason is increasingly lacking in substance. The military activities of the Palestine Liberation Organisation are a matter for international concern, no matter what one thinks of the PLO's claim to nationhood. The seizure of the Grand Mosque in Mecca raised the spectre of Saudi instability and loss of access to oil. The rise of urban guerrillas or terrorists in Western nations poses many questions of relevance to those concerned with international strategic problems: can they be met effectively without international action; are they in any way linked to the east-west rivalry through Soviet sponsorship; do they carry implications for world order, particularly in terms of the strained relationship between developed and developing societies?

It is not the prime purpose of this examination to treat these questions; rather it is concerned with the ways in which violence is applied by sub-national groups and how it is resisted by national authorities. However the two sets of issues are inextricably linked, not least because many of those who apply violence at the sub-national level have international aims. The ends influence the means and vice-versa.

The problem of sub-national violence is becoming steadily more serious. According to figures recently released by the Central Intelligence Agency, the 587 deaths due to terrorism in 1979 represent the highest annual number since the Agency began keeping such statistics in 1968 (Middleton, 1980, p. 2). Half of these killings occurred in Western Europe and North America; many were the work of outside groups who had chosen targets in this region for reasons of their sensitivity and the degree of impact likely to be achieved by publicity.

In discussing these activities it must be remembered, as in the case of major insurgencies, that the aims of such groups are political and therefore most of their activities are political. It is absurd to concentrate attention on the visible tip of the iceberg, the violence they cause. Almost inevitably such limited treatment leads to overly complacent conclusions for established authority. Although sub-national groups can rarely confront the forces of law and order and win, it must be remembered that in embarking on such confrontations, their aim is to undermine popular respect for the established order by forcing it to show the ugly side of its face. The accompanying publicity is also valuable; any following trials and imprisonment also offer important opportunities to be exploited in societies which do not execute suspected terrorists on the spot.

However, at least in liberal societies, the offence which these groups commit is not political but physical. Their political differences with the established order can be tolerated, even though they desire its overthrow, but their violence cannot be. Dissident groups may campaign and proselytise for members; they may rail against the iniquities of the established order. The problem of such liberality for some dissidents is that they do not wish to be seen as just another political party. They need identification with violence to give themselves distinction and to impress the world, rather than having to moderate their views and compete for followers from the main stream of political opinion. They are frequently romantics and perfectionists, to whom such open competing for support, for voters, is anathema. In many cases they despise those for whose good they claim to be striving.

Consequently it seems unlikely that terrorism will be dissipated by a liberal society's warm embrace of the dissidents. Of course it can be exacerbated by an illiberal response, by government incompetence or by the existence of major social injustices to which insufficient attention is being paid. High unemployment amongst educated young people provides a rich seedbed of frustrated hopes which will promote the growth of violent groups. For as long as this type of economic problem persists, we may look during the 1980s to see a rising incidence of such trouble in western societies. Governments should bear in mind that in promoting employment they are not only decreasing their expenditure on welfare but also may be making savings in spending on security measures, quite apart from reducing risks to the lives and limbs of their members and employees.

The techniques employed by sub-national groups in the 1970s have been very diverse, ranging from bomb attacks, assassinations and kidnappings through to airport and aircraft incidents. Improved airport security appears to have lowered the occurrence of skyjacking and random killings in terminal buildings, but determined terrorists will find ways around the existing measures. Two groups of people are now subject to a much higher degree of risk than in the early 1970s: diplomats and those engaged in the pursuit and administration of justice. Embassy security is particularly difficult to tighten, given that an embassy is a small enclave in a foreign nation which is meant to be accessible to that nation's citizens. The situation is not helped when the host government appears to be indifferent towards the security of some of the diplomats accredited to it. Protection of government buildings and courts, although needing improvement around the world, is not such a difficult matter because a government's formidable security resources are ready to hand. Individual security in homes and private offices and while travelling is extremely difficult to guarantee without making intolerable intrusions into the privacy of those requiring protection. Nonetheless, a burgeoning industry has arisen to meet the problems of individual and industrial security.

The international implications of terrorist and sub-national violence are many and complex. Most international terrorist incidents relate to bilateral and irridentist issues and are not worth discussion in the context of broad trends in strategic thinking. There are two exceptions, however: those which are related to the east-west rivalry; and those which are related to the north-south relationship. The super-powers and their allies have an interest in assisting, or even creating, groups which, directly or indirectly will further their interests by the selective application of violence in other nations. There has been ample evidence of such assistance in the past, although the political climate within the United States in the latter half of the 1970s has strongly discouraged American involvement in these activities. The Russians and their allies accordingly have lengthened their lead in this field, presenting a problem to the West of whether to react offensively or defensively in target areas. While incidents of systematic terrorism have not yet begun to form a strand of the complex north-south relationship, it would be foolish to ignore the possibility as frustrations rise, means of violence proliferate and international travel becomes easier.

Prospects for the 1980s

Insurgency and counter-insurgency warfare has been one of the most, if not *the* most, dominant modes of conflict in the past two decades. The wave of nationalistic struggles which was set in motion by the Second World War and its aftermath in South and South-east Asia and the Middle East, appeared to have largely spent itself by the close of the 1950s, with the ending of the Malayan Emergency, the departure of the French from Indo-China and their imminent departure from Algeria, and the ending of the Mau-Mau emergency in Kenya. For a short period in the 1960s a general optimism prevailed amongst Western political and military leaders that first, because the political causes of insurgencies, or wars of national liberation, depending on one's point of view, were understood, they would be judiciously avoided in future, and second, because some of these conflicts had been settled following the defeat of the insurgents in a military sense, the techniques of fighting insurgencies to a successful conclusion were readily available.

These comforting thoughts were shown, by the end of the 1960s, to be of limited value. Clearly experience of the 1960s and 1970s has shown that insurgencies of various kinds remain major forces in world politics and no reliable panaceas have been developed for defeating them. This is not to say that fortune always favours the insurgents. Events in Rhodesia, the Horn of Africa, Oman, Kampuchea and East Timor have shown that insurgents have no magic formula for success simply because they are rebelling against what they claim to be oppression. Insurgencies and counter-insurgencies are usually deeply rooted in individual cultures, in religious, racial and social differences within individual nations or sub-national groups. It is hence extremely difficult to generalise about them. What may have been useful to Che Guevara would not necessarily have helped the Viet Cong or the PLO. What the British learned about counter-insurgency in Malaya was not automatically applicable to the problems of the Americans in Vietnam or the French in Algeria. Nonetheless there are some concepts, on both sides of the insurgency – counter-insurgency relationship, which are recognisably applicable to a wide range of individual situations, which will remain relevant in the 1980s. For insurgents these are typified by the ideas embodied in Giap's doctrines and for counter-insurgents they are exemplified by the notions developed by the British during the Malayan Emergency. While these concepts may undergo continual refinement, there is no escaping from the primacy of politically-oriented activities for both insurgents and counter-insurgents and the need for economy of effort in fighting a long engagement.

Before concluding this discussion, it is pertinent to examine the likely future potential for international intervention in such conflicts. Throughout the post-1945 period, the Soviet Union has probably been the major supplier to insurgent forces, establishing the AK47 automatic rifle as standard form of guerrilla equipment from Vietnam to the Middle East and Southern Africa. Soviet rockets, grenades, machine-guns, sub-machine guns, mortars and artillery have all been supplied in copious quantities to insurgent forces. Heavier equipment, such as tanks, artillery, fighter and transport aircraft, frigates and patrol craft has been provided to those clients whose local successes have reached the point at which such equipment can be used offensively against their opponents or, at least, defensively to protect their main support bases. China has also played a leading role in supporting the Viet Minh, the North Vietnamese, the forces of Mr Mugabe in Rhodesia and various other smaller insurgent groups in areas adjacent to its borders, particularly in South-east Asia.

More recently, the Soviet Union has become involved in supporting established governments, such as in Afghanistan and Ethiopia. The Soviet power to provide such assistance far outweighs that of China, particularly when the theatre of conflict lies at any great distance from their borders. Nonetheless, both Communist great powers have been compelled by their own interests to regard insurgency as an activity of imperfect virtue. They can no longer profess that right is always on the side of those struggling against some constituted authority. Rather they have had to come to grips with the realisation that in some senses, although to a different degree from the West, they are *status quo* powers. Just as China does not wish to see violent upheavals within the ASEAN states, neither does the Soviet Union wish to see the regimes of clients such as Mengistu and Babrak Karmal overthrown by the Eritreans, the Ogaden rebels and the Mujahidin in Afghanistan.

Countervailing change in Western policies, or at least the policies of Western governments, is more difficult to detect. Generally speaking, there are few tendencies to side with insurgent movements, and in cases where there is clear Western sympathy for guerrillas, such as in Ethiopia and Afghanistan, there is little evidence of direct Western assistance to the extent given to insurgents in Angola and Rhodesia by the Cubans, the Eastern Europeans and the Soviets. Although some military supplies of Western origin percolate through to insurgents who are fighting the Soviets or Soviet-backed regimes, they are frequently provided by sympathetic neighbouring states, such as the Sudan, from their own arsenals.

This Western reluctance to become involved on the side of insurgents perhaps reflects the increased unwillingness to support counter-insurgents which swept the West in the 1970s, when the hopelessness of the American situation in Vietnam became clear. The opposition of both Houses of the United States Congress to Kissinger's design for major assistance to the FNLA and UNITA groups in Angola, in their struggle against the MPLA, punctuated a long tradition. United States support for governments which were resisting Marxist-oriented insurgents had been one of the more permanent features of the post-1945 era. The Americans have not been alone in their support for counter-insurgency operations. The British, French, Portuguese and Spanish governments have all been involved in such struggles in their colonies. The British and the Americans have been assisted by Australia and New Zealand in the South-east Asian region. While the imperial powers were forces to be reckoned with in their colonial domains, they can scarcely be regarded as such in dealing with insurgencies in the post-colonial era. They lack not only the means to undertake such ventures but also, and more importantly, the motivation to do so. Britain's junior partners, Australia and New Zealand, were never significant counter-insurgents in their own right. They became involved in the Malayan Emergency and the Vietnam conflict chiefly to retain the interest of their 'great and powerful friends' in being militarily involved in a nearby and troubled region. Now that these allies show no sign of becoming similarly involved in the near future, and South-east Asia has become a relatively stable region, it is difficult to imagine that Australia and New Zealand will become involved in counter-insurgency operations in the future.

Thus the likelihood of future Western involvement in such conflicts would seem to depend entirely on whether the Americans re-enter the field. What then are the prospects for this development? It must be said that they are not high. It is most unlikely that the United States will commit large numbers of troops to such operations, having learned from the Vietnam experience that these undertakings can detract heavily from American capabilities to protect national interests elsewhere. The resources of a sixteen-division army have to be applied carefully, given that the major potential opponent has over one hundred. The United States has also learned from both the Korean and Vietnam wars that lengthy, indecisive commitments become most unpopular politically. Finally, it should be recognised that the United States armed forces are not highly effective in counter-insurgency operations. While some parts of the US Army and Marine Corps did achieve high proficiency in these operations in Vietnam, the major components of these forces have to be concerned primarily with conventional operations and lack the knowledge and skills necessary to master this most intricate and intensely political form of warfare.

The contribution of American material support to a threatened friendly government whose political system and armed forces are capable of meeting the challenge of insurgents is a separate issue. Many of the factors which militate against the use of human resources do not apply to the provision of food, money and the machines of peace and war. But, as the Congress showed in 1975 with respect to Angola, the United States' ability to supply this type of assistance cannot be taken for granted. In the wake of increased Soviet – United States tensions, Congressional attitudes are likely to moderate in this regard, although not to become totally permissive of Administration desires. The potential recipient of United States assistance will have to appear worthy of it. It will not be sufficient simply to mouth anti-Communist slogans to make America, which is increasingly aware of the limitations of its military and economic strength, willing to ship millions of dollars worth of supplies to a friendly government which has an insurgency problem. Counter-insurgents will have to rely much more on their own political, economic and military resources than in the 1960s and early 1970s. The pendulum is unlikely to swing back fully. Of course, such potential recipients will not be easy to find. Governments with these attributes are not likely to be faced by serious insurgent threats.

The Soviet Union, while not always as generous to insurgents as the United States has been to counter-insurgents, appears unlikely to stint its support in future. Furthermore, its resources are augmented by those of its allies, particularly Cuba and East Germany. If the insurgencies in Angola, Mozambique and Zimbabwe may be considered as concluded, there may not be many potential recipients of any consequence of Soviet and allied assistance in the coming decade. Key areas to watch will be Baluchistan, North-east Thailand, Somalia, Morocco, Iran, Yemen and Central America. Although some of these, particularly Baluchistan and Iran, are of high strategic importance to the West, the notion that Western-supported counter insurgency operations will be conducted there is simply unfeasible from many points of view. Consequently, it is difficult to see this type of warfare returning to the prominence it enjoyed in the 1960s as a form of proxy conflict between East and West. External involvement will still continue, but it is unlikely to rend the fabric of super-power relations.

The Soviets are not about to surrender their advantage of claiming, and acting, to champion the cause of the oppressed, or whoever it suits them to define as such. But the United States, still smarting from Vietnam, is not going to reciprocate as fully as in the past. While appreciating that the Soviets would like to dominate the Third World for their own ends, various episodes such as the Iranian Revolution, Arab reaction to the Soviet invasion of Afghanistan and the outcome of the struggle in Rhodesia show us that the Third World states have wills of their own and do not wish to become pawns in any super-power game if they can avoid such a fate. Consequently in these circumstances, the interests of the West lie more in the direction of consolidation of interests with the Third World, helping to increase the powers of the latter to resist Soviet pressures rather than intervening in their affairs simply to prop up an unpopular but friendly regime. The prime means of such consolidation will be political and economic rather than military. There is a strong Western interest in world society remaining a plurality. Ultimately, provided that the direct super-power relationship remains stable, the Soviets will come to appreciate that they also have an interest in a pluralistic world order, but they seem likely to get their fingers burned in the process.

Section Four
Political Problems in the Management and Application of Military Force

14 Clear and Future Danger Managing Relations with the Soviet Union in the 1980s

RICHARD NED LEBOW

Much has been written of late concerning Soviet strategic capability and the shield it allegedly provides for Soviet leaders to carry out aggression. Some students of foreign affairs (Luttwak, 1980; Podhoretz, 1980) have cited the Soviet invasion of Afghanistan as a case in point, arguing that the Soviets would never have dared to subjugate that country in the absence of at least strategic parity with the United States. Such an analysis is based on the premise that Soviet aggression is primarily a function of the *opportunity* Soviet leaders perceive to carry it out. This chapter advances a contrary thesis: that aggression is more often a function of the perceived *need* to conduct such a policy. This need arises when policymakers face a combination of international and domestic threats which they believe can be overcome only by a forceful foreign policy.

The motivation of aggression is more than a question of theoretical interest; it has important implications for the future pattern of East-West relations. Many of those who attribute aggression to opportunity see the next few years as particularly dangerous by reason of a "window of opportunity" they ascribe to the Soviets, a period during which they believe the Soviet Union will possess a strategic advantage. But if need motivates aggression, the crisis in East-West relations is more likely to come in the late 1980s and early 1990s, when Soviet perceptions of their strategic and domestic weakness may encourage them to pursue risky foreign policy ventures. The two interpretations of the causes of aggression also suggest quite different prescriptions for coping with the problems posed by the Soviet Union. Adherents to the opportunity notion urge greater immediate defence expenditures to beef up existing strategic forces in order to deny the Soviets any strategic advantage. Those who see aggression as the result of need also tend to believe in a strong deterrent but place greater emphasis on developing sensitivity to the Soviet's security dilemma in order to avoid, if possible, pushing them into the kind of corner from which they are likely to strike out irrationally.

The contention that a "window of opportunity" will exist for the Soviet Union is the early 1980s is open to serious criticism. In the first place it is doubtful that the Soviets have any kind of overall strategic advantage. The United States has a far greater number of deliverable reentry vehicles (RVs), a relatively invulnerable submarine-launched ballistic missile (SLBM) force and more reliable and ready systems, assets that will continue to give it an edge even in the absence of the MX. Force comparisons that result in a Soviet advantage (see, for example, Pipes, 1977; Gray, 1978; Nitze, 1979) invariably assume extremely unrealistic conditions. They posit exaggerated performance characteristics for many Soviet systems, take for granted that all these systems will function as the Soviets intend and that just about anything that can go wrong for the United States will go wrong. Such force comparisons also ignore the existence of allied nuclear arsenals and American theatre systems which, as vocal Soviet concerns for the latter indicates, considerably augment American strategic capability.

Worst case scenarios may be useful as a first step in the force planning process, but it is misleading to pretend that they accurately relect the reality of any strategic exchange. It is even more absurd to believe that the Soviets subscribe to such a distorted picture of the strategic "correlation of forces". Past evidence suggests that Soviet military planners are extremely conservative in their estimates of the forces required to achieve specified missions. There is every reason to assume that their strategic analysts, for the same reason as do ours, weight the scenarios they design in the direction of the worst possible case for themselves. If so, they undoubtedly end up with a greatly exaggerated notion of American strategic advantage. To the extent that both superpowers engage in a conservative analysis of the strategic balance, they draw asymmetrical but equally anxiety provoking conclusions, conclusions that encourage the purchase of new arms which lead to the development of new anxieties.

The more fundamental objection to the notion of a "window of opportunity" is its assumption, already noted, that aggressive foreign policy in general, and Soviet policy in particular, is motivated by opportunity. This view of the motivation of aggression is by no means a novel one. It underlies the concept of deterrence, the most widely accepted strategy of conflict avoidance in international relations.

Deterrence is based on the Hobbesian notion that adversaries will take advantage of each other's every weakness. It assumes that aggression will occur when an adversary perceives the opportunity to get away with it. To pass up such an opportunity might actually encourage others to question that state's strength or resolve. Ole Holsti (1962) observes that even the occasional friendly gesture risks being interpreted as an indication of submission. For these reasons deterrence seeks to discourage aggression by denying an adversary the opportunity to carry it out. It seeks to raise the perceived cost of aggression and thereby to remove the incentive for it. It is with this end in mind that those who subscribe to the idea of a "window of opportunity" advocate a rapid buildup of the Western strategic arsenal.

Deterrence Reconsidered

My own research (Lebow, 1981) indicates that deterrence is far from an efficacious strategy of conflict avoidance. I studied the origins of thirteen Brinkmanship crises – confrontation in which a state challenges an important commitment of an adversary in the expectation that the adversary will back down – to determine what encouraged policymakers to pursue foreign policies that entailed the risk of war. The case histories indicated that political leaders who might otherwise have opposed an adventurous foreign policy became willing to assume the risks of Brinkmanship because they were convinced that it was essential to overcome serious foreign and domestic problems.[1]

The most important external threat appears to be the expectation of a dramatic impending negative shift in the balance of power. In seven Brinkmanship crises the confrontation was preceded by the widely shared perception among policymakers in the initiating nation that such a shift was imminent. Brinkmanship in these cases was conceived of as a forceful response to this acute danger; as a means of preserving one's strategic position before time ran out and such a response was no longer realistic. The Cuban missile crisis offers an interesting illustration of this point. Its origins can be traced, at least in part, to acute feelings of strategic insecurity on the part of Soviet leaders (Abel, 1966; Horelick and Rush, 1966; Hilsman, 1967; Tatu, 1968; Allison, 1971; Kahan and Long, 1972).

According to this interpretation, the Russian decision to put missiles in Cuba was triggered by the sudden realization that the United States was capable of launching an effective first strike against the Soviet Union. At that time the Soviets possessed a very small fleet of long range bombers, a sizable number of MRBMs and IRBMs and a small number of ICBMs. All of these weapons were based in the Soviet Union and were of limited use in any retaliatory strike against the United States. The bombers were slow and possessed no ECM capability. They could not be expected to penetrate American air defences. The medium and intermediate range ballistic missiles were excellent weapons but incapable of reaching the continental United States, and the first generations ICBMs, for which the Soviets had great hopes, proved too bulky to serve as a practical weapon. Only a few of them were actually deployed.

American estimates of the size and effectiveness of the Soviet missiles force had been highly speculative after May 1960 when U-2 overflights of the Soviet Union had been discontinued. This situation was rectified in the late summer of 1961 by the introduction of satellite reconnaissance which made the American intelligence community aware of the true strategic situation. At that time a far-reaching political decision was made to tell Moscow that Washington knew of their vulnerability.

The risk inherent in such a course of action was appreciated by President Kennedy who feared that the Soviets would now speed up their ICBM program. But the President and his advisors were more concerned with moderating Khrushchev's bellicosity, alarmingly manifest in his several Berlin ultimata, and thought this could be accomplished by communicating their awareness of American strategic superiority. The message was first conveyed by Roswell Gilpatric, Deputy Secretary of Defence, in a speech delivered in November 1961 and was subsequently reinforced throught other channels.

For Soviet leaders the political implications of this message must have been staggering. Almost overnight the Kremlin was confronted with the realization that its nuclear arsenal was not an effective deterrent. In the words of Roger Hilsman (1967, p. 164):

It was not so much the fact that the Americans had military superiority – that was not news to the Soviets. What was bound to frighten them most was that the Americans knew that they had military superiority. For the Soviets quickly realized that to have reached this conclusion the Americans must have made an intelligence breakthrough and found a way to pinpoint the location of the Soviet missiles that had been deployed as well as to calculate the total numbers. A 'soft' ICBM system with somewhat cumbersome launching techniques ... is an effective weapon for both a first strike ... and a second, retaliatory strike, so long as the location of the launching pads can be kept secret. However, if the enemy has a map with all the pads plotted, the system will retain some of its utility as a first-strike weapon, but almost none at all as a second-strike weapon. The whole Soviet ICBM system was suddenly obsolescent.

The Soviets were in a quandary. The missile gap could be closed by a crash program to develop more effective second generation ICBMs and perhaps a submersile delivery system. Such an effort was extremely costly and likely to meet strong opposition within the Soviet hierarchy. More importantly, a crash program did nothing to solve the short-term but paralyzing Soviet strategic inferiority that could be exploited by American leaders. The deployment of missiles in Cuba can be interpreted as a bold attempt to resolve this dilemma.

The forty-eight MRBMs and twenty-four IRBMs earmarked for Cuba represented at least a doubling of Soviet first-strike capability, and there is no reason to believe that the buildup would have stopped at seventy-two missiles. These missiles gave the Soviets limited second-strike capability, permitting them to launch a devastating attack against the Southern United States after having been attacked themselves. The IRBMs, which were liquid fueled and required fixed installations, were extremely vulnerable but the 1,000 mile range MRBMs were a mobile "field type" missile designed for use by ground forces in combat. They required only a flat area large enough to manoeuvre two vehicles back to back, a missile erector to lift the weapon into firing position and a trailer to transport the missile to location. They could be deactivated, moved and reactivated in a matter of days. Sufficient numbers of MRBMs in Cuba would have considerable deterrent value. They circumvented the United States Ballistic Early Warning System (BMEWS) as well as the DEW and Pinetree lines. They were also certain to be more accurate than missiles fired from the Soviet Union because of the greater proximity to American targets. Finally, by doubling the first strike capability of the Soviet Union, the Cuban missiles would have forced the United States to deploy its own striking force against a larger number of launch strikes, making the entire Soviet arsenal a little less vulnerable.

While concern for their security encouraged Soviet policymakers to assume the risks of Brinkmanship, they no doubt aspired to do more than merely counter the threat to their strategic arsenal. Soviet leaders must have been aware of the political rewards they would reap from putting their missiles into Cuba: Castro would be strengthened, Soviet resolution would be demonstrated to the Chinese and American influence throughout Latin America could be expected to decline. Brinkmanship is thus more than a defensive reaction to threatening developments in the international environment. It is an attempt to secure a significant, perhaps even decisive hedge against such developments in the future. Such a payoff may be necessary to convince policymakers that the risks associated with Brinkmanship are warranted.

A second motivation for aggressive foreign policy derives from the weakness of a state's political system. In four cases, Korea (1903–04), Bosnia (1908–09), July 1914 and the Arab-Israel War (1967), domestic political instability or the frangibility of the state itself was instrumental in convincing leaders to provoke a confrontation. They resorted to the time honoured technique of attempting to offset discontent at home by diplomatic success abroad. In 1903–04, Russian leaders looked with favor upon a confrontation with Japan because they expected that a war scare would strengthen nationalist sentiment and weaken the revolutionary movement. Viascheslav Plehve, the influential minister of interior, is alleged to have confided to the minister of war, General Kuropatkin: "What this country needs is a short victorious war to stem the tide of revolution" (Pokrovskii, 1925, p. iv). Some French leaders expected similar political benefits to arise from the Fashoda confrontation. While domestic politics was not paramount in minds of German leaders at the time of the First Morocco and Agadir crises, they nevertheless hoped that a successful demarche with France would arouse nationalist sentiment and weaken the power of social democracy. The same concern made German leaders more willing to risk war in 1914. Perhaps the best example of the extent to which Brinkmanship can be motivated by need to overcome internal difficulties are the Bosnian and July crises. Both were desperate attempts to shore up the stability of the Austro-Hungarian Empire.

The political weakness of leaders as distinct from the instability of the political system as a whole can provide another incentive for Brinkmanship. It can encourage leaders to seek political success abroad in order to buttress their position at home. Political weakness can also lead to confrontatory foreign policies because leaders feel too insecure to oppose policies they know to be very risky or ill-conceived. One or the other of these manifestations of political weakness appear to have played a part in the origins of ten Brinkmanship challenges. These are Fashoda (1898), Korea (1903–04), First Morocco (1906), Bosnia (1909), Agadir (1911–12), July (1914), Korea (1950), Sino-Indian (1962), Cuba (1962) and Arab-Israeli (1967).

A fourth incentive for Brinkmanship is associated with intra-elite competition for power. When the stakes are great and the competition intense, players may feel less bound by the normal rules of the game. Historically, this has most often happened when competition for influence within the policymaking elite reflects a broader social political struggle and the factions involved represent divergent views about the nature and structure of society. When this occurs, foreign policy issues may be assessed in terms of how they affect the balance of power between or among competing factions. French politics in the 'thirties is a case in point. Class antagonism so dominated politics that the cry of the French Right became "Better Hitler than Blum", and national interests in Europe were sacrificed to the domestic interests of a political coalition. Intense intra-elite competition was a primary cause of three Brinkmanship crises, Fashoda (1898), Korea (1903–04) and the Sino-Indian (1962). It was probably a secondary cause of several others. A bureaucratic sub-unit or political coalition can engineer a confrontation with a foreign power in the expectation that it will enhance their domestic influence or undermine that of their adversaries. Intra-elite competition can also induce actors to pursue policies calculated to enhance their domestic influence which have the side effect of provoking a crisis with another state. The Fashoda crisis is an example of the former and the Russo-Japanese crisis in Korea of the latter.

Sometimes leaders pursue aggressive foreign policies for irrational reasons that have little or nothing to do with their political needs or those of their state. "Hitler trod that path," Gerhard Weinberg (1970, p. 350) observes, "with a combination of caution and bravado, of opportunism and consistency, that leaves the observer torn between wonder and fear". The example of Hitler ought not to detract from the finding that the overwhelming majority of Brinkmanship crises could be attributed to strategic or domestic problems which encouraged or even compelled leaders to challenge commitments of their adversaries. A case by case approach would reveal that, Hitler aside, *several* incentives were operative in each instance and appear to have reinforced each other. The Cuban missile crisis might once again be cited as an example.

Earlier, we attributed the secret placement of Soviet missiles in Cuba to perceived strategic necessity: they offered Soviet leaders a "cheap" means of compensating for American nuclear superiority. But, as Graham Allison (1971, pp. 237–44) observes, putting missiles in Cuba may have been perceived as a solution to a number of different problems confronted by influential groups within the Soviet hierarchy. It may have appealed to the foreign ministry as a means of dramatizing Soviet support for Castro while also demonstrating resolve to Peking. It promised to achieve strategic goals cheaply, freeing funds for the industrial sector of the economy. If successful, it would also give Khrushchev more chips to play in Berlin. Finally, it promised to advance the domestic political interests of Khrushchev and his supporters who must certainly have felt the need for a major success after the failure of their two Berlin offensives and domestic agricultural programs. For all of these reasons, Allison (1971) suggests, a powerful coalition emerged in favor of putting missiles into Cuba, a coalition that consisted of bureaucrats and political leaders who envisaged the move as the solution to their particular problems. This is even more true of Brinkmanship because of the perceived risks it entails. Brinkmanship scenarios are not embarked upon casually or frequently. They normally require some kind of consensus within the policymaking elite, something which may presuppose the presence of several different kinds of incentives. Taken individually, these incentives build support for Brinkmanship by making it appear as the solution to a number of parochial problems. Taken together, they hold out the promise of sufficient return to make policymakers more willing to run the risks that Brinkmanship entails. As Roger Hilsman (1959) observes: "The test of a policy is not that it will most effectively accomplish an agreed-upon value but that a wider number of people decide to endorse it".

Deterrence theory assumes that credible commitments will not be challenged unless an adversary does so purposely to start a war.

Initiators of Brinkmanship crises expect to achieve their objectives short of war; they count on their adversaries to back down rather than fight. This, after all, is a defining characteristic of Brinkmanship crises. It follows that the initiators of Brinkmanship crises, rightly or wrongly, do not perceive the commitments they challenge to be credible. The historical record of our cases bears out this contention. We found that while the actual willingness of initiators to face the prospect of war varied considerably from case to case, policymakers in every instance expected their adversary to back down from his commitment when challenged. None of them were deliberately trying to provoke a war. The really interesting question is the extent to which it was reasonable for initiators of Brinkmanship crises to hold these expectations. Were there good reasons for them to suspect the credibility of their adversary's commitment? If so, what were these reasons? If not, why did they conclude that their adversaries would back down?

Credibility is a subjective notion because it concerns policymakers' perceptions of the *intentions* of other actors. Clearly, a commitment seen as credible by one policymaker may be questioned by another. Hitler, for example, correctly surmised that France and Britain would not go to war to defend Czechoslovakia. Most of his generals and foreign policy advisors thought otherwise. The subjective nature of credibility constitutes a serious problem for the analyst. As Christer Jonsson (1975, p. 86) laments: "Just as there is no sure way for an actor to make a commitment credible, there is no unequivocal criterion by which the researcher – or the actor – can make credibility estimations". The perceptions of policymakers in the state that might wish to challenge a commitment are the only ones that possess operational significance. But to determine credibility on the basis of an adversary's restraint or lack of it would be tautological. There must be some independent test of credibility if the concept of deterrence is to make any claims as a strategy of conflict avoidance. But until recently, proponents of deterrence had made very little effort to analyse its underlying assumptions or the criteria for its success. George and Smoke (1974, p. 62–64) concluded that deterrence theorists took its logic for granted and focused their efforts on the technical means of implementing it.

The literature on deterrence is nevertheless suggestive of four conditions that most analysts have come to regard as fundamental requirements of deterrence. Nations must (1) define their commitment clearly, (2) communicate its existence to possible adversaries, (3) develop the means to defend it or to punish adversaries who challenge it, and (4) demonstrate their resolve to carry out the actions that this entails. Successful deterrence also presupposes a degree of rationality on the part of a potential adversary in estimating the gains and losses arising from his challenge of a commitment.

The four conditions provide the criteria for assessing the credibility of the commitments that were challenged in our thirteen cases. They are the templates against which the accuracy of the initiator's judgement can be measured. This was done in three ways. The first involved the author's own estimate of the extent to which the commitments in question met all four conditions. Afterwards, the judgements of the historians and other social scientists were examined. In many cases this literature revealed a surprising degree of consensus about the apparent credibility, or lack of it, of the commitments involved. Third parties, policymakers whose states were not participants in the crisis, also formed opinions as to the likely outcome of a Brinkmanship challenge. Whenever possible, their estimates of credibility were incorporated into the assessments.

Imperfect as these judgements might be, they are nevertheless revealing. Naturally, in this chapter they can only be summarized, and the reader is referred to Lebow (1981) for a more detailed presentation of these findings and additional documentation on the origins of Brinkmanship crises. The data indicate that, more often than not, Brinkmanship challenges were initiated in the absence of any good evidence suggesting that the adversary lacked the resolve to defend his commitment. In many cases, the available evidence pointed to just the opposite conclusion, as the commitment in question appeared to meet all four conditions we have postulated as necessary for deterrence. Initiators of the Brinkmanship crises in our sample actually challenged more commitments that appeared credible than they did those whose credibility could reasonably have been questioned. In only five cases, First Morocco (1905–06), Bosnia (1908–09), Rhineland (1936), Munich (1938) and Berlin (1948) did initiators have compelling reasons for suspecting that their adversaries would back down from their commitments once challenged. In each of these instances the states whose commitments were challenged had given reasonably clear indications of their lack of resolve. In the Morocco, Bosnian and Berlin crises, they had failed to develop adequate means to defend their commitments. In the Rhineland, Munich and Berlin crises, they also appeared to lack the will to do so. In Berlin, the Western failure to make any serious effort to define their commitment may also have contributed to Soviet preceptions of its vulnerability. It is more difficult to explain how the initiators of the remaining Brinkmanship crises could have concluded that their adversaries would back down. Each of these commitments appears to have met the conditions for deterrence and initiators should have expected challenges of them to encounter strong resistance. At the very least, they should have been alert to the likelihood that such resistance would develop. In every one of these cases, in fact, the initiators were forced to back away from their challenge or face war. Even allowing for the ambiguity, uncertainty and confusion of the real world in contradistinction to the clarity, certainty and order of historical retrospection, the expectations that underlay these crisis scenarios seem difficult to account for on a rational basis.

These findings suggest that the presence of a vulnerable commitment does not appear to be a precondition of Brinkmanship. What counts is the perception by the initiator that such a vulnerable commitment exists. This judgement, as we have discovered, was more often than not erroneous in the cases we examined. These cases also suggest that faulty judgement was most often related to the perceived need by policymakers to pursue a Brinkmanship challenge. We found that when policymakers perceived the necessity of achieving specific foreign policy objectives they became predisposed to see these objectives as attainable. In the study, this is documented in the July, Korea (1950) and Sino-Indian crises. In all three cases, political leaders in the initiator felt compelled to pursue aggressive foreign policies in response to strategic and/or domestic political imperatives. They convinced themselves that they could achieve their respective policy objectives without provoking war with their adversary. Because they knew the extent to which they were powerless to back down, they expected that their adversaries would have to. Some of these leaders also took comfort in the illusion that they would emerge victorious at relatively little cost to themselves if war in fact developed. German, American and Indian policymakers maintained these beliefs despite the accumulation of considerable evidence to the contrary both before and during the crisis. They resorted to elaborate personal and institutional defences to avoid having to come to terms with this information. The most prevalent defence mechanism was denial. The Kaiser and those around him used it to discredit reports that Britain would intervene in a continental war. Acheson and Nehru and their advisors resorted to it to discount the possibility that American or Indian policies would provoke a Chinese military response. On an institutional level, denial took the form of structuring feedback channels to filter out dissonant information and to reinforce the preconceived notions of political leaders. In such a closed decisionmaking environment events during the crisis did little to disabuse policymakers of their unrealistic expectations. These case histories suggest the pessimistic hypothesis that those policymakers with the greatest need to learn from external reality appear the least likely to do so.

Our empirical findings raise serious questions about the utility of deterrence. If policymakers rationalize the conditions for the success of a foreign policy to the extent they feel compelled to pursue it, efforts to impart credibility to commitments may have only a marginal impact on an adversary's behaviour. Even the most elaborate efforts to demonstrate prowess and resolve may prove insufficient to discourage a challenge when policymakers are attracted to a policy of Brinkmanship as a necessary means of preserving vital strategic and domestic political interests. Fashoda, July and Korea (1950), the Sino-Indian crisis and Cuba all attest to the seriousness of this problem. In each of these cases, the defending state not only did its best to buttress the credibility of its commitment but the commitments in question represented interests of sufficient political or strategic magnitude to have given any adversary consideration to pause. The Russian challenge of Japan in 1903–04 and the Japanese attack on Pearl Harbour can probably be cited as further evidence of wishful thinking. In the latter case, Japanese leaders realized that the disparity in economic power and access to resources between themselves and the United States meant that Japan could only succeed in winning a limited war of short duration. They accordingly convinced themselves that the United States would fight such a war. Pearl Harbour was the consequence of this delusion (Snyder and Diesing, 1977, p. 301).

These cases and others point to the importance of motivation as the key to Brinkmanship challenges. To the extent that leaders perceive the need to act they become insensitive to the interests and commitments of others that stand in the way of the success of their policy. The converse may also hold true. In the absence of compelling domestic and strategic needs most leaders may be reluctant or unwilling to pursue confrontatory foreign policies even when they hold out a reasonable prospect of success. The existence of a Hitler, the one policymaker in our sample whose Brinkmanship ventures could not easily be attributed to reasons of state, should not detract from what may be a generally valid conclusion.

If our analysis of the origins of Brinkmanship is correct, it not only indicates that deterrence is a less than satisfactory strategy of conflict avoidance but points to two reasons why this is so. The first of these we have already noted; when policymakers feel compelled to act they may employ denial, selective attention or other psychological sleights of hand to dismiss indications of an adversary's resolve. The complex and ambiguous nature of the international environment does not make it a breeding ground of restraint but rather of irrational confidence. The second reason is that aggression is less a function of opportunity than it is of need. We found reasonable opportunity for aggression (i.e., a vulnerable commitment) in only one-third of our cases but discovered strong needs to pursue an aggressive foreign policy in almost every instance. This suggests that policymakers, at least in Brinkmanship crises, are more responsive to internal imperatives than they are to external opportunities.

Because deterrence attempts to prevent aggression by removing the opportunity for it, it is most germane to situations characterized by pure conflict where overt hostility is muted only by perceptions of cost. Such situations are hard to find; the closest contemporary approximation may be Syrian-Israeli relations as seen from Damascus. Most international conflicts are less extreme. They contain an important element of defensive motivation (i.e., concern for security) on both sides as well as offensive goals. Deterrence becomes less relevant to the extent that a conflict can be described as a mutual security dilemma. Deterrence can even be dysfuntional in such a situation because it does nothing to defuse hostility. It may actually intensify it by appearing to confirm mutual suspicions of aggressive intent. The Soviet-American arms race has probably functioned in this manner.

The finding that motivation is a more important source of aggression than opportunity suggests a corresponding shift in the focus of our efforts to prevent aggression. It may be that we devote too much attention, in theory and in practice, to the credibility of our commitments and not nearly enough to trying to understand what might actually prompt an adversary to challenge these commitments. It is an article of faith among many American strategists that deterrence is difficult to achieve and that its success turns on fine technical details. Some strategists have made careers out of detecting alleged American strategic vulnerabilities. They have dreamed up scenarios in which the Soviets exploit some asymmetry in the strategic balance in order to launch a crippling first strike that destroys our land based deterrent. These strategists generally assume that the United States will not respond with its sea based nuclear forces for fear of having its cities destroyed by a retaliatory Soviet strike *and* that the Soviets know this with certainty – this is after all what makes their attack possible.

These scenarios are not only very far fetched in a technical sense but they also assume that the Soviet ability to launch such an attack is limited only by the number and performance characteristics of their delivery systems and warheads. They overlook the entire range of constraints, social and political as well as technical, that probably prevent the Soviet leaders from seriously contemplating such a strike. Despite the political and even military unreality of these scenarios, billions of dollars have been authorized to correct the perceived deficiences they point to. This has been done on the further assumption that the Soviets could somehow exploit any kind of strategic edge to their political advantage or might even be tempted to launch a first strike if they believed that they would suffer relatively less damage from a nuclear exchange. Concern for the nuclear balance has become even more acute in recent years in response to the growing sophistication of the Soviet nuclear arsenal. Fear for the possible vulnerability of the Minuteman missile system was offered by the Carter administration as justification for their support of the MX missile and the multiple protective shelter (MPS) mode for its deployment. In theory, this would enhance the survivability of the American land based deterrent by forcing the Soviets to target a finite number of warheads against several times the number of launch pads than would otherwise be the case. A number of telling arguments have been made by the opponents of these systems to demonstrate that they would do little to enhance our security and might even detract from it (Callahan et al, 1978; Tsipis, 1979). Objections can also be raised with regard to the premise upon which these systems are based: that even a marginal Soviet advantage would tempt them to pursue a more aggressive foreign policy. What we have learned about Brinkmanship suggests that strategic advantage, which the Soviets are far from achieving in any case, rarely provides the incentive for a foreign policy challenge. This arises instead from a combination of political and strategic insecurities which push leaders in the direction of aggressive foreign policies. The Cuban missile crisis, it should be remembered, was not precipitated by a Soviet perception of their strategic advantage – quite the reverse. According to most students of the crisis, Moscow put missiles into Cuba as a way of overcoming their unacceptable strategic *inferiority*. Kahan and Long (1972, p. 585) argue that the crisis was actually caused by American insensitivity to the Soviet's strategic dilemma:

The Kennedy administration's early emphasis on superiority can be said to have helped cause the crisis by tilting the nuclear balance so far against the Soviets that they were forced to emplace missiles in Cuba in order to rectify the strategic relationship. Had the U.S. become more sensitive to the Soviet needs – both political and military – for equality, it might have not pressed its advantage as far as it did and have avoided the risks of the Cuban confrontation.

It is unwarranted and perhaps even dangerous to dismiss deterrence totally or to ignore the strategic balance between the United States and the Soviet Union. If only for its political effect upon third parties, the United States must be careful not to convey the impression that it is falling behind its rival in military prowess. In this regard, retired admirals and generals who make post-military careers for themselves by questioning American strength and resolve probably do more damage than any new Soviet strategic system. In sum, American strategists should probably pay less attention to arcane calculations of equivalence and more to the kinds of circumstances, both domestic and foreign, that would encourage an adversary to challenge and important American commitment. Just what combination of internal and external incentives would lead the Soviets to pursue policies that might risk a major confrontation or even a war with the United States? How could these conditions come about? What, if anything, could American leaders do, consonant with their own interests, to discourage the development of these conditions?

Confrontation in the 1980s?

Our study of Brinkmanship points to motivation as the key to aggressive foreign policy, that is to the combination of foreign and domestic problems that leaders believe can only be surmounted through the successful challenge of an adversary's commitment. In the foreign sphere, the most important of these problems arises from a dramatic shift in the balance of power in an adversary's favor. Domestic incentives for Brinkmanship are provided by fear for the survival of the state, its political system or leaders. To what extent are such problems likely to develop in the Soviet Union in the course of the coming decade? Are they likely to become sufficiently acute to push Soviet leaders into pursuing a more aggressive foreign policy?

Soviet concern for their security can certainly be expected to intensify in the next ten years. The primary reason for this is that the United States and China, the Soviets' two major adversaries, are likely to become relatively more powerful and more closely linked together in efforts to oppose the Soviet Union. In all likelihood, Russian leaders will exaggerate the extent of both developments.

In the case of China, the Soviets were disappointed but probably not surprised that the passing of Mao brought no improvement in relations. Mao's successors insisted on the same terms for reapprochement: demilitarization of Mongolia and the Sino-Soviet border. The Soviet-Chinese Friendship Treaty expired in April 1980 and was not renewed. Bilateral contacts have continued to decline and contacts in international forums remain cool and formal. Chinese propaganda efforts against the Soviet Union have increased in scope and intensity as have the Chinese attempts to foster subversion within the USSR. More importantly, the Chinese seem on the road to putting their own house in order and are intent on pursuing more pragmatic policies aimed at rapid economic development. At the same time, they have continued with their strategic weapons program and have begun efforts to modernize their largely obsolescent conventional forces.

The Chinese currently possess perhaps five hundred nuclear warheads and a small number of operational MRBMs with a range of 600–700 miles (IISS 1979, p. 59). Peking has recently tested a new ICBM, the CSS-4, with sufficient range to reach any target in the Soviet Union (*Aviation Week*, 25 August 1980, p. 16). This system and perhaps the "Long March 4", will become operational in the course of the next several years. The People's Liberation Army

(PLA), the largest armed force in the world, consists largely of infantry; only 11 of its 129 Main Force divisions are armoured (IISS 1979, p. 59). As its recent performance in Vietnam indicates, the PLA has only limited offensive capability. However, this capability can be expected to improve over the course of the coming decade. Chinese airpower, although numbering over 5,000 warplanes, remains weak as even their most advanced platforms are no match for Soviet aircraft in performance. There is little likelihood that the Chinese can significantly close this gap unless they are able to procure advanced Western weapon systems.

In response to the sharp deterioration in Sino-Soviet relations in the 1970s the Soviets moved to strengthen their military position in the Far East. Before Mao's death, the buildup along the Chinese border reached forty-three divisions supported by numerous modern combat aircraft, prepositioned munitions and an expanding communications and transportation network. The Soviets also began work on the Baikal-Amur Railway (BAM) to provide a second and more secure route to the Maritime Provinces than the single track Trans-Siberian Railway, long stretches of which run close to the Chinese border.

The Soviet buildup, designed to moderate Chinese policy, failed to achieve its objective. Rather, it encouraged Peking to seek a rapprochement with the United States. The Chinese also shifted the bulk of the PLA from the South, where it had faced the American forces in Indochina, to the North, opposite major Soviet force deployments. These moves, along with the apparent Chinese commitment to modernize their forces, have only heightened Soviet concern for China as recent Soviet military moves along the Chinese border make apparent. In the Spring of 1978, Moscow publicly identified China as her primary enemy. In April of that year Brezhnev visited the Far East and resurrected the Far Eastern Theatre of Operations, established in 1945 prior to the invasion of Manchuria and disbanded in 1953 at the end of the Korean War. A month later, Marshal Nikolai Ogarkov, chief of the general staff, was sent out to oversee the integration of several military districts, the Pacific Fleet and the area's strategic forces into the new command (FBIS (China), 13 August 1980, p. 1). In the course of the last two years, the Far Eastern Theatre has received additional ground and air forces and much modern equipment, including the aircraft carrier *Minsk*.

On China's southern flank the Soviet Union has provided billions of dollars of military assistance to Vietnam. Since the Soviet-Vietnamese Friendship Treaty of March 1978, the Russians have become ever more deeply involved in the training, resupply and logistics of their Vietnamese ally. Soviet aid, estimated to represent some 25% of the Vietnamese GNP, has enabled that country to pursue the conquest of Indochina. The intensity of Chinese-Vietnamese hostility, which remains acute in the aftermath of their 1979 war, paralleled by the increasing closeness of Vietnam to the Soviet Union, bodes ill for the future of Sino-Soviet relations. For the duration of the 1980s, relations between the two giants of the Eurasian landmass will continue to deteriorate even if they do not lead to hostilities.

If the Soviets have become more concerned for their security in the East, they must also be more alarmed about their situation in the West. Détente, in which Brezhnev in particular seems to have put great store, is dead. It became a political liability in the United States even before the Soviet invasion of Afghanistan. There is very little chance that Soviet-American relations will improve so long as the Soviet military operations in Afghanistan continue.

Soviet interest in détente derived from political, strategic and economic concerns. Closer relations with the West were expected to moderate Chinese expressions of their hostility, enhance Soviet security through an arms control agreement with the United States and revive their flagging economy through the infusion of imported technology. For the most part, these aspirations remain unfulfilled, a situation that will exacerbate some of the serious problems the Soviets can be expected to face in the coming decade.

American defence spending can be expected to increase over the next few years in response to the widely shared perception that the international political situation has become more unstable and threatening. This means that the Soviet military advantage in Europe, which became even more pronounced in the 1970s, will be diminished considerably. Even in the absence of higher defence budgets, Western force improvements mandated by NATO heads of government in 1978, will begin to take effect in 1982–83 as new weapons, doctrines and organization come on line. Most of the new weapons systems will incorporate state of the art technology such as Chobham armour and "fire and forget" munitions, developments not yet available to the Soviets. No serious analyst alleges that the Long-Term Defence Program will give NATO an edge over the Warsaw Pact but it will raise considerably both the cost and uncertainty of the outcome of any Soviet attack on Western Europe. Of equal importance politically, it will cause a shift in the perception of the military relationship that has shaped East-West relations in Europe since the end of World War II. For the first time in three decades the salient perception will be that militarily, things are getting better for the West. The greatest absolute growth in military capability will occur in the West, not in the East. The highest rate of military improvement will be in the West, not in the East. And the gap between Western and Eastern capabilities will narrow, not widen. This can be expected to have the same kind of impact upon the thinking and calculations of Europeans on both sides of the divide as Soviet force modernization and expansion did in the last decade.

In the strategic realm the correlation of forces can also be expected to shift in the direction of the West. As with conventional systems, Soviet development programs in the 'seventies led to the deployment of systems which significantly improved their position vis a vis the West. The SS-18 and SS-19, versions of which were first deployed in 1975, gave the Soviets an effective second strike capability, something they had lacked before. More ominously, both systems can carry MIRVs – the SS-18 mod 4 has been tested with up to ten – greatly enhancing the number of warheads the Soviets can deliver against the continental United States. Both the SS-18 and SS-19 are also far more accurate than their predecessors, something that gives them a certain capability against hardened targets, including missile silos.

Despite the warnings of some self-appointed strategic Cassandras, the United States still retains a margin of strategic superiority measured in terms of the number and accuracy of the warheads it can deliver against the Soviet Union. Even after a "sneak" Soviet first strike – at best a theoretical possibility – the United States would have sufficient forces left to carry out a wide range of retaliatory options. US ability to do this will increase considerably in the 1980s. The MX missile, regardless of its ultimate mode of deployment, will enhance US delivery capability because it carries ten MIRVs instead of the three of Minuteman III and is also more accurate. If deployed in a mobile mode, as the Carter Administration intended, it will complicate the Soviet targeting problem. The new Ohio class submarines, equipped with the Trident missile, will improve US seaborne deterrence because of the greater range, payload and accuracy of its missiles. By 1985, seventy percent of US MIRVed missiles will be at sea where they will be largely invulnerable for the foreseeable future. By way of contrast, seventy-five percent of the Soviets MIRVs will remain in stationary silos where they will be vulnerable not only to MX but also to Trident II, the first sea launched intercontinental missile to have the accuracy to serve as a counterforce weapon.

The Soviets will also confront the deployment by the West of airborne (ALCM), ground launched (GLCM) and possibly sea launched (SLCM) cruise missiles. A low flying terrain hugging sub-sonic platform, the cruise missile is designed to penetrate Soviet air defences by virtue of its numbers and low radar profile. An effective Soviet defence against cruise missiles will require interceptors equipped with very sophisticated "Look-down shoot-down" radars and a fleet of airborne warning craft, similar to our AWACS. They are not expected to field such a capability for some years to come. The Soviets must also contend with the strategic force modernization now being carried out by France and Britain, the latter committed to replacing its obsolescent Polaris missiles with the new Trident system. Finally, the United States might conceivably deploy a number of new weapons based on advanced technologies. Secretary of Defense Harold Brown's recent revelation of the progress that has been made on a "Stealth" aircraft invisible to radar is a case in point (*Washington Post*, 21 August 1980, p. 1). American breakthroughs in the field of anti-ICBM weapons, something the Soviets must at least contemplate, would be even more threatening to them.

Whatever the actual extent of the strategic shift in favor of the West it is almost certain to be perceived by the Russians as greater and more threatening than reality warrants. There are two reasons for this. The first pertains to the way in which strategic calculations are made. Analysts are generally more sensitive to their adversary's strength and their own country's weakness rather than *vice versa*. Strategic calculations, as we noted earlier, are usually based on worst case or at least conservative scenarios that posit all kinds of advantages for the adversary. This kind of force comparison invariably leads to over-valuation of the threat. It also tends to make analysts insensitive to the fears that an adversary has for his security, fears derived from *his* worst case estimates of the strategic balance. Insensitivity to an adversary's strategic anxieties encourages analysts and policymakers to impute aggressive intentions to any increment or improvement in his forces. After all, if, by their calculations, he has more than enough capability for his "legitimate" defence needs, then any further military buildup must be for aggressive purposes. The current alarm in the United States over the Soviet strategic buildup is to a great extent the result of such a process. The mirror image is likely to prevail in the mid-1980s when new American strategic forces are deployed. Any further force improvements will only intensify Soviet concern.

This brings us to the second reason why it is probable that the Soviets will exaggerate the threat posed by our strategic forces. This is the political context in which the meaning of these forces must be assessed. It is likely that Soviet leaders will see the international environment in the second half of the decade as fraught with dangers for themselves.

The primary Soviet fear, fanned by the events of the last few years, is that Sino-American rapprochement will develop into a full-blown alliance directed against themselves. In the past, Soviet leaders have characterized Chinese-American cooperation as "opportunistic collusion", by which they meant sporadic tactical collaboration against the USSR. In the last year they have begun to accuse their adversaries of plotting against them, militarily and politically, on a coordinated long-term basis. Understandably, they are nonplussed by the prospect of the world's most populous nation in alliance with the most technologically advanced. In this regard, the Soviets must be particularly concerned with the possibility that a massive infusion of American or Western technology into China will enhance her military capability and perhaps encourage Peking to pursue a more aggressive foreign policy. The ultimate Soviet nightmare is, of course, encirclement: a United States-Japan (rearmed)-PRC-NATO coalition directed against themselves and capable of being exploited by the Chinese for their revanchist goals.

Encirclement is nowhere close to becoming a reality. NATO countries are reluctant to enter into any commitment outside of Europe and become positively nervous when the United States does; Japan is not on the verge of rearming and has been very cautious about being drawn into the Sino-Soviet dispute; and the United States, while anxious to use China as a means of offsetting the Soviet Union, has carefully avoided entering into any kind of formal alliance with Peking and, to date, has refrained from selling her arms. Encirclement is likely to remain a dark fear in the back of Soviet minds unless they act in ways to bring such an alliance into being. Here, an analogy to pre-1914 Germany is appropriate.

Ever since the creation of the German *Reich* in 1871, the nightmare of German leaders was encirclement by hostile neighbours. In the West, French antagonism was taken as given. In the East, Bismarck maintained friendly relations with both Russia and Austria-Hungary, a task that required considerable finesse. His sucessors possessed neither his skill nor wisdom and allowed Russo-German relations to deteriorate to the point where Russia moved closer to France. The Franco-Russian alliance of 1893 touched off German fears of encirclement. German anxieties intensified between 1893 and 1905. Italy loosened her ties with the *Reich* and moved closer to France. Anglo-German relations, carefully nurtured by Bismarck, also deteriorated by reason of German naval and colonial pretensions. Worst of all, the Anglo-French *Entente* of 1904 raised the spectre of Britain joining the Franco-Russian alliance against Germany. It was this fear that prompted desperate German leaders to provoke a confrontation with France, the Moroccan crisis of 1905–06, in the hope of separating France from Britain. However, the crisis had the opposite effect; it brought Britain and France closer together and encouraged them to initiate staff talks with the purpose of coordinating their military planning in case of war with Germany. Subsequent crises provoked by Germany in 1909 and 1911 to break the ring of encirclement were similarly self-defeating and actually brought into being the very combination of alliances that she had feared.

The Soviets appear to have a similar fear of encirclement and alas, a similar propensity for diplomatic clumsiness. The Russo-

Finnish War and the Stalin-Hitler Pact, it should be remembered, were part and parcel of the Soviet's last response to the threat of encirclement. If the Soviet Union's relations with her neighbours continues to deteriorate it is conceivable that some future Sino-American or perhaps Sino-Japanese security initiative will arouse such extreme anxiety in Moscow as to convince Soviet leaders that drastic action is required to preserve their strategic position. As did the Germans in 1904, 1909, 1911 and 1914, they may resort to Brinkmanship in the hope of breaking up the coalition of hostile states they see arrayed against them. However, such heavy-handed efforts, as is the case with their invasion of Afghanistan, are just as likely to strengthen their adversaries' resolve which in turn can only exacerbate Moscow's insecurity. The danger here is that such a charged environment would encourage the Soviets, as it did the Germans in 1914, to contemplate even more desperate measures hoping that they could keep matters from getting too far out of hand.

In our study of Brinkmanship we found that such a policy was almost invariably associated with domestic as well as foreign incentives. Both seem necessary in order to mobilize support within the policymaking elite in favour of risky foreign ventures. The most important domestic incentives arise from policymakers' concern for the survival of their state, political system or their own position for power. Such concerns are likely to become more pronounced in the minds of Soviet leaders in the years ahead.

The major internal threat to the Soviet Union derives from the restlessness of the peoples of Eastern Europe. Eastern Europe can be considered an internal problem in the sense that these countries are within the confines of what might be considered the Soviet Empire. For this reason, the Soviets have long recognized that developments in Eastern Europe usually have immediate repercussions with the USSR and thus have important implications for its internal stability. In 1968, for example, Brezhnev is reported to have told Wladyslaw Gomulka that all the Warsaw Pact nations must contribute forces for the invasion of Czechoslovakia because in the absence of East bloc solidarity the unrest might spill over into the Ukraine (*New York Times*, 28 August 1980, p. 8). Recent evidence of the extent to which the Soviets see their Western border as permeable is provided by their insistence that television coverage of the Pope's visit to Poland not be broadcast in northeastern Poland because it could then be picked up in Soviet Lithuania. At the moment of writing, the Soviets, for the same reason, are jamming broadcasts from the West describing the strikes in Poland. The magnitude of Soviet concern is attested to by the fact that this is the first time in the last seven years that they resorted to jamming Western broadcasts (*New York Times*, 28 August 1980, p. 8; 1 September 1980, p. 1).

The Soviets appear to subscribe to their own "domino theory", and one that makes more sense than the American fear in the 1960s of falling dominos in Southeast Asia. As did the czars before them, Soviet leaders fear that political liberalization anywhere within their Eastern European empire will lead to demands for similar freedoms with the Soviet Union itself. The actual loss of a satellite to socialism or the Warsaw Pact would have even more serious repercussions given the difficulty all of the communist governments of Eastern Europe have with respect to legitimacy. If one Eastern European state pursues too independent a course all are endangered. If all or even part of Eastern Europe ever succeeded in breaking away, Soviet control of the Baltic republics and the Ukraine would be threatened. Both these areas, and most of the other border provinces of the Soviet Union, are populated by nationalities that are antagonistic to Russian domination and quiescent only because of their respect and fear of Soviet power. This is why the Soviets felt the need to crush the workers' uprising in East Germany in 1953 and invaded Hungary in 1956 and Czechoslovakia in 1968.

The communist governments of Eastern Europe have an even more difficult time of maintaining themselves. They must satisfy two masters: the Kremlin and their own people. Most have attempted to do this by following Soviet guidance with respect to internal structure and foreign policy but at the same time attempting to win popular support by raising the living standards of their people. Hungary, Poland and East Germany all follow this strategy which Khrushchev derisively dubbed "goulash communism". Since the Prague Spring came to an end, the Czech government has attempted to pursue this approach as well. Roumania has developed its own variant which consists of ideological rigidity at home coupled with a semi-independent foreign policy designed to appeal to the national feelings of the Roumanian people. Bulgaria, with no religious or national strains, and a history of close relations with Russia, is a special case.

In the years ahead it will become increasingly difficult for Eastern European governments to satisfy simultaneously their two different constituencies. For a start, most of these governments have never really succeeded in holding out affluence as a substitute for political freedom and meaningful national independence. As recent events in Poland demonstrate, Eastern Europeans are far from satisfied with their standard of living and attribute much of the problem to mismanagement. Even in East Germany, certainly the most properous of the satellites, people are disgruntled over the differences between their standard of living and that of the West. They are also well aware of the differences as 60–65% of East Germans watch West German television every night (*New York Times*, 28 August 1980, p. 8). Dissatisfaction is almost certain to increase as the economic prospects for Eastern Europe are not encouraging.

The German Institute for Economic Research estimates that Eastern European economies only expanded 2% last year compared with their planned goal of 4.3%. Moreover, much of this growth was financed through foreign loans. Between 1979 and 1980, the combined Eastern European debt rose from 41 to 48 billion dollars (*New York Times*, 21 August 1980, p. 11). The Poles alone owe 19.4 billion dollars, the servicing of which has become a severe burden. The rising cost of energy will become the greatest constraint upon growth. East Europeans have been accustomed to cheap and plentiful energy from the Soviet Union; this year the Soviets will supply 70% of their energy at 40% below the world market price as there is an agreed upon five year lag in Soviet oil pricing (*New York Times*, 20 August 1980, p. 20). But the Soviet Union is itself expected to become a net importer of energy by 1985 and has already put the members of Comecon on notice that they will have to find alternative sources of energy supply. The Soviets are expected to provide no more than 50% of Eastern Europe's energy by 1990. They are also likely to cut back on their supply of raw materials. Increasing energy costs, uncertain access to raw materials and a declining labour force will all contribute to economic malaise in Eastern Europe.

Economic problems in Eastern Europe will almost certainly have political consequences, as the current troubles in Poland make apparent. Widespread unrest in more than one satellite will compel its government to make concessions of an economic and perhaps even of a political nature in order to keep the lid on protest. However, Eastern European governments can go only so far in this direction without running afoul of Moscow. And to the extent that Soviet leaders feel threatened by international developments the latitude they allow the Eastern Europeans is likely to diminish. The point may be reached where these governments can no longer satisfy their two constituencies. The Soviets will then face the choice of intervening directly or of allowing their satellites to become more responsive to popular demands. Both alternatives have dire consequences for Soviet security.

Moves towards liberalization or repression in Eastern Europe will be watched carefully by all the restive nationalists in the European provinces of the Soviet Union. However, the most serious nationality problems the Soviets ultimately will confront are in Central Asia. Since the early 1920s the Soviets have tried to win the support of these peoples by transforming their societies. In sixty years they have succeeded in modernizing the Caucasus and Central Asia. Traditional elites have been supplanted by a growing class of intelligentsia and, to a lesser extent, skilled workers, enjoying a degree of relative prosperity. However, this new elite has resisted Russification and has increasingly come to resent Russian domination of the political and economic life of their respective Republics or autonomous regions. In effect, education and urbanization, instead of eradicating traditional cultures appear to have reinforced them. The mass of Central Asians, the overwhelming majority of whom are Muslims, continue to adhere to traditional values. Their knowledge of Russian is actually declining. Everywhere in Central Asia, life is becoming more nationalized (Allworth, 1971; Azrael, 1978; D'Encausse, 1979).

Developments in Central Asia probably pose a long term threat to the very survival of the Soviet Union. Soviet Muslims, who now number about forty million, are experiencing a population explosion; their estimated growth rate is 3.03%. By way of contrast, the Russians, now a minority within the Soviet Union, have a growth rate of only 1.20%, slightly above the very low 1.06% rate of the Soviet European population as a whole (D'Encausse, 1979). Between the late 1980s and the end of the century, non-Europeans will come to constitute 40% of the labour force and an even higher percentage of the 18 year old cohort available for military training. Most of these young people are expected to have only a rudimentary grasp of the Russian language. The size, demographic dynamism, political alienation and geographic position of the Central Asians along the Chinese border, already make Soviet leaders uneasy.

The extent to which the nationality problem becomes acute will be influenced by economic developments. Economic progress and greater affluence could be expected to mute to some degree expressions of nationalist dissatisfaction. Conversely, economic stagnation would be likely to intensify the pace and scope of demands for autonomy. Soviet economic growth, both predicted and actual, declined throughout the 1970s. The five year plan adopted in 1971 calls for a growth rate of 6.9%. This figure was revised downwards to 4.4% in the following five year plan, approved in 1975. Even so, the real growth was less than half this figure, and in 1978–79, it dropped to 2.1%, the worst performance since the end of World War II (CIA, 1980).

Economic growth in the 1980s faces even greater obstacles. The Soviets will no longer be able to count on an abundant energy supply. The United States Central Intelligence Agency estimates that they will become a net importer of energy by 1985 (1977). Bad harvests, resulting in lower agricultural production, will also require the expenditure of scarce foreign currency assets. Both the energy and agricultural problems will reduce the foreign exchange available to pay for the importation of Western technology upon which economic growth heavily depends. Growth will further be constrained by the lower rate of growth and different composition of the labour force.

Between the end of World War II and the present, increased industrial output in the USSR has been a function of the increase in the size of the European workforce, not the result of any increase in *per capita* productivity. The latter has increased only marginally despite major efforts devoted to the goal. Given the demographic trends already noted, the Soviets will be forced gradually to shift their industrial base to Central Asia or to train and import ever larger numbers of Central Asians to Europe. Either strategy will prove very costly and fraught with political danger.

We have described a less than encouraging future for the Soviet Union. While the author believes that such a prospect is very real one can nevertheless hope that neither the domestic nor the international situation deteriorates to the point where Soviet leaders feel so threatened that they are increasingly attracted to risky foreign policies. But even less dramatic setbacks at home and abroad will still leave Soviets in a less favorable strategic position and facing intensified Chinese hostility and greater Sino-American collaboration. Within her empire, Eastern Europeans will become more restive and difficult to control as will many of her own national minorities. Finally, a lower growth rate, and possily even economic stagnation, will make it impossible for Soviet leaders to continue their current level of military spending and still hope to satisfy growing domestic demands for greater material well-being. A cut back in either area – a reduction in military spending seems the most likely of the two – will have detrimental implications for Soviet security.

At the very least therefore, Soviet leaders are likely to see themselves as vulnerable and on the defensive. Historically, policy makers in such situations have usually exaggerated not minimized the extent of their own weaknesses. They have also tended to exhibit an exaggerated concern for their credibility, convinced that any sign of weakness on their part will only encourage more aggressive behaviour by their adversaries. American policymakers are currently displaying such a neurotic response to a decline in their international position brought about by their failure in Indochina, the Soviet strategic buildup and, more recently, events in Iran. The Soviet dilemma, which objectively is likely to be greater in magnitude and more enduring in its consequences, can be expected to engender an even more irrational and pessimistic outlook among Soviet leaders. Such fear for the future on their part does not bode well for the security of either superpower.

Conclusions

The preceding analysis, while critical of deterrence, should not be construed as a call for the renunciation of that concept. Deterrence can make a positive contribution toward regulating conflict. It encourages leaders to define and articulate commitments and thus to make decisions about the nature of their interests and which among them are sufficiently vital to risk war to defend. Firm efforts to define and impart credibility to commitments may also reduce the probability of a challenge through miscalculation on the part of an adversary. But, as we have argued, even elaborate efforts to impart credibility to a commitment by no means preclude self-deception.

Our findings point to the conclusion that most adversarial relations are best managed by a combination of firmness *and* sensitivity to the security concerns of an adversary. Firmness is necessary to give a clear indication of resolve, sensitivity to avoid, if possible, putting the adversary in a position where he feels compelled to embrace confrontatory foreign policies. Finding the right mix of overt confrontation and tacit cooperation is by no means and easy task. In situations where an adversary's power base is fragile or his concern for its maintenance borders on paranoia it may prove impossible. Could Britain, for example, have convinced Wilhelmian Germany that her fear of encirclement was neurotic? We will never know as British statesmen never made a sustained effort to this end. At the very least, it might prevent Soviet anxiety from becoming even more acute. The Soviets would be equally well advised to consider such a foreign policy objective vis a vis the United States.

A shift, even a subtle one, in the focus of our approach to conflict avoidance is certain to meet considerable opposition from the self-styled adherents of *Realpolitik* because of its emphasis on political sensitivity instead of military hardware. It is also certain to require a very different set of skills. Neither problem should detract from the elemental truth that efforts to understand and mitigate the sources of conflict are likely to be more effective in the long run than attempts to suppress their manifestations.

15 Arms Control
The Record of the 1970s and the Outlook for the 1980s

J. OWEN ZURHELLEN JR.

The Soviet dissident Andrei D. Sakharov says that 'negotiations on disarmament are possible only on the basis of strategic parity' (*New York Times Magazine*, 15 June 1980), an idea that seems to have wide concurrence. Making strategic parity a basis for arms control negotiations is hampered by a time constraint, the difference in the rate of weapons development in the Soviet Union and the United States. The problem is that a surge on one side is not necessarily matched on the other side; quite the contrary, the United States and the USSR in past decades have been very much out of phase and remain so.

A possible judgment on the decade of the 1970s in the area of arms control may well be that a rapidly expanding Soviet force approached and gained parity with the force of the United States at some point in the decade, that an opportunity then existed for meaningful arms control results, that that opportunity was missed, and that it is problematic whether the parity, if it still exists, will last much longer. Thus, the future of strategic arms control in the 1980s is doubtful, at the least.

By the early 1960s the agenda for arms control was already well established. At the top of the list stood the control of nuclear weapons, so much more destructive than all other weapons that their control is one of the primary concerns of mankind. While the United Kingdom, France and subsequently China also had nuclear weapons, it was the United States and the USSR which had the power to destroy the world and it was to these two powers that the world looked for meaningful leadership in the control of nuclear weapons. By the beginning of the 1970s, when the Strategic Arms Limitation Talks (SALT) got down to serious business, a significant groundwork had already been laid.

As early as 1963, the USSR and the US signed an agreement establishing a 'hot line' between their capitals for rapid and direct communication between the governments in time of crisis. In 1971 this agreement was brought up to date to make use of the new satellite technology and make the circuits more reliable.

Also in 1963 the United States, the USSR and the United Kingdom signed and ratified, and invited other nations of the world to do the same, a Limited Test Ban Treaty prohibiting nuclear weapons tests in the atmosphere, in outer space and under water. Though more than 100 nations have adhered to this agreement, the other two nuclear powers, France and China, have not. (France, however, has discontinued all but underground nuclear tests.) By limiting tests to under ground, the test ban treaty makes testing more difficult, more costly and more time-consuming.

The 1967 Outer Space Treaty, open to signature by all nations, prohibited the placing of nuclear weapons or other weapons of mass destruction in space orbit. It banned testing and the establishment of bases as well as military manoeuvres in outer space.

The Seabed Treaty of 1971, finally, prohibited the emplacement of nuclear weapons and other weapons of mass destruction on or below the seabed beyond the 12-mile limit. Again, many of the world's nations have adhered to this treaty.

The Limited Test Ban Treaty and the agreements prohibiting nuclear weapons in outer space and on the seabed are based on the concept that the existence of nuclear weapons tends to promote the possibility of nuclear war and that, conversely, anything that inhibits, limits or finally prevents the production and proliferation of nuclear weapons contributes to peace. Thus the agreements are linked to the idea of disarmament. While this idea is espoused in principle by most nations, including the United States and the USSR, it does not conform in practice to the current rationale for the control of nuclear weapons. On the contrary, there is considerable opinion, and governmental policy based on it, that under present world conditions the possession by each of the two superpowers, at least, of nuclear arsenals capable of destroying the other, after having absorbed a first strike, not only deters these superpowers from initiating nuclear war against each other but places considerable, if not always definable, limits on their freedom to use military force in other situations. This concept in effect says that the cause of peace would not necessarily be advanced if the USSR and the United States (and, of course, other nuclear powers), were suddenly deprived of all nuclear weapons and the world was left with a conventional war capability exceeding that of the Second World War as the only alternative to the peaceful settlement of international disputes.

This dilemma has been a fundamental problem of SALT. In the 1950s and 1960s the superiority of the United States over the Soviet Union in nuclear technology and weapons made negotiations on bilateral limitations impractical; the United States would hardly have agreed to stand still and let the Soviets catch up, while the Soviets would hardly have agreed to a permanent condition of second class.

As the US efforts slowed and those of the Soviet Union speeded up, a rough parity was probably reached some time in the 1970s. As the 1980s begin, the momentum of the Soviet Union in nuclear arms expansion will carry on for a number of years even if no new decisions are taken, while the lethargy of the American economy and political will will have delayed or prevented similar moves on the part of the United States. In the perception of a large part of the American public, at least, and of American military leaders, if parity has not already been breached in favour of Soviet superiority that will inevitably happen in the mid-1980s, and attitudes towards SALT are deeply affected thereby.

A further fundamental problem of SALT has been the definition of parity or equality in military terms that will then provide a basis for the negotiation of force levels. Should the end result of SALT be a mathematical equality of the forces on the two sides, or should it be an equality of security in a subjective sense?

Even if this question is resolved, there remains a further problem of how to count. Does a smaller but more accurate missile count the same as a heavier but less accurate one? Is a noisy submarine that needs frequent repairs the same as a silent one that can stay at sea longer? Is a bomber than can fly to the target and back again for another load the same as a bomber that can make only a one-way flight? And, especially, should SALT cover *all* the nuclear weapons with which each side can strike the other, or only those weapons located on its own territory with that capability? A noteworthy aspect of the SALT negotiations is that it appears to take more time to resolve questions such as these than it does to develop weapons which pose new questions. Thus the process never catches up with itself.

In spite of these many difficulties, it was the SALT agreements on the number, size and characteristics of nuclear weapons in their respective arsenals that constituted far and away the main achievements of the superpowers in the 1970s in the category of arms controls.

The only actual treaty which has come into force in this series so far is the Antiballistic Missile (ABM) Treaty of 1972, part of the SALT I package, which limited each side to the deployment of two ABM sites (reduced by a 1974 Protocol to one site each). This treaty establishes clearly the basic premise of the doctrine of deterrence: each side agrees to leave itself open and therefore in a sense helpless in the face of the inevitable (so it was considered) retaliation by the invulnerable second strike forces of the other side that would follow any nuclear attack. The ABM Treaty posits the existence of nuclear weapons, and specifically of a second-strike capability, as a stabilising factor and, conversely, stigmatises defence against a second strike as possibly destabilising. In this context it is not merely the size, number and capability of nuclear weapons which have to be dealt with in arms control concepts, but their disposition in terms of stabilising or destabilising a crisis situation.

Part of the importance of the ABM Treaty was the emphasis which it placed not only on being essentially defenceless against a nuclear attack but also on ensuring that the other side knew that this was the case. This made possible and desirable an openness to the so-called national technical means of verification, including satellites with sensitive cameras and other sensing mechanisms, that did not exist before.

The other part of the 1972 SALT I package, the Interim Offensive Weapons Agreement, in effect simply froze the aggregate number of US and Soviet strategic launch vehicles, including ICBMs, submarines and heavy bombers, for a five-year period ending in the Fall of 1977. As its name implies, it was thought of as an interim agreement, not a permanent treaty, stopping both sides where they were while further negotiations went on to refine the concepts involved and arrive at longer-range limitations that would be qualitative as well as quantitative.

The Interim Agreement served as a first step in bringing the US and the Soviet Union, each deeply suspicious of the other, to disclose to each other detailed data about their nuclear forces. As in the case of the ABM Treaty, the need for verification led to an opening up of the skies and the air waves on each side so that the other could have an unimpeded look and listen. The experience in this area became an important part of the negotiating climate for SALT II. While the Interim Agreement limited the total number of launch systems on both sides, it did not prevent the production of new systems and the replacement by them of older systems. As new submarines were built, for instance, old submarines had to be dismantled or changed so that they could no longer carry nuclear missiles; as new ICBMs were installed, old launchers had to be dismantled, and so on. The mechanism set up to establish procedures for these highly technical measures, the Standing Consultative Commission (SCC), which also has the task of receiving and resolving complaints under the ABM Treaty and the Interim Agreement, may turn out to be one of the most important consequences of the SALT I agreements. According to official American statements, all occasions on which Soviet actions were questioned in the SCC resulted either in cessation of the action concerned or a satisfactory explanation of it. The SCC is carried over in the SALT II treaty.

Soon after the conclusion of the SALT I agreements, negotiations began on SALT II. Perhaps because of strong criticism in the United States that SALT I simply froze what might have been inequalities in nuclear forces in favour of the USSR, there was great emphasis on the part of the American delegation on obtaining agreement in SALT II to 'equal aggregates' of ICBMs, SLBMs and heavy bombers in the new treaty. This initial emphasis on equal numbers of systems, however, conflicted with the fact that the size and capability of individual weapons were not the same on the two sides.

The United States had led in the development and production of multiple warheads mounted on a single missile, each of which could be directed independently to a different target (MIRVs), and this gave it an advantage at the time of SALT I. By the time SALT II was nearing completion, however, the USSR was also able to deploy MIRVs and the much larger size of its heavy missiles gave it the potential of placing perhaps as many as 20 or 30 MIRVs on each missile, compared with the three MIRVs on an American Minuteman II ICBM and the maximum of 14 on the largest American submarine missile tested. It was this great number of potential warheads, coupled with highly improved accuracy, that was believed to give the Soviet Union the potential in the 1980s to carry out a disarming first strike effectively against all American land-based ICBMs, thus bringing into doubt the concept of deterrence by mutual assured destruction.

By the end of 1974, the two superpowers had established the broad outlines of the SALT II agreements. There was to be a common overall ceiling on the aggregate number of heavy bombers and ICBM and SLBM missile launchers, with a sub-ceiling on MIRVed missiles. There would also be qualitative limitations on the weapons themselves. There were two principal sticking points, however: how to treat cruise missiles (essentially unpiloted aircraft flying at aircraft altitudes and speeds and able to avoid air defences and zero-in accurately on targets), in which the United States was well ahead; and the Soviet *Backfire* bomber, which the US thought should be considered an intercontinental bomber subject to SALT limitations, while the Soviets maintained that it should not.

To negotiate these points and to surmount a host of other problems, not the least of which was the political climate in each of the countries and the question of 'linkage' between general US–Soviet relations and the SALT process, required the rest of the decade. The SALT II Treaty and its accompanying Protocol signed in 1979 reflected closely the decisions of 1974. An aggregate ceiling of 2,400 strategic launch vehicles for each side was established, and would be reduced further in 1981 to 2,250, thus for the first time requiring actual reductions in forces – a number of missiles on the Soviet side and of moth-balled B-52s on the American. A system of sub-ceilings limited the number of launchers permitted in the more sensitive categories. Heavy bombers equipped to carry long-range, air-launched cruise missiles were to be counted in the aggregate total; the parties agreed not to test any long-range, sea-launched or ground-launched cruise missiles before the expiration of the Protocol at the end of 1981. ICBMs would be limited to a maximum of 10 MIRVs and SLBMs to 14. The *Backfire* was not to be counted within the Soviet ceiling, but the USSR undertook not to give that aircraft an intercontinental capability and not to produce more than 30 per year. Each side was to be allowed one, but only one, new ICBM system. A number of other provisions reaffirmed the verification provisions of SALT I, exchanged agreed and detailed data on the current forces held by each party, provided agreed definitions and otherwise rounded out the package.

In a formal statement the parties agreed to go on with further SALT negotiations for quantitative and qualitative reductions in nuclear arms and cited strategic stability, equality and equal security as the principles that would guide them. They pledged themselves to work for a Comprehensive Test Ban (CTB), to strengthen nonproliferation, to continue the Mutual and Balanced Force Reduction talks between NATO and the Warsaw Pact (MBFR), to seek agreements on anti-satellite systems, conventional arms transfers, chemical weapons and on the Indian Ocean. They confirmed agreement on the major elements of a radiological weapons agreement, and finally agreed to pursue other questions of arms limitations and general disarmament. Long though it had taken, SALT II wound up with significant steps forward in the control of nuclear weapons between the US and the USSR. By listing all the other arms control measures in which the two superpowers were interested, it may have linked progress on them to implementation of SALT, which in turn may cause wider and multilateral problems if SALT remains in suspension.

When SALT II was signed in June 1979, it was expected that the ratification process in the US would be completed within five months or so, before the adjournment of the US Senate for the year. By September, however, it was clear that the treaty was in jeopardy. A number of respected retired officers, including the military representative on the SALT II delegation, openly and strongly opposed ratification on the basis that it confirmed a situation in which the Soviet Union was rapidly drawing ahead of the United States in nuclear strength and would, by the mid-1980s, have the capability of destroying the entire American ICBM arsenal in a first strike. Political leaders who had favoured SALT began to drop off as popular attitudes shifted, and the treaty was not brought to a vote in the Senate before the end of 1979 lest it not receive the required two-thirds vote for ratification. The Soviet intervention in Afghanistan in late December put the final end to hopes for early ratification, and the Administration itself backed away, with the President asking the Senate to suspend action on the treaty.

Newly-elected President Reagan has withdrawn the SALT II agreements from the Senate in their present form, but has indicated his intention to continue the SALT process in an attempt to produce new agreements that would provide guarantees for the US that the USSR could not achieve strategic superiority. Any re-opening of negotiations, however would likely cause a negative reaction on the part of the USSR which would delay or end the chances for SALT II to come into effect before the end of 1981. By that time, the Protocol as presently worded would already have expired. If the validity of the treaty were thus overtaken by delays in its coming into force, it would lose whatever attraction it might still have for the parties.

While the ratification and coming into force of the SALT II Treaty and Protocol in their present form cannot be completely ruled out, what would the strategic arms limitation situation be in the absence of this agreement? Unquestionably, the basic interests of the Soviet Union and the United States require further efforts in this area. Their underlying caution and appreciation of the dangers that would result from a complete collapse of the SALT process have been shown by the fact that the two powers continue to participate in pro-forma meetings of the SCC and other bilateral arms control negotiations, and neither has indicated any immediate intent to depart from observance of the terms of both SALT I and SALT II.

If SALT II does not come into force, what are the prospects for the 1980s? First is the coming superiority of the USSR, as perceived by the United States, which must be prevented. This could be done, in theory, by agreement of the Soviets to limit their arms expansion more than is specified in SALT II; this is, however, a most unlikely prospect. Alternatively, the United States could recover its sense of equality by significantly increasing defence budget appropriations over the next several fiscal years. Definitive decisions on the MX missile program; a speed-up in the Trident submarine and missile programs; perhaps a beginning of a new heavy bomber program, such as the B-1; decisions such as these, taken in principle in the next year, could restore American confidence which was lost, after all, not so much by an actual gaining of superiority by the Soviets as by an American perception that the momentum of Soviet plans and programs, contrasted to an American malaise, would lead to such superiority during the life of the SALT II Treaty.

In any event, whatever the fate of the SALT II Treaty itself, the principles which it establishes and perhaps even the quantitative and qualitative restrictions which it spells out may well be the actual guidelines for the development of the American and Soviet strategic forces in the 1980s.

A category of nuclear arms control which is also of great interest to the nuclear powers and to the nations of the world in general is that of non-proliferation, the avoidance of any increase in the number of nations possessing nuclear weapons. By 1968, when the Non-Proliferation Treaty was negotiated (it came into force in 1970) five states had nuclear weapons: the United States, the USSR, the United Kingdom, France and the People's Republic of China. While only the first three signed and eventually ratified the NPT, all five would qualify for the status of 'nuclear weapon state' under the treaty which, in effect, recognises the right of these states to continue to possess nuclear weapons. In return for certain promises on the part of the nuclear weapon states, principally a pledge to work for nuclear arms control and eventual disarmament and to provide the non-nuclear weapon states fully with the peaceful fruits of nuclear progress, including peaceful nuclear explosions (PNEs), the non-nuclear weapon states undertake to refrain from developing nuclear explosive devices of any kind and to place their entire nuclear processes under the safeguards of the International Atomic Energy Agency (IAEA) in order to ensure verification of compliance. While the question of the supply of PNEs by the United States and the USSR to non-nuclear weapon states was an important issue for several years, the finding by the United States that PNEs would be neither efficient nor economical, and steps toward agreement between the superpowers to apply to PNEs the same controls which apply to nuclear weapons tests, have tended to lessen interest in this subject.

India exploded a nuclear device in 1974. Although this was stated to be an experiment for peaceful purposes, a nuclear explosive device can be used for either peace or war. While no other state is known to have tested a nuclear explosive device, there are several whose capabilities may have enabled them to proceed far along the path of production, if not to the final assembly, of nuclear weapons.

The problem of non-proliferation has been greatly complicated in the 1970s by developments in the use of nuclear reactors for power generation, which in turn has been spurred by rising oil prices and the approaching depletion of oil reserves. From an ideal non-proliferation standpoint, all fuel enrichment for power reactors and all processing of spent fuel, plus certain other processes, would be done by nuclear weapon states which, together with IAEA safeguards on the reactors during the use of the fuel, would assure against diversion of any material to other purposes. Many states believe that there are valid economic and political reasons, however, to become independent in the production and enrichment of nuclear fuels and in the processing of spent fuels.

The Review Conference of the NPT, called for by the Treaty every five years, met in 1975 and again in 1980. The failure of the nuclear weapon states, as perceived by others, to carry out the terms of the NPT in regard to their own nuclear disarmament and their attempt, again as perceived by others, to maintain unfair economic and political domination through the control of the peaceful uses of nuclear energy have been sources of dissension among the members of the NPT, and will, no doubt, continue to be so.

Significant progress was made during the 1970s on the question of controlling nuclear weapons tests. As noted above, the Limited Test Ban Treaty, preceding the conclusion of the SALT I agreements, had ended, for the parties to it, nuclear tests in the atmosphere and under water. Within two years after SALT I, the United States and the USSR succeeded in negotiating the Threshold Test Ban Treaty, limiting underground nuclear weapons tests to a maximum yield of 150 kilotons. In 1976, the Peaceful Nuclear Explosions Treaty extended the same limitation to individual peaceful nuclear explosions (PNEs) and added an overall limitation of 1,500 kilotons to any group explosions of PNEs, such as might be used for large-scale earth-moving projects. These two treaties succeeded for the first time in putting an actual ceiling on the size of nuclear weapons tested. The significance of this fact lies in the argument that military decision-makers, faced with a choice between an older but tested weapon and a newer, theoretically more capable weapon that has not been tested, will opt for the tested weapon. The Threshold Treaty would thus put a permanent cap on the development of new types of nuclear warheads of more than 150 kilotons yield.

The second treaty went far towards settling a long-standing disagreement between the USSR and the United States regarding the possible use of PNEs. The US had maintained that explosions of nuclear devices must all be considered as potential weapons tests, since it might be impossible to detect the weapons factors that were being tested in an explosion conducted ostensibly for peaceful purposes such as earth-moving.

The Threshold and PNE Treaties continued verification provisions of high significance. In the case of the former, tests were to be limited to prescribed test areas, and detailed geological data on these areas were to be communicated to the other government, in order to facilitate estimates of yield. In the PNE Treaty, the verification procedures were expanded greatly to include full information about the type, yield and time of explosion as well as access by designated personnel of the other party to the explosion site, witnessing the emplacement of explosives and measuring scientifically the yield and other factors to their own satisfaction.

Though both of these treaties were signed personally by the President of the United States and were submitted to the US Senate in 1976 for ratification, the Senate has taken no action.

In spite of the lack of ratification of the Threshold and PNE

Treaties, negotiations began in 1977 on a Comprehensive Test Ban Treaty (CTB) which would go the further step of ending all nuclear weapons tests. The United Kingdom was brought in as a negotiating partner and the treaty was designed to be one of universal adherence, rather than among the nuclear weapon states alone. By the end of 1979, agreement had been reached that the treaty would have a fixed duration and would include a moratorium on PNEs for the same period. Significant progress had been made on verification by on-site inspection and tamper-proof seismic stations located on the territory of the parties.

Though a CTB would stop further nuclear tests, it would not affect non-explosive improvements in guidance, accuracy and other factors concerning nuclear weapons. Because of these other factors a CTB is closely related to other negotiations, such as SALT, on questions of numbers and sizes of weapons and their disposition. More directly, a CTB would obviously be connected in the minds of the leaders of the United States and the Soviet Union with continuing progress on SALT. Ratification of SALT II and the restoration of a climate of détente would clearly make the possibility of a CTB greater. Conversely, if the linkage between SALT II and the Soviet actions in Afghanistan, for instance, causes the US government to delay or refuse to ratify SALT II, then it is most unlikely that the two powers, committing themselves to competition through an arms build-up rather than through arms control, would tie their hands at the same time by agreeing to cease tests.

During the 1970s there began another set of negotiations of a strategic nature, those between the members of the North Atlantic Treaty Organisation (NATO) and of the Warsaw Pact, called the Talks on Mutual and Balanced Force Reductions (MBFR). (The Soviet Union prefers not to use the term 'balanced'.) Held on a continuing basis in Vienna, these talks concern proposed reductions in the forces of the two sides in a restricted area of central Europe, the Federal Republic of Germany and the Benelux nations on the NATO side and the German Democratic Republic, Poland and Czechoslovakia on the Warsaw Pact side. Begun in the Fall of 1973, these talks are now in their seventh year and show no signs of proceeding more rapidly in the 1980s than they did in the 1970s. As in the case of the SALT talks, difficulties of both concepts and counting exist. The Warsaw Pact forces in the reductions area are larger in manpower and tanks than those of NATO, and the full might of the Soviet Union lies behind a border only 400 miles away, while the US is eight times as far. Withdrawals of equal numbers or equal percentages by the United States and the USSR would therefore not produce a balance of remaining forces, and the US forces would be far more difficult to re-introduce to the area if that were ever required. While the

Warsaw Pact accepted the NATO contention that the final result of MBFR should be, in principle, common ceilings on the two sides and that these should be reached in phases, this acceptance was based in turn on an acceptance by NATO of the Warsaw Pact figures for its own forces as being now roughly equal to those of the West. The West continues to maintain that the Eastern figures are actually higher and that there must therefore be appropriately larger reductions by the East if common ceilings are to be reached.

Rather than showing signs of reaching an early conclusion, the MBFR talks appear more to be becoming an institutionalised mechanism for bilateral contacts between the opposing treaty organisations with the concomitant necessity for mechanisms on both sides for coordinating national approaches, not only of those countries located in the reductions area but of other members of their alliances as well. In this sense, it may be that the MBFR talks are serving at least two fundamentally useful purposes: first, simply by continuing to talk and thus to describe to each other the problems as they see them, the two alliances are gaining a better understanding of each other, and the habit of talk is better than the habit of crisis-making. Second, the experience of the individual nations, perhaps more on the NATO side but probably not completely lacking on the part of the Warsaw Pact, of having to discuss common problems and arrive at common positions within their own groups must give all of the parties a better appreciation of the overall difficulties. The conclusion of a final MBFR agreement seems unlikely in the absence of a relaxation of conditions in central Europe, which might well bring about reductions on both sides even in the absence of an agreement. If such a time comes, however, the existence of the MBFR mechanism will provide an opportunity for more rapid and efficient agreement, including provisions for inspection and verification. Meanwhile, neither side is likely to choose to terminate an arrangement which at least keeps the alliances talking to each other.

A further arms control move in the European area was the Helsinki agreement in 1975, which provided for advance notification of large-scale military manoeuvres anywhere in Europe and for other discretionary confidence-building measures, such as the exchange of observers or announcement of smaller-scale manouevres. While perhaps not a matter of great significance, this attention to arms control is symptomatic of the desire of all nations to have some part in and to bring some influence to bear on the principal confrontation between East and West in Europe.

That desire of a large number of nations to share a role in the general attempt to limit armaments has been reflected by the work of the First Committee of the United Nations General Assembly (UN-GA) each year during the 1970s, by the 1978 Special Session of the

UNGA on Disarmament, by the re-establishment of the dormant UN Disarmament Commission in 1978, (in which the People's Republic of China has taken an active part) and most particularly by the sessions during the 1970s of the Conference of the Committee on Disarmament (CCD), which became in 1979 the Committee on Disarmament (CD). Meeting several times a year in Geneva, the CD is composed of the five nuclear-weapons states (the United States, USSR, United Kingdom, France and China), and 35 others representing the more active nations in the arms control and disarmament field. While China has not taken its seat in the CD, it has requested that the seat be kept available for it.

The CCD, and later the CD, served during the 1970s as a forum for debate and for the presentation of ideas on arms control and disarmament by a number of nations. It was also the forum to which the USSR and the United States presented draft treaties on a number of general arms control subjects, which were then debated in the CCD and referred to the UN General Assembly for approval and signature. The NPT (1968), the Seabed Treaty (1971), the Biological Weapons Convention (1972), and the Environmental Modification Convention (1977) are in this category. At the present time, the CD has before it a joint initiative by the United States and the USSR on a treaty to prohibit radiological weapons, and has formed a working group to negotiate effective arrangements to protect non-nuclear weapons states against the threat or use of nuclear weapons. A long-term interest in a treaty prohibiting the use of chemical warfare has been shown in the CCD and the CD, and bilateral negotiations between the US and the USSR on an agreed initiative for presentation to the CD are continuing.

Given the widely varying interests, sizes and military capabilities of the nations participating in the CD and other UN-connected arms control efforts, it is not likely that these will have a decisive effect on the international situation. The fact that the United States, the USSR and the United Kingdom, however, often find themselves sharing positions against the considerable opposition of other countries, including both advanced industrial states and developing states, helps to bring home to the two superpowers that they do, in fact, share many interests and that they are looked upon by much of the rest of the world, at least in the area of arms control, as similar rather than contrasting dangers.

Finally, but certainly far from least in its world impact, a major subject of arms control discussion, if not action, in the 1970s was the transfer of conventional weapons among nations, especially transfer from the advanced industrial powers to the developing world. While total expenditures for health and education in the developed world exceed military expenditures by more than 50 per cent, health and education expenditures in the developing world generally amounted to little more than half the cost of military expenditures. There can be no doubt that the developing world, taken as a group, devoted assets to military purposes at rates that severely handicapped social and economic development, thus tending to perpetuate, rather than alleviate, the basic North-South economic division among nations.

On the supplier side, the United States led with approximately a 40 per cent share of world arms exports (1977), while the Soviet Union was second with a 30 per cent share. France took about 7 per cent of the export market, the United Kingdom and the Federal Republic of Germany about 5 per cent each. Arms constituted some 10 per cent of Soviet exports as the decade ended (from a high of 25 per cent in 1973, with the percentage decline largely attributable to increases in other exports), while the arms proportion of American exports was about 5 per cent. In 1979, the sudden withdrawal of Iran (until then by far the largest importer) from the arms import market brought about a sharp decline in US exports.

Over the years, economic aid extended by the United States to the developing world, while less than military aid, was generally comparable in amount. French economic aid was almost three times greater than France's military exports to developing nations; the United Kingdom gave 50 per cent more in economic aid than it supplied in arms exports; and the Federal Republic of Germany extended more than three times as much economic assistance. The Soviet Union, at the other extreme, supplied more than five times as much in arms exports to the developing world as it gave in economic aid.

While a supplying power might, especially if all or most all other suppliers were in agreement, undertake to restrict arms exports to the developing world for political or economic developmental reasons, these considerations were of little validity in determining, for instance, US and Soviet exports of arms to their respective friends in the Arab-Israel conflict.

Moreover, from the point of view of the developing nations, international efforts to restrict their freedom to make their own decisions on the use of whatever economic assets they had and on the relative importance to them of arms, as compared with other items, were an unwarranted interference in their sovereignty.

Against this relatively unpromising background, the United States and the Soviet Union initiated talks in 1977 on a common effort to limit the transfer of conventional arms. One meeting was held in 1977, and three more in 1978. No meeting was scheduled in 1979 and it does not appear that any real progress has been made on this subject between the two principal arms suppliers. As long as nations desire to buy arms and other nations profit from selling them as well as, in some cases, furthering their strategic objectives, it seems unlikely that international agreement will override national interest as perceived by the countries concerned.

As the 1970s ended thus, and the world faced the uncertain decade of the 1980s, several significant successes in strategic arms control could be counted, but the progress had largely come to a standstill, and it could not be foreseen when and in what manner it would be resumed, though world interests clearly are bound up in such a resumption. Of all the new factors that must be taken into account, the position of the People's Republic of China looms as the largest and most important. China has now essentially switched from being an ally of the USSR to being its enemy, and although it has not become an ally of the United States it might well like to do so if the United States were willing. While all possible opponents of China must take into account China's nuclear capability, particularly in ICBMs, it is the Soviet Union that must face the threat of nuclear attack from China (and *vice versa*) in the short term. Whatever the Soviet disposition may be to continue and even press ahead on nuclear arms limitations with the United States, it will reach a point where the nuclear capability of China must also be brought into the equation.

A further complication will be the role of those nuclear systems which have so far remained outside the SALT process, the so-called 'forward-based systems' or 'theatre' nuclear weapons. In a triangular relationship for which no one has yet found a ready answer, the Soviet Union maintains intermediate-range missiles, aircraft and other weapons that can reach and threaten Western Europe; the United States, France and the United Kingdom, in turn, maintain nuclear weapons in Western Europe not only of battlefield usefulness in central Europe but capable of reaching the Soviet Union. SALT has so far concerned itself only with those weapons located in the United States or the USSR, or in their submarines on the high seas, capable of reaching the other country, although each side has tried to include some, at least, of the other side's shorter-range weapons. To make the absurd comparison, if the SALT negotiations resulted in a zero level for ICBMs, submarines and heavy bombers, the Soviet Union would have no weapons capable of striking the United States while the United States would have weapons of its own in Western Europe capable of striking the USSR, as well as United Kingdom and French weapons which might be used similarly. Obviously the more the SALT process succeeds, the closer the superpowers will come to the point where all nuclear weapons, including short-range ones, must enter into the equation. From the point of view of arms control, it might be a happy outcome if this point is reached in the 1980s, but it will bring additional difficulties and needs for multilateral negotiations with it whenever it comes.

The general political situation also poses difficult problems for arms control in the 1980s. Since the revolution in Iran and the Soviet intervention into Afghanistan, the United States and the USSR have moved apart politically. The movement of the allies of the United States, especially in Western Europe and to some extent in Japan, has not coincided with that of the US government in direction or speed. As Soviet-American relations have deteriorated, there has been an indication of some desire on the part of Western Europe to differentiate its position from that of the United States; to show Europeans as being not as extreme, not as anxious or even willing to take countermeasures against the Soviet Union, while still sharing to a large degree the political views of Americans regarding Soviet behaviour. This is probably not simply a difference in reaction to the current Soviet stance, but to some extent also reflects a long-standing European desire to move out from under the shadow of the United States as well as a European dismay at what is thought to be a lack of both policy and leadership on the part of the American Administration. These Western European attitudes have, in turn, affected and been affected by the results of the Presidential election in the United States. One consequence will probably be increased pressure from Western Europe for a return to détente and negotiations with the Soviets. If this is met by a similar attitude on the part of the Washington Administration, the situation may improve; if the contrary occurs, then a wider gulf may open up among the NATO allies.

President Brezhnev has already shown signs of being unable to function as effectively as in the past, and it is obviously only a question of time, perhaps a short time, before the Soviet government also has to decide upon new leadership. Whether that will mean further progress along the lines of (comparative) liberalisation seen in the past decade, or a retrogression, remains to be seen, but it will certainly have a major effect on the Soviet position in the world, on Soviet-American relations, and on the future of arms control between the superpowers.

16 Warfare and Policy
The Political Control of Military Force

J.D.B. MILLER

Any consideration of the political control of military force involves a great many questions. They include those of how control of military force is sustained by civilian government, how and when that control is lost, and what happens when it is. They also include questions of what sort of political force the military[1] is, what happens to civilian-military relations as a result of technological changes in warfare and all that goes with it, and what can be done to get the military, the civilian governments, and the people at large into some sort of effective relationship. Again, there are questions of how the political climate differs as between peace and war, and of what part the military play in beginning and ending wars.

Each of these questions would justify a paper in itself, even if it applied only to a particular state or group of states. For any attempt at general statement, however, the range and diversity of evidence are frightening. There is no single model of proper or actual relationships between politicians, officials and the military. People in the democracies of Western Europe and North America (and in such derivative countries as Australia) like to think that there is, but they are wrong. In terms of their own fairly recent experience, one need mention only the names of Napoleon, Petain, De Gaulle, Hindenburg, Churchill, Lloyd George, Franco and Badoglio in order to recognise what a variety of patterns can emerge. Americans should recognise that their own practices with the Washingtons, Jacksons, Grants, Eisenhowers and MacArthurs have also created patterns of consequence. When one turns to Asia, Africa and Latin America, the contemporary situation displays a far greater variety of possibilities. There is no clear norm, whether we try to suggest one or not. (For the Australian situation see Millar, 1978).

This is because the military everywhere are not identical machines, but part of the societies in which they operate. Their roles and significance vary greatly from one country to another, and from time to time. In every country they constitute political forces, whether in the restricted intra-governmental sphere of budget provision, or in the wider sphere of national leadership and control. Their possession of the instruments of ultimate force gives them (in the abstract, at any rate, and often in the concrete) a kind of ultimate veto over political action. Their disciplined procedures given them plausibility as an alternative form of government; they know it, and so do the politicians. There is thus a basic tension between civil and military authorities, whether the actual waging of war is a factor in the situation or not. What form this tension takes will depend very much upon the past history and the governmental traditions of the country in question. It would be possible to construct a spectrum with, say, Sweden and Switzerland at one end, and Latin American countries at the other – a spectrum ranging from assumptions of political supremacy to expectations of military rule. Yet there would not be constancy over time in relative positions on such a spectrum. Switzerland, for example, has experienced considerable civil-military tension in both world wars.

I think it best to ask, in terms as general as possible, what sort of social and political force the military represents, and to proceed from there to consider the prospects of the next decade or so in the countries of the West, so far as civilian control of military force is concerned. This will mean glancing at most of the questions mentioned above. It is advisable to keep in mind throughout discussion of civil-military relations that they have two aspects. One is the acceptability of the military within the society of which they are part (which includes the question of the acceptability of armed force as such); the other is the degree of responsibility for policy, held respectively by civil and military authorities. The second depends to a considerable extent upon the first.

Historically, armed forces have evolved from small-scale assemblies of seasoned soldiers and raw recruits, using primitive weapons, into large-scale, essentially technical and basically professional entities, by way of the *levée en masse* and modern technology. They have become more and more expensive, and more arcane in character at the same time. In this way (if in no other, although, as suggested below, there are other ways too) a gulf has widened between civil and military attitudes. Civilian governments, accustomed to public pressures and a steady increase in provision by the state of domestic services which will increase their popularity, are confronted by military demands for weapons and equipment which they do not fully understand, and which seem outrageously expensive for the public benefit which the *materiel* appears to bestow. Military demands are couched in terms of long-term estimates of threats to the security of the state; like all long-term estimates of the future they are liable to be wrong, and even if broadly correct are liable to be overtaken by events, so that the people who made them are likely to go unrewarded for prescience which was reasonable on the basis of knowledge available when it was exercised.

While it is true to say that military forces have often in the past been difficult for civilian governments to handle – whether in ancient Rome or 17th Century England, and whether there were questions of pay or of the vaulting ambitions of particular generals – it may also be true that the problems of today are potentially more acute because of the increasingly deadly and expensive character of the weapons and equipment which the military possess. These problems arise directly between the civilian government on the one hand and military leaders on the other; but further problems derive from the effects on the forces of the conditions of civil life.

Traditionally, armies have provided a whole way of life and the facilities needed to maintain it – food, clothes and shelter for the professional soldier and his family, education where necessary for his children, medical care, transport and the like. The US and Indian services, if likely to agree on little else, would be fully agreed on the need to maintain these separate ways of life, and to ensure that they are not eroded by comparison with what is available to civilians. Yet, in advanced consumer societies there is no way of sealing off the services from the rest of the community, or of ensuring that there is no erosion of standards or of the continued attractiveness of military life – unless the military themselves become the governors, and put the services at the top of the list for pay, housing, and whatever else is required. Something like this happens in war, with the shift of the economy towards military needs; but in peacetime the contrast between civil and military conditions may become acute, especially if the economy is booming and military spending lags behind it.

The effects upon civil-military relations of such a situation in peacetime will differ from high-standard to low-standard countries. Broadly speaking, comparisons are likely to work to the disadvantage of armies in high-standard countries, and to their advantage elsewhere. If we assume that national armies, navies, etc., have become increasingly alike in expense because of their demands for equipment of the same type (that is, it costs much the same to equip any country with missiles, destroyers, fighter planes, etc.), and because they need many people with skills and educational qualifications to go with the equipment, then these forces will look very attractive to ambitious young men in countries where other opportunities for employment are scarce and ill-paid. The acceptability of the services will be high. Conversely, the traditional habit of advanced countries of paying servicemen less than civilians, combined with peacetime reluctance to meet all the expensive demands made by the services, will lead to less attractiveness in military life, especially if the economy is growing or even simply stable. Acceptability may well be low in these conditions.

The fact that armies have traditionally provided an especially attractive way of life is presumably one of the reasons for the Latin American syndrome of the impending possibility or actual existence of military rule: the army promises advancement and opportunity (with little likelihood of getting killed, since wars are scarce in Latin America), while civil life is marked by poverty or unstable economic growth, and by political forces which are often evanescent, corrupt and confused. These conditions rarely if ever exist in the high-standard countries of the west. Instead, the contrast is normally the other way. Armies often lack the attractiveness which would enable them to avoid conscription, and conscription creates its own problems of contrast. The point should not be overdrawn, since high-standard countries sometimes experience periods of depression in which army life may become more attractive; but even these are periods in which the services (notably the US Army at the present time) (see *Time*, 9 June 1980) may find great difficulty in finding and holding the recruits who can man sophisticated equipment.

It follows from what has just been stated that in peacetime armies will have more social significance in low-standard countries than in high. This helps, perhaps, to explain why military regimes occur so often in the one case, and so seldom in the other. For high-standard countries, peacetime is normally a period in which the military are held in check, their expenses scrutinised by Treasuries and their quest for manpower curtailed, as much by the attractions of civil life as by government decision. In low-standard countries the military may benefit from whatever misfortunes overtake the civil government – such as financial crisis, guerrilla disturbance, ethnic quarrels and foreign pressure – and may supersede it.

The situation in the high-standard countries may alter radically in and after war. The Petains, De Gaulles, Hindenburgs and Eisenhowers have little or no leverage before war begins, unless there has been a clear and prolonged military threat which strengthens their influence in government circles; even a Churchill needed a war to make his essentially military approach, his pugnacious temperament, and his strategic ideas, acceptable to his fellow countrymen. The military gain opportunity from war and its aftermath because war threatens completely the maintenance of high standards of living, and leaves behind it periods of disturbance and uncertainty in which the personification of military virtue may become politically attractive. The nearer any country gets to actual war, the more significant soldiers become, because there is so much to protect, and also (in the case of high-standard countries) because the economy is capable of substantial readjustment so as to provide the sinews of war on a massive scale. The low-standard countries accustomed to military rule do not experience this substantial change in the significance of the military, because the military are already in the seat of power – and these countries do not, in any case, often indulge in actual fighting.

In high-standard countries the military do have some opportunity to gain esteem and influence in peacetime, whether it be through their control over forms of intelligence-gathering or through civil activity such as has traditionally been carried on by the US Army Corps of Engineers, but it is broadly true that prolonged peace is the worst thing that can happen to them in terms of influence. Huntington refers to the condition of the US Army after the Civil War, when influence was largely lost by the military. (He says also, however, that 'the very isolation and rejection which reduced the size of the services and hampered technological advance made these same years the most fertile, creative and formative in the history of the American armed forces'; (1964, p. 229) so there may also be some long-term gains.)

In low-standard countries, on the other hand, peace may be a time of cheerful prosperity for the armed forces, because of the contrast between their conditions and those of the general population, together with their disciplined capacity to perform civil tasks, and the possibility that their leaders may become rulers.

What all this means is that armies do not operate as given quantities within the balance of social and political forces of any sovereign state; neither can they be regarded as technical services to be turned on and off like a tap. Nothing has been said so far about the *symbolic* significance of armed forces as emblems of patriotic feeling, demonstrations of national power, non-political elements devoted to the public good, and the like; but this role in society, while difficult to measure, must always be kept in mind when one is trying to estimate the acceptability of the military within its society. If acceptability on symbolic grounds is high, the military obviously have reason to demand that they be fed, clothed, sheltered and equipped at a high level. Even at periods of the deepest peacetime depression, they are major elements in the budget. Whatever demands they make about manpower and equipment have implications for the state of the economy. If they have to struggle for resources, this is likely to increase their 'otherness' within the society of which they are part, by emphasising the special nature of their demands, and their dependence upon civilians who do not sympathise with their aims.

As already indicated, war is the time when the military necessarily gain in significance, even though they run the risk of disgrace and destruction. The closer the approach of war, and the more aware the public is of this fact, the more advantage will lie with the military, for the following reasons:

★ if there is a strong sense of public danger (or, presumably, if there is a growing sense of exultation because of the anticipated spoils of war), the military will gain in acceptability because of their role as guardians and their possible role as heroes and conquerors. This will make it easier for them to gain the resources they want, and will provide them with greater political 'clout';

* conversely, the politicians will have to make obeisance to the need for military power, even if they doubt the likelihood or the need for war. This will be especially so if they are from political groups identified in the public mind with attitudes of pacifism (for example, Labour parties in Britain, Australia and New Zealand);

* as the risk of war grows, foreign policy will be dominated more and more by strategical considerations, about which the military are assumed to know more than the politicians. There may be politicians who conceive themselves capable of better strategic judgement than their generals (like Lloyd George and Churchill), but they need remarkable charisma in their own right if they are to overcome the public view that the military know their own business best. It is when the generals fall out (as with Marshall and MacArthur in the Second World War), or when attention is concentrated upon *post*-war possibilities while the war is still on (as with Roosevelt at Yalta), that the politicians are likely to be given their heads;

* because of the need to transfer scarce resources to military purposes, there will be curtailment of governmental civilian programs, and in due course of civilian consumption. Politicians have to bear the brunt of this, so far as public opinion is concerned;

* actual war requires a process of deification or at least sanctification of the generals, admirals, etc., in order to inspire public confidence and provide some justification for the sacrifices required from soldiers and civilians. A political leader may despise his generals (as Clemenceau and Lloyd George evidently did in the First World War, and Churchill in the Second World War), but it is a long and uncertain step to denounce them in public. 'Political' generals, like Kitchener and MacArthur (and Montgomery?) may cause grave concern to politicians, as Abraham Lincoln found more than once;

* as war approaches, the public may become more susceptible to military-style metaphors in regard to politics ('we must all pull together', 'don't argue with the man on the bridge', 'no dissension in the ranks', etc.). While these may be helpful to politicians, since the President or Prime Minister can be represented as 'the man on the bridge', they also involve dangers. The garrison state may not seem so far away; there is the prospect that martial law, a logical concomitant of war, may supersede the normal processes. Military viewpoints may be publicised as both realistic and morally imperative. This process did not lead to martial law in the USA in the Second World War, but it did lead, both there and in Britain, to a tendency to assert publicly that military attitudes must prevail until the war was actually over – that is, to the declaration that 'Victory is our war aim', when in fact there was much argument within the government about war aims of a

more specific nature (see, for example, Thorne, 1978);

* in fact, however much military considerations may seem to elbow normal domestic politics out of the way, the result is not likely to be a simple reproduction of military orders and military actions, within the governmental system as a whole. Military men, faced with the need to make decisions going far beyond the resolution of a particular military situation, are no more likely to agree than any other men. The arguments between 'Easterners' and 'Westerners' in Britain in the First World War, and those between the exponents of Atlantic and Pacific strategies in the United States in the Second World War, are examples of how the conduct of a war can induce extreme differences of opinion. The military may find it easy to agree that civilians should do what they are told, but beyond that there is room for military politics on a large scale. Inter-service rivalry will provide an ample source of disagreement, even if there is unanimity on ultimate strategy. The politicians may well find themselves restored to significance as arbiters between services and between differing strategic concepts.

In effect, we have now arrived at the core of the problem, which can arise for civilian governments of every kind, for Russians, Chinese and Pakistanis as well as for French, Germans and Americans. How does a civilian government control armed forces at a time when these are greatly favoured by circumstance – when they are widely seen as guardians, and when that role as guardians may actually be the one which they perform?

There are certain obvious policies which the politicians and their officials may adopt towards the generals. They can:

* bribe them, that is, give them all the resources which they ask for, and leave them relatively unhindered in preparations for war and its eventual conduct. This is, in effect, a recognition that war is on the way, and that the generals should take the responsibility for it in return for getting what, as professionals, they want. The politicians may hope (or, while not hoping, may find that events decide) that they will retain nominal power until the generals, as it were, run out of steam; in this event the civilian government may be able to reassert full authority;

* divide them, that is, exploit the natural divisions amongst them. The divisions may be between one general and another, or one service and another, or (perhaps in chaotic, semi-revolutionary situations), generals *vs.* colonels or officers *vs.* NCOs and other ranks;

* appeal to tradition, that is, exploit any tradition which involves the loyalty of the forces to the Crown or other symbols which the politicians can manipulate;

* appeal to the electorate, that is, ask for parliamentary and public confidence in order to demonstrate that the people really believe in the

leadership of the politicians, not the generals. This is risky, because of the divine quality which, as already suggested, it has been necessary to ascribe to the generals, and because generals of some kind are needed to retain the loyalty of the forces, and to fight the war;

  ⋆ embrace them, that is, take generals into the cabinet (as with Kitchener in the First World War), and either show their deficiencies when confronted with non-military issues, or use them to support potentially unpopular policies;

  ⋆ abdicate to them, that is, accept either direct military rule or the pre-eminence of a charismatic military figure, as with Petain in France in 1940.

The actual participation of generals in government has often been the Achilles heel of the military in political matters. Intelligent soldiers in the high-standard countries of the West are aware of this, and normally think of military intervention as at the best a short-term expedient intended to deal with some extraordinary situation. Armies are good at running their own affairs and regulating their own enclosed ways of life, and they are good at occasional public relations, in the sense that they can affect public opinion by vague statements about threats, and by planting military views in the civilian media. They are much less good at general civilian government. This is because it is a matter of reconciling interests, rather than giving orders. The military know about satisfying interests, so far as their own ranks are concerned, and they are accustomed to reconciling the interests of the different services, except in situations of budgetary crisis in which they may seek separate access to the Presidential or Prime Ministerial ear. They are not good at the business of judging the significance of civilian interests in terms of their relevance to the community's needs, and of their possible appeal to public opinion. The military tendency has normally been to increase coercion when public dissatisfaction makes itself felt. This can be quite effective, but involves becoming more unpopular. Unless there is a kind of choreography of coercive positions, involving some stylisation and general understanding of what can be done without too much damage to the community at large – as sometimes appears to be the case in Latin American states – the army is unlikely to be a permanent solution to governmental problems. The in-and-out circumstances of the military in some African states, such as Ghana and Nigeria, seem to reinforce this point.

The incapacity of most generals to run governments is due in part to lack of the specific skills required, but also to the fact that garrisons and most states are run on different lines. The machinery of state in most cases is messy, undisciplined, negative in purpose, wasteful and confusing, compared with the running of armies, ships and aircraft stations. In a sense, the garrison state, whether it is run by armies or by revolutionaries, is a contradiction in terms: only by deliberately approximating the state to a garrison, and taking the steps necessary to provide efficiency, discipline, positive purpose and simplicity of operation, can the notion of a garrison state acquire some plausibility. In practice, the attempt is rarely made, and is generally a failure when it is made. What military rulers do is to suppress dissident political groups and then allow other interests in the community a fairly free rein, so long as the army and other services receive the resources they need. In effect, the military do not rule, except for short periods in extraordinary circumstances, and they have no theory of how to turn the whole polity over to military standards. Instead, when apparently ruling, they use coercion in order to reduce opposition, and otherwise let things take their course, except for a good many speeches and military parades.

Such considerations may mean that civilian government will win out in the end over military rule, as Spain's recent example suggests. Except where military rule has become institutionalised, with its own specific style (as in Latin America), most military regimes do not last long. So far as the West is concerned, however, military rule is very much the pathology of civil-military relations. We need to consider at greater length the more normal situations in stable, Western industrial democracies, and how these situations are likely to develop in the 1980s. It seems clear that they will be affected by the increasing technical complexity and expense of weapons, communication systems and the like; by the fact that the military will demand more and more technical skill and the money with which to pay for it; by public opinion demanding more or less spending on the military, in accordance with what is thought for the moment about the moves likely to be made by possible adversaries; by alliances in which partners, because of their perceptions of possible threat, and because of the exigencies of their own domestic politics, make demands upon the other states involved; and, above all, by the problems of whether to go to war in an age of nuclear weapons promising mass destruction.

It seems most unlikely that the answers to these problems will be found in military rule, or that anyone will try to find them there. Instead, we are likely to see considerable anxiety amongst the military about whether civilians will accept what the military say, and whether the temper of western societies is now such as will give the military profession any credence at all. The 1973 Conference of the International Institute for Strategic Studies, held at Travemünde, devoted its time to 'The Future of Military Forces in Modern Societies'. Much doubt was expressed about the acceptability of the use of military force in advanced industrial societies; the military, as the key paper said, 'appears to many as a blunt, insensitive, and immoral instrument'. (Gard, 1973, p. 1) Rarely can soldiers have tip-toed so quietly in the presence of civilians. The emphasis was on making the forces more acceptable, not on their absolute indispensability. Probably the climate of opinion has changed somewhat since 1973, since Vietnam is further away, and Iran and Afghanistan are closer; but it is still difficult to regard the military as other than somewhat diffident when they see the gap between their traditional values and those manifest in the societies around them.

The movement of public opinion about the military profession is amongst the variables which will affect civil-military relations in the near future. Another is the extent to which the military can impose upon the civilian authorities their views of how the world is going. If NATO's intelligence report were all that members of the alliance had to rely on, every country in Western Europe would be spending twice as much on military force, and the United States would have done all that the Republicans demanded in the 1980 Presidential Election, and more. In fact, the NATO members' governments have had access to a variety of other sources of information which moderate the lurid picture of Soviet espionage, subversion and military preparation – information which, at the political and economic levels, modifies to some degree the stark picture which military planners paint on the basis of their intelligence findings and their own need for manpower and equipment. If the military were the only source of information, they would become a state within a state, able to dictate the size of the forces and the measures to be taken towards any act which the supposed enemy undertook. This is not the case; but the closer it gets in any Western society, the nearer to power the military may find themselves. One of the dilemmas of any government is that, once war has actually begun, it looks like disloyalty to take any advice about the enemy except that which the military offer. At the same time, as Clausewitz noted, since

war springs from some political purpose, it is natural that the prime cause of its existence will remain the supreme consideration in conducting it ... Policy, then will permeate all military operations, and, in so far as their violent nature will admit, it will have a continuous influence on them. (Clausewitz, 1976, p. 87)

If politicians cannot control the sources of information about the enemy, either before or during a war, they will be left with a strictly military vision in which tactics overcome ultimate strategy, and policy becomes subject to military whim. On the whole, Western countries do not seem likely to fall into this trap.

Another variable is the extent to which the military have direct access to the centres of civilian power. There is a widespread tradition (exemplified in different ways in Britain, Germany, Japan and the United States) that military chiefs have direct access to the monarch, president or other highest officer of government, and do not need to present their cases through ministers like other senior officials. The working of such a system will determine whether the military are able, in this respect as in respect of intelligence, to operate as a state within the state. To by-pass cabinets and the whole apparatus of inter-departmental consultation and bargaining is to exercise independent jurisdiction to a considerable extent. In war the practice is probably unavoidable. In peace it gives the military the kind of veto over policy which every arm of government would wish to possess but rarely does. The Hore-Belisha case in Britain in 1939, which saw the Minister for War dismissed because of military access to the Monarch and the Prime Minister, is a case to remember (see Taylor, 970, p. 561).

A further variable is the extent to which the state has become habituated to an arms race with its most obvious antagonist, and what form this takes. Once they get under way, such races have often involved continued increments of power to the military in their control over resources. It is unwise to assume, however, that this must automatically be accompanied by a similar increase in control over policy.

The limiting case (that is, that in which a massive increase in armaments does not necessarily lead to military control over policy) is that of nuclear weapons. So long as a state possesses weapons of mass destruction, the use of which would involve large civilian casualties and assured response of the same kind from an adversary, the decision to use the weapons will remain firmly in civilian hands. (The extraordinary lengths to which the USA goes to provide for presidential decision about launching nuclear weapons illustrates the point.) There is a sense in which the military, in all nuclear countries, would like these instruments to be classed as 'just another weapon', since this would give them the operational control which they possess over other arms (though not, of course, over the actual decision to wage war; it is because a nuclear strike represents the most momentous warlike initiative in history that such extreme precautions are taken to keep nuclear decision in civilian hands). The growth of tactical nuclear weapons and of such devices as the neutron bomb, which herald the use of nuclear instruments as 'battlefield' weapons, represents a threat to civilian control; the further this sort of refinement of nuclear weaponry goes, the nearer states approach to the condition of 'just another weapon'. The bigger the bomb, the less likely the military are to be allowed by public opinion to decide its use; whether the situation is reversed, so that the smaller the bomb (that is, the nuclear weapon), the more likely military control is to be accepted, we have yet to see.

Nuclear weapons, and the communications systems which they entail, have also created a new variable out of an old problem which has troubled civilian and military authorities for centuries: that of how much independence should be permitted to minor allies whose territory is regarded as essential to the security of a major power. An example is the Canadian political crisis of 1963, (see Lyon, 1968, ch. 3) during which it became clear that the US government was actively interfering in Canadian politics – in effect, taking sides and pushing one side in preference to the other – because of the Diefenbaker government's reluctance to have US nuclear weapons on Canadian soil. It is not impossible that something similar might occur over the US facilities in Australia, such as Pine Gap; indeed, there are suggestions that it did occur in 1975, but not with the same resounding effect as in the Canadian instance. The relevance of these examples to this paper is that connections between the military in the major and minor allies may involve questions of where ultimate loyalty lies. Are Canadian, Australian or conceivably German soldiers to regard their allegiance to their own governments as absolute, or are they to believe that the cause of resistance to Communism or to the Soviet Union must not be prejudiced by some anti-American action based on local political circumstances? The global confrontation between the super-powers makes the question likely to crop up, while the immediacy inseparable from nuclear warfare can give it the sharpest edge.

Looking at the future of civil-military relations as a whole, one can distinguish, from the standpoint of traditional Anglo-Saxon notions of the desirability of civil control, both a 'worst case' and a 'best case' situation. The worst case would be one in which danger seemed near, weapons and equipment were hideously expensive but had to be provided, knowledge about likely action by adversaries was largely confined to the military, public opinion was hostile to 'the politicians', nuclear weapons were widely regarded as battlefield devices, and allies, through both military and diplomatic means, placed constant pressure on the civil authorities to do what the military told them. Under these circumstances it would not matter much whether there was a military government in name or not; there might as well be one. Civilians might prove quite powerless in practice, and there would be a lack of what has traditionally been regarded as typical civilian caution when decisions were being made.[2]

A best case would be one in which the tradition of the military was of constant assent to civil control, the agencies of military intelligence were matched by civilian institutions, the military needed to go through civil departments in putting their views, and were fully aware of the problems created by arms races; in which, also, allies kept largely to themselves except at the political level, and public opinion was both informed and sceptical about the devilish nature of adversaries. This best case is not dissimilar to that which most western democracies have experienced in the past. The key question for the 1980s is whether present tendencies make worse or better the prospect of its appearing again.

Broadly speaking, there are two *universal* dimensions of change which will affect all powers: the development of political relationships between the major powers, and the development of technology in weapons and the other systems which constitute military force. There is also a *local* dimension for each power, involving its domestic politics, which may include such influences upon civil-military relations as the British have encountered in the disturbances in Northern Ireland, or the Italians from urban terrorists. More advantage is probably to be gained from consideration of these three dimensions in each national instance than from any attempt at generalisation, since Western countries differ greatly in tradition and experience, as was suggested at the beginning of this chapter. The forms of the existing civil-military relationship in the United States, for example, contrast to a considerable extent with those in Britain and France.

The essence of the matter is not, of course, the day-to-day relations between civilian and military authorities so much as the extent to which each would contribute to any decision to go to war. In this sense, the problem has not changed greatly from the past, except in scale: for one super-power to go to war against another is not unlike the decisions made by the European powers in 1914 and 1939, except in terms of the vastly more destructive consequences. Going to war against Third World states today entails the possibility of an adverse propaganda barrage not unlike those which greeted the British ultimatum to the Boers or the attempt to discipline the Boxers, but is still a viable policy, as China's actions in Indochina and France's in Africa have shown. In all these decisions there has been a mixture of civil and military influence. Whether one outweighs the other must depend upon variables within the three dimensions mentioned above, together with the dimension applicable to all political decisions, that of time.

Conclusions:
Of Means and Ends

HEDLEY BULL

Strategy is the art or science of shaping military means so as to promote the ends of policy; it is an art or science of means, more particularly of military means. A feature of discussions that concentrate on strategy is that they direct one's attention towards means but away from ends, and also away from means other than military means. The discussion in this book has been eminently and properly strategic, but more attention should be paid to the basic premises of military policies in the 1970s and 1980s, to the question "What ends should we be prepared to use force for, and what are the circumstances in which it is appropriate to choose military means rather than other kinds of means?".

The international political setting in which these questions arise is dominated by two great and new realities. The first is the emergence of the Soviet Union as a military power equal to the United States in strategic nuclear capacity, possessing local military superiority in Europe and established as a global, no longer merely a regional power, by its naval strength and capacity for military intervention in the Third World. We have to begin by recognising that this is a major new development. I do not feel that this was sufficiently brought out in Geoffrey Jukes's highly informative account of "Soviet Strategy 1965–1990". I have had the privilege of listening to Geoffrey Jukes's analyses of defence policy for the best part of twenty years. They are always brilliant, always loaded with fresh and original insights, and always completely convincing in showing that we in the Western world have a systematic tendency to exaggerate the growth of Soviet military power, to find grand designs behind Soviet military activity that are not there, to forget that in the Soviet Union (as in life generally) much of what goes on is more humdrum than one would think from reading the newspapers. Nevertheless, one cannot help noticing that during the twenty years in which Geoffrey Jukes has been saying this kind of thing, Soviet power has been constantly growing, not only absolutely but also relatively to the Western world. I have a fantasy about a world a decade or so hence, when the Red Army is marching up Anzac Parade in Canberra to the strains of the *Internationale*, and

Soviet tanks are exercising on the banks of Lake Burley Griffin, Geoffrey Jukes will be in the Coombs Lecture Theatre at the Australian
National University giving his lecture and, his voice barely audible
above the tramp of marching feet, will be explaining that if you look
at the teeth-to-tail ratio of the Soviet forces, it is really not very impressive. I know that this is unfair to Geoffrey Jukes, who has heard
me say this before, but I do think we have to recognise the wood as
well as the trees.

The other great reality is the strong reaction against the Soviet
Union on the part of all the other major industrialised powers of the
world – the United States, Western Europe, Japan and China – and
their tendency to combine with one another in a grand alliance
against the Soviet Union. If there are reasons for concern about the
growth of Soviet military power, there are reasons for being alarmed
about this incipient grand alliance also. We need to remember that the
dominant power throughout the postwar period – the 'threat', if this is
the right term, to the world balance of power – has not been the
Soviet Union, but the United States. By this I do not mean to endorse the thesis of the 'revisionist' historians that it is the United
States that has been expansionist in its objectives and the Soviet
Union that has reacted defensively to this expansionism. I mean simply
that it is the United States – because until recently it was the leading
military power in the world as a whole, and is still the leading power
economically – which, quite apart from its intentions or objectives,
has come closest to being in a position of universal preponderance and
so upsetting the system of balance of power upon which the system of
independent states ultimately rests. If Britain were really faithful to its
historic policy of maintaining a balance of power in the international
system, it would be in alliance today with the Soviet Union against the
United States, and not vice versa (in fact, Britain's historic policy has
only applied to the European region, not to the world as a whole, and
in Europe it is the Soviet Union, not the United States, that since
1945 has been the potentially dominant power).

The Soviet Union, until recently, has been merely a regional
power – in no sense the equal of the United States, but more able than
any other state to check the latter's position as a potentially dominant
power. To Third World states, for which the main objective has been
to struggle against Western and especially American dominance, the
check provided by the Soviet Union to the latter has appeared to be
vitally important: on issues such as the elimination of colonial rule,
white supremacism and neo-colonial dependency, most Third World
states have conceived themselves as being in alliance with the Soviet
Union against the dominant, Western element in international society –
a point stressed by Dr. Ayoob in his chapter. For countries like
Australia and Britain, which have felt comfortable in the era of Amer-

ican primacy, the growth of Soviet power is an unsettling development, but for those countries basically in opposition to the international *status quo*, the growth of Soviet power has been perceived as a constructive development. Now that the Soviet Union is powerful enough to pose threats of its own to the independence of neighbouring Third World countries, such as it has long done in the Eastern European region, these perceptions are beginning to change, but for most of the post-1945 period the combination of the Soviet Union and the Third World grouping on certain key issues has represented a natural alliance of the two weaker sections of international society against the strongest section.

There is a need to focus attention upon the emergent grand alliance against the Soviet Union, and raise certain questions about it. First, how far is such an alliance likely to develop? It does not yet meet the strict criteria of formal alliances discussed in Dr. Millar's chapter on this subject, and we have to note the very different reasons that each of the parties to this potential combination has for its present posture of antagonism towards the Soviet Union: the United States seeking to restore a vanished primacy which would not in fact be welcome to any of the other potential allies; Western Europe, seeking to ensure that the Soviet Union will face pressure on its eastern as well as its western frontiers, but concerned also not to undermine the political arrangements that have stabilised its relations with the Soviet Union and Eastern Europe; Japan, attached to a policy of "equidistance" as between the Soviet Union and China, but compelled to abandon it by the Soviet intransigence over the northern island dispute, in itself of no interest to the other parties; China, locked in its own border dispute, ideological disagreement and power rivalry with the Soviet Union, which the other parties regard with indifference and seek only to exploit for their own purposes. The essence of an alliance, however, is not common goals, and still less common values, but (as the British Chief of Defence Staff, Sir Neil Cameron, said in his celebrated speech in Peking) the existence of a common enemy; and while we should not think that the Soviet Union, by choosing different policies, is in a position to detach one or more of the members of the grand alliance from committing themselves further to it (a concession to Japan on the northern island issue, as mentioned by Dr. Millar in his chapter, to West Germany on the issue of German unity, or to China on the border question), in the absence of such Soviet policies there is good reason to expect the present trend to continue.

Secondly, is it desirable that the grand alliance should continue to take shape? It is not only from the Soviet Union that the dangers come that at present menace the peace of the world. The United States public mood is marked by a new mood of belligerence that has been gathering force since 1975 and is now sweeping all before it, including the previously pacific Administration of President Carter. Some see this new mood as a welcome and overdue reaction to Soviet intransigence but I confess that I cannot view it in this way. The new United States policies have themselves contributed to the collapse of détente; they express the difficulties the United States public is experiencing in adjusting to its loss of international primacy and novel dependence upon the international economy; and they have given rise among America's allies to fears of irrational or impulsive actions, that are resuscitating neutralist sentiment.

We also have to ask ourselves whether there is not a causal connection between, on the one hand, the growth of Soviet military power, and on the other hand, the shaping of a grand alliance against the Soviet Union, a causal connection that operates both ways, and carries with it the danger of a vicious spiral of insecurity, as each side fears that the balance is shifting against it and takes remedial action, whose effect is to confirm the fears of the other. Dr. Coral Bell, in the course of the conference which helped to shape this book, said that there are signs at present of the existence of a "crisis slide". If this is so, one way of arresting it might be to tackle the interconnection between the Soviet military build up and the formation of the grand alliance, and seek to transform the vicious circle into a virtuous one.

Thirdly, if the incipient grand alliance carries dangers with it, how can these be moderated? I believe that there may be a constructive role here for Europe. One of the encouraging developments in world politics at present is the increasing tendency of the West European powers, despite their failure to make any progress towards a European supra-national community, to collaborate more and more in basic matters of defence and foreign policy. The ability of Chancellor Helmut Schmidt to assert the leadership of Western Europe and to receive backing from other Western European leaders in his willingness to be more assertive in matters of foreign policy, to be more forthright in criticism of the current drift of American foreign policy, is a constructive development. It is obvious that there are profound differences of approach between Western Europe and the United States, both on the issue of détente in Europe, and over the matter of how to go about securing oil supplies from the Gulf. It is not true, as is widely asserted on the American side, that the Europeans are simply back-sliding and failing to pull their weight; rather it is the case that there are genuine differences of method and philosophy underlying the West European approach to these matters, and on these questions of method it is the European which is right and the American one which is wrong.

There may also be some constructive role for India in relation to the formation of the grand alliance. The more the latter is solidified, the more India will be forced to align even more closely with the

Soviet Union. There is a certain reluctance on the Indian side to do this; an attempt on India's part to mend its bridges with China would restore some flexibility into that country's diplomacy, and militate against the emergence of the classic danger of a confrontation between two armed camps.

The theme I introduced in the second chapter was that world politics in the 1980s was likely to become more Hobbesian, less moderated by the rules and institutions of international society than it has been in the 1960s and 1970s. I drew a contrast between the beginning of the 1970s when there was a widespread expectation that the role of force in international politics would decrease, and the present expectation that it will increase. I mentioned five assumptions made at the beginning of the decade, which in the course of it have come to be moderated or abandoned. I must say that nothing in the subsequent chapters gives reason to alter this judgement.

No one has challenged the proposition that détente between the super powers has collapsed, although Coral Bell and others have raised the question whether it might not be revived at some point in the future, and Mohammed Ayoob has reminded us that despite the collapse of detente the super powers still recognise some common interests. Owen Zurhellen's chapter shows, I think, that arms control is still a serious enterprise, but not that there is any momentum behind the arms control negotiations between the superpowers; indeed, the American "arms control community", once so fertile a source of schemes and suggestions, is at present barren of them, and it is French and West German students of arms control, addressing themselves to the strategic implications of the détente in Europe, that seems set to persist as super power détente fades away, that have been providing fresh ideas on this subject. Warner Schilling's chapter shows us how far, in their absorption with the irrelevant issue of "parity", SALT negotiations were from promoting the classic goals of arms control, even when they were under way during the 1970s.

The transition during the 1970s from the old assumptions of abundant resources and the continuation of a liberal international economic order, to the new assumptions of scarcity and neomercantilism, have not been challenged either, although a good deal was said in the conference, especially in discussion of Dr. Ayoob's contribution, about the inutility of military force as a means of securing oil supplies. A basic question we explored a little in the conference is how far military means are appropriate in relation to the goals of access to resources. Some fundamental distinctions here should be underlined. We need to distinguish between the use of force to coerce oil producers, as implied in the 1974 Kissinger statement, and its use to deter seizure of the oil resources by others, as implied by the Carter Doctrine in response to the Soviet invasion of Afghanistan. We need to distinguish between the use of force to prevent strangulation of the economy, and its use simply to protect a particular standard of living -or to prevent price rises. Above all, we need to ask ourselves whether military means are in fact the most feasible ones to secure the result of securing access to oil – whether the use of force really offers more hope than a policy of allowing radical political changes to take place and seeking to do business with new, radical governments, a policy that has worked well in black Africa, and which is the policy towards which West European governments now lean, in preference to reliance on force.

The revival of belief in the utility of military intervention in the affairs of weaker states, to which I referred, was discussed further by Dr. Ayoob in his chapter. He concentrated on super power intervention in the affairs of Third World countries; it needs to be said, however, that the stronger Third World countries have also built up an impressive record of military intervention of this kind. I am not thinking simply of the long-standing commitment of some Third World countries to intervene against colonial and white supremacist governments that always sat uneasily alongside their commitment to a principle of non-intervention so as to protect themselves against dominance by the super powers. There is also a record of intervention by states such as India, Indonesia, Iran and Vietnam in the affairs of neighbouring, weaker Third World states. The abortive intervention by Egypt in the attempt to relieve hostages a Larnaca in Cyprus is also of interest here, in that it showed that the doctrine of a right to intervene to protect citizens abroad is no longer the monopoly of the Western powers.

No one has challenged the proposition I put forward that there has been a weakening of perceived legal obstacles to resort to force, or the proposition that the use of force has become less unacceptable to Western societies – although Professor Miller in touching on the latter theme in his chapter, indicates that in his view the analysis of the acceptability of force provided in the papers of the 1973 Conference of the International Institute for Strategic Studies is still applicable today. I believe that while, today, Western societies are still very far from being militarised, the role of the military in them has become more comfortable than it was then, there is a greater willingness to shoulder defence burdens and to adopt military perspectives. The phenomenon which in my chapter I called "expressive" interventionism, and which Professor Lebow in his refers to as "the Mayaguez syndrome", shows that in the United States, at least, there is a will to see military force used as a demonstration of national pride.

Professor Ropp reminded us at the beginning of this book that our conference in Canberra coincided with the bicentenary of the birth of Clausewitz, the founder of modern strategy. It has often seemed to me that all of the concepts of contemporary strategic thinking – notions such as deterrence, crisis management, limited war, insurgency, arms control – are no more than a series of variations on Clausewitz's theme of the need to subordinate war to the political object. In the sense that they recognise the danger that war will get out of hand, and seek to devise ways in which war can still serve the political object, even in an age in which war can quickly give rise to dislocation of an interdependent international economy, social and political revolution and nuclear destruction, strategists are "all Clausewitzians now". Unfortunately, however, Clausewitz does not have anything to say to us as to what the political object in war should be. This is why the study of strategy should not ever be allowed to become separated from the study of international politics, international law and international ethics.

The Determinants of Defence Policy for a Medium Military Power

ADMIRAL SIR ANTHONY SYNNOT

The questions examined in this book are highly relevant to the formulation of strategic guidance, and should increase understanding of strategic matters across a broad spectrum. By arranging the conference from which this book developed, and by many other activities, the Strategic and Defence Studies Centre deserves much credit for contributing significantly to defence policy making in Australia.

Other chapters discuss topics ranging from strategic concepts and international relationships to various forms of warfare and arms control. I will not attempt to compete with them, but will comment on the principles involved in the practical business of determining defence policy and structuring a defence force, noting in passing that defence policy is one of a number of products of a nation's strategy.

This chapter addresses not the super powers, nor Australia in particular, but is directed to the medium and smaller military powers, the problems of which have not been covered in detail in other chapters. In discussing armed forces, I am thinking of them being used for national defence purposes, and not for aggressive purposes. I am not addressing internal security, which nevertheless sometimes has an important influence on the characteristics of a defence force.

The defence policy-maker has to avoid being either over-optimistic or over-pessimistic; he may learn from past trends, but he must do more than speculate on the future. He has to weigh up possibilities and likelihoods against risks. In essence he has to be practical, rather than theoretical, about a very complex subject.

Defence policy should flow from a country's strategic circumstances. To start with, therefore, it is necessary to develop strategic guidance covering political, economic and military circumstances and their trends. As a starting point for this process a searching intelligence assessment will be required, even though its forecasts may be relatively short compared to the time span of defence planning. We must decide whether there is a threat now or foreseeably. It is generally accepted that there are two basic elements of threat; first, capability and second, intention. Until and unless a potential enemy has the necessary capability, he cannot be a threat; his capability is open to assessment and there are limitations on how quickly he can change it. The second element, intention, can change much more quickly. The degree to which it can change will be more a matter of judgement than assessment. The nature of a threat can range from involvement in a global war, through a regional conventional war, to relatively low-level but nonetheless damaging contingencies.

The state of the strategic environment, particularly whether there is a threat now or foreseeably, or no foreseeable threat but a situation of general instability, must have a big influence on our defence planning. An assessment of no identifiable threat indicates that greater emphasis should be given to developing long lead-time equipment and skills, at the expense of a high state of operational readiness. On the other hand a clearly identifiable threat indicates a requirement for readily available trained manpower, in-service equipment and an effective logistics organization. In either case one should have the capacity to deal with current and foreseeable lesser tasks. For contingencies more remote in time and probability, one should have the ingredients in one's defence force which can be expanded to the level needed within the likely warning time.

Next, one should identify principal national interests of defence concern. Examples might be protection of off-shore resources and maintenance of sovereignty over island territories. One should then look at the enduring features of the environment. To give some superficial examples: there are enduring geographic features, such as whether one lives on a island, or has land frontiers with other countries; there are enduring economic features, for instance, the dependence of a country on trade or on overseas supplies; there can also be enduring political features such as whether a country is non-aligned or has particular alliances.

Alliances may help to share the burden if one is under the sort of threat which could seriously affect an ally also. In such instances, the importance of being able to operate with one's ally and of having done so in exercises will be evident. Also one must not overlook the fact that, in some low-level contingencies, one's ally or allies may be prepared to help from the sidelines, but not wish to become directly involved in the action.

Taking these factors into account, it is then necessary for a government to decide on its broad military strategy. Will it depend on a deterrent strategy, or a defensive strategy, or a mix of each? Much has been written in the earlier chapters about nuclear deterrence, but it is important to understand what is meant by a deterrent strategy in the non-nuclear arena. The generally accepted military definition is – "to prevent action by fear of the consequences. It is a state of mind brought about by the existence of a credible threat of unacceptable counter-action". The potential enemy must be convinced of one's will to retaliate offensively and of one's capability to inflict damage. To do this one needs offensive forces capable of exploiting enemy vulnerabilities. The term "offensive" is used here rather than "aggressive" as there is an important difference between them.

A deterrent strategy based on fear of retaliation may not be effective in low-level situations below the threshold where punitive operations could be justified. Such a strategy could serve to limit escalation of low-level situations, but in any case some defensive forces will be needed. With regard to higher level contingencies, modern conventional weapon systems give a better potential for deterrence than used to be the case.

The alternative of relying on a defensive strategy may be more attractive to some countries where there are large reserves of manpower, or where the costs of buying and maintaining complex offensive weapons systems might prove impracticable. Nonetheless, it is worth remembering that it is better to deter war, rather than to plan on winning it after it has started.

In summary, in formulating a defence policy, one should assess one's strategic circumstances, identify the degrees of threat which may have to be faced, and analyse enduring features and national interest. One's broad operational concept would then flow from these considerations. It is then possible to plan the structure, size and characteristics of the armed forces, and to consider the part that civil infrastructure, industry, research institutes and other defence-related bodies might play.

At this stage a word of warning should be sounded. R. James Woolsey, a former United States Under Secretary of the Navy, has written recently:

There are some – very few – weapon systems decisions that profit from lengthy study of the specific scenarios in which the weapon might be used. But for many, and especially for a weapon system as widely useful and as badly needed, for example, as the general-purpose submarine, their utility is so general that agonizing studies of specific scenarios are a waste of time. (1980)

He goes on to point out that modern technology enables us to change the weapon systems in existing platforms. It is after all the performance of the weapon system rather than of the platform which is of prime importance.

There has been a tendency in the past for the land, sea and air forces of a country to operate in peacetime with a high degree of independence. More than ever before, it is important to recognise the interdependence of the arms of a defence force. In significant operations it is now most unlikely that any one Service will operate independently of the others. It is therefore important in peacetime to exercise joint operations, particularly land operations involving army and air force units, and maritime operations involving navy and air force units.

One will need to decide on how much self-reliance is necessary and practicable. It is expensive to acquire; only the super powers can hope to be fully independent in equipment development, procurement and support. Most governments want to be able to operate independently; this entails a capability to maintain own forces in operations for a period of time without reliance on others. Therefore when buying new equipment, one must examine how it is to be supported. An effective logistics organization would be essential. If supply and support problems are to be minimised, it would be important to avoid proliferation in types of equipment. Standardisation in basic equipments sometimes achieves less than the ideal result, but, if it helps to achieve effective logistic support, it cannot but be a very important aim to pursue. It may also be necessary to improve the extent to which a nation's industry can support particular weapon systems and equipments.

In recent times there has been an electronic revolution, exemplified by advances in computer technology, data processing, microcircuitry, fibre optics and the terminal guidance of weapons. These and other developments are making possible the production of high capacity, light, reliable and relatively cheap equipment which is within the capacity of many medium powers to support, despite the significant costs of items such as computer software.

Consideration must therefore be given to the level of technology one should seek. I suggest that the level sought should be one which relates to other countries in the neighbourhood, rather than to other powers worldwide. When seeking to develop a higher level of technology one should try to avoid high complexity, because, while advanced technology may offer reliability, high complexity may cause software and logistic support problems. Good arguments can be made for increased use of modern technology where a saving of manpower is important, and it can reduce early obsolescence in equipments. It can be very expensive in initial capital cost, however. In relation to technology, it is therefore wiser to strive for adequacy rather than excellence. If there is an identifiable threat of particular importance to a country, one can structure one's defence force to meet it. Many countries, however, face a variety of threats and must look for versatility in their weapons systems rather than a better but narrower capability.

The degree of mobility required in a defence force will depend to a large extent on geographical features. Some countries may have their defence force deployed along threatened borders. Other, larger, countries may have to depend on moving a relatively small defence force quickly to wherever an unexpected threat develops; for a continental country this can be achieved largely by air and land transport, but for an archipelagic country sea transport would be particularly important. In either of these latter cases some specialised military transport will be necessary even though most countries nowadays have national air and shipping lines which can be used for the movement of personnel and of bulk cargoes.

The degree of endurance required in one's platforms will also depend on geographic factors. For instance, some countries require equipment with a long radius of action for operating over vast land and sea areas, whilst other countries find high performance rather than great endurance important.

In the future more emphasis will need to be given to electronic warfare. It will affect all forms of warfare through its potential both to render weapons systems ineffective and to disrupt communications links. While modern command systems permit a commander to control military activities effectively from a distance, they depend on high quality communications. But because of the possibility of disruption of communications, commanders at all levels must be trained to use their initiative and continue to fight intelligently in accordance with broad directives.

The importance of commanders being able to take initiatives emphasises the value to a defence force of well-trained manpower. This, of course, encompasses not just the Regulars, but also the Reserves. Whether Reserves serve voluntarily or compulsorily, their utility is not so much a question of numbers, but rather of whether they are well trained in modern weapon systems and tactics. The complexity of military systems now calls for intensive training and regular exercising. Personnel should have a sense of purpose and an understanding of the importance to national security of their task. There is no substitute for sound leadership and good morale. The serviceman will continue to be the most important single factor in the effectiveness of any defence force.

In conclusion, the development of defence policy and refinement of force structure options is a complex and demanding process. A comprehensive and well structured strategic assessment, encompassing the theme of this book, provides the basis for such policy development.

The World in the 1980s
Strategic Problems and Responses

ROBERT O'NEILL

In their conclusions, Professor Bull and Admiral Synnot have addressed major themes relating to their own fields of expertise. The former
has reminded us that strategy is the servant of policy and has invited
us to question the wisdom of current trends in great-power attitudes:
the latter has outlined the principal factors to be considered and some
of the methods which are being used by strategic planners to meet
expected challenges of the 1980s. It falls to me to offer an overview of
the major problems discussed by the contributors and important
trends in the techniques which might be applied to their solution.

Global Problems

Two particular issues of world-wide significance stand out from the
previous analyses: the nature of international relations in the 1980s
seems certain to be harsher than in the 1970s; and, this trend notwithstanding, the disincentives for the super-powers to go to war with
each other are as high as ever. The increasing international tensions of
the 1980s are not simply a by-product of the Soviet invasion of Afghanistan but are caused more by the deep-seated rivalry of the two super-powers. The Afghanistan issue has sharpened the contest but
solution of that problem will have little effect on more fundamental
divisions, which can be managed only within a framework of East-
West negotiations. While each side will continue to believe in the next
few years that it must stand up to the other, they both show signs of
awareness that unmoderated confrontation can lead only to an increasingly less manageable balance between them. Similarly doctrinal
and force structure asymmetries, at both the nuclear and conventional levels, should be recognised, their causes understood and their magnitude reduced in the interests of world peace.

Regional Influences on the Super-Powers

Despite the widening gap between the super-powers and the remainder of the international community in terms of weapons technology
and strategic power, each will have to pay more attention to the views

of its allies and to those of non-aligned states than in the 1970s. The strategic stalemate between the Soviet Union and the United States has always provided opportunities for others, such as Britain and India, to acquire some moderating influence. While not always welcome to the giants, initiatives by other powers can play a major constructive role.

As Dr T.B. Millar reminds us, the natures of alliances are changing as the less powerful members in a military sense increase their political and economic significance and become more anxious about the directions in which their major allies are leading. These tends have long been evident within NATO: the independence shown by Rumania and recent events in Poland, in which the Soviets have thought it wiser not to intervene militarily, emphasise that there are real problems of co-operation within the Warsaw Pact also. The European powers of both alliance systems are likely to play a bigger role in the conduct of East-West relations than ever before. Opportunities for them to make contributions, such as the European Conference on Security and Cooperation, will probably be widened. Europe remains the theatre in which the greatest concentration of opposing military forces exists and it is vital for the remainder of the world that those particular forces should never be used for their prime purpose. Fortunately the European powers have the strongest of all incentives to see that these forces should not be pitted against each other, and they should act on it vigorously.

Elsewhere in the world other powers are becoming increasingly assertive. China, India and Japan in particular are playing a bigger role in international relations then ever before, particularly in a strategic sense. While there are great differences in their perspectives, there is a growing commonality of interests between them. All three see a need to increase their strategic strength and independence. China and Japan, and perhaps India also, are concerned about the speed with which the Soviet Union is increasing its military power, particularly with regard to the deployment of conventional forces in the East Asian region. China and Japan also have doubts regarding United States capacity and willingness to deploy countervailing force in an emergency.

The turn-about which has occurred in Chinese policies since 1976 and the recently announced Japanese willingness to make long-term increases in defence capability are harbingers of greater changes to come in the 1980s. These changes are more likely to occur in the form of implementation of these new policies than as any radical extensions of them: each, particularly China, acknowledges severe limits on the speed with which it can develop strategic power. Nonetheless strategic thinkers the world over will have to pay increasing heed to these new centres of influence. While Indian policies under Mrs Ghandhi in the

1980s may not be very different from what they were in the 1970s, under the same leadership, Professor Rao has pointed to a growing capacity to use seapower in the Indian Ocean. India seems likely to increase its power to influence its own strategic environment. In view of the continuing growth of American forces, bases and facilities in the Indian Ocean region, Washington will have to pay particular heed to this concern of India if it is not to force Mrs Gandhi more firmly into the arms of the Soviets.

Other non-aligned states, particularly those which control key resources or are located in positions of major strategic influence, seem most likely to both demand and receive a voice in determining the regional and global policies of the super-powers and their allies. As Third World states increase their political determination, economic strength and military capabilities, they will become more difficult for the external powers to ignore or manipulate than in the 1970s. Similarly their support or co-operation will be more important. Both the Middle Eastern and African states in particular are going to play a greater role in world affairs, while riven by disputes amongst themselves and, in many cases, with governments which are threatened domestically. They are likely therefore to offer the super-powers opportunities for intervention which, if followed up, may prove expensive or even counter-productive in the long term, despite the attractiveness of such options to the super-powers in the short term.

The Modes of Conflict in the 1980s

In this situation, all four recognised major modes of conflict appear to remain relevant to the 1980s, although with differing emphases from the 1970s. Nuclear confrontation, wide-ranging conventional force deployment, limited warfare and insurgency conflicts all will continue to occur in the coming decade, fostered by a more competitive international political climate and an increasing array of potential actors, but moderated by widening concern regarding the vital importance of avoiding a direct super-power clash.

In the nuclear field there can be little room for complacency regarding the prospects for avoiding such a clash as doctrines for limited nuclear warfare, such as that approved in 1980 by President Carter, gain currency. At present the Soviets have shown little inclination to develop this option, preferring to rely on full-scale nuclear retaliation to deter the Americans from such steps. Nonetheless, as the Soviets' nuclear technology continues to evolve they are likely to acquire means similar to those of the Americans for precise, limited strikes. These means may well give rise to a similar body of doctrine, which would then appear to make limited nuclear warfare increasingly feasible from the super-power standpoint. It is an extremely difficult game

for only one power to play for long without causing the other to escalate to full-scale attack. Where such conflicts might lead, how escalation might be prevented, is totally unclear. Nonetheless, if they become real options for both super-powers, rather than merely one as at
present, these will be questions which must be examined soon. As
Professor Lebow warned, major Western initiatives in the strategic
field in the wake of the Afghanistan crisis can have complex consequences. Additions to military strength and development of new doctrines can lead to countervailing changes on the other side which only
complicate the management of a stable world order.

In the field of major conventional war, we face similar, although
less dramatic, problems. Brigadier Hunt pointed to a high probability
that technological change will continue rapidly. This trend will affect
different nations in different ways, improving the stability of some
existing strategic balances and decreasing that of others. Areas for particular concern in this regard are again the Middle East and Africa,
where fast rates of political and economic change are both fuelling the
development of military power and sharpening enmities between and
within the states of each region. In most developing countries professional military competence is rising, and their governments will probably develop it further, but such changes can have both positive and
negative effects on regional stability. All of these developments create
more ways in which external states, particularly the super-powers, can
gain undesirable influence. Hence it is very important that Third
World states should maintain strongly based political independence to
prevent increasing polarisation of the world. Despite its complications, the world is in a more agreeable condition for most powers and
most people through retaining a pluralistic power structure.

Limited warfare strategies, as Professor Kolkowicz reminded us,
are likely to remain relevant for all great powers in the 1980s. The
possibilities of their being drawn into local disputes in the Third
World remain so significant that they must confront the question
'what then?'. The growing lethality of new conventional weapons
makes even more serious the prospect that what is but a limited war
for a major external power is a life and death struggle for the regional
participants. Whether in a future clash of interests the Soviet Union
will not be the first to blink, as Kolkowicz forecasts, remains to be
seen, irrespective of who is the President of the United States.
Perhaps of greater applicability to the world of the 1980s are his
thoughts relating to Soviet development of a strategy of limited disturbance, in which they can pursue similar ends to those of limited
warfare, but at less risk and cost.

Insurgency and counter-insurgency techniques do not look to be
as relevant to the affairs of the world in the 1980s as they were in the
past decade. The United States appears unlikely to become directly

involved in situations like Vietnam in the 1980s, although it may give indirect support. Without direct American involvement, other Western powers are unlikely to participate directly themselves. By contrast, the Cubans and East Germans show no such reluctance to intervene on behalf of 'progressive forces' as they see them in the Third World, and the Russians themselves face a difficult situation in Afghanistan. It is difficult, however, to credit the Russians with any major, lasting advantages out of such involvement, either by themselves or by their allies. This judgement may have to be changed if they manage to de-stabilise the Saudi regime or create chaos in South Africa, but neither prospect can be given a high degree of probability at this point. There will certainly be internal trouble in both areas but whether the Russians will be able to turn it to their own lasting advantage is very open to question.

Resolution and Containment of Disputes

Preservation of a stable international order in the 1980s will obviously require greater efforts both to resolve disputes before they erupt into violence and to limit the consequences of those which are not resolved in this way. Although the climate of international politics in the 1980s looks to be unkind, and hence the problems in the way of maintaining peace are unusually formidable, there is at least a wider understanding amongst leaders of the consequences of failure. There is also a greater degree of acknowledgement of the constructive roles which can be played by diplomacy, both bi-laterally and multi-laterally, arms control agreements and sensible military policies. The SALT II treaty may prove to be a dead letter, but both sides may continue to observe its terms because the alternatives are so unattractive. Arms control serves not only broad, humanitarian purposes: it also serves to reduce waste and to trim military forces of some of their less effective elements. Unless either the American or Soviet governments commit a major breach of the implied terms for their continued co-existence, it is difficult to believe that there will not be some moderation of East-West tensions in the coming five years, which will enable discussion of new, albeit limited, arms control agreements. Such agreements will need to cover both conventional and nuclear forces, if they are to have real prospects of success because of the existing asymmetries in the super-power balance in both dimensions.

As part of the process of maintaining a stable international order, which nonetheless can accommodate changes in the interest of social justice, close attention must be given by individual states to the development of sound politico-military relationships. Political and military leaders are each dependent on the other for effectiveness, as Professor Miller has indicated, and each must understand the other's problems and the limitations of his power. Politicians and their civilian advisers must further develop their competence in modern strategy: military leaders, besides maintaining their professional competence, must study more closely the problems and aims of their political masters in order to serve them better.

Finally, the preservation of peace at a time of high rates of political, social, economic and technological change will be aided by a more expert public opinion, both nationally and internationally. While these thoughts are not so relevant to the Soviet Union, some of its allies and some states of the Third World which circumscribe the scope of public discussion of strategic issues, they are of increasing importance to other countries. Hence it behoves all who are professionally concerned with strategic thinking, particularly those who work in universities and the media, to make a major effort to stimulate wider discussion of these problems in the 1980s. Just as war is too serious to be left to generals, so is thinking about international relationships and the preservation of peace too important to be confined to the ranks of analysts, government advisers and the military.

Notes

1 Strategic Thinking Since 1945   *Theodore Ropp*

1. For comparisons between Sun Tzu and classic Greek military sophists I am indebted to Mr. Ong Chit Chung of the University of Singapore and Dr. Everett L. Wheeler of the University of Indiana. For comments on air power, I am heavily dependent on the ideas of Col. David MacIsaac, USAF. The completed work will also be edited by Prof. Donald M. Schurman, Royal Military College of Canada. Professors Felix Gilbert and Gordon Craig, the sub-editors, have confirmed our suspicions that Earle never tried to define Makers, Modern, or Strategy.
2. He had already shown that Japanese cities had been destroyed at "1 square mile for 3 million dollars", and that future costs would be "less than half a million", a fine statistical argument. (Arnold, 1946, p. 26).
3. After the sense of crisis has brought forth plausible alternatives, the revised paradigm normally incorporates "much of the [old one's] vocabulary and apparatus ... But they seldom employ [them] ... in quite the traditional way ... [as] old terms, concepts, and experiments fall into new relationships". Kuhn sees no reason why this intellectual process in the natural sciences should be regularly cyclical. In the case of strategy, any reason would be related to the generational struggle for power within large, hieratic organizations, and to the complexity and multiplicity of factors which changed over time even in those Berber societies described by the great historian Ibn Khaldun (1332–1406) who has a three-generation 120 year cycle. The first modern Western historian to take cycles seriously was Jakob Burckhardt, whose 1869–71 *Reflections on History* were translated by J. Hastings Nicholas as *Force and Freedom* (Boston, 1964).

3 US Strategic Nuclear Concepts in the 1970s   *Warner Schilling*

1. This chapter is an edited version of a transcript of a lecture given to the Conference on the Development of Strategic Thinking in the 1970s: Prospects for the 1980s. The author was unable to provide a full written text.

4 Soviet Strategy 1965–1990   *Geoffrey Jukes*

1. The Soviet tank inventory in 1939 totalled about 20,000, which was approximately three times the combined total of Germany, France and Great Britain, and in 1941 the Soviet Union had between 12,000 and 14,000 aircraft, considerably more than the British and the Germans then had between them. But less than 10% of the aircraft were of up-to-date design.
2. Soviet calls for superiority in military technology were observed in six publications by or for military officers between 1966 and 1976, including the Defence Minister (Marshal Grechko) in *Kommunist* in 1970, and Volume 2 of the *Soviet Military Encyclopaedia*, (Sovetskaia voennoia entsiklopediia) p. 253. However, calls for the retention of a presumed superiority by senior government or military leaders in NATO countries are so frequent that it is doubtful whether any real significance can be attached to military rhetoric of this kind, whatever its source.
3. For example in a speech on 14 January 1960 and in his memoirs (1972, pp. 13–53), Khrushchev indicates that cost considerations were uppermost.
4. This is reflected in the pattern of major Warsaw Pact exercises, which almost always combine conventional with nuclear operations.
5. *Military Balance* (International Institute for Strategic Studies, London), for various years from 1960 onwards shows the entire inventory of the Afghan armed forces to be of Soviet origin.

6 Deterrence and Stability in the NATO-Warsaw Pact Relationship   *Johan Jörgen Holst*

1. The views expressed in this chapter are the personal views and assessments of the author and do not necessarily reflect official Norwegian views.
2. For a comprehensive discussion of the role of arms control in the current international environment see the author's "Arms Control Revisited" to be published in a volume on arms control policy issues edited by Uwe Nerlich (forthcoming).
3. Public Law (PL) 93–365 was enacted by the US Congress on August 5, 1974. It directed that the Secretary of Defense shall study the overall concept for use of tactical nuclear weapons in Europe; how the use of such weapons relates to deterrence and to a strong conventional defence; reduction in the number and type of nuclear warheads which are not essential for the defence structure of Western Europe; and the steps that can be taken to develop a rational and coordinated nuclear posture by the NATO Alliance that is consistent with proper emphasis on conventional defence forces. (For background see Hearings, 1974; Schlesinger 1975; Congressional Budget Office, 1977; Hearings, 1976.) The reports from the NATO studies on the implications of advances in modern conven-

tional weapon technologies, the MIT (Military Implications Team) (1976) and PIT (Political Implications Team) (1977) provided a basis for assessing the interplay of conventional and nuclear defence options.

4. I am indebted to Phillip A. Karber for first suggesting this basic approach.

7 Autonomy and Intervention   Mohammed Ayoob

1. The term "Third World" is used in this paper in a generic sense and deliberately so. I am sure it will lead to the criticism that there is too much diversity within the "Third World" for the term to be used in such a generic sense. While this criticism is partially valid, it is one which attempts to elevate a half truth to the position of the whole truth. It is no doubt true that there are diverse elements which constitute the Third World; it is also true that there are intra-mural problems, conflicts and antagonistic relations prevalent within the Third World. But this does not necessarily invalidate the thesis that given the immense disparity in power (economic and military) between the Third World on the one hand and the developed North, and particularly the superpowers, on the other, there does prevail a major conflict of interests which, in fact, forms what one can call the "principal contradiction" within the international system as it is presently constituted. Since the disparity in power in this case (as in other cases within domestic political systems) almost automatically translates itself into an exploiter – exploited, dominant – subservient relationship (for which the euphemism "interdependent" has been coined), it adds to the feelings of exploitation and deprivation on the part of one party and of self-righteousness and aggressiveness on the part of the other. It is my contention that this contradiction will become increasingly sharp and more visible in the 1980s than has been the case so far – and it is to this phenomenon that, at least in part, this paper addresses itself.

2. Notable examples of non-official views were: Tucker, 1975, pp. 21–31; Ignotus, 1975, pp. 45–62. Secretary of State Kissinger's comments in an interview to *Business Week*, 23 December 1974, can be treated as representative of official US thinking on the subject (Kissinger, 1975).

3. Pre-eminent among these studies was the one prepared by the Congressional Research Service of the United States Library of Congress, 1975.

4. President Zia-ul-Haq of Pakistan, no great friend of the Soviet Union, expressed these sentiments, while opening the Islamic Foreign Ministers' Conference in Islamabad in May 1980, when he declared that while "we vehemently oppose the Soviet military presence in Afghanistan, we also oppose the presence of U.S. naval forces which have been deployed in a threatening posture in the vicinity of Iran". *Mansuri*, 24–30 May 1980, p. 2.

5. The Iranian Revolution has made a remarkable contribution to this process by demonstrating that a revolution – in both its internal and external dimensions, namely, restructuring of the domestic order and rejection of foreign domination – can take place in 'native' terms without the help of external (Marxist or liberal) agents of legitimacy. I have developed this argument in my article, Ayoob, 1979b.

6. This development is somewhat analogous to what has been happening in the Indian countryside recently. With the increase in political consciousness among the Harijan (untouchable) landless labourers and, consequently, their attempts to act autonomously of the traditional power elite (and, on occasion, in defiance of the existing power structure), there has been a marked increase in acts of repression committed by the dominant peasant castes in order to prevent this "infection" from spreading. While, frequently, the dominant caste groups, for example the Jats and the Rajputs, compete for dominance in a village community, they are usually not averse to acting jointly to contain the threats posed by the landless elements to the established order. Again, when one of the dominant caste groups is engaged in repressive measures against the Harijan landless, the other(s) often adopt a stance of 'benevolent neutrality', that is benevolent from the dominant group's point of view. The parallels with the way the super powers act vis-a-vis the Third World are remarkable.

8 Alliances in the 1970s and 1980s   T.B. Millar

1. The different expectations from alliances is examined in more depth in the author's monograph, *Contemporary Alliances*, to be published during 1981 by the Department of International Relations, Australian National University, in the series Canberra Studies in World Affairs.

2. Occasionally the "revisionist" case is made that the Soviet Union has merely reacted to American initiatives. e.g. see Garrett, 1977. Hedley Bull wrote recently: "If there has been a threat to the general 'balance of power' in the post-war international system, limiting the freedom of manoeuvre of other actors, this has come from the United States rather than the Soviet Union. The Soviet Union has provided the principal check to the power of the United States . . .". *Quadrant*, vol. XXXIV, no. 7, July 1980.

3. In an article which appears largely to ignore the real world, Mancur Olson Jr and Richard Zeckhauser have drawn up a model for alliance defence expenditure (1970, pp. 121–40).

4. One wonders how many Europeans were misled by the Oxford Union resolution of 9 February 1933 that the Union would "in no circumstances fight for King and Country". In these times an off-the-cuff statement by a European left-wing (or even more, a right-wing) politician can be extremely disturbing to the authorities in Washington.

5. In 1979 US press reports that the United States policy, undeclared to Japan, was to "swing" naval forces from the Western Pacific to the North Atlantic in the event of trouble there.
6. Japan has been reluctant to become involved in joint military planning with the United States, and only in November 1978 did it even agree to consider guidelines for conducting studies on such planning.
7. Britain and France were members of SEATO, but it was a very ineffectual alliance, i.e. not really an alliance at all.
8. Including Iceland, which provides only the use of its territory for US and NATO facilities.
9. Except for the Baltic states, whose incorporation into the Soviet Union has not been recognised by Britain or the United States.
10. On 16 July 1980 Britain announced that it would equip its new submarine force with US Trident missiles.
11. The "window" is supposed to be a time – probably between 1981 and 1985 – when the Soviet Union will be able to destroy virtually all the American land-based intercontinental ballistic missiles, whereas the United States will not have a similar (reciprocal) capacity and would not wish to compensate by using less accurate "counter-value" weapons that would presumably bring retaliation against American cities.
12. Robin Remington analyses the origins of the Pact, and the relevance of the inner-party struggle in Moscow after the death of Stalin in her book, 1971.

9 The Evolution of Chinese Strategic Thought   *Jonathan D. Pollack*

★The views expressed in this chapter are entirely the author's own, and should not be attributed to the Rand Corporation or any of its governmental sponsors.
1. One is reminded of the conversation between Vice Premier Deng Xiaoping and Senator Edward Kennedy during the Senator's 1978 visit to China. When comparing notes on their respective experiences as military men, Kennedy remarked that he had been a private in the Korean War. Deng responded that "I have been a general since 1927".
2. I am indebted to Dwight Perkins for this observation.
3. In this essay, the designation of PLA will be used to encompass all Chinese forces, irrespective of service sector.

10 Strategic Thinking in India in the 1970s   *R.V.R. Chandrasekhara Rao*

1. A quasi-official research body the Institute and its staff, in their individual capacities, have not only contributed to a wider public

discussion of strategic issues but also took definite stands on major issues. For example, they have been early advocates of India's acquiring nuclear capability as also of the need of India's asserting its position in the region.

2. Many publicists and scholars wrote about the need for and feasibility of India's manufacturing atomic weapons. Some of these have been included in *Nuclear Weapons* compiled by the Department of Atomic Energy. (1970)

3. This was the theme of the Institute's Annual Conference held in Baden bei Wien, Austria, in September 1976.

4. This had been Mrs. Gandhi's stand during the Indian election campaign in early June 1980. After assuming the Prime Ministership she too was more inclined to appreciate the circumstances of Russian intervention. See also *The Times of India*, (Bombay, 24, 25 January, 3 April 1980 and *The Hindu*, (Hyderabad, 5 March, 1980)

14 Clear and Future Danger   *Richard Ned Lebow*

1. These cases are: Fashoda (1898), Korea (1903–04), First Morocco (1905–06), Bosnia (1908–09), Agadir (1911), July (1914), Rhineland (1936), May and Munich (1938), Berlin (1948), Korea (1950), Sino-Indian (1962), Cuba (1962), Arab-Israeli (1967).

16 Warfare and Policy   *J.D.B. Miller*

1. To solve problems of nomenclature, I shall use 'the military' and sometimes even 'armies' to include land, sea and air forces, except where some specific differentiation is required. 'The military' seems to me capable of being used with both singular and plural verbs.

2. This is not meant to suggest that the military are always 'hawks' and the civilians 'doves'. Hitler was no dove. Generals (especially Alanbrooke) certainly had to restrain Churchill at times. There are other cases in which civilian authorities have been more bellicose than their military advisers, though most evidence seems to give a mixed answer to the question whether there is anything inherently aggressive about military attitudes. The point implied above is not that politicians are pacifists, but that the range of interests which they have to take into account is wider than that which usually presents itself to generals.

References

1 Strategic thinking Since 1945

Arnold, H.H. (1946) "Air Force in the atomic age" *in* Masters, Dexter & Way, Katharine (eds.) *One World or None*. (New York: McGraw-Hill).

Brodie, Bernard. (1973) *War and Politics*. (New York: Macmillan).

Clark, John Bates. (1916) Introduction to Bodart, Gaston. *Losses of Life in Modern Wars, Austria-Hungary; France*. (Oxford: Clarendon Press). This was among the first volumes of the *Economic and Social History of the World War* (c. 150 vols.) eventually published by the Canadian-American "new" historian, James T. Shotwell.

Clausewitz, Carl von. (1976) *On War*. (Princeton: Princeton University Press). (Edited and translated by Michael Howard and Peter Paret). This splendid edition and translation is, by itself, a sign of strategists' return to first principles, as is the German Democratic Republic's rehabilitation of Clausewitz.

Douhet, Giulio. (1943) *The Command of the Air*. (London: Faber and Faber). (Translated by Dono Ferrari)

Foch, Ferdinand. (1921) *The Principles of War*. (London: Chapman & Hall). (Translated by Hilaire Belloc)

Fuller, John Frederick Charles. (1942) *Machine Warfare: an Enquiry into the Influences of Mechanics on the Art of War*. (London: Hutchinson).

Guibert, Jacques Antoine Hippolyte. (1803) *Oeuvres Militaires de Guibert*. (Paris: Magimel).

Jomini, Henri. (1947) *Jomini and his Summary of the Art of War*. (Harrisburg: Military Science Publishing Co.). (Edited by J.D. Hittle)

Kuhn, Thomas S. (1962) *The Structure of Scientific Revolutions*. (Chicago: University of Chicago Press).

United States Air Force Basic Doctrine (1964). (Washington).

2 Force in International Relations

Aron, Raymond. (1958) *War and Industrial Society*. (Auguste Comte Memorial Trust Lecture; no. 3) (London: Oxford University Press).

Aron, Raymond. (1978/79) 'War and industrial society: a reappraisal',

Millenium: Journal of International Studies, v. 7, (3) Winter.
Buchan, Alastair. (1974) *Change Without War: The Shifting Structures of World Power*. (The BBC Reith lectures; 1973) (London: Chatto and Windus).
Hoffmann, Stanley. (1968) *Gulliver's Troubles; or the Setting of American Foreign Policy*. (New York: McGraw Hill).
Keohane, Robert, O. & Nye, Joseph S. (eds.) (1972) *Transnational Relations and World Politics*. (Cambridge, Mass.: Harvard University Press).
Knorr, Klaus. (1966) *On the Uses of Military Power in the Nuclear Age*. (Princeton, New Jersey: Princeton University Press).
Knorr, Klaus. (1977) 'Is international coercion waning or rising?', *International Society*, v. 1 (4) Spring.
Martin, Laurence. (1973) 'The Utility of Military Force', *in* International Institute for Strategic Studies. Annual Conference, 15th, Travemünde, 1973. *Force in Modern Societies, Its Place in International Politics*. (Adelphi Papers; no. 102) (London: International Institute for Strategic Studies).

4 Soviet Strategy 1965–1990

Grechko, A. (1970) 'Na strazhe mira i sotsializma', *Kommunist*, No. 3, p. 51–64.
Khrushchev, N.S. (1974) *Khrushchev Remembers. Vol. 2: The Last Testament*. (London: Deutsch).
The Military Balance (1960) (London: International Institute for Strategic Studies).
Quarterly Economic Review: Pakistan, Bangladesh, Afghanistan. Annual Supplement 1979. (1980) (London: Economist Intelligence Unit).
Sovetskaia voennaia entsiklopediia (1976) (Moskva: Voenizdat).
United Nations (1979) *Statistical Yearbook 1978*. (New York: United Nations).

5 On Limited War

Adoratskii, V.V., Molotov, V.M. and Savelev, M.A. (eds) (1931) *Leninskii sbornik (Lenin Miscellany)*, 2nd edn. (Moscow).
Arbatov, G.A.(1974) 'Problemy mira i sotsializma', *World Marxist Review*, no. 2.
Bondarenko, V.M. (1968) *Kommunist Vooruzhennykh Sil*, December.
Clausewitz, Karl von. (1953) *On War*, (Washington: Combat Forces Press).
Deutscher, Issac, (1976) *The Prophet Armed: Trotsky, 1879–1921*. (Oxford: Oxford University Press).
Douglass, Joseph D. (n.d.) 'The Soviet theater nuclear offensive', *Studies in Communist Affairs*, vol. 1.
Earle, Edward Mead. (ed.) (1966) *Makers of Modern Strategy: Military Thought from Machiavelli to Hitler*. (New York: Athenaeum).

Epishev, A.A. (1975) *Nekotorye Voprosy Ideologicheskoi Raboty v Sovetskikh Vooruzhennykh Sikakh*, (Moscow: Voenizdat).

George, Alexander L. and Smoke, Richard. (1974) *Deterrence in American Foreign Policy: Theory and Practice*, (New York: Columbia University Press).

Gouré, Leon, et al. (1974) *The Role of Nuclear Forces in Current Soviet Strategy*, (Coral Gables, Florida: Center for Advanced International Studies, University of Miami).

Grechko, A.A. (1974) 'Rukovodiashchaia rol' KPSS v stroitel'stve armii razvitogo sotsialisticheskogo obshchestva', *Voprosy Istorii KPSS*, no. 5.

Grechko, A.A. (1977) *The Armed Forces of the Soviet Union*, (Moscow: Progress Publishers).

Halperin, Morton H. (1963) *Limited War in the Nuclear Age*, (New York: Wiley).

Kaufmann, William W. (ed.) (1956) *Military Policy and National Security*, (Princeton, N.J.: Princeton University Press).

Kissinger, Henry. (1960) 'Limited war: nuclear or conventional? – a Reappraisal', *Daedalus*, Fall.

Kissinger, Henry. (1961) *The Necessity for Choice: Prospects of American Foreign Policy*, (New York: Harper).

Kolkowicz, Roman. (1967) *The Soviet Military and the Communist Party*, (Princeton, N.J.: Princeton University Press).

Kolkowicz, Roman. (1970) Submission to Senator Albert Gore *in* United States. Congress. Senate. Committee on Foreign Relations. Subcommittee on Arms Control, International Law and Organization. *ABM, MIRV, SALT, and the Nuclear Arms Race: Hearings*, (Washington: USGPO).

Krylov, N.I. (1969) 'The Instructive Lessons of History', *Sovietskaia Rossiia*, August.

Lambeth, Benjamin S. (1975) *Selective Nuclear Operations and Soviet Strategy*, (Santa Monica: The Rand Corporation).

Lambeth, Benjamin S. (1979) 'The political potential of Soviet equivalence', *International Security*, v. 4(2) Fall.

Marxism-Leninism on War and Army, (1972) (Moscow: Progress Publishers).

Nerlich, Uwe. (1980) 'Theatre nuclear forces in Europe: is NATO running out of options?, *Washington Quarterly*, Winter.

Osgood, Robert E. (1957) *Limited War: The Challenge to American Strategy*, (Chicago: University of Chicago Press).

Savkin, V.Ye. (1972) *Osnovnye Printsipy Operativnogo Iskusstva i Taktiki*, (Moscow: Voenizdat).

Schelling, Thomas C. (1966) *Arms and Influence*, (New Haven, Conn.: Yale University Press).

Scott, Harriet Fast and Scott, William F. (1979) *The Armed Forces of the USSR*, (Boulder: Westview Press).

Snyder, Jack L. (1977) *The Soviet Strategic Culture: Implications for Limited Nuclear Operations*, (Santa Monica: The Rand Corporation).

Sokolovskii, V.D. (ed) (1963) *Soviet Military Strategy*, 3rd edn. (Santa

Monica: The Rand Corporation).
Sokolovskii, V.D. (ed) (1968) *Soviet Military Strategy*, 3rd edn. (New York: Crane, Russak & Co).
Talenskii, N. (ed.) (1966) 'Anti-missile systems and disarmament', *in* Erickson, John. (ed.) *The Military Technical Revolution: its Impact on Strategy and Foreign Policy*, (New York: Praeger).
Wolfe, Thomas W. (1965) *Soviet Strategy at the Crossroads*, (Cambridge, Mass: Harvard University Press).
Zhilin, P. (1972) 'The military aspects of detente', *International Affairs*, (Moscow) no. 12.

6 Deterrence and Stability in the NATO-Warsaw Pact Relationship

Bertram, Christoph & Holst, Johan J. (eds.) (1977) *New Strategic Factors in the North Atlantic*. (Oslo: Universitetsforlaget for the Norwegian Institute of International Affairs).
Canby, Steven L. (1980) 'Solving the defense riddle', *New Republic*, v. 182 (17) 26 April, pp. 20–23.
Carter, Jimmy. (1980) Letter to Prime Minister Margaret Thatcher, 14 July, *The Times* (London) 16 July, p. 6.
Coffey, Kenneth J. (1979) *Strategic Implications of the All-Volunteer Force: the Conventional Defense of Central Europe*. (Chapel Hill: University of North Carolina Press).
Holst, Johan J. & Nerlich, Uwe. (eds.) (1977) *Beyond Nuclear Deter-Doctrines, and Arms Limitation*' *in* Kaplan, Morton A. (ed.) *SALT: Problems and Prospects*. (Morristown, New Jersey: General Learning Press).
Holst, Johan J. (1976) 'SALT and East-West Relations in Europe' *in* Andren, Nils & Birnbaum, Karl E. (eds.) *Beyond Detente: Prospects for East-West Co-operation and Security in Europe*. (Leyden: Sijthoff).
Holst, Johan J. & Nerliche, Uwe. (eds.) (1977) *Beyond Nuclear Deterrence: New Aims, New Arms*. (New York: Crane-Russak).
Holst, Johan J. (1978) *Var Forsvarspolitikk: Vurderinger og Utsyn*. (Oslo: Tiden Norsk Forlag).
Holst, Johan J. (1979a) 'Defence Planning and the Politics of European Security' *in* Hemily, Philip W. & Ozdas, M.N. (eds.) *Science and Future Choice: Volume 2: Technological Challenges for Social Change*. (Oxford: Clarendon Press).
Holst, Johan J. (1979b) *SALT-II og var sikkerhet*. (Oslo: DNAK).
Holst, Johan J. (1980) 'The Northern region – key to Europe'. (A paper prepared for the SEA LINK 80, Annapolis, Md., June 17–19)
Holst, Johan J. (1981?) 'Arms Control Revisited' *in* Nerlich, Uwe, a volume on arms control policy issues to be published early in 1981 in English and German for Stiftung Wissenschaft und Politik, Munich.
Painton, Frederick. (1980) 'The great nuclear debate', *Time*, v. 116 (3) 21 July, pp. 4–10.

Rowen, Henry S. (1979) 'The Evolution of Strategic Nuclear Doctrine' in Martin, Laurence. (ed.) *Strategic Thought in the Nuclear Age*. (London: Heinemann).

Schlesinger, James R. (1975) *The Theater Nuclear Force Posture in Europe*, A Report to the US Congress. (Washington: USGPO).

Schmidt, Helmut. (1978) 'The 1977 Alastair Buchan memorial lecture', *Survival*, v. 20 (1) January/February, pp. 2–10. 'The tempter of Paris' (1980), *Economist*, v. 276 (7142) 19 July, pp. 13–15.

United States Congressional Budget Office. (1977) *Planning U.S. General Purpose Forces: the Theater Nuclear Forces*. (Washington: USGPO).

United States Department of Defense. (1980) *Annual Report Fiscal Year 1981*. (Washington: USGPO).

United States House of Representatives, Committee of International Relations, Subcommittee on International Security and Scientific Affairs. (1976) *First Use of Nuclear Weapons: Preserving Responsible Control: Hearings* (94th Congress, 2nd Session). (Washington: USGPO).

United States Senate Foreign Relations Committee, Subcommittee on U.S. Security Agreements and Commitments Abroad and Subcommittee on Arms Control, International Law and Organization (1974) *Nuclear Weapons and Foreign Policy: Hearings* (93rd Congress, 2nd session). (Washington: USGPO).

7 Autonomy and Intervention

Allan, Col. (1980) 'Special US rapid strike force ready', *Weekend Australian*, 21–22 June: 8.

Ayoob, Mohammed. (1979a) 'Super powers and regional 'stability': parallel responses to the Gulf and the Horn', *World Today*, v. 35(5) May.

Ayoob, Mohammed. (1979b) 'Two faces of political Islam: Iran and Pakistan compared', *Asian Survey*, v. 19(6) June.

Ayoob, Mohammed. (1980) 'The Indian Ocean Littoral' in Bell, Coral (ed.). *Agenda for the Eighties*. (Canberra: ANU Press).

Ayoob, Mohammed. (1981) 'Oil, Arabism and Islam: the Persian Gulf in World Politics' in Ayoob, Mohammed (ed.). *The Middle East in World Politics*. (London: Croom Helm).

Ball, George W. (1979–80) 'Crisis in Israeli-American relations'. *Foreign Affairs*, v. 58(2) Winter.

Benningsen, Alexandre A. and Wimbush, S. Enders (1979) *Muslim National Communism in the Soviet Union: a Revolutionary Strategy for the Colonial World*. (Chicago: University of Chicago).

Benningsen, Alexandre. (1980) 'Soviet Muslims and the world of Islam'. *Problems of Communism*, v. 29(2) March-April.

Bull, Hedley. (1971) 'World Order and the Super Powers' in Holbraad, Carsten (ed.). *Super Powers and World Order*. (Canberra: ANU Press).

Conant, Melvin, A. and Gold, Fern R. (1978) *Geopolitics of Energy*.

(Boulder, Colorado: Westview Press).
Critchlow, James, (1972) 'Signs of Emerging Nationalism in the Moslam Soviet Republics' in Dodge, Norton T. (ed.). *The Soviets in Asia*. (Mechanicsville, Maryland: Cremona Foundation).
'The doctrine's acid test'. (1980) *Newsweek*, 18 February: 11–12.
El-Khawas, Mohamed A. and Cohen, Barry (eds.). (1976) *The Kissinger Study of Southern Africa*. (Westport, Connecticut: Lawrence Hill).
Goldman, Marshall I. (1980) 'What is the Soviet Union up to in the Middle East? The unfortunate case of Afghanistan', *Middle East Review*, v. 12(3) Spring.
Ignotus, Miles. (1975) 'Seizing Arab Oil', *Harper's* v. 255(1550) March.
Kissinger, Henry. (1975) 'Kissinger on oil, food, and trade', *Business Week*, 13 January.
LeoGrande, William M. (1980) 'Evolution of the non-aligned movement', *Problems of Communism*, v. 29(1) January–February.
Mansuri, M.A. (1980) 'President opens Islamic Foreign Ministers' Conference in Islamabad', *Dawn Overseas Weekly*, v. 5(21) 24–30 May.
'The marines aren't here, yet'. (1980) *Economist*, v. 275(7136) 7 June.
Rywkin, Michael. (1979) 'Central Asia and Soviet manpower', *Problems of Communism*, v. 28(1) January–February.
Stobaugh, Robert and Yergin, Daniel. (1980) 'Energy: an emergency telescoped', *Foreign Affairs*, v. 58(3).
'Stuck in Afghanistan'. (1980) *Economist*, v. 275(7137) 14 June.
Tucker, Robert. (1975) 'Oil: the issue of American intervention', *Commentary*, v. 59(1) January.
United States. Library of Congress. Congressional Research Service. (1975) *Oil Fields as Military Objectives: a Feasibility Study*. (Washington: Library of Congress).

8 Alliances in the 1970s and 1980s

Garrett, Stephen. (1977) "Detente and military balance", *Bulletin of the Atomic Scientists*, April v. 33(4).
Hudson, G.F. (1976) "Collective Security and Military Alliances", in Butterfield, Herbert and Wight, Martin (eds.), *Diplomatic Investigations. Essays in the Theory of International Politics*. (London: George Allen and Unwin).
Kissinger, Henry. (1979a) *The White House Years*. (London: Weidenfeld and Nicolson and Michael Joseph).
–(1979b) "The future of NATO", *The Washington Quarterly*, v. 2 (4): Autumn.
Langdon, F.C. (1973) *Japan's Foreign Policy*. (Vancouver: University of British Columbia Press).
Okita, Saburo. (1979) "Japan, China and the United States", *Foreign Affairs*, v. 57(5): Summer.
Olson, Mancur Jr and Zeckhauser, Richard. (1970) "An Economic

Theory of Alliances", *in* Beer, Francis, A. (ed.) *Alliances: Latent War Communities in the Contemporary World.* (New York: Holt, Rinehart and Winston).

Remington, Robin. (1971) *The Warsaw Pact. Case Studies in Communist Conflict Resolution.* (Cambridge, Mass.: MIT Press).

Schwarz, Hans-Peter. (1979) "Atlantic Security in an Era without Great Alternatives", *in* Kaiser, Karl and Schwarz, Hans-Peter. (eds.) *America and Western Europe, Problems and Prospects of European-American Relations.* (Lexington: Lexington Books).

Spanier, John. (1972) *Games Nations Play. Analyzing International Politics.* (New York: Praeger).

9 The Evolution of Chinese Strategic thought

Boorman, S.A. (1972) "Deception in Chinese Strategy", in Whitson, W.W. (ed.) *The Military and Political Power in China in the 1970s.* (New York: Praeger).

Editorial Department, *Renmin Ribao* [People's Daily] (1977) "Chairman Mao's Theory of the Differentiation of the Three Worlds is a Major Contribution to Marxism-Leninism". *Peking Review*, No. 45, 4 November.

Huang Hua (1978) "Speech to the Special Session of the U.N. General Assembly on Disarmament". *Peking Review*, No 22, 2 June.

Liddell Hart, B.H. (1964) *Strategy.* (New York: Praeger).

Mao Zedong [Mao Tsetung] (1963) *Selected Military Writings of Mao Tsetung.* (Beijing: Foreign Languages Press).

Mao Zedong (1977) "On the Ten Major Relationships", 25 April 1956, in *Selected Works of Mao Tsetung*, Volume V. (Beijing: Foreign Languages Press).

Middleton, D. (1978) *The Duel of the Giants.* (New York: Charles Scribner's Sons).

Pollack, J.D. (1977) "China as a Nuclear Power", in Overholt, W. (ed.) *Asia's Nuclear Future.* (Boulder, Colorado: Westview Press).

Pollack, J.D. (1979) "The People's Republic of China in a Proliferated World", in King, J.K. (ed.) *International Political Effects of the Spread of Nuclear Weapons.* (Washington: US Government Printing Office).

Pollack, J.D. (1980a) "China as a Military Power", in Marwah, O. and Pollack, J.D. (eds.) *Military Power and Policy in Asian States.* (Boulder, Colorado: Westview Press).

Pollack, J.D. (1980b) *Security, Strategy, and the Logic of Chinese Foreign Policy.* (Berkeley, California: University of California, Institute of East Asian Studies, Policy Studies Monograph).

Pollack, J.D. (1981a) *Strategy and Policy in Chinese Security Debates.* (Santa Monica, California: Rand Corporation).

Pollack, J.D. (1981b) *The Sino-Soviet Conflict in the 1980s, Its Dynamics and Policy Implications.* (Santa Monica, California: Rand Corporation).

Special Commentator, *Renmin Ribao* (1980) "The Military Strategy of the Soviet Union for World Domination" in *Foreign Broadcast Information Service Daily Report – People's Republic of China*. 8 August.

Su Yu (1977) "Great Victory for Chairman Mao's Guideline on War", in *Foreign Broadcast Information Service Daily Report – People's Republic of China*. 8 August.

Sunzi [Sun Tzu] (1963) *The Art of War*. (trans. S.B. Griffith) (New York: Oxford University Press).

Whiting, A.S. (1972) "The Use of Force in Foreign Policy by the People's Republic of China". *The Annals of the American Academy of Political Science*, v. 402, July.

Whiting, A.S. (1975) *The Chinese Calculus of Deterrence, India and Indochina*. (Ann Arbor: University of Michigan Press).

Xinhua [New China News Agency] (1976) in *Foreign Broadcast Information Service Daily Report – People's Republic of China*. 23 December.

Xu Xiangqian (1978) "Heighten Our Vigilance and Get Prepared to Fight a War". *Peking Review*, No 32, 11 August.

Xu Xiangqian (1979) "Strive to Achieve Modernization in National Defense – In Celebration of the Thirtieth Anniversary of the Founding of the People's Republic of China" in Joint Publications Research Service, *Translations from Red Flag* No 10, October.

Ye Jianying (1978) "Developing Advanced Military Science of Chinese Proletariat". *Peking Review*, No 12, 24 March.

10 Strategic Thinking in India in the 1970s

Brown, Neville. (1977) *The Future Global Challenge; a Predictive Study of World Security*. (London: Royal United Services Institute for Defence Studies).

Chakravarti, P.C. (1962) *India's China Policy*. (Bloomington: Indiana University Press).

Doder, Durko. (1980) 'Soviet thank India with huge arms deal and cut rates', *Guardian Weekly*, 8 June; and *The Statesman* (Calcutta) 14 July.

Hackett, Sir John. (1978) *The Third World War: a Future History*. (London: Sidgwick & Jackson).

India, Department of Atomic Energy. (1970) *Nuclear Weapons*. (New Delhi: Government of India).

International Institute for Strategic Studies. (1979) *The Military Balance, 1979–1980*. (London: IISS).

International Institute for Strategic Studies. (1980) *Strategic Survey 1979*. (London: IISS).

Jain, R.K. (1976) *Detente in Europe: Implications for Asia*. (New Delhi: Radiant Publishers).

Jukes, Geoffrey. (1973) *The Soviet Union in Asia*. (Sydney: Angus & Robertson).

Kapur, Ashok. (1970) 'Power politics and co-alignment in India's approach to strategy', *U.S.I. Journal* (New Delhi), October/December.

Kapur, Ashok. (1976) *India's Nuclear Option: Atomic Diplomacy and Decision Making.* (New York: Praeger).

Kaushik, B.M. and Mehrotra, O.N. (1980) *Pakistan's Nuclear Bomb.* (New Delhi: Government of India).

Kissinger, Henry. (1979) *The White House Years.* (New Delhi: Vikas).

Kohli, S.N. (1975) *Sea Power and the Indian Ocean.* (New Delhi: Tata McGraw Hill).

Laqueur, Walter. (1977) *Guerrilla: a Historical and Critical Study.* (London: Weidenfeld and Nicolson).

Larns, Joel. (1978) 'The Indian Navy: the neglected service expands, modernises and faces the future' (Paper presented at a seminar or 'Foreign Policy Perspectives U.S. and India' at Bangalore, June 1978 under the auspices of the United States Educational Foundation in India).

Liu, Leo Yueh-yun. (1972) *China as a Nuclear Power in World Politics.* (London: Macmillan).

Niesewand, Peter. (1980) 'Indians ready to ditch low flying Jaguar', *Guardian Weekly*, 24 August.

Noorani, A.G. (1967) 'India's quest for a nuclear guarantee', *Asian Survey*, v. 3(7) July.

Palit, D.K. and Namboodiri, P.K. (1979) *Pakistan's Islamic Bomb.* (New Delhi: Vikas).

Rao, R.V.R. Chandrasekhara. (1973) 'Brezhnev plan and the Indo-Soviet treaty: expectations and frustrations', *Economic and Political Weekly* (Bombay), v. 8(46) 17 November.

Rao, R.V.R. Chandrasekhara. (1978) 'Janata and Indian foreign policy', *The World Today*.

Rao, R.V.R. Chandrasekhara. (1979) 'Indian defence policy at cross roads: a plea for public debate', *in* Khanna, D.D. (ed.) *Strategic Environment in South East Asia during the 1980's.* (Calcutta: Prakash).

Rao, R.V.R. Chandrasekhara. (1980) 'Sino-Indian ties, time for issues', *Financial Express* (New Delhi), 23 July.

Sen, Chanakya. (1960) *Tibet Disappears: a Documentary History of Tibet's International Status in the Great Rebellion and its Aftermath.* (Bombay: Asia Publishing House).

Singh, K.R. (1977) *The Indian Ocean: Big Powers Presence and Local Response.* (New Delhi: Manohar).

Singh, Sukhwant. (1980) *India's Wars since Independence: the Liberation of Bangla Desh.* Vol. 1. (New Delhi: Vikas).

Sinha, P.B. and Subramanian, R.R. (1980) *Nuclear Pakistan.* (New Delhi: Vision Books).

Stockholm International Peace Research Institute. (1979) *World Armaments and Disarmament: SIPRI Yearbook 1979.* (London: Taylor & Francis).

Subrahmanyam, K. (1974) *Defence and Development*. (Calcutta: Minerva Associates).
Subrahmanyam, K. (1980) 'Non-alignment and the struggle for peace and security' (Paper presented at the Indo-Yugoslav Symposium on Non-Alignment at New Delhi, May 1980).
Thomas, Raju G.C. (1978) *The Defence of India*. (New Delhi: Macmillan Co. of India).

11 Strategic Thinking in Japan in the 1970s and 1980s

Momoi, Makoto. (1977) 'Basic Trends in Japanese Security Policies', in Scalapino, Robert A. (ed.), *The Foreign Policy of Modern Japan*. (Berkeley, California: University of California Press).

13 Insurgency and Sub-National Violence

Arbuckle, Thomas. (1979) 'Rhodesian bush war strategies and tactics: an assessment', *RUSI*, v. 124(4) December.
Brodie, Bernard. (1976) 'A Guide to the Reading of '*On War*' in Clausewitz, Carl von. *On War* (edited and translated by Michael Howard and Peter Paret). (Princeton, New Jersey: Princeton University Press).
Clausewitz, Carl von. (1976) *On War*. (Princeton, New Jersey: Princeton University Press).
Downie, Nick. (1979) 'Rhodesia – a study in military incompetence', *Defence*, v. 10(5) May.
Gottman, Jean. (1943) 'Bugeaud, Gallieni, Lyautey: the Development of French Colonial Warfare' *in* Earle, Edward Mead (ed.) *Makers of Modern Strategy: Military Thought from Machiavelli to Hitler*. (Princeton, New Jersey: Princeton University Press).
Greene, T.N. (ed.) (1967) *The Guerrilla – and How to Fight Him*. (New York: Praeger).
Middleton, Drew. (1980) 'Year's terrorism killing highest on record', *Canberra Times*, 20 May, p. 2.

14 Clear and Future Danger

Abel, Elie (1966) *The Missile Crisis*. (Philadelphia: Lippincott).
Allison, Graham T. (1971) *Essence of Decision: Explaining the Cuban Missile Crisis*. (Boston: Little, Brown).
Allworth, Edward (ed.) (1971) *Soviet Nationality Problems*. (New York: Columbia University Press).
Aviation Week & Space Technology (1980).
Azrael, Jeremy R. (ed.) (1978) *Soviet Nationality Policies and Practices*. (New York: Praeger Publishers).
Callahan, M. *et al.* (1978) "The MX Missile: An Arms Control Impact

Statement", (Cambridge: Department of Physics, Massachusetts Institute of Technology).

United States Central Intelligence Agency (1977) *Soviet Prospects for Oil Production*. (Washington, D.C.: US Government Printing Office).

United States Central Intelligence Agency (1980) *The Soviet Economy in 1978–79 and Prospects for 1980*. (Washington, D.C.: US Government Printing Office).

D'Encausse, Helène Carrère (1979) *Decline of an Empire: The Soviet Socialist Republics in Revolt*. (New York: Newsweek Books).

Foreign Broadcast Information Service (1980) *China*. 13 August.

George, Alexander L. *et al.* (1974) *Deterrence in American Foreign Policy: Theory and Practice*. (New York: Columbia University Press).

Gray, Colin S. (1978) "The Strategic Forces Triad: End of the Road?", *Foreign Affairs* v. 56 (July).

Holsti, Ole R. (1972) "The Belief System and National Images: A Case Study", *Journal of Conflict Resolution* v. 6 (September).

Hilsman, Roger (1959) "The Foreign Policy Consensus: An Interim Research Report", *Journal of Conflict Resolution* v. 3(4) (December).

Hilsman, Roger (1967) *To Move a Nation: The Politics of Foreign Policy in the Administration of John F. Kennedy*. (New York: Doubleday).

Horelick, Arnold and Myron Rush (1966) *Strategic Power and Soviet Foreign Policy*. (Chicago: University of Chicago Press).

International Institute for Strategic Studies (1979) *The Military Balance: 1979–1980*. (London: International Institute for Strategic Studies).

Jonsson, Christer (1975) *The Soviet Union and the Test Ban: A Study in Soviet Negotiating Behaviour*. (Lund: Studentlitteratur).

Kahan, Jerome H. and Anne K. Long (1972) "The Cuban Missile Crisis: A Study of Its Strategic Context", *Political Science Quarterly* 87 (December).

Lebow, Richard Ned (1981) *Between Peace and War: The Nature of International Conflict*. (Baltimore: Johns Hopkins University Press).

Luttwak, Edward N. (1980) "After Afghanistan, What?", *Commentary* 69 (April).

Nitze, Paul (1979) "Viable U.S. Strategic Missile Forces for the Early 1980's", in William R. Van Cleave and W. Scott Thompson, *Strategic Options for the Early Eighties*. (New York: National Strategy Information Center).

Pipes, Richard (1977) "Why the Soviet Union Thinks It Could Fight & Win a Nuclear War", *Commentary* v. 64(1) (July).

Podhoretz, Norman (1980) "The Present Danger", *Commentary* 69 (March).

Snyder, Glenn H. and Paul Diesing (1977) *Conflict Among Nations: Bargaining, Decision Making, and System Structure in International Crises*. (Princeton: Princeton University Press).

Tatu, Michel (1968) *Power in the Kremlin: From Khrushchev to Kosygin*. (New York: Viking).
Tsipis, Kosta M. (1979) "The MX Missile: A Look Beyond the Obvious", *Technology Review* 81 (May).
Weinberg, Gerhard L. (1970) *The Foreign Policy of Hitler's Germany: Diplomatic Revolution in Europe, 1933–36*. (Chicago: University of Chicago Press).

16 Warfare and Policy

Clausewitz, Carl von. (1976) *On War*, (Edited and translated by Michael Howard and Peter Paret). (Princeton: Princeton University Press).
Gard, Robert G. (1973) 'The future of the military profession' *in* International Institute for Strategic Studies. Annual Conference, 15th, Travemunde, 1973. *Force in Modern Societies: Its Place in International Politics*. (Adelphi papers; no. 103) (London: IISS).
Huntington, Samuel P. (1964) *The Soldier and the State: the Theory and Politics of Civil-Military Relations*. (New York: Vintage Books).
Lyon, Peyton V. (1968) *Canada in World Affairs: v. 12: 1961–1963*. (Toronto: Oxford University Press).
Millar, T.B. (1978) *The Political-Military Relationship in Australia*. (Working paper; no. 6) (Canberra: Strategic and Defence Studies Centre, Australian National University).
Taylor, A.J.P. (1970) *English History, 1914–1945*. (Harmondsworth: Penguin).
Thorne, Christopher. (1978) *Allies of a Kind: the United States, Britain and the War against Japan, 1941–1945*. (London: Hamilton).
'Who'll fight for America?' *Time*, 9 June (1980).

Conclusions: The Determinants of Defence Policy for a Medium Military Power

Woolsey, R. James. (1980), 'Studying Defense to Death', *Washington Post*, 3 July.

Index

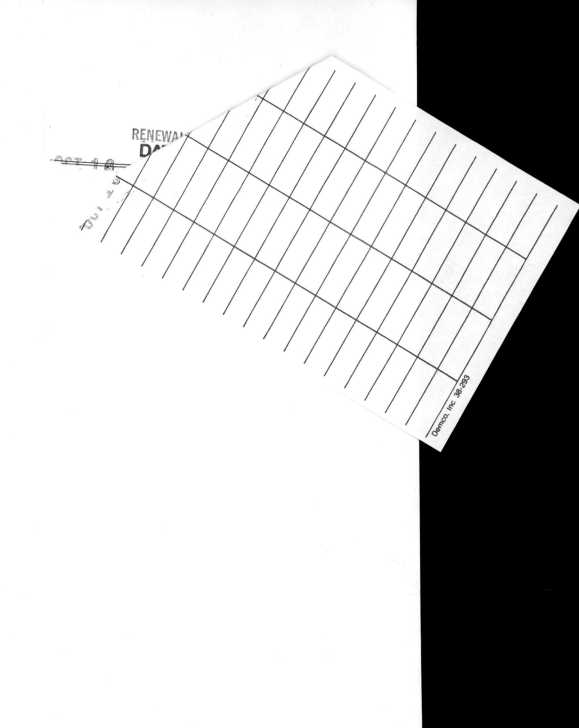